D1083034

THE THEORY OF
INTERNATIONAL ECONOMIC POLICY
VOLUME ONE

THE BALANCE OF PAYMENTS

The Royal Institute of International Affairs is an unofficial body which promotes the scientific study of international questions and does not express opinions of its own. The opinions expressed in this publication are the responsibility of the author.

THE THEORY OF

INTERNATIONAL ECONOMIC POLICY

VOLUME ONE

THE BALANCE OF PAYMENTS

BY

J. E. MEADE

Nuffield Senior Research Fellow
Christ's College, Cambridge

Issued under the auspices of the
Royal Institute of International Affairs

OXFORD UNIVERSITY PRESS

LONDON   NEW YORK   TORONTO

Oxford University Press, Ely House, London W. 1

GLASGOW   NEW YORK   TORONTO   MELBOURNE   WELLINGTON
CAPE TOWN   SALISBURY   IBADAN   NAIROBI   DAR ES SALAAM   LUSAKA   ADDIS ABABA
BOMBAY CALCUTTA MADRAS   KARACHI   LAHORE   DACCA
KUALA LUMPUR   SINGAPORE   HONG KONG   TOKYO

SBN 19 214553 3

FIRST EDITION 1951
REPRINTED (WITH CORRECTIONS) 1952, 1954, 1956,
1960, 1962, 1963, 1966 AND 1970

PRINTED IN GREAT BRITAIN

TO K. M.

Preface

THIS volume is the first of a series which I hope to prepare on the Theory of Economic Policy. It deals with the international aspects of the closely related problems of preserving a balance in the financial payments between nations and, at the same time, of maintaining full employment domestically within each nation.

It is to be followed by a second volume dealing with such matters as the control of foreign trade, of the international migration of labour, of international capital movements, and of other international transfers of purchasing power; but this will be done from the point of view of the effects of controls, not upon levels of employment and balances of international payments, which form the subject-matter of this volume, but upon the efficient use of the world's economic resources, upon the total supply of those resources, and upon the distribution of the total of world income among the citizens of the various countries.

The second volume is planned as a second part of a Theory of International Economic Policy. The preparation of such a work, as will become clear to the reader of this volume, is possible only if much of the analysis of the domestic effects of different economic policies is taken for granted. For this reason it would be desirable to complete the study with a Theory of Domestic Economic Policy which would cover the domestic aspects of economic policies designed for the maintenance of full employment, for assuring the economically most effective use of resources, for achieving a socially desirable distribution of income and property, and for producing the optimum supply of economic resources of various kinds. The second volume of the *Theory of International Economic Policy* is in active preparation; but whether any of the volumes of the *Theory of Domestic Economic Policy* will ever pass beyond the stage of vague aspiration is most uncertain.

My interest in economics has always been in considering the contribution which pure economic analysis can make to the formation of economic policy; and this volume undertakes that task in one limited field. It does not claim to make any significant contribution of original work in the fundamentals of pure economic analysis. Nor, on the other hand, is it a factual study of our present problems. It is the work neither of a tool-maker nor of a tool-user, but of a tool-setter. I have attempted, that is to say, to take over the modern techniques of economic analysis and to set them out in a form in which they can subsequently be applied most usefully to the particular issues (such as the dollar shortage, the intra-European payments scheme, the depreciation of sterling, etc.)

which may present themselves in balance-of-payments problems.

But I must confess frankly that there is one piece of modern technique in economic analysis which is very relevant to the problems discussed in this volume, but of which I have made no use. I refer to the analysis of the dynamic process of change from one position of equilibrium to another. The method employed in this volume is first to consider a number of countries in at least partial or temporary equilibrium, domestically and internationally; next to introduce some disturbing factor (which is often an act of government policy) into this equilibrium; then to consider the new partial or temporary equilibrium which the economies will attain when the direct and indirect effects of the disturbing factor have fully worked themselves out; and finally to compare the new position of equilibrium with the old. In other words, this is a work not on dynamics, but on comparative statics, in economics.

As I have made clear in the text (pp. 55–59) there may be cases in which the dynamic process of change will itself significantly affect the static position which is ultimately reached. In such cases the method of comparative statics is inadequate. And yet I have had to be content with it, because I was trained on the old static tools and still find these new dynamic tools with their difference equations and differential equations too complicated to be set up for the solution of international problems. Perhaps some time later, when my own skill is improved and —possibly—the dynamic tool-makers have passed a little further from the prototype stage, I may be able to return with more success to this question.

Whether it is true, as I believe, that the results of pure economic analysis have an important contribution to make in the formation of international economic policy, I leave to the reader of this book to decide for himself. But I would make it clear that, while I put forward serious claims on behalf of such a study, I realize that it remains incomplete unless it is supplemented by appropriate factual studies of a descriptive and quantitative character. Indeed, the final answer to the central issue discussed in this volume depends upon just such a question of fact. Should the ultimate reconciliation of domestic and of international equilibrium be brought about through price adjustments (e.g. exchange depreciation) or through direct controls (e.g. import restrictions)? It is perhaps the main thesis of this book that if demand in international trade is reasonably sensitive to changes in relative prices, so that one country's products will displace another's if the price of the former's falls relatively to that of the latter's, then the methods of price adjustment are greatly to be preferred. But if demand in international trade is insensitive, then, perforce, reliance must be placed on direct controls.

This is a question of economic fact on which bold and suggestive pioneering work has already been done.[1] But this work is still inconclusive for at least three reasons. First, as is suggested by recent work,[2] the statistical basis of these computations is most uncertain. Secondly, the sensitiveness of international demand to price changes is likely to be much greater if time is allowed for producers and consumers to adapt themselves to the new price relationships than it will be immediately after the change; but the studies which have so far been made do not allow for the gradual working out of such long-run adjustments. Thirdly, to answer the question of policy, we want to know how sensitive demand would be to price changes in the absence of rigid trade controls; but the studies which have been made of the sensitiveness of international demand to price changes all relate to periods in which the existence of artificial barriers to international trade has reduced such sensitiveness in a smaller or greater degree. The presumption remains that, if adequate time is allowed for adjustment and in the absence of rigid and serious artificial barriers to changes in the channels of trade, international demand would be reasonably sensitive to price changes. But much more work needs to be done on this central question of fact.

My indebtedness to other economists in the preparation of this book is very great. I fear that my mind often absorbs an idea without remembering the source from which the idea came. For this reason I find it particularly difficult to make proper acknowledgement; and I hope that I shall be forgiven by those of my colleagues who see ideas of their own embedded in my book without any acknowledgment. My indebtedness to the ideas of Lord Keynes is, I imagine, too obvious to need any emphasis. Much of my analysis, of course, is derived from the standard works on the theory of international trade, such as Gottfried von Haberler, *The Theory of International Trade*, J. Viner, *Studies in the Theory of International Trade*, R. F. Harrod, *International Economics*, and B. Ohlin, *Interregional and International Trade*. I have also been much helped by more recent work on the general theory of international trade such as the application of J. R. Hicks's type of analysis to international trade contained in Jacob L. Mosak's *General Equilibrium Theory in International Trade*, and by such articles as W. F. Stolper and P. A. Samuelson, 'Protection and Real Wages', Tibor de Scitovszky, 'A Reconsideration of the Theory of Tariffs', and A. P. Lerner, 'The Symmetry between Import and Export Taxes'. I have been much

---

[1] For example, T.-C. Chang, 'International Comparisons of Demand for Imports', 'The British Demand for Imports in the Inter-War Period', 'A Statistical Note on World Demand for Exports'; R. Hinshaw, 'American Prosperity and the British Balance of Payments Problem'; J. Tinbergen, 'Some Measurements of Elasticities of Substitution'.

[2] For example, Guy H. Orcutt, 'Measurement of Price Elasticities in International Trade'; and W. Corlett and D. J. Morgan, 'The Influence of Price in International Trade: A Study in Method.'

helped on the subject of international trade multipliers and the conflict between internal and external equilibrium by F. Machlup's *International Trade and the National Income Multiplier*, L. A. Metzler's two articles, 'The Transfer Problem Reconsidered' and 'Underemployment Equilibrium in International Trade', R. Nurkse's 'Domestic and International Equilibrium' (in *The New Economics*, edited by S. E. Harris, 1948); on the subject of exchange depreciation by Joan Robinson's 'The Foreign Exchanges' (in her *Essays in the Theory of Employment*), A. J. Brown, 'Trade Balances and Exchange Stability', J. J. Polak, 'Exchange Depreciation and International Stability', and A. O. Hirschman, 'Devaluation and the Trade Balance'; on trade controls by H. Heuser's *Control of International Trade*; and on the problem of discrimination by the article by R. Frisch entitled 'On the Need for Forecasting a Multilateral Balance of Payments', and by G. D. A. MacDougall's *Notes on Discrimination*.

My method of work in constructing this book has been to make a simple mathematical model of most of the problems before writing about them. Rigid proofs of many assertions made in this volume are not given in the text. I have, therefore, thought it useful to prepare a mathematical supplement which is being published separately and in which I have set out my mathematical models. This has been read by Dr. W. J. Baumol who gave me invaluable help on some problems in which I was out of my depth; but he is not to be held responsible by any mathematician for the clumsy piece of work which I have finally produced. I wish to thank the editor of *Economica* for permission to use in this supplement my article on 'A Geometrical Representation of Balance-of-Payments Policy' from the November 1949 issue. Professor L. C. Robbins has given me great help in Part I of this book. As a result of his comments I have completely revised my way of defining a balance-of-payments deficit, though I doubt whether I shall have fully satisfied him. I would like to thank Mr. M. A. Rudzki and Mr. J. Serafin for preparing the index.

I owe a very special debt of gratitude to Professor R. G. Hawtrey of the Royal Institute of International Affairs, who has taken immense trouble in giving me detailed comments on the typescript of my book. Many of his suggestions have enabled me to remove serious blemishes from my text. Yet I fear that on his main point I have left Professor Hawtrey's criticism largely unanswered. For he emphasized strongly the inadequacy of dealing with these problems by the method of comparative statics rather than dynamically; and yet for the reasons which I have stated above I have felt obliged to confine myself essentially to the static method.

This study has been undertaken for the Royal Institute of International Affairs who, by means of a generous grant from the Rockefeller

Foundation, have made it possible for me to devote the whole of my leisure in the last two years to this subject. I believe that it is something of an innovation in the policy of the Institute to supplement their admirable series of studies with a work which is so frankly theoretical as this. In principle, I feel strongly that both types of work are necessary; I can only hope that my work will be found to have sufficient merit to justify the Institute's initiative.

J. E. MEADE

London School of Economics
and Political Science
April 1950

Contents

PART V. DIRECT CONTROLS

PART VI. THE NETWORK OF WORLD PAYMENTS

List of Tables

PART I. DEFINITIONS

PART I. DEFINITIONS

CHAPTER I

THE MEANING OF A COUNTRY'S BALANCE OF PAYMENTS

A COUNTRY'S balance of international payments is said to be 'favourable' or 'in surplus' when the total receipts from its exports, etc., to the rest of the world exceed the total payments for its imports, etc., from the rest of the world. Conversely, its balance of international payments is said to be 'unfavourable' or 'in deficit' if its receipts fall short of its payments. Its balance of payments may be said to be in equilibrium when its receipts are equal to its payments on account of its transactions with other countries. A country whose balance of payments is in surplus or in deficit we shall call for short a 'surplus' or 'deficit' country. When a country is neither in surplus nor in deficit we shall talk of it as being in 'external balance'.

One of the basic problems of international economic policy is to find effective means for restoring external balance to a country whose balance of payments is seriously in surplus or in deficit. But this problem, as the argument of this volume will attempt to demonstrate, is closely bound up with the problem of maintaining a high and stable level of economic activity—or what is more colloquially called 'full employment'—in the country suffering from the disequilibrium in its balance of payments. This volume will, accordingly, be devoted to an examination (i) of the reactions upon the level of economic activity in the various 'deficit' and 'surplus' countries of the world of alternative means of removing the disequilibrium in their balances of payments, and (ii) of the reactions upon their balances of payments of various national measures adopted in order to achieve or to maintain full employment.

But the term balance of payments is an ambiguous one. It is often used loosely without any precise definition of what it is intended to cover, and such loose usage of the term is the cause of much muddled thinking on the subject. It is not possible to proceed without a full discussion of the various possible meanings of this term.

There is, of course, one sense in which the balance of payments can never be out of equilibrium. As with any other account, the total receipts of a country are bound to be equal to the total payments of that country, if one includes all the receipts and all the payments of the country in the account, including—for example—in a country's receipts not only the value of the goods which it exports but also the value of the gold or other monetary reserves which it exports in order to obtain purchasing power over that part of its imports which is not covered by its normal commercial exports. Consider the example given in Table I. The left-hand side of this account enumerates all the ways in which residents in the country in question have received purchasing power over foreign goods and services in the course of the period under examination. Such receipts of external purchasing power may come from the sale of the country's exports to foreign countries, from the sale of services (such as shipping or financial services) to foreign countries, from the receipt of gifts from foreign governments or individuals, from the borrowing of money from foreigners or from the repayments by foreigners of loans previously made to them, or from the sale of part of the country's monetary reserves or other assets to foreigners. The right-hand side of the account shows how, in the same period, the total of external purchasing power was used, whether for acquiring imports of foreign goods, for purchasing services from foreigners, for making gifts to foreigners, for lending to foreigners, for repaying capital previously borrowed from foreigners, or for acquiring additional monetary reserves or other assets from foreigners. Since the payments side of the account enumerates all the uses which were made of the total of foreign purchasing power acquired by this country in a given period, and since the receipts side of the account enumerates all the sources from which foreign purchasing power was acquired by the same country in the same period, the two sides must balance. They are merely different ways of enumerating the same thing.

TABLE I

An Account of a Country's International Receipts and Payments

Receipts	$ m.	Payments	$ m.
(i) Trade Items			
1. Visible exports (i.e. exports of commodities) . .	650	5. Visible imports (i.e. imports of commodities) .	900
2. Invisible exports (i.e. exports of services) . .	160	6. Invisible imports (i.e. imports of services) . .	90
(ii) Transfer Items			
3. Unrequited receipts (i.e. gifts, indemnities, etc. received from foreigners) .	110	7. Unrequited payments (i.e. gifts, indemnities, etc. paid to foreigners) . . .	30
4. Capital receipts (i.e. borrowings from, capital repayments by, or sale of assets to, foreigners) .	180	8. Capital payments (i.e. lendings to, capital repayments to, or purchase of assets from, foreigners) . .	80
Total receipts	1,100	Total payments	1,100

Before we proceed to a discussion of the senses in which a country's balance of payments may be in surplus or in deficit, it will be useful to discuss in a little more detail the contents of Table I.

Items 1 and 5 show respectively a country's receipts from the sale of the goods which it exports and its payments for the goods which it imports in the period in question. These two items account for what is often called the country's 'visible' trade.

Item 2 enumerates the receipts of the country from the sale of current services to foreigners in the period in question. If residents of the country in question have lent capital to foreigners in the past or own land or other income-bearing property in foreign countries, they will during the period in question be receiving interest, dividends, or rent on these foreign investments. Such payments are regarded as the payments made by foreigners for the current services which they obtain from the capital of the residents of the country under examination, i.e. services obtained from use of the land or other assets which in effect belong not to them but to the residents of the other country. The country in question is, therefore, selling to foreigners (or exporting) the services of this amount of the capital which belongs to it; and the payments by foreigners for such services accordingly appear as one element in item 2.

Item 2 also contains the other 'invisible' receipts which the residents of the country in question obtain from the sale of other current services to foreigners in the period in question. The following are examples of such services: the receipts of foreign money which residents of the country obtain from foreign tourists visiting the country, and who purchase goods and services within the country during their stay in the country, goods and services which do not appear in the 'visible' exports of the country; the receipts of the country's banks and other financial institutions (other than such interest as has been already covered in the previous paragraph) from foreigners in respect of banking and similar services rendered by them to foreigners, and the receipt by the shipping concerns of the country in question from foreigners for the transport of goods on behalf of foreign traders.

Item 6 would cover the payments which the residents of the country in question make to foreigners for similar services: such as interest on capital used by the residents of the country but owned by foreigners; payments for goods and services consumed by the residents of the country in question when they are touring abroad; and payments for financial or shipping services provided by foreigners for the residents of the country in question.

In items 1, 2, 5, and 6, we have enumerated all the receipts and payments made in respect of the current trade in goods or services. There remain for enumeration all those payments from the residents of one country to those of another which are not payments for a simultaneous flow of goods and services in the opposite direction. Such payments we shall call transfers. They fall into two main categories: first, gifts, reparations, indemnities, etc., which we shall call 'unrequited transfers', i.e. payments from some person or body in one country to another person or body in another country in respect of which no present or future *quid pro quo* is demanded; and secondly, 'capital transfers', i.e. payments made by way of loan or for the purchase of capital assets for which no current return in the form of an immediate import of goods and services is obtained but from which some future benefit is expected.

Let us deal first of all with 'unrequited transfers'. Residents of the country may receive gifts from residents in foreign countries. For example, emigrants from a country may, after they have settled down in the foreign land, remit part of their earnings for the support of their parents in their old home country. Or the government of a country may receive a reparation payment or some other indemnity from the government of a foreign country. All such unrequited receipts are entered in item 3 and all such unrequited payments from residents in the country in question to the residents of other countries are entered in item 7.

We are left now with the items enumerating the movements of capital funds into (item 4) and out of (item 8) the country. Such capital transfers may take very many different forms. The following are the ways in which the residents of a country may receive on capital account (item 4) funds which give them purchasing power over foreign goods and services:

(i) The government or a corporation, company, or individual resident in the country in question may have borrowed money from the government or a corporation, company, or individual resident in a foreign country. Such borrowings may take many forms. They may consist of direct borrowing by the government of the country in question from the government of another country; or of the issue of new securities by the borrowing agency in the capital market of the lending country; or of borrowing by the borrowing agency from the banks of the lending country. The debt may be long-term or short-term and the interest and the principal to be repaid may be fixed in the currency of the borrowing or of the lending country or in terms of some third currency or measure of value.

(ii) The government or a corporation, company, or individual resident in the country in question may receive sums from abroad in repayment of some loan which it had previously extended to some borrowing agency in the foreign country.

(iii) The government or a corporation, company, or individual resident in a foreign country may acquire capital assets from the government or a corporation, company, or individual resident in the country in question. Such acquisition of assets may take many forms. Some agency or person in the foreign country may acquire land or machinery or existing securities or bank deposits or gold from some agency or person in the country in question; and these assets may consist either of assets physically situated in the country in question or of assets physically situated in the foreign country (or some third foreign country) but previously owned by an agency or person in the country in question. Provided the assets so purchased are not commodities which are exported from the country from which they are bought, they will not appear as commodity exports (item 1 of Table I) and must be included here. This is, of course, an enormously wide category. It is possible here to give only a few typical examples. A resident of a foreign country may invest money in land or in existing securities on the capital market of the country in question. The central bank of the country in question may sell a holding of deposits of money in the foreign country to the central bank of the foreign country. A company in the foreign country may buy up a productive plant in the country in question, or the materials and labour necessary to construct such a productive plant in the country in question, for the purpose of operating a subsidiary company in the country in question. A merchant in the country in question may dispose of a stock of commodities which he is holding in a foreign country to some purchaser in that foreign country.

We are now in a position to distinguish between certain senses in which the term 'balance of payments' may be used, though not—as it will turn out—yet in a position to define a disequilibrium in a country's balance of payments. We may illustrate this from the position of our imaginary country whose external account is re-arranged in Table II. This country is importing $900 m. worth of goods and exporting goods to the value of only $650 m. It has a deficit in its balance of visible trade of $250 m. (row 1 of Table II). But this in no sense measures the disequilibrium in its balance of payments. Part of its excess imports are being financed by a net receipt of $70 m. (row 2) in respect of the excess of its receipts of interest on capital or of fees, commissions, etc., charged for services provided to foreigners, so that its deficit in respect of trade in goods and services is only $180 m. (row 3). This balance we shall call the 'balance of trade'.

This balance of trade is, as will be shown in Chapter III, a most important concept; but it still in no sense measures the disequilibrium in the country's balance of payments. In order that a country should be in international equilibrium, it is by no means necessary that its balance of visible and invisible trade should be neither in deficit nor in surplus. For example, the government of a country may be receiving an annual reparations payment from the government of another country. Unless, in such circumstances, there is an excess of invisible and visible imports into the former over the visible and invisible exports from it, it may be difficult for the government paying reparations to transfer the payment. In row 4 of Table II the net receipts of our country on account of unrequited transfers from abroad of $80 m. is set against its deficit in its balance of visible and invisible trade of $180 m.

Even so, the remaining deficit of $100 m. does not necessarily represent a disequilibrium in its international position. The country in question may, for example, be an undeveloped country in which there is a great scarcity of capital and in which, for that reason, the yield on capital development is much higher than in the other more developed countries. In such circumstances there may well be a natural flow of capital funds from other countries into the country in question, which will provide the finance for the excess imports into the country during its period of capital development. If, as is done in row 5 of Table II, the whole of the net capital inflow into our country (items 4 and 8 of Table I) is set against the remaining deficit of the country, the net deficit disappears completely—as indeed it was bound to do since we have again merely enumerated all the net receipts of foreign purchasing power of our country and set against this all the net uses which the country makes of that purchasing power.

TABLE II
The Balance of Trade and the Balance of Transfers
Notes: + means surplus of receipts.
            — means deficit of receipts.

			$ m.		
1. Balance of visible trade (Table I, items 1 and 5)	. . . .	650—	900	=	—250
2. Balance of invisible trade (Table I, items 2 and 6)	. . . .	160—	90	=	+ 70
3. Balance of trade		810—	990	=	—180
4. Balance of unrequited transfers (Table I, items 3 and 7)	. .	110—	30	=	+ 80
5. Balance of capital transfers (or net foreign disinvestment) . . . . . . (Table I, items 4 and 8)		180—	80	=	+100
6. Balance of transfers		290—	110	=	+180
7. Balance of trade and transfers . . .		1,100—	1,100	=	Nil

The categories of 'balances of payments' enumerated in Table II have their uses. As we shall see in Chapter III the balance of trade (row 3 of Table II) is of importance when we are considering the repercussions of external changes on the domestic economy of a country or the repercussion of domestic changes in a country's economy upon its external position. Moreover, the simple truism represented by the relationship between rows 3, 4, and 5 of Table II, namely, that a country's balance of trade and its balance of unrequited transfers must be exactly offset by its balance of capital transfers is important. If a country purchases more goods than it sells ($180 m.) and can only offset part of this ($80 m.) by way of gifts from abroad, then the difference ($100 m.) must represent the extent to which its capital position vis-a-vis the rest of the world has worsened in the period in question. The balance of capital transfers (row 5 of Table II) is often called that country's 'net foreign disinvestment' when it is desired to draw attention to the fact that it means a net worsening to that extent of the country's external capital position.

But clearly we have not yet found any meaning for the phrases a 'deficit' or a 'surplus' in a country's balance of international payments. If we include all items in the account, then, as we have just seen, the account must balance; there can be no 'deficit' or 'surplus'. We must search along some other lines for a meaning for these terms.

Let us proceed by considering what happens when for one reason or another there is an increased demand for foreign currencies to make increased payments abroad. Suppose that the country starts in full international equilibrium, but that for one reason or another importers decide to spend $1,000 m. per year instead of $900 m. per year (as in item 5 of Table I) on the purchase of foreign currencies in order to obtain a larger volume of imports from abroad.

Now there are many things which may happen as a result of this change of plans on the part of the importers. The authorities in the country in question might take immediate steps (e.g. by exchange control regulations or by import restrictions) to *prevent* the importers from spending this additional amount on imports; or they might take immediate steps (e.g. by a deflationary fiscal policy involving the raising of higher rates of taxation on the people who wished to purchase imports) to *dissuade* importers from spending additional sums on imports; or the increased demand for foreign currencies by the importers might be allowed to cause the price of foreign currencies in terms of the domestic currency to rise so that the importers did not in fact obtain any increased amounts of foreign purchasing power over imports, even though their demand expressed in terms of their domestic currency had increased.

Let us suppose, however, for the moment that none of these things happen. The increased demand by importers for foreign currencies to finance an increased volume of imports is not prevented by direct governmental intervention, and at the same time the price of foreign currencies is not allowed to go up in terms of the domestic currency.

For this to be possible someone must be prepared to provide the additional amounts of foreign currencies to the importers at the existing rate of exchange. To a limited extent and for a limited period of time these additional sums of foreign exchange may be provided more or less automatically by private dealers in foreign exchange. Such dealers are likely to hold reserves of the home currency (say, dollars) and of foreign currencies (say, pounds); and they may conduct their business by announcing a price (e.g. $4 to £1), at which they are willing to deal; and they may change this price only occasionally as they change their plans from time to time in view of the changing market conditions for foreign currencies. In this case American importers who decide to spend $1,000 m. instead of $900 m. a year on the purchase of foreign currencies will for a time be able to obtain additional pounds at the rate of £25 m. a year from the foreign exchange dealers who will be receiving in exchange additional dollars at the rate of $100 m. a year. The exchange dealers are in fact purchasing dollars with pounds in order to hold their capital in the home currency, dollars; and this represents a capital receipt in the balance of payments of that country. There will thus be an additional $100 m. in item 4 of Table I to offset the additional $100 m. in item 5. But this movement of the exchange dealers' capital from pounds to dollars was unplanned and in fact took place only as an incidental and unforeseen result of the increased demand for foreign means of payment by the country's importers. It will last only until the exchange dealers readjust their plans.

A more important and more lasting source of the same type of financial operation exists when the monetary authority of a country undertakes itself to buy and sell a foreign means of payment (e.g. gold or the notes or deposits of foreign countries) at a fixed price in terms of the national currency. In this case the American importers who have decided to spend $1,000 m. instead of only $900 m. a year on imports will obtain the additional £25 m. at an unchanged price of $4 for £1 by purchasing the additional pound notes or deposits (or the gold with which pound notes or deposits can be obtained) from the central monetary authority. If the central monetary authority can command large reserves of foreign money and has determined to maintain a fixed rate of exchange, this movement of funds (unlike the movement of funds by exchange dealers) may continue on a large scale for a long time. As it loses gold or reserves of foreign money, the central monetary authority will, like the exchange dealers in the previous example, find that it is holding less foreign money or less gold and more domestic money among its assets. If the export of gold is shown in item 1 of Table I or the loss of a holding of foreign money in item 4, then once again Table I will balance. But these movements have once more taken place merely as an incidental and unforeseen result of the increased demand for foreign means of payment by the country's importers.

This type of financial transaction can continue only so long as the central monetary authority of the deficit country can command the necessary reserves of foreign purchasing power (i.e. reserves of gold or of foreign exchange). But there is one type of governmental transaction which may prolong this period more or less indefinitely. The government or the monetary authorities of one country may advance money to the government, monetary authorities, or other residents in another country simply because an excess of foreign payments over foreign receipts in all the other items of the balance of payments of the latter country is foreseen, and it is desired to meet this deficit without exchange rate variation, import restriction, or other alternative methods of closing the gap.

In what follows we shall call payments of this kind 'accommodating' payments to distinguish them from all other payments which we shall call 'autonomous'. 'Accommodating' payments may be made by private persons (like the automatic changes in the balances of private exchange dealers to which reference is made above) or they may be made by public authorities (like the loss of gold by a central bank or the provision of special aid by the government of a surplus country). They may be automatic, i.e. unplanned and unforeseen (like the changes in the balances of private exchange dealers or the loss of gold reserves by a central bank) or they may be discretionary, i.e. planned and foreseen (like special governmental aid). Their distinguishing feature is that they have taken place only because the other items in the balance of payments are such as to leave a gap of this size to be filled. On the other hand, the distinguishing feature of autonomous payments is that they take place regardless of the size of the other items in the balance of payments.

Some examples may help to clarify the distinction. Thus the category of autonomous receipts would contain all normal commercial exports, gifts such as emigrants' remittances or reparations payments which are made for motives quite other than to put the balance of payments into balance, as well as all those normal capital movements which are taking place on the initiative of private enterprise because it appears more profitable to invest capital in one country rather than in another. For example, the sale of a security in a foreign country and the use of the proceeds to purchase a security in the home country because the yield on the second is higher than that on the first, or the purchase by a foreign company of a subsidiary plant in the home country because this appeared to the foreign company the most profitable way of expanding its own business, would be unequivocal examples of autonomous capital receipts.

Some unequivocal instances of accommodating receipts are: the loss by a central bank of its holding of gold or the sale of its holdings of foreign currencies in order to provide to importers in the country in question at the current rate of exchange the foreign currencies needed to finance their purchases from foreign countries; or the receipt by the government of the country in question of funds from a foreign government either by way of loan (such as the Anglo-American Loan of 1946) or by way of gift (such as much of the aid under the European Recovery Programme) for the express purpose of acquiring foreign currencies to meet an existing gap in the other receipts and payments on the balance of payments; or the compulsory acquisition by the government of the country in question of foreign assets owned by its citizens in order to sell them to realize funds for the finance of such a balance-of-payments gap.[1]

TABLE III

Autonomous and Accommodating Transactions

Receipts	$ m.	Payments	$ m.
1. Autonomous receipts		3. Autonomous payments	
(a) Autonomous exports (visible and invisible) .	790	(a) Autonomous imports (visible and invisible) .	990
(b) Autonomous unrequited receipts from foreigners . . .	10	(b) Autonomous unrequited payments to foreigners . . .	20
(c) Autonomous capital receipts from foreigners	40	(c) Autonomous capital payments to foreigners	50
2. Accommodating receipts		4. Accommodating payments	
(a) Accommodating exports (visible and invisible) . . .	20	(a) Accommodating imports (visible and invisible) . . .	Nil
(b) Accommodating unrequited receipts from foreigners . . .	100	(b) Accommodating unrequited payments to foreigners . . .	10
(c) Accommodating capital receipts from foreigners	140	(c) Accommodating capital payments to foreigners	30
Total	1,100	Total	1,100

[1] There may, of course, be intermediate cases in which, for example, a government borrows money from abroad for capital development at home partly because it thinks that such development, financed by external borrowing, is—as it were—commercially profitable for the country as a whole, but partly because it knows that the country is threatened by a balance-of-payments gap which such borrowing will help to finance. Theoretically, however, the distinction is reasonably clear. If in this case there had been no prospective difficulty of financing a balance-of-payments gap, how much would have been borrowed? The excess over this is the amount of the accommodating capital receipt.

TABLE IV

The Balance of Payments

		$ m.	
1. Balance of autonomous trade . .		790−990	= −200
(Table III, items 1a and 3a)			
2. Balance of autonomous transfers . .		10+40−20−50	= −20
(Table III, items 1b and c and 3b and c)			
3. Balance of payments		840−1,060	= −220
4. Balance of foreign accommodation .		20+100+140−10−30	= +220
(Table III, items 2 and 4)			
5. Balance of autonomous and accommodating transactions		1,100−1,100	= Nil

In Tables III and IV an attempt is made to rearrange the figures given in Tables I and II so as to make allowance for this distinction between autonomous and accommodating transactions. By way of illustration it may be useful briefly to compare the items of receipts in Tables I and III. Thus of the visible and invisible exports of $810 m. (items 1 and 2 of Table I), we suppose $790 m. to be normal commercial exports (item 1a of Table III) and $20 m. to represent an accommodating transaction (item 2a of Table III) to find foreign funds to close a balance-of-payments gap (e.g. an export of gold by the monetary authorities). Of the receipt of gifts of $110 m. (item 3 of Table I) we assume $10 m. to be autonomous (item 1b of Table III), (e.g. emigrants' remittances home) and $100 m. to be accommodating (item 2b of Table III) (e.g. aid under the European Recovery Programme). Of the foreign disinvestment of $180 m. (item 4 of Table I) we assume $40 m. to be autonomous (item 1c of Table III) (e.g. foreign companies setting up subsidiaries in the country) and $140 m. to be accommodating (item 2c of Table III) (e.g. sale of its holdings of foreign deposits by the central bank).

We are now in a position to define an actual surplus or deficit in the balance of payments of a country. For this purpose the figures of Table III are rearranged in Table IV. Our country has a deficit in its balance of autonomous trade of $200 m. It has a further deficit on account of autonomous transfers of $20 m. Our country has, therefore, a deficit of autonomous trade and transfers of $220 m.; and this is a true balance-of-payments deficit. In future when we talk of an actual surplus or deficit in the balance of payments we shall have in mind this balance of autonomous trade and transfers. It is this sum which must be matched by what we have called accommodating finance.

But the existence of an actual net balance of accommodating finance would be much too narrow a criterion of a disequilibrium in the balance of payments. So far we have discussed the position only on the assumption that the authorities do not take special steps to prevent the excess demand for foreign currency and are prepared to provide any accommodating balance of foreign currency which may be required to meet the full demand at the current rate of exchange. But, of course, the governmental authorities may be driven to take other measures.

Thus, a country may well have no actual deficit or surplus in its balance of payments as defined in Table IV, but the authorities may nevertheless be avoiding such a deficit only by the most strict controls and restrictions over its trade and transfers. By rigid exchange control which prevents a natural export of capital or by rigid import restrictions which prevent the natural inflow of goods they may be avoiding any loss of monetary reserves or other need for foreign accommodation. But the country is certainly in acute balance-of-payments difficulties and it is unnatural to say that there is no balance-of-payments disequilibrium.

Similarly, a country may be avoiding an actual deficit in its balance of autonomous trade and transfers by the adoption of some internal policy which is specially devised for this purpose. As we shall see in what follows, the most important example of this is when the authorities in a country deflate the domestic national expenditure and income in order thereby to reduce the demand for imports, so as to avoid the need to find foreign accommodation even at the expense of mass unemployment at home. In this case again it would be most unnatural to say that the country was not in balance-of-payments difficulties merely because there was no actual deficit on its balance of autonomous trade and transfers.

We have still to allow for the fact that an excess demand for foreign currency may not be met by the provision of accommodating finance at the current rate of exchange nor by governmental import restrictions or other policies devised to restrict the demand for foreign currencies. It may merely be allowed to have its natural effect in causing the price of foreign currencies to rise in terms of the home currency. Such a mechanism will once more effectively prevent the appearance of any actual deficit in the balance of payments. The foreign exchange value of the country with the excess demand for foreign currencies will depreciate. Such a depreciation will have many effects which will be discussed at length in Part IV. During the period in which it is actually taking place the alteration which is occurring in the prices of imports and of exports will disappoint the expectations and frustrate the plans of the traders at home and abroad. They will be constantly modifying their plans until a new equilibrium is reached at which they are content to continue to trade at new levels at a new and stable rate of exchange. But for our present purpose we need only realize that at each moment of time, even in the disequilibrium of the process of adjustment, a market rate of exchange between the home currency and foreign currencies will appear at which the demand for foreign currency is just equal to the supply of foreign currency. There is no actual deficit or surplus.

A variation in the exchange value of a country's currency is thus itself a symptom of a disequilibrium in the country's balance of payments. A depreciation, for example, suggests that the demand for foreign currencies is in excess of the supply, and that there would have been an actual deficit requiring some accommodating finance if the rate of exchange had not been allowed to depreciate.

We may, therefore, define an 'actual' balance-of-payments deficit as the actual amount of accommodating finance used in any period of time (see row 4 of Table IV), and a 'potential' balance-of-payments deficit as the amount of accommodating finance which it would have been necessary to provide in any period in order to avoid any depreciation in the exchange rate without the employment of exchange controls, import restrictions, or other governmental measures specially devised to restrict the demand for foreign currencies. It is, of course, this 'potential' deficit (or the corresponding 'potential' surplus) which is the proper measure of a balance-of-payments disequilibrium.

It is, however, important to realize that a disequilibrium of this kind may be temporary or may be more or less permanent; and it is the latter, of course, which presents the really serious problem. For example, a country may be momentarily in external balance because of some special uncontinuing item in its balance of payments, but its long-period prospects may be very different. Thus, an agricultural country may be fundamentally in a long-continuing balance-of-payments deficit, but just this year its balance of payments (as shown in row 3 of Table IV) may not be in deficit because it has had a peculiarly good crop of the product on which it mainly relies for export while its competing suppliers have had peculiarly bad crops.

This distinction between temporary and continuing movements is perhaps particularly important in considering the size of any autonomous capital transfers (items 1c and 3c of Table III). The movement of long-term capital funds into a country year after year because that country is undeveloped and is for that reason a continuing field for profitable foreign investment by other countries may differ in this respect very markedly from the receipt of short-term funds. For example, short-term funds may be moving from one country to another because the rate of interest which can be earned on them in the first country has been reduced, while that in the latter has not fallen. Even if the new relationship between rates of interest on short-term funds in the two countries is likely to be permanent, the movement of short-term funds is not likely to continue at its present rate; for when once the available *corpus* of short-term capital has moved from the one centre to the other the flow is likely to cease or at least to slacken.

Here is an autonomous but temporary movement of capital. Even a speculative movement of hot money from a particular country, when the funds are moving because of a speculative—and possibly very short-lived—scare that there is going to be a political revolution or a currency depreciation in the country from which the funds are coming, constitutes in our terminology an autonomous and not an accommodating transaction. It is not taking place in order to find the funds to finance a surplus or deficit in the other items of a country's balance of payments; on the contrary, it may be causing an acute strain on international balances of payments. But it is not only a temporary movement; it may soon reverse itself and flow as quickly in the opposite direction. A country with a deficit on its balance of autonomous trade (row 1 of Table IV) covered by an autonomous capital transfer (included in row 2) is in quite a different position if that capital receipt is a reliable continuing item than if it is a very temporary affair which may even be suddenly reversed. In those parts of the argument of this volume in which it is necessary to bear this distinction in mind we shall distinguish between temporary and continuing elements in the balance of payments and shall speak of the size of the temporary and of the continuing deficit or surplus on a country's balance of payments.

In our terminology, then, perhaps the most basic measure of balance-of-payments disequilibrium is the country's surplus or deficit of potential and continuing payments for autonomous trade and transfers. For short we shall often refer to this simply as the surplus or deficit on the country's balance of payments.

There remains one further preliminary matter of definition. When we talk of a country's balance of payment we are personifying the country in a way which often leads to carelessness of thought. A country does not demand imports; it is the private traders or the State importing organizations of the country who do so. A country does not impose import restrictions; it is the government of the country which does so. In order to analyse balance-of-payments problems usefully it is essential to bear in mind at every stage what class of persons or institutions is responsible for the action which we are discussing. The chief distinction will be between the action of private traders on the one hand and the action of governmental authorities on the other. For example, an argument which concludes with some phrase such as 'the country will then have an incentive to increase its imports' has failed to make it clear whether the situation is one in which private traders will wish to import more (e.g. because foreign products have become cheaper) or one in which the government of the importing country is likely to be willing to relax its restrictions on imports (e.g. because its monetary reserves of foreign currency have risen). These are obviously two very different situations.

In what follows we shall avoid, as far as possible, the personification of a country in its economic relations with other countries. We shall talk of the 'residents' of a particular country when we want to refer to all persons or institutions which are held to belong to that country and which may have economic relations with the residents of other countries. We shall talk of the 'producers' in a particular country when we wish to refer to those persons and institutions who are residents of that country and who make goods or services whether they be for export or home consumption, whether they be capital goods or goods and services for current consumption, and whether they be for sale to private individuals or to governmental or other public authorities. We shall talk of the 'purchasers' in a particular country when we wish to refer to those residents of the country who are purchasing goods and services for final use in that country,[1] whether the goods and services purchased be home-produced or imported, whether they be capital goods or goods and services for current consumption, and whether the purchasers be private individuals, business concerns, or public authorities. We shall sometimes talk of the 'importers' and 'exporters' of a particular country when we wish to refer specifically to purchasers or their agents who are purchasing imported as opposed to home-produced products or to producers or their agents who are selling their products in foreign countries as opposed to the domestic market. Finally, we shall talk of the 'authorities' in a particular country when we wish to refer to those institutions which determine the governmental economic policy of the country. Authorities will thus include (i) the 'banking system', by which we shall mean those institutions which determine the total supply of money in the economy, (ii) the 'fiscal authorities', by which we shall mean the central and local authorities in their capacities of raising and spending public funds, (iii) the 'commercial authorities', by which we shall mean the government in its capacity of determining such commercial matters as the restriction of imports, and (iv) the 'exchange control', by which we shall mean the authority responsible for instituting and operating any governmental controls over payments by residents of the country to residents of other countries.

It would be unbearably pedantic never to personify any country. For example, to insist always on saying the 'balance of payments between residents in country A and residents in other countries' instead of 'country A's balance of payments' would hardly be acceptable. But by the liberal use of the above terminology for the various persons and institutions which the phrase 'country A' may cover in various contexts we shall hope to avoid much confusion of thought.

[1] In other words, purchasers are those persons and institutions responsible for the 'domestic expenditure' of the country as defined on p. 35 below.

CHAPTER II

THE INTERNATIONAL CONSISTENCY OF
BALANCE-OF-PAYMENTS DEFINITIONS

IN the last chapter we examined the meanings that can be attached to a single country's balance of international payments. But a balance of payments must involve more than one country, any country's balance of payments being a statement of the transactions between it and the rest of the world. Our next task is, therefore, to ensure that all countries attach consistent meanings to the items which make up their balance of payments.

The first point to observe is that each international transaction has a double aspect: while it is a payment (e.g. for imports or to finance a loan abroad) for the residents in one country, it must simultaneously be a receipt (e.g. from exports or from borrowing from abroad) for the residents in another country. In Tables I and II given in the previous chapter each payment in the account of the country in question must be a receipt in the account of some other country; and each receipt in the account of the country in question must be a payment in the account of some other country.

But there is a further question which needs careful examination. Given that a payment by residents of country A must be a receipt by residents of country B, does it follow that the receipt by residents of country B must (or should be made to) fall under the category corresponding to the payments by residents of country A? Must, for example, an autonomous import of a commodity into country A be matched not merely by a receipt by residents of country B but by an autonomous commodity export from country B? In what follows in this volume it will be seen that it is of the greatest convenience if each single international transaction can be recorded in the same category of transactions both when it is paid from the paying country and when it is received into the receiving country. Is this always possible?

In this connexion we have two sets of classification to consider: first, that adopted in Tables I and II where transactions were divided into four main groups as payments or receipts for trade in commodities, for trade in services, for unrequited transfers, and for capital transfers; and secondly, that adopted in Tables III and IV where a twofold classification of payments and receipts was adopted by distinguishing between autonomous and accommodating transactions. Reflection suggests that with a little care a transaction can, and indeed should, always be entered into the same category for receiving and paying country so far as the first classification into commodities, services, unrequited transfers, and capital transfers is concerned, but that a transaction may be genuinely autonomous for the receiving (or paying) country but accommodating for the other.

Let us first consider this latter distinction between autonomous and accommodating transactions. Transactions involving the import and export of gold present a good case in point. Consider a movement of gold from country A to country B. Now, if this gold is part of the normal monetary reserve of the central bank of country A and is moving to form part of the normal monetary reserve of the central bank of country B and if the movement is taking place simply because there is an excess of payments from A's residents to B's residents equal to this amount on all the other items in the balance of payments, the receipt from the sale of the gold by A's central bank is an accommodating receipt and the payment for the purchase of the gold by B's central bank is an accommodating payment.

But what if the gold is being imported into B as a raw material for the production of gold fillings by B's dentists and (what is more important in reality) is being exported from A as part of the normal annual produce of the gold mines in A, which provide what is to A's producers a normal industrial product for sale to other countries? Clearly in these cases the sale of the gold represents an autonomous receipt for A and payment for B. In this case, the gold is not being moved in order to find the finance to 'accommodate' a deficit or surplus on the other items of the balance of payments of either country.

But unfortunately for the tidiness of any scheme of balance-of-payments statistics, there is no reason to expect these two categories to coincide. The annual output of the gold of the gold-exporting countries is likely in fact in large measure to be imported for addition to the monetary reserves of the gold-importing countries. It is an autonomous export for A but its purchase represents an accommodating payment for B. Country B has a surplus without country A having a deficit, on the balance of autonomous trade and transfers.

Another example of a similar divergence would be if the authorities of country A were to mobilize foreign securities held by the residents of country A for sale on the capital market in country B to the residents of country B in order to raise the funds necessary to finance a deficit in country A's balance of autonomous trade and transfers. Such a sale would be a clear case of accommodating foreign disinvestment to country A. But the private purchasers of the securities on the capital market in country B would be buying them because their price would fall until their purchase represented a normal profitable investment. Their purchase would represent an autonomous foreign investment in country B, and there would be no reason for anyone in country B to feel that country B had a surplus, although country A had a deficit, on the balance of autonomous trade and transfers.

There is no clever way round this divergence. To the extent that one country may have a surplus (deficit) without any other having a deficit (surplus) on the balance of autonomous trade and transfers, the world total of autonomous receipts will exceed (fall short of) the world total of autonomous payments. In such circumstances the authorities in one country of the world will feel as if they have a balance-of-payments surplus (deficit) to face, without the authorities in any other country feeling that they have a corresponding deficit (surplus); and this is a real fact for which allowance must be made in our analysis. This possibility is not unreal; but it is unlikely in fact to be quantitatively as important as the fundamental disequilibria in balances of payments which develop when one country's surplus is matched by another's deficit. Accordingly, in what follows we shall neglect this case unless we make specific mention of it. We shall assume that one country's accommodating payments are matched by another's accommodating receipts except in those cases where the argument demands that special notice should be taken of the possibility of divergence between the two.

But when we come to the principle of classification of transactions adopted for Tables I and II, namely, into transactions in commodity trade, in services, in unrequited transfers, and in capital transfers, there is no need for any divergence. If each transaction is carefully and consistently defined, what is a payment for an import of a commodity for country A must be a receipt for an export of a commodity for country B, and so on. Each transaction has obviously the two aspects, that of a payment and that of a receipt; and if for both purposes it is carefully defined in exactly the same way it must fall into the same category both in the payer's and the receiver's account.

Nevertheless care is needed to achieve such an international consistency. The sort of problems which arise may be illustrated by two examples from the choice of various methods of recording commodity imports and exports for purposes of balance-of-payments statistics.

First, how should the imports and exports be valued? Here the most obvious example of the many possible causes of divergence is the question whether imports should be recorded as including the insurance and freight involved in shipping them from the country of export (c.i.f.) or whether they should be recorded as including only the value of the goods when put on board the ship at the exporting country's port (f.o.b.).

As far as the self-consistency of any one country's balance-of-payments record is concerned, either method of recording is possible provided that the other items in the balance of payments are suitably adjusted. Consider the following figures, reproduced from items 1, 2, 5, and 6 of Table I:

	$ m.		$ m.
Exports of goods . . .	650	Import of goods . . .	900
Export of services . . .	160	Imports of services . .	90
Balance of visible and invisible trade	180		
Total	990	Total	990

Let us suppose that both the commodity exports of $650 m. and the commodity imports of $900 m. are recorded f.o.b. in this table. What difference would now be made to the figures if the commodity imports were recorded c.i.f.? Let us suppose that the cost of the insurance and freight of shipping the $900 m. worth of goods into this country is $80 m., of which sum $20 m. represents a payment to foreign shippers, insurance agents, etc., and $60 m. a payment to shippers, insurance agents, etc., of the importing country. Then the following would be the figures with imports valued c.i.f.:

	$ m.		$ m.
Exports of goods . . .	650	Imports of goods (900+80) .	980
Exports of services (160+60) .	220	Imports of services (90−20) .	70
Balance of visible and invisible trade	180		
Total	1,050	Total	1,050

Commodity imports are now $80 m. larger. Of this $20 m. represents a payment to foreign shippers, etc. Previously this $20 m. must have been included in the $90 m. of imports of foreign services to account for the foreign shipping services needed to bring the goods to the importing country. Now this $20 m. is already included in the gross purchase price which is paid to foreigners for the imports and must be excluded from the separate record of imports of foreign services, which thus falls to $70 m. The remaining $60 m. of the increased value of imports represents a payment made to domestic shippers, etc. for bringing the goods to the country. Since the gross purchase price paid to the foreigners for the imports now includes the total cost of bringing the goods to the shores of the importing country, the domestic shippers, etc., must be represented as selling this $60 m. worth of their shipping and similar services to the foreign suppliers of the country's imports in order to help them to bring these goods to the importing country's shores. Exports of services must, therefore, be raised by $60 m. to $220 m.

It will be observed that the change leaves the balance of visible and invisible trade unaltered. It is merely a reshuffle as between visible and invisible items within this balance. But if it is desired to maintain an international consistency between all the constituent elements in all countries' balances of payments (in the sense that the total of all importing countries' visible imports should equal the total of all exporting countries' visible exports and the total of world invisible imports should equal the total of world invisible exports) it is by no means a matter of indifference how the items are valued for the purpose of definition and record. Either all imports and all exports should be valued c.i.f. or all imports and all exports should be valued f.o.b. In the former case a movement of goods from A to B will be recorded both as A's export and as B's import inclusive of all shipping and insurance charges needed to deliver the goods to B, and any shipping services rendered by residents of B to help to achieve the delivery of the goods to B will be recorded as an invisible export of services from B to A. In the latter case the movement of goods from A to B will be recorded as A's export and as B's import exclusive of the cost of getting the goods from A to B and any shipping services rendered by residents of A to help to achieve the delivery of the goods will be recorded as an invisible export of services from A to B.

Since in practice exports are recorded f.o.b. by all countries and imports are also recorded f.o.b. by a large number of countries it will accord more closely with reality if, in order to achieve international consistency in the argument, we treat all visible exports and imports as f.o.b.

A second and similar problem arises in determining the point of time at which commodity trade should be valued. Goods are exported from country A to country B. Should this appear in the exports of A and the imports of B when payment is made for the goods, when the liability for the transaction is incurred, or when the goods actually move from A to B, and in this last case should it be when the goods leave A or when they reach B? Unless a coherent basis is more or less universally adopted for statistical purposes in this matter, it will not be possible to compare one country's imports with the net exports of the rest of the world; and unless we adopt a single basis of definition, our analysis cannot proceed on the assumption that one country's imports is the same thing as the net exports of the rest of the world. If in A exports are expressed as the value of the goods which leave its shores and in B imports are expressed as the amount paid for imports, and if the importers of B are obtaining additional credit from the exporters of A, B's recorded imports from A will fall short of A's recorded exports to B. Part of what is recorded in A's balance of payments as a receipt from autonomous commodity exports and as a payment for an autonomous loan to B will appear neither in B's payments for autonomous imports nor in her receipts from autonomous borrowing.

(i) *The payments basis*. In some circumstances it may be most convenient statistically to record imports and exports on the basis of the payments actually made for imports and exports. This may well be so, if the statistics are obtained from a foreign exchange control whose administrative task involves the recording of payments and receipts of foreign exchange for various purposes. And for some purposes it may be convenient to have a cash account. But this is not, of course, the proper basic account for a country any more than it would be for a firm or an individual. Suppose the residents of country A to be importing a great deal more than usual for which they have not yet paid. On a cash basis the external account in Table I would show no exceptional items. Yet the position would be much more truly recorded if the imports of goods (item 5 of Table I) included the value of the exceptionally large imports and if this were offset by the inclusion in item 4 of the borrowing from abroad which the credits obtained by country A's importers from country B's exporters truly represented.

(ii) *The transactions basis*. One method of getting rid of these inadequacies of a cash account would be to record imports and exports when the contract was signed, or the liability was otherwise incurred, for the purchase of the goods in question. But this raises other difficulties. Suppose that importers in country A (whether private merchants or a State importing agency) enter into a long-term contract to purchase supplies of a commodity in B to be imported into A over the next five years. In such cases it may be right and proper to enter in item 4 of Table I a figure representing the liability to pay so and so much to B in the future for these goods and in item 8 a corresponding figure representing the liability of A to provide so and so much in value of this commodity. But to enter the whole of the five years' imports of the commodity in the imports (item 5 of Table I) of the year in which the contract was signed would be altogether unnatural. If this were done one would, as it were, be pretending that the goods had already been imported; that they had not all been consumed, so that part were stored at home; and they had been imported on credit. This would involve the recording of the whole value of the transaction in imports (item 5 of Table I); the treatment of the whole of the unconsumed part of the 'imports' as if they had been added to the domestic stocks of commodities[1]; and the inclusion in item 4 of Table I of the liability to pay in the future for the supplies as they were in fact provided by the exporting country.

But suppose that the goods for the next five years were in fact actually purchased now on credit and were stored in the exporting country. The record would not, of course, be so unnatural. It would

[1] They would need to be added to item 3 in Table VI (see p. 34).

merely involve recording as an import something which had been actually bought abroad but not yet shipped, and as an item in domestic stocks (item 3 of Table VI) something which had been in fact stored abroad. But even in this case the record would be unnatural in certain respects. If a company in country A purchases a subsidiary plant in country B, this is not recorded as an import and as an addition to the domestic stock of plant and machinery (item 3 of Table VI). It is recorded merely as an element of foreign investment in item 8 of Table I. If merchants in country A purchase stocks of a commodity in country B and store it there, why should it not be similarly treated?

(iii) *The movements basis.* This suggests that the best course is to define imports and exports as the value of the goods which actually move from the one country to the other in the period in question. This gives a reasonably precise definition of imports and exports. It also gives a reasonably precise definition of foreign and domestic investment and disinvestment (item 5 of Table II and 3 of Table VI) in so far as changes in the ownership of goods are concerned. Country A's foreign investment would then include the addition to the stock of goods owned by residents of A but situated outside A and the reduction of the stock of goods situated in A but owned by residents of countries other than A; and country A's domestic investment would include the addition to the whole stock of goods situated inside A.

If this basis of definition is adopted, there is no need to make any exception even in the case of gold movements. A movement of gold from A to B is, according to our definition, a commodity export from A to B when it actually moves from A to B. Whether or not it is an autonomous or an accommodating transaction (broadly speaking, a monetary or a commercial movement) is, as we have seen, altogether another matter. If when the gold moves from A to B it does not change ownership (e.g. the central bank of A now owns it under earmark in country B), then it represents: (i) a reduction in domestic investment in A and an increase in domestic investment in B (less gold stock in A and more in B); (ii) a commodity export by A and import by B; and (iii) an increase in A's and a decrease in B's foreign investment (an increase in the stock of gold situated in B but owned by A).

Even if this basis of recording commodity imports and exports when the goods actually move from one country to another is adopted, certain tiresome subsidiary problems would remain of which we may give two examples.

In the first place, what is meant by a country? For example, is country B's embassy in country A part of country B or of country A? If the former, then the goods sent from B to its embassy in A are not part of B's exports and should not be recorded in A's imports. If the latter, then they should appear in both countries' foreign trade statistics; and in this case the expenditure of B's embassy staff in A on these goods must be recorded as an invisible service (comparable to a tourist service) provided by A to these residents of B, or alternatively B's embassy staff in A must be regarded as residents in A whose incomes are part of the national income of A, in which case their incomes must be regarded as being earned by selling to the government of B that particular 'invisible' service which bureaucrats may be supposed to provide. In a case like this little matters except consistency of definition.

Secondly, to which country do the high seas belong? When goods are shipped from A to B are they in A or in B when they are on the high seas between the two countries? If goods are all valued f.o.b. then the logical course would be to define them as being in the importing country B as soon as they leave the shores of the exporting country A. But this would mean that B's imports should be recorded not as the f.o.b. value of the goods imported into B in the period in question but as the f.o.b. value of the goods exported from other countries in the period in question for the destination of B; and any additional goods on the high seas in transit to B should be included as part of the addition to B's domestically held stocks of commodities. This point is, however, likely to be of minor significance unless very rapid changes in prices or the volume of trade are taking place.

A coherent basis is also required for the other elements in the balance of payments besides imports and exports in order to ensure that A's payments under any heading of Table I should be the same as B's receipts under the same heading. Let us take one illustration from the items for transfers.[1]

On what principle should one decide whether to treat a particular transaction as an item of invisible trade or as an item of transfer in the balance of payments? To take an example, in Chapter I interest received by the residents of country A on capital invested in country B has been treated as part of A's invisible exports, i.e. as representing the sale by owners of capital in A to users of capital in B of the current services of part of A's capital stock; but remittances from B to A of money by persons who have in the past emigrated from A to B, to their relatives still left in A are treated as a transfer from B to A. Why should we not treat the capital as having emigrated from A to B and the income earned on it in B and paid to creditors in A as a transfer?

---

[1] In general it will probably be best to adopt the principles that invisible trade should be recorded at the value and at the point of time at which the actual service is rendered, and that transfers should be recorded at the value and at the point of time at which the gift is legally handed over, or at which the liability for a debt is actually incurred or discharged, or at which the ownership of an asset actually changes.

Is there any difference, in actual economic fact, in the internal or external position of A or of B between the case where the residents of A receive $100 m. a year from the residents of B by way of interest on capital and the case where the same people receive the same sum from the same sources by way of emigrants' remittances? Yet if a distinction is drawn we should seem to be assuming that there is an essential difference, because the one (i.e. interest payments) would increase the balance of autonomous trade of A, whereas the other (i.e. emigrants' remittances) would not; and in Chapter III we shall suggest that a change in the balance of autonomous trade affects a country's domestic expenditure and national income in a way in which a change in its balance of transfers does not.

Such distinctions as we have been drawing are inevitably somewhat arbitrary at the margin where it is always difficult to draw a line which does not fail to separate some instances that are more alike than unlike. But the clue to the logical and formal consistency of what we have done is to be found in the definition of the national income. Is the interest on A's capital invested in B part of A's or of B's national income? And are the emigrants' remittances from B to A part of A's or of B's national income? There must be international consistency on this point. These items must be treated as either A's or B's income; they must not be treated as the income of both or of neither. We have treated the interest payment to A as an invisible export by A because we shall treat the interest on this capital as part of A's national income and not as part of B's national income. If this is done, the receipt of a larger interest on A's foreign investment in B will represent an increase in A's national income; and the payment to A must be treated as in return for an export from A, since A's net visible and invisible exports to B are meant to represent all those payments by residents of B to residents of A which directly generate national income in A.

Emigrants' remittances from B to A we have, on the other hand, treated as part of B's national income and not as part of A's national income. That is to say, when an individual in B transfers $100 m. to an individual in A we have not represented that as a fall in B's and a rise in A's national income, but as a transfer out of a given national income in B to supplement the purchasing power obtained from a given national income in A. For this reason the transaction must be treated as a transfer and not an item of invisible trade; it does not directly generate income in A.

Formally, therefore, it all depends upon the definition of the national income; and for this purpose a consistent set of definitions must be adopted for all the countries in our world system, so that every element of income is counted once but once only. The general basis on which we have proceeded is to decide that income from all the factors of production owned by the residents[1] (or the State) of A is A's national income, no matter where the factors themselves may be situated nor to whom the income may ultimately be transferred. The element of rent, profit, and interest in A's national income is the rent, profit, and interest earned on the instruments of production owned by A's residents or public authorities, and this may be greater or less than the rent, profit, and interest earned on the instruments of production situated in A. Reparations paid by the government of B to the government of A we treat as a transfer from B to A and not as an invisible export from A to B, because the income from which the payment is raised in B (by way of taxation or borrowing by B's government) is treated as part of B's and not of A's national income.

The formal problem is soluble on these lines. It remains true, of course, that the actual difference in economic effect between a receipt of interest on a foreign investment and a receipt of an emigrant's remittance may be negligible. This we have to treat *ad hoc* as we discuss each problem. For example, in what follows we shall often have to allow for the fact that a transfer from B to A may cause an increase in domestic expenditure in A because the national income of A is now supplemented by the increased purchasing power represented by the transfer. This will correspond to the effect which an increased receipt of A from increased visible or invisible exports will have in increasing the national income in A and so (by way of rule i on p. 37 below) leading to an increase in domestic expenditure. Things which are formally treated in different categories can thus be explained as having very similar effects.

If the world were made up of two countries only, this sort of consideration would be all that need be discussed on the formal matter of the inter-connexions of national balances of international payments. For many problems we can treat the world as if it were made up of two countries, namely, of the country in which we are interested on the one hand and of the rest of the world on the other. In Parts I to V of this volume we shall confine our attention to these problems, i.e. of balance between one country on the one hand and the rest of the world on the other. But a number of problems of economic policy, in particular those connected with the choices between bilateralism and multilateralism or between discrimination and non-discrimination, arise simply because the world is made up of a system of more than two

---

[1] It remains, of course, to determine what constitutes 'residence'. For logical consistency everyone must be a resident in one and only one country. When he is staying in another country and spending money there he is a 'tourist' and giving rise to tourists' expenditure. Are members of foreign embassy staffs or of armies of occupation 'residents' or 'tourists'? And if you live three months in each year in each of four countries, of which are you a 'resident' at any given time?

countries. We shall, however, postpone until Part VI of this volume all the formal and analytical problems which arise specifically because we have to deal with problems involving more than two countries. Until we reach Part VI we shall confine ourselves to the relationships between two countries A and B, of which A may be taken to represent one particular country (or group of countries, e.g. the sterling area) and B to represent the rest of the world.

CHAPTER III

NATIONAL INCOME, DOMESTIC EXPENDITURE, AND THE BALANCE OF TRADE

IN Chapter I we considered the definition of a country's balance of international payments. In Chapter II we examined the way in which the items in the balance of payments must be defined in order to obtain an internationally consistent system. In this chapter we shall complete our preliminary observations on the meaning of the balance of payments by considering how a country's balance of international payments fits into its own domestic economy.

Let us first consider the relationship between the national income and the national expenditure of a 'closed economy', i.e. of a country without any international economic or financial relationships with other economies. This subject would have to receive extensive treatment if we were writing a Theory of Domestic Economic Policy; but for our present purpose we must confine ourselves to a brief description of the most salient points.

The national income of a country may be defined as the income which the different factors of production receive from the production and sale of the goods and services which these factors of production produce. Thus the national income is made up of the wages and salaries received by persons for the work which they do, of the rents received on the land and other similar assets which the landlords hire out for use in productive industry or for the immediate satisfaction of consumers' needs, of the interest paid by entrepreneurs or other producers on the capital which is borrowed and employed by them in the production of goods and services, and of the profit which is left over to the entrepreneur when he has sold his product and out of the sale price has paid his wages and salary bill, his rent, his interest, and other current expenses of production.

These incomes are all generated by the demand for the goods and services which the labour, land, capital, and enterprise of the country produce. A first way to enumerate the national income of a country is to enumerate the incomes earned by all these factors of production; but a second way to enumerate the same national income is to add up all the expenditures on the goods and services produced by these factors of production. If care is used in defining the terms appropriately, the value of the goods and services sold must be equal to the value of the incomes received by everyone engaged in the production of those goods and services. The amount of money paid by the purchaser is the same as the amount of money received by the seller. These are merely two ways of enumerating the same total.

The final demand for goods and services which generates the incomes of those engaged in the production of these goods and services may, in a 'closed economy', be conveniently divided into four main parts. First, there is the demand of private individuals for goods and services for personal consumption. This figure will include the total expenditure by private persons on food, drink, tobacco, clothing, rents of dwelling houses, holidays, haircuts, etc. Secondly, there is the demand of the public authorities, including local as well as the central government, for goods and services to provide the current services of defence, police, justice, education, and the like. Thirdly, there is the demand by private industry and private enterprise in general for goods and services for the purpose of adding to the capital equipment of the community—for the building of new factories, the installation of new plant and machinery, the construction of additional dwellings, the accumulation of greater stocks of raw materials, of goods in process, or of finished goods, and so on. Finally, there is the demand of public authorities for goods and services for the purpose of adding to that part of the community's capital equipment which is under the control of such authorities—for example, for the construction of new roads, for the building of new schools, for the capital development of socialized industries, and so on.

If we add up the expenditure in any period of time on goods and services purchased under these four heads, the total should be equal to the total of rent, interest, profit, salaries, and wages earned in the production of the community's output of goods and services. But in order to make sure that these two sums are identically the same, care must be taken in the treatment of the various items. To treat this subject in detail would involve a long and laborious discussion which would not be relevant to our discussion of the balance of payments. But the following salient points may be noted here.

First, there may be certain elements of the national income and national expenditure which do not give rise to an actual monetary purchase. For example, a man who is living in his own house does not, as occupier, actually pay himself, as landlord, a money rent for the house; but his real economic position is best described as if his income were greater by the annual value of his house and as if his expenditure on consumption (under the heading of cost of renting a dwelling) were greater by a similar amount. No damage is, of course, done to the balance between the national income and the national expenditure, provided that the addition is made both to the national income (under the heading of rents received by landlords) and to the national expenditure (under the heading of payments for rent of dwellings).

Secondly, there is the problem of 'transfer incomes', i.e. of incomes received, but not in payment for any productive services rendered. Compare, for example, the benefit paid by the State to an unemployed man and the wages paid by the State to a policeman. The latter is, and the former is not, normally regarded as the purchase of a service by the State. The wage of the policeman is, therefore, included in the figure for public expenditure on goods and services (under the heading of the provision of police services) and also in the figure of national income under wages. The 'transfer income' paid by the State to the unemployed is, however, not included in the figure for public expenditure on goods and services nor in the figure of wages in the national income. Interest on the national debt is usually treated in a similar way, being excluded both from the figures of public expenditure on goods and services and from the figures of interest received in the national income. The balance between the national income and national expenditure will be preserved provided that, once a decision has been reached on any element of public expenditure that it is a 'transfer payment', it is excluded both from the figures of national expenditure and from those of national income.

Thirdly, in the national expenditure we must include only expenditures on goods and services for final use for consumption by persons or public authorities or for adding to the net stock of capital equipment by private or public enterprise. Consider the expenditure by an individual of $8 on the purchase of a shirt. The shirt-maker receives $8, of which he keeps as his own profit or pays in wages or salaries to his workers or in rent or interest to his landlord or creditors $3, passing on the other $5 in purchase of the cloth. The manufacturer of the cloth receives $5, of which he keeps as profit, or pays in wages, salaries, rent, or interest $4, passing on the other $1 for the purchase of the raw material. The producers of the raw material thus receive an income of $1. The total income earned is the $1 in the production of the raw material plus the $4 in the working up of the raw material into cloth and the $3 in working up the cloth into a shirt—a total of $8. Against this must be set the personal expenditure of $8 on the final product, the shirt, when it is ready for consumption. The national expenditure on goods and services must not include the expenditure of $5 by the shirt-maker on the purchase of the intermediate product 'cloth' nor the expenditure by the maker of the cloth of $1 on the raw material.

This principle that the national expenditure must include only the final and not the intermediate demands for goods and services has a special application in the case of the demand for capital goods and for productive equipment in general. Suppose that, as in the above example, the manufacturer of cloth receives $5 for his cloth and pays $1 for his raw material, keeping $4 in his own business. But suppose now that only $2½ of this $4 represents his own profit or the rent, interest, wages, or salaries which he pays out, and that the remaining $1½ represents a depreciation allowance which he puts aside in order at some later date to replace his machinery as it wears out. The balance between national income and national expenditure is now upset since national expenditure totals $8 (personal expenditure on a shirt) and the national income totals $6½ ($1 in the production of the raw material, $2½ in the working up of the material into cloth, and $3 in the working up of the cloth into the shirt). The depreciation allowance of $1½ must be deducted from the national expenditure to preserve the balance. The meaning of this should be clear. Some producer, who might, of course, be the manufacturer of cloth himself, or might be another manufacturer in the same industry or in another industry, is—we may suppose—installing new machinery worth $9 in the period of which we are speaking. This expenditure of the $9 on new machinery will, of course, directly or indirectly generate incomes of $9 in the industries producing machinery. But of this $9 only $7½ can be regarded as a net addition to the community's capital equipment, since part of the $9 gross increase in the community's capital equipment is offset by the $1½ depreciation of the equipment of our shirt manufacturer which is not being replaced this year. The national accounts might be shown as follows:

National Expenditure	$	*National Income*	$
Personal consumption (purchase of shirt)	8	Wages, salaries, interest, rent, and profit in—	
Gross domestic investment (purchase of new machinery) .	9	(i) production of raw material	1
Less Depreciation allowances .	1½	(ii) production of cloth .	2½
Net domestic investment . .	7½	(iii) production of shirt .	3
		(iv) production of machinery	9
Total net national expenditure .	15½	Total net national income .	15½

Fourthly, the existence of indirect taxes or of subsidies on the goods and services purchased means that there is a divergence between the amounts of money actually paid by the final purchasers of the goods and services and the amounts received in profits, interest, rent, wages, and salaries in their production. Thus, suppose that of the $8 spent on the shirt in the previous example, $1 represented a purchase tax which accrued directly to the government. There would remain only $7 to generate income for the factors of production engaged in the industries directly or indirectly involved in the production of the shirt. Or suppose that in addition to the $8 paid by the final consumer of the shirt, the producers received $1 by way of subsidy from the State; in this case the total amount of income generated for the factors of production engaged in the industries directly or indirectly involved in the production of the shirt would be $9. In other words, we must add any indirect taxes to, and subtract any subsidies from, the rent, interest, profit, salaries, and wages received by the factors of production in order to obtain a figure for the value of the national income which will correspond to the market value of the products produced by those factors.[1]

With these explanations we may present Table V in illustration of the balance between national income and national expenditure in a closed economy, i.e. in a country which has no economic contacts with any other country. Our picture is as follows. Persons demand goods and services for personal consumption to the extent of $3,000 m. at market prices (item 1); the central government and other public authorities spend on goods and services for current purposes $2,000 m. (item 2); there is a gross private and public demand for goods and services for

TABLE V

The National Income and National Expenditure of a Closed Economy

National Expenditure	$ m.		National Income	$ m.
1. Private consumption	3,000		7. Rent	320
2. Public consumption.	2,000		8. Interest . . .	810
3. Gross private and public home investment . .	1,200		9. Profit	340
			10. Salaries . . .	730
			11. Wages	1,800
4. *Less* depreciation allowances . .	700			
5. Net home investment . . .	500			
			12. Net national income at factor cost . . .	4,000
			13. *Add* indirect taxes . . +1,700⎱ 1,500	
			14. *Deduct* subsidies . . − 200⎰	
6. Net national expenditure at market prices	5,500		15. Net national income at market prices . .	5,500

[1] Let us call indirect taxes less subsidies 'net indirect taxes'. Then we can add net indirect taxes to the incomes of the factors of production to obtain the net national income 'at market prices'; and this will be comparable to the national expenditure on goods and services valued at the market prices at which they are bought (i.e. including net indirect taxes). This is the procedure adopted in the text and illustrated in Tables V and VI. Alternatively, we could deduct indirect taxes from the national expenditure to obtain the net national expenditure 'at factor cost' (i.e. valued at the cost of production before adding indirect taxes to obtain the market prices); and this would be comparable directly with the incomes earned by the factors of production, i.e. with the net national income 'at factor cost'.

TABLE VI

The National Income and National Expenditure of an Open Economy

National Expenditure	$ m.	National Income	$ m.
1. Private consumption .	3,000	8. Rent	300
2. Public consumption. .	2,000	9. Interest . . .	800
3. Net home investment .	500	10. Profit	320
		11. Salaries . . .	700
		12. Wages	1,700
4. Net domestic expenditure at market prices . .	5,500	13. Net national income at factor cost . . .	3,820
5. *Deduct* net imports . .	−800	14. *Add* indirect	
6. *Add* net exports . .	+620	taxes . . +1,700⎫	
		15. *Deduct* sub- ⎬ 1,500	
		sidies . . −200⎭	
7. Net national expenditure at market prices . .	5,320	16. Net national income at market prices . .	5,320

adding to the capital equipment of the community of $1,200 m. (item 3), but against this must be set allowances for the depreciation of existing equipment of $700 m. (item 4), so that there is a net demand for capital goods to represent the net additions to the community's capital equipment of $500 m. (item 5). These items add up to a final demand for goods and services at current market prices of $5,500 m. (item 6). But of these market prices $1,700 m. (item 13) represents indirect taxes which go straight to the taxing authority and do not generate rents, interest, profit, wages, or salaries for the producers; but to these market prices must be added $200 m. (item 14) to allow for the receipts of the producers from government subsidies. There remains a net sum of $4,000 m. (item 12) to generate incomes for the producers of these goods and services; and this generates $320 m. rents (item 7), $810 m. interest on capital (item 8), $340 m. profits of enterprise (item 9), $730 m. salaries (item 10), and $1,800 m. wages (item 11).

What difference is made to this picture by removing the assumption that the country under examination is a closed economy, and by assuming that it is an open economy, i.e. by making allowance for the fact that it makes payments to, and obtains receipts from, the rest of the world? In principle, the necessary adjustment is a very simple one. The left-hand side of Table V enumerates all those demands for goods and services which directly or indirectly cause a demand for factors of production (i.e. for the productive services of land, capital, enterprise, and work) whose incomes are enumerated on the right-hand side of the table. The total demand for goods and services for the main purposes enumerated on the left-hand side of Table V (i.e. for personal or public consumption or for private or public net investment) would, however, in an open economy include the demand for imported as well as for home-produced goods. But the demand for imported goods does not directly lead to a demand for the country's own productive resources, but for the productive resources of other countries. Expenditure on imported goods and services must, therefore, be deducted from the expenditures on the left-hand side of Table V. On the other hand, the amount which foreigners spend on the export of goods and services of the country under examination is just as effective in generating income within the country as is any other form of expenditure upon its products. We must accordingly add the value of the country's exports of goods and services to the left-hand side of Table V to obtain a complete enumeration of the income-generating demands for its products.

If $5,500 m. (item 4 of Table VI) is the value at market prices of the net demand for goods and services (whether imported or home produced) for domestic purposes (i.e. for private or public consumption or investment domestically), and if this sum includes a demand for $800 m. of imports (item 5), and if the foreigners are buying $620 m. of the country's exports (item 6), then the net national income at market prices (item 16) generated by this demand for goods and services would be $5,320 m., i.e. $5,500 m. — $800 m. + $620 m.[1] In other words, if the country has an excess of imports over exports of $180 m. then the net national income at market prices will be $180 m. less than its market demand for goods and services (whether imported or home produced) for all purposes of final consumption and investment at home. If we use the term 'domestic expenditure' for the net demand at market prices for imported and home-produced goods for purposes of final use in domestic consumption or investment, then we have the simple relationship

domestic expenditure *less* imports *plus* exports =
net national income,

where exports *less* imports is the balance of visible and invisible trade as shown in row 3 of Table II.

This relationship holds good, of course, for both of our two countries or groups of countries, A and B, into which our world is divided. Remembering that A's imports are equal to B's exports and vice versa we can express the relationship between A's and B's national incomes, domestic expenditures, imports, and exports simply in the manner shown in Table VII.

[1] For the reason why we have shown imports at $800 m. and exports at $620 m. instead of at $990 m. and $810 m. as in row 3 of Table II, see pp. 38–9, below. It will be observed that the deficit on the balance of visible and invisible trade is in any case $180 m.

TABLE VII

A's and B's National Income, Domestic Expenditure, and Foreign Trade

$ m.

		Spending Countries		Total, i.e. national income
		A	B	
		(*a*)	(*b*)	(*c*)
Receiving Countries	A (1)	4,700	620	5,320
	B (2)	800	3,000	3,800
Total, i.e. domestic expenditure	(3)	5,500	3,620	

In this table we represent the amount of expenditure in each country on home products and on the products of the other country. Thus, reading down the figures in column *a* of the table we see that purchasers in country A are represented as spending $4,700 m. on A's products and $800 m. on B's products. Total domestic expenditure in A is therefore $5,500 m. of which $4,700 m. represents a demand for A's products and $800 m. a demand for imports from B. Similarly in column *b* purchasers in country B are represented as spending $620 m. on A's products and $3,000 m. on B's products, making a total domestic expenditure of $3,620 m. of which $620 m. represents a demand for imports from A and $3,000 m. a demand for home produce.

But these demands in each country for each country's products will determine the national income earned in each country; and these national incomes can be found by reading the figures in each row of the table. Thus in row 1 we see that producers in A receive $4,700 m. from the sale of home-produced goods and services to meet the home demand for A's products, and $620 m. from the sale of home-produced goods and services for export to B to meet the demand of B's purchasers for A's products. A's total national income is, therefore, $5,320 m. Similarly, B's national income is $3,800 m., of which $800 m. is received from the sale of goods and services for export to A and $3,000 m. from the sale of goods and services for home consumption in B.

Table VII is based upon the facts that for each country domestic expenditure *less* imports *plus* exports = the net national income and that each country's imports is the other country's exports. In what follows we shall make considerable use of these simple relationships, in order to analyse problems which are concerned (i) with the way in which the balance of foreign trade may affect the demand for home-produced goods and services and so the net national income of any country, or (ii) with the way in which a change in the net national income and the domestic expenditure in a country may affect the demand for imports and so the balance of trade.

These reactions of the balance of trade upon the national income and of the national income upon the balance of trade will come about in various ways which will be discussed in greater detail at a later stage. At this point it may be useful to summarize briefly the main factors at work.

(i) First, an increase in the national income is in itself likely to cause an increase in domestic expenditure. When people have larger incomes from rent, interest, profit, salaries, or wages they may not spend all of it on demanding more goods and services for final use. Part of the increased income may be saved without being spent on new capital goods, part may go in increased tax payments without the State purchasing more goods with the money, and so on. But a part at least of the increase in national income is likely to be spent in increased demand for imported and home-produced goods and services for final use in the country, i.e. is likely to represent an increase in domestic expenditure.

(ii) Second, an increase in domestic expenditure is likely to represent partly an increase in the demand for imports (which will generate incomes in the other country) and partly an increase in the demand for home-produced goods and services (which will generate incomes domestically and thus raise the net national income). That is to say, other things being equal, a larger demand for goods and services in general for final use domestically will normally lead to a larger demand both for home-produced goods and for imports, although the actual proportion between imported and home-produced goods and services may not, of course, remain constant.

(iii) Third, an increase in exports (i.e. in the imports of the other country) will cause an increase in the national income of the exporting country. Since an increased demand by foreigners for a country's products represents an increased demand by foreigners for the services of the factors of production of that country, it will generate a larger national income in that country.

In order that these simple relationships should be true we wish (i) to treat imports as the demand for goods and services in any country, expenditure on which will not generate any income at home but will generate income abroad, and (ii) to treat exports as the foreign demand for the country's products, expenditure on which does not come out of the exporting country's domestic expenditure but does generate income in the exporting country.

It is clear that imports and exports are normally of this character.

There are, however, two qualifications which should be borne in mind.

(i) First, in some cases goods may be exported out of stocks held in the exporting country. When goods are sold out of stock, the purchase of the goods creates income at home only in so far as the stockholder gives orders to the producers to replace his stock. This will normally be the case; but there are occasions on which it will not happen.

The most obvious case is that of the export of gold from the gold reserves of the central monetary authority to find the accommodating finance necessary to pay for a country's imports and other payments abroad. Suppose, for example, that our country is importing goods and services worth $990 m. and exporting goods and services worth $810 m. (the position assumed in Table II); but suppose that of this export of $810 m., $20 m. represented an accommodating export of gold and only $790 m. represented an autonomous export of goods and services, because the country was exporting $20 m. from the gold reserves of its central bank to help to finance a part of its deficit on other items in the balance of payments. We have already explained (p. 24) that this export of gold may properly be recorded as a commodity export. It will also represent an item of domestic disinvestment—the country's domestically held stock of this metal being reduced by this amount. But this export of gold does not, like the ordinary exports of the country's produce, represent a demand by foreigners for the produce of the country and so, directly or indirectly, for the services of the country's productive resources; nor does the accompanying disinvestment in the domestically held stock of gold represent in any way a decline in the domestic demand for goods and services of a sort which will lead to a reduction in the domestic demand for the services of the country's productive resources. Our simple relationship—domestic expenditure *less* imports *plus* exports equals the net national income— still holds good; but here is a case where an increase in exports has caused a reduction in domestic expenditure and not an increase in the national income. In using the relationship it is necessary to remember that there are cases of this kind, in which rule iii above does not hold good.

(ii) Secondly, to some extent a demand by foreigners for a country's exports may generate incomes in the foreign country and not in the home country (thus modifying rule iii above) and a demand by home purchasers for imports may generate incomes in the home country and not in the foreign country (thus modifying rule ii above). This may happen because of what may be called the import content of exports and the export content of imports. Let us consider the illustrative figures of Table II where the country's visible and invisible imports are $990 m. and exports $810 m. But for the production of these exports of $810 m. the country needs to import, say, $100 m. of foreign raw materials. The $810 m. demand for its exports represents in fact only a $710 m. net demand by the foreigners for the country's own production, the other $100 m. being an indirect demand for the foreigner's own raw materials; and the $990 m. demand by the country for imports represents only a $890 m. demand for foreign goods to satisfy its own final needs enumerated in its own domestic expenditure, the remaining $100 m. being the demand for imported raw materials for re-export. Thus one may eliminate this $100 m. import content of exports from both exports and imports, in which case one obtains figures of $710 m. exports and $890 m. imports. But of this remaining $890 m. of demand for imports some part (say $90 m.) represents the raw materials which the foreigners have to obtain from the country in question to make the goods which they are sending to the importing country. In this case only $800 m. of the $890 m. imports represent a demand by our country for the use of the foreigner's productive resources, the remaining $90 m. representing a demand for its own home-produced raw materials; and of the exports of $710 m., only $620 m. represents a demand in the foreign countries for goods for the satisfaction of the true domestic needs of those foreign countries, the remaining $90 m. representing a demand for our country's raw materials for manufacture for re-export to our country. In what follows we shall wish to treat the imports and exports of each country as both net of both the import content of exports and the export content of imports. In future for all balance-of-trade purposes we define imports and exports as net imports and exports in this sense.[1]

Much of the analysis of the immediately following chapters will be concerned with the interactions of the three rules on p. 37 and of the inter-relationships illustrated in Table VII. Some primary change or disturbance takes place. We must then allow for the repercussions in both of our two countries of national income on domestic expenditure, of domestic expenditure on imports and on national income, and of exports on national income, and for the fact that A's imports are B's exports and vice versa. Our problem is, then, to determine the final outcome of the disturbance, first, on the general level of economic activity within each country (i.e. on the national incomes of A and B) and, secondly, on the external economic position of each country (i.e. on the balance of payments between the two countries).

This, broadly speaking, will be the subject matter of Part II.

---

[1] This principle has a multilateral application. If country A imports raw materials from B to manufacture goods to export to C, then C's demand for the imports represents a demand for B's production so far as the raw material content is concerned and a demand for A's production so far as the making up of the raw materials is concerned. In Part VI, where we are dealing with patterns of world trade in terms of net imports and net exports, we shall be using the above definition.

PART II. THE NEUTRAL ECONOMY

PART II. THE NEUTRAL ECONOMY[1]

CHAPTER IV

SPONTANEOUS DISTURBANCES AND
THE NEUTRAL ECONOMY

OUR next task is to consider the nature of the disturbances which may initiate some change in country A's or country B's domestic or external economic position. We start, let us assume, with the position described in Table VII, with a given national income and domestic expenditure in each country and a given flow of trade between them. What are the primary changes or, as we shall call them, the 'spontaneous disturbances' which, by their direct action and their indirect repercussions, may cause a change in the world system of national incomes and balances of payments, and by what mechanisms do they work?

Let us start by making clear certain definitions. In what follows we shall draw a distinction between 'spontaneous', 'policy', and 'induced' changes in the various quantities (such as national incomes, domestic expenditures, balances of trade, and balances of payments) which we are examining. By a 'spontaneous disturbance' we shall mean any change in the underlying conditions, the cause of which we are prepared to take for granted and do not wish to examine, but the effect of which on the domestic and external position of our two countries we wish to examine. By a 'policy' change we shall mean a change which the State or some public authority brings about as a result of a definite decision of State policy in order to achieve some given end of general economic policy and in particular to offset some of the effects of a 'spontaneous disturbance'.[2] Finally, by an 'induced' change is meant a change in some quantity which occurs on purely commercial principles because of the repercussions of some previous 'spontaneous' or 'policy' change.

[1] In the Note at the end of Part III (p. 125) will be found some numerical examples of the operations of the international-trade 'multipliers' which form the subject matter of much of Parts II and III.

[2] It is important to realize that this does not imply that all changes made by public authorities are 'policy' changes. Suppose, for example, that the public authorities are carrying out a school-building programme. There is an invention which makes it cheaper to use home-produced steel rather than imported timber for building, and on purely commercial principles the authorities shift from importing timber to purchasing home-produced steel. This is the 'induced' effect of a 'spontaneous' change. But if they do so in order to reduce imports in order to improve the balance of payments, although on commercial principles imported timber is cheaper than home-produced steel, then this is a 'policy' change.

It may be useful to illustrate these distinctions. A 'spontaneous' increase in domestic expenditure in any country would occur if, for example, private enterprise changed its ideas about future prospects of profit and decided to spend more money on new capital installations of machinery, plant, buildings, etc., or if consumers for one reason or another decided to spend a larger proportion of their incomes on consumption goods and services and to save a smaller proportion. Here would be 'spontaneous' changes which meant that the domestic demand for goods and services increased although there had been no change in the national income or any other of the quantities which we are examining to 'induce' the change. A 'policy' decrease in domestic expenditure would occur if, in order to offset the effects of such a 'spontaneous' increase in domestic expenditure, the authorities decided to decrease their public expenditure on goods and services or to raise the taxes which are levied on private incomes in order to restrain the private demand for goods and services. An 'induced' increase in domestic expenditure would occur when, for example, as a result of a 'spontaneous' or 'policy' increase in domestic expenditure the national income rose as a result of the increased demand for home-produced products and when, as a secondary repercussion, a further increase in domestic expenditure on goods and services was 'induced' as a result of the fact that consumers now had larger incomes to spend.

Similarly, a 'spontaneous' increase in imports would occur when, as a result of a change in taste, private consumers out of any given level of total domestic expenditure shift from purchasing home-produced to purchasing imported goods. A 'policy' decrease of imports would occur if the State, for other than commercial reasons (e.g. in order to give employment at home), decided, out of a given level of total public expenditure, to purchase less imports and more home-produced goods. An 'induced' increase in the volume (or value) of imports would occur if, as a result of a rise in the national income, purchasers decided to buy a larger amount of (or to spend a larger sum on) imported goods.

A similar distinction can be drawn between 'spontaneous', 'policy', and 'induced' changes in foreign transfers. A decision on the part of private lenders to lend abroad rather than at home because of a spontaneous change in their expectations about the relative profitability of foreign and domestic industry or the imposition of a reparations payment on the country in question would be examples of a 'spontaneous' increase in a country's foreign transfers. The imposition of exchange control by a country in order to prevent a flow of lending abroad would represent a 'policy' decrease in foreign transfers. An increased lending abroad because savers had larger resources from which to lend as a result of a rise in the national income at home—itself the result of a 'spontaneous' or 'policy' increase in the demand for the country's products—would afford an example of an 'induced' increase of foreign lending.

Now there is an almost unlimited number of possible types of spontaneous disturbance whose effects we may wish to examine. A's or B's authorities might depreciate their exchange rate, impose an import duty, or offer an export subsidy; and we might wish to examine the effects of such action upon the national incomes of A and B and the trade between them. The wage-rate might be increased in one or more of A's or B's industries. The banking system in A or B might increase the supply of money and thereby reduce the rate of interest in one or other of the countries, which might have direct repercussions upon the domestic expenditure and the net foreign lending of the country concerned. And so on. For our present purpose we can choose only one or two typical instances of spontaneous disturbance in order to examine their effects as an illustration of the method which might be adopted to analyse the effects of other disturbing factors.

(i) The first type of spontaneous disturbance which we shall examine is a spontaneous increase or decrease of domestic expenditure in one of our two countries. This involves an increased or decreased demand for goods and services for domestic consumption or for domestic investment by the public authorities or by the private consumers or entrepreneurs in the country, due in the latter case to a change in their choice between spending their incomes on consumption goods instead of saving or in their expectations of future profit on domestic investment. The change is not due to any previous change in their incomes which has 'induced' the larger expenditure. It is 'spontaneously' generated, as it were. It should be observed that a spontaneous increase (or decrease) in domestic expenditure of a given amount does not mean a spontaneous increase (or decrease) in expenditure on home-produced goods and services of the same amount. On the contrary, it will be assumed that there is some normal net import content in any increment of domestic demand for consumption goods or capital goods, so that a spontaneous increase in domestic expenditure may be broken down into two parts: a spontaneous increase in the demand for home-produced goods and a spontaneous increase in the demand for imported goods, the two parts having some natural relationship depending upon the circumstances of each country and of each particular form which the spontaneous increase in domestic expenditure may have taken.

(ii) The second type of spontaneous disturbance which we shall examine is an increase in productivity in one of our two countries. In country A, for example, the general level of output per head goes up by 10 per cent because of a series of technical inventions. What effect will this reduction in costs in country A have directly and indirectly upon the trade between A and B and upon the national incomes of A and B?

(iii) The third spontaneous disturbance which we shall consider is a spontaneous shift of demand, within any given level of domestic expenditure in the country concerned, from the products of that country on to the products of the other, thereby increasing the demand for the second country's products and reducing the demand for the first's without there being any direct change in the total demand for all products. Such a change might be due to a simple change of tastes on the part of consumers.

(iv) Our fourth case is a spontaneous change in foreign transfers. This occurs, for example, when a change in stock-exchange expectations at home and abroad causes persons to purchase foreign rather than domestic securities.

In the real world the spontaneous disturbances with which we have to deal are hardly ever of the 'simple' types enumerated above. They are more likely to be 'complex' in the sense that the given disturbance directly affects not only one of the quantities in which we are interested, but a number of them at the same time. A few examples may serve to illustrate this point.

First, consider a reparations payment from country A to country B. This is a spontaneous increase in foreign transfers from A to B (Type iv above). But the government in A may raise taxation to finance the reparations payment not for the policy purpose of affecting the level of the national income, domestic expenditure, or balance of payments (though it will, of course, have repercussions in those directions), but for the narrowly fiscal purpose of raising the money to transfer to B. Similarly, the government of B may use the reparations receipt to increase its expenditure or to remit taxation. These fiscal changes in A and B will have the effect of causing a decrease in domestic expenditure in A and an increase in domestic expenditure in B, the size of these changes in the two countries in relation to the reparations payment itself depending upon the actual fiscal policy adopted. The whole operation is best regarded as a spontaneous increase in foreign transfers from A to B (Type iv above) combined with a simultaneous spontaneous decrease in domestic expenditure of a certain size in A and an increase in B (Type i above).

Or, consider an important invention or geographical discovery in a certain region of the world which opens up a large new field for profitable investment opportunities in that territory. This may cause people to lend any funds which they have available to this country rather than to invest them at home, and this will represent a spontaneous increase in foreign transfers to the country in question (Type iv above). Simultaneously, the change will probably mean an increased demand for capital goods for developmental projects to take advantage of the new profitable opportunities in the country in question, which will represent a spontaneous increase in domestic expenditure in that country (Type i above). The change may reduce the prospects of profitable exploitation of the same or a competing product in the rest of the world, and thus cause some simultaneous spontaneous reduction in the domestic expenditure of other countries (Type i above). The increased capital development in the one country and the reduced capital development in the rest of the world might mean that one type of equipment (e.g. for exploiting oil resources) was required in place of another (e.g. for exploiting coal resources). This might mean a shift in demand on to the exports of a country which produced the former away from the exports of a country which produced the latter, which would represent a spontaneous increase in the exports of the former and reduction in the exports of the latter (Type iii above). Finally, the invention itself might immediately reduce the costs of production in that country relatively to costs of production in the rest of the world (Type ii above). Thus a change of this kind might involve simultaneous spontaneous disturbances of all the kinds which we have enumerated above.

All that can profitably be done in a general treatment of this subject is to examine the effects of a limited number of typical disturbing factors in order to elaborate a type of analysis which, by suitable adaptations, can be applied to any real problem which may present itself.

We must next consider the institutional setting in which these spontaneous disturbances are assumed to occur. The possible institutional settings are, like the spontaneous disturbances themselves, almost numberless. Our procedure will be to adopt one set of institutional assumptions, which we shall name the 'neutral economy'; to discuss in some detail the effect of some typical spontaneous disturbances in the conditions of the 'neutral economy'; and then to consider what differences would be made by changes in the institutional setting of the 'neutral economy' and, in particular, by changes in the assumptions made about governmental policy.

The following are the five main assumptions which we shall make about the 'neutral economy'.

(i) *Constant fiscal policy.* We assume that there are no policy or induced changes in rates of taxation or in the demand by the public authorities for goods and services. We may treat a change in rates of taxation or in the governmental demand for goods and services as a spontaneous disturbance, the effects of which we wish to examine; but we shall assume that no changes in rates of taxation or in governmental demand for goods and services are made as a matter of policy in order to offset the effects of other spontaneous disturbances and that no such changes are induced as a result of changes in the rest of the economy. This assumption allows, of course, for induced changes in the government's budget surplus or deficit, because as the national income rises or falls, constant rates of tax will raise a larger or smaller total revenue and as prices of goods and services rise or fall a given level of real governmental demand will require a larger or smaller total public expenditure in terms of money.

(ii) *Constant monetary policy*. We assume that the banking system so operates as to prevent any induced changes in the rates of interest and the other terms on which money can be lent or borrowed for given periods of time. This means that the banking system must be prepared to expand (or contract) the total supply of money to the extent necessary to prevent any scarcity (or plenty) of funds in the capital market which may be induced by any other disturbing factor, from causing a rise (or fall) in interest rates. We should be prepared to examine the effect of a spontaneous change in monetary policy (i.e. in interest rates), but we assume that the authorities do not change the rates as a means of offsetting the effect of other disturbing factors nor allow other disturbing factors to affect the rate of interest.

(iii) *Constant money wage rates*. We assume that the trade unions and employers' federations or the State wage-regulating bodies do not alter money wage rates as a result of what happens to the demand for labour and the volume of unemployment or to the general level of prices and the cost of living. In other words, while we may examine the effects of a spontaneous change in money wage rates we assume that they do not vary as a result of variations in other factors.

(iv) *Constant rate of exchange*. We assume that the rate of exchange between A's currency and B's currency is pegged and that this rate is not changed because of what happens to the supply and demand for A's currency in terms of B's currency as a result of any other spontaneous disturbance. Any such divergence between supply and demand in the foreign exchange market (i.e. any deficit in A's or B's balance of payments) is assumed to be met by an accommodating movement of monetary reserves (e.g. gold) from the deficit to the surplus country, and, in accordance with assumption ii above, the internal effects of any such movement of monetary reserves on interest rates is assumed to be offset by the monetary authorities, who vary the total internal supply of money in such a way as to keep such domestic interest rates constant. We may, of course, examine the effects of a spontaneous change in the rate of exchange; but we are assuming that no such change occurs merely as a result of other disturbing factors.

(v) *Constant commercial policy*. We do not necessarily assume complete free trade between A and B. There may be moderate duties on imports or subsidies on exports in either country. But we assume that there are no rigid obstacles (e.g. comprehensive exchange controls or import controls) which prevent changes in conditions of demand or supply in either country from having any effect at all upon the flow of trade and payments between A and B. Moreover, we assume that there are no policy or induced changes in existing rates of duty or subsidy; or, in other words, while we may consider the effects of a spontaneous change in commercial policy we assume that there are no changes in rates of import tax or export subsidy which are induced by other changes or which are adopted as a means of policy to offset the effect of other spontaneous disturbances.

We do not make the above assumptions about the nature of the institutional arrangements in the neutral economy because we suppose them to be the most realistic or most probable assumptions. We choose these assumptions merely in order to have a standard or reference case the working of which we can fully analyse, so that we can then see what would be the effect upon our results of introducing variations of fiscal policy, monetary policy, wage rates, exchange rates, and commercial policy.

The above assumptions are all concerned with social policies or institutions, and we make them provisionally merely in order to have a standard against which we can assess the effects of changes in these institutional arrangements. But in addition to these institutional assumptions we shall have to make one further assumption about the nature of the goods and services produced in the world in order to simplify the analysis. We shall in general divide the products of our two countries into certain broad groups and shall assume that within any one of these broad groups the prices of the various products move up or down together.

At first we shall divide products into only two of these broad groups, namely, into A's products on the one hand and B's products on the other hand; we shall, in other words, be assuming that the prices of all of A's products move up or down more or less in line together, and that the prices of all of B's products move similarly up or down more or less in line together. This will enable us to concentrate attention in the first place upon the most important and obvious international implication of price changes, namely, the extent to which a fall in the price of the products of one country relatively to those of another country will enable the products of the former to be substituted for those of the latter. This assumption will allow us to examine some of the most important international implications of price changes with very great simplification of the argument; but it also, unfortunately, blurs some important issues.

At a later stage (Chapter XVIII) we shall, therefore, modify it by distinguishing[1] between the products of each country's sheltered trades, which we shall call its 'home-trade products', and which are incapable of entering into international trade, and the products of its unsheltered trades or its 'foreign-trade products' which are capable of being exported to the other country or liable to face the direct competition of imports from the other country. But until that point is reached we shall continue to assume that the only price changes with which we are concerned are those between the products of A treated as one single homogeneous group and the products of B treated as another single homogeneous group.

In examining the effects which any spontaneous disturbance will have on these institutional and technical assumptions we shall be most interested in four things: the volume of employment in A; the volume of employment in B; the balance of payments between A and B; and the real terms of trade between A and B.

As far as the effects upon the general level of employment in either country are concerned, we shall be interested in considering the effect of any spontaneous disturbance upon the total money demand (whether internal demand or a foreign demand for the country's exports) for the country's products, i.e. upon the total money expenditure on the country's produce which, as we have seen, is the same as the total national income of that country. For, on the assumption that money wage-rates are constant, an increase in total money expenditure upon the country's products is likely to represent an increase in the demand for that country's labour.

As far as the effects of any spontaneous disturbance upon the balance of payments between A and B is concerned, we shall be interested not only in the effect upon the demand in A for B's products and the demand in B for A's products, which will determine the effect upon the balance of trade between them. We shall also be interested in the effects of the spontaneous disturbance upon the flow of capital funds or of any other transfers between A and B, since these too must be taken into account before we can conclude what effect the change will have upon the total balance of payments between them.

Moreover, as far as the trade items are concerned, we shall not merely be interested in the total balance of trade between A and B; we shall also be interested in the terms of trade, i.e. in the price which A has to pay in terms of her own products in order to obtain a given amount of B's products. Thus, let us suppose that there is some spontaneous disturbance which leaves the balance of trade between A and B unchanged. A's exports remain equal to B's exports before and after the change. But the change might nevertheless mean that the prices

---

[1] Following Professor R. G. Hawtrey. See his *The Balance of Payments and the Standard of Living* (London, Royal Institute of International Affairs, 1950).

of A's products have fallen and those of B's have risen, so producers in A must export a greater *volume* of products to obtain the same *value* of exports, while producers in B can export a smaller volume of products to obtain the same export value. Residents in A will be getting less of B's products in exchange for each unit of their own produce. By the terms of trade between A and B we shall mean the amount of B's produce which is exchanged for a unit of A's produce. The terms of trade therefore move in A's favour if the prices of A's exports rise relatively to the prices of B's exports.

Our programme is then as follows. In the rest of this Part we shall examine the effect of various spontaneous disturbances upon employment and national incomes in A and B and upon the balance of payments and terms of trade between them, on the assumptions of the neutral economy. In Parts III, IV, and V we shall proceed to modify the policy assumptions of the neutral economy in order to see how the adverse effects of various spontaneous disturbances can best be avoided.

CHAPTER V

THE INCOME EFFECTS OF A SPONTANEOUS CHANGE IN DOMESTIC EXPENDITURE[1]

IN this and the following chapter we shall analyse in some detail the secondary repercussions (or what we have called the induced effects) of one particular and simple spontaneous change: namely, a spontaneous increase in domestic expenditure in country A. This will enable us to examine carefully the main interconnexions, and thus in Chapter VII to consider the induced effects of other spontaneous changes more rapidly and in less detail.

Let us then start with an examination of the following problem. There is a spontaneous increase in domestic expenditure in country A. This may occur, for example, because entrepreneurs in A take a more optimistic view than before about the prospects of profit in the future; and accordingly at the given rate of interest at which they can borrow funds for capital development and at the given rate of demand for their products they spend at a higher rate on new capital equipment. What ultimate effects will this boom in country A have upon the total demand for the home-produced goods (i.e. upon the national income) of country A, upon the total demand for B's products, and upon the balance of payments and the terms of trade between A and B, on the assumptions that in neither country is there any change in tax rates, in government demand for goods and services, in rates of interest, in wage rates, in the rate of exchange, or in commercial policy?

Suppose for a moment that country A were a closed economy, i.e. that it had no relations at all with the rest of the world but produced all its own supplies at home, exported nothing, and in no circumstances engaged in any foreign transfers.[2] Then the spontaneous increase in the entrepreneurs' demand in A for capital equipment would directly cause an exactly equal increase in the national income of country A, since the national income is the sum total of the amount earned through the sale of the goods and services produced in A to the final purchasers of goods and services in A. This rise in A's national income would induce some further rise in domestic expenditure; but this secondary rise in domestic expenditure would, for a variety of reasons, probably be less than the rise in the national income which occasioned it.

In the first place, when the demand for A's products rose this would

---

[1] The subject matter of this and the two following chapters is considered in Section VIII (i) of the separate mathematical supplement.

[2] It would be necessary in any Theory of Domestic Economic Policy to treat these problems of the 'closed economy' at considerable length. Here only a very brief sketch is appropriate.

cause an increase of output and employment in A.[1] But the unemployed receive unemployment benefit, and the incomes which wage-earners have to spend do not, therefore, rise as much as the rise in the wages earned in productive industry. Secondly, some part of the rise in the incomes of consumers (whether wage-earners, salary-earners, or the recipients of interest, rent, and dividends) will lead to an increase in the payment of direct taxes (income-tax, surtax, profits-tax, and the like) to the public authorities, and it is only the remainder which represents a rise in the tax-free income available for expenditure on consumption goods. Thirdly, not all of this net increase in tax-free spendable incomes will in fact result in an increase in expenditure on goods and services for consumption. Some part of it will represent an increase in savings. Companies will put more profits to reserves when their profits increase; they will not pass the whole of their increased earnings on in the form of an increased distribution of dividends to their shareholders. And individuals when their incomes rise will not raise their demand for goods and services for consumption by the whole of that amount; part of it they will add to their savings. Fourthly, the remainder of the primary increase in national income (i.e. that part which does not merely replace unemployment benefit or which does not lead merely to increased payments of direct taxes or an increased volume of savings) will, of course, cause a secondary rise in the demand for goods and services for consumption; but if some of these goods or services are subject to indirect taxation (e.g. purchase tax or the duties on beer and tobacco) not the whole even of this will represent a further rise in the incomes earned in productive industry. For the purchase price of these goods and services which are now purchased in greater quantities will have included an element of taxation which will mean merely an increase in the tax revenue of the public authorities and will not cause any secondary rise in the wages, salaries, interest, profits, or rents earned in the production of the goods.

On the other hand, there may be some other factors at work further increasing the demand for goods and services. We are for the moment assuming that the public authorities' demand for goods and services and tax rates remain unchanged, so that we have not now to allow anything for the fact that the increased revenue of the State from direct and indirect taxes or the reduced expenditure by the State on

---

[1] This assumes, of course, that there is an appreciable volume of unemployment in A to start with. But it is only on such an assumption that we can reasonably assume that money wage rates do not rise in spite of an increased demand for labour. If there were no unemployment the increased demand would show itself entirely in higher prices and not at all in increased output. The analysis of the text would, however, work in the case of a 'spontaneous' decrease of domestic expenditure even if there were full employment at the outset; for a decline in the demand for labour in such a case might well cause a decline in employment at constant wage rates.

unemployment benefit may lead to fiscal changes (e.g. increased public expenditure in other directions or reduced rates of taxation) which will further increase the demand for goods and services. We assume that it merely adds to the budget surplus. But it is probable that, consistently with our assumptions, the primary rise in the national income will lead to some induced increase in the demand for goods and services for capital development for which we have not yet allowed. For we are assuming that the banking policy is such as to keep rates of interest constant so that the terms on which funds can be borrowed for capital development remain unchanged. On the other hand, the general increase in the demand for finished goods and services which has caused the rise in the national income is bound to have increased the profitability of industry, particularly since—as we are assuming—there has been no rise in money wage rates when the prices offered for the finished products are improved. Each increase in the demand for finished goods is, therefore, likely to induce some further increase in the demand for capital goods.

Now it is possible that this factor is so important that it outweighs all the other factors (the replacement of unemployment benefit by wages and the increase in tax payments and savings) which tend to make the secondary increase of expenditure less than the primary increase in national income by which it is induced. In this case a primary increase of national income of 100 would induce, say, a secondary increase in demand of 110, and so in national income of the same amount. This secondary increase in national income of 110 would induce, say, a tertiary increase in demand of 121 and so in national income; and so on. The primary increase in national income would then give rise to a chain reaction by which the unstable economy would go soaring into an uncontrolled inflation by ever-increasing waves of increased demand and national income.

But this could not, of course, go on indefinitely. Sooner or later something would have to be done to put a stop to the rollicking inflation. The action that might have to be taken would probably be incompatible with our assumptions. There would have to be some deflationary offsetting factor such as a reduction of government expenditure or a rise in interest rates or tax rates. We shall discuss the effects of such action in later chapters. We must proceed now with our argument on the assumption that the inflationary forces are not of this extreme explosive character, and note in passing that if they are, the necessity for some of the policy measures which we shall discuss later would quickly become apparent.

Accordingly we may assume that of any given primary increase in national income a certain proportion (namely, that which represents the amount which merely replaces unemployment benefit or which leads only to increased savings or increased tax payments *less* the amount by which the increase in national income induces a further increase in demand for goods for capital development) represents what we will call a net 'home leakage' in that it does not generate any secondary net increase in demand and so in national income. But the remainder does cause a secondary increase in demand and national income. It follows that in our closed economy any spontaneous increase in the demand for capital goods or for consumption goods will cause an increase of that magnitude in the national income and will thereby induce a series of successive waves of further increases in demand and in national income. Each wave of inflation will be smaller than the last because of the net home leakage, and the economy will finally settle down at a new equilibrium at which the national income will have risen by an amount greater than the primary spontaneous rise in demand, the size of the rise being smaller the larger is the home leakage.

In the above analysis we have compared the new equilibrium which will ultimately be reached after the spontaneous increase in domestic expenditure has taken place with the old equilibrium which existed before that spontaneous increase occurred. We have not considered at all fully what may happen during the process of change, because we have entirely neglected the effect of two types of factor which can operate only during a process of change.

The first set of neglected factors comprises all forms of time-lag. Let us give examples of three types of time-lag.

(i) First, there may be a lag between a rise in income and the resulting decision to increase domestic expenditure. Thus, when purchasers' tax-free incomes rise, they may, as was assumed above, increase their purchases of goods and services for final use by a definite proportion of the increase in their spendable incomes; but they may take time to react, and the increase in domestic expenditure may lag behind the increase in income by a certain interval of time. Similarly, when the profitability of industry has been increased by a certain amount as a result of an increase in the demand for goods and services, entrepreneurs may increase their demand for goods and services for the capital development of their business; but in fact this secondary increase in the demand for capital goods may lag somewhat behind the primary increase in the profitability of industry which caused it, because entrepreneurs may take time to adjust their plans for capital development as a result of an improved market for their products.

(ii) There may be a lag between an increase in the demand for goods and services and the decision on the part of entrepreneurs to produce more to satisfy that demand. Thus when purchasers spend more on goods and services, the immediate effect may be either (*a*) that stocks of goods are run down as purchasers take more goods from the shops at the given prices, or (b) that the same amount of goods or services are sold and the increased demand merely drives up the price at which they are sold. In neither of these cases is there any immediate increase in production or employment. It is only in case (a) when the shopkeeper gives larger orders to the producer in order to replenish his stocks, or in case (b) when the supplier realizes that at the higher price it would pay to produce more, that the increased demand has its effect upon production and employment.

(iii) There may be a lag between increased receipts from the sale of products and the distribution of the money so earned to the final income earners. Thus profits may be distributed in dividends only at the end of the year. Increased profits earned in a firm because the demand for that firm's products has increased will, therefore, be received by the final income earners only after a delay; and it is only after this time-lag that such increases in income can in turn have their effect in inducing a further increase in domestic expenditure.

Because of such time-lags we must relate the level of induced domestic expenditure at one point of time not to the level of the national income at that same point of time but to the level of the national income at some previous point of time. When a new equilibrium has been reached[1] the existence of such time-lags will, of course, cease to have any significance. If the national income is constant at a new and higher level, then induced domestic expenditure will be constant at its new and appropriately higher level. Whether it is related to yesterday's or today's national income makes no difference when the national income is no longer changing from day to day.

There is a second important set of factors at work during the process of change, which we can neglect when we are simply comparing the new equilibrium with the old. The absolute level of some induced quantity may in fact depend not only upon the absolute level of the factor on which it depends, but also upon the rate at which that factor is increasing or decreasing.

Let us consider three possible examples of such relationships.

(i) The amount of stocks which a merchant holds may need to bear a certain relation to the turnover of his business. Thus, when a shop has a turnover of 1,000 pairs of shoes a year it may need to hold a stock of 100 pairs of shoes; and when its turnover is 2,000 a year, its stock may be raised to 200. In such a case the demand of the shopkeeper for shoes from the manufacturer of shoes will depend not only upon the level of his turnover (which will determine his demand to replace his stock of shoes) but also upon the rate at which his turnover is increasing (which will determine his demand to build up his stock of shoes),

---

[1] If it is ever reached. See below p. 58,

Thus he will give orders for 1,000 or 2,000 pairs of shoes a year to replace his stock, according as his sales are at a constant level of 1,000 or 2,000; but if in any year his turnover increases in the course of the year from 1,000 per annum to 2,000 per annum, he will order an additional 100 pairs in order not merely to replace his initial stock but to raise it by 100 (from 100 to 200). In so far as this factor is at work, that part of domestic expenditure which represents expenditure on goods for stocks will depend not merely on the size of the national income but also upon the rate at which the national income, and so demand, is increasing.

(ii) This principle (that the demand for products may depend upon the rate at which the national income is rising) is known as the 'acceleration principle'. Its clearest application is probably in the case of stocks which has been discussed above. But this is not necessarily its only application. The amount of new machinery or other fixed plant which is being installed in an enterprise may depend not only upon the absolute level of the demand for the products of that firm, but also upon the rate at which the demand for the firm's products is increasing, since this may be one of the important factors determining the rate at which the firm must expand. In so far as this is the case, here is another reason why the level of induced domestic expenditure may depend upon the rate at which the national income is rising.

(iii) There are other possible ways in which the rate at which the demand for products is changing may affect the absolute level of induced expenditure. For example, as we shall see in the next chapter, an increase in domestic expenditure is likely to cause some increase in the general level of money prices as well as some increase in output and employment. During the process of change prices will be rising. Now the fact that prices are rising may cause purchasers to expect them to rise still further; and in this case they are likely to increase their expenditure above the amount which would normally correspond to their present levels of income in order to buy durable products before their price has risen still further. The fact that prices are rising at a certain rate will thus cause induced domestic expenditure to be higher than it would otherwise be. This factor may conceivably work in the opposite direction. When prices are rising, purchasers may have in mind some idea of a previously 'reasonable' or 'normal' level of prices; and they may expect prices to fall in the future back towards this more reasonable norm. In this case they are likely to postpone their purchases as much as possible. In so far as this happens, the fact that prices are rising will cause domestic expenditure to be lower in relation to the national income than would otherwise have been the case.

These relationships between the absolute level of domestic expenditure and the rate at which the national income or the level of prices is changing can also be neglected once we have reached the new position of equilibrium.[1] In the new position of equilibrium the national income will have reached a new and constant level, and in consequence the price level will also have reached a new and constant level. Since there will be no change still going on in these levels, induced domestic expenditure will have reached once more its normal relationship with the absolute level of the national income and will no longer be subject to influences which depend solely upon the fact that income is changing at a certain rate.

In the remainder of this volume we shall neglect these processes of change. We shall confine ourselves to a comparison of the new position of equilibrium which results when some spontaneous disturbance has occurred and has had time to work out all its repercussions, with the old position of equilibrium which existed before the disturbance occurred. We shall not concern ourselves with the process of change.[2] This procedure is satisfactory enough provided that the process of change does not affect the final position of equilibrium which is ultimately reached.

Unfortunately this is not always the case. Time-lags and the 'acceleration principle' may bring it about that a small spontaneous disturbance, instead of causing the economy to move by a moderate amount from one position of equilibrium to another, may cause it either to fall into an ever-increasing inflation or deflation or to start an oscillating movement, swinging first upwards and then downwards with a diminishing, a constant, or an ever-increasing amplitude of swing. There will, of course, in reality be some limits ultimately set to these upward and downward movements. For example, an inflationary movement, when it has progressed a sufficient distance and has mopped up all unemployed resources, will lead to a continuous rise in the general level of prices. At some point to prevent any further rise in prices the banking system is likely to stop the creation of the new money which will be being demanded to finance the ever-higher level of monetary transactions. At this point a relative scarcity of monetary funds will develop, and the rate of interest will rise, so that one of the assumptions of our neutral economy will no longer be preserved. All that is asserted is that, with certain time-lags and certain 'acceleration principles' at work in the process of adjustment to a spontaneous disturbance, there might develop an almost endless upward or downward movement if the assumptions of our neutral economy were strictly maintained.

It is, however, very probable that in fact even with time-lags and the

[1] Assuming, of course, that we do ever reach such a position. See the following paragraphs.

[2] In technical language, this volume is on comparative statics and not on dynamics.

'acceleration principle' at work, the economy will ultimately settle down to a new equilibrium. This is likely to be so if the 'home leakage' is sufficiently large. In the rest of this volume we shall suppose this to be the case, and shall confine ourselves to the comparison of the new with the old position of equilibrium. Our analysis, even when it is restricted in this way, is complicated enough; and it will enable us to understand a great number of the real forces at work. It must, however, be borne in mind that it is incomplete in the way indicated above. In fact the economic system may in some cases be less stable than we shall assume it to be, so that more extensive measures of governmental policy than those which we shall recommend may in some cases be necessary in order to maintain full equilibrium.

We have indicated above (p. 55) that, assuming a new equilibrium to be attained, a spontaneous increase in domestic expenditure in A will raise the national income by more than the spontaneous increase in domestic expenditure itself. But nevertheless, because of the 'home leakage', this increase in national income will be limited in amount; it will be the smaller, the larger is the 'home leakage'.

So much for our closed economy. We have now to make allowance for the fact that our country A which is experiencing this spontaneous increase in domestic demand has trading and financial relations with the rest of the world. In particular we must allow for the fact that with every spontaneous or induced increase in domestic expenditure in A the purchasers in A are likely to increase their demand for imported goods and services as well as for their home-produced goods and services. We will designate as the 'marginal propensity to import' in A, the proportion of any increased domestic expenditure in A which represents a net increase in the demand for imports as opposed to home-produced goods. From the point of view of A's economy this marginal propensity to import represents a leakage which we will call the foreign leakage and which, in addition to the home leakage examined above reduces the induced inflationary effects of a primary spontaneous increase in domestic expenditure. The mechanism operates in this way: a primary increase in the national income causes a secondary but smaller rise in the demand for home-produced goods not only because some part of the increased purchasing power merely replaces unemployment benefit or merely goes to waste, as it were, in increased tax payments and savings (the home leakage) but also because a part of the remainder, depending upon A's marginal propensity to import, represents an increased demand for imported goods (the foreign leakage). Only the rest represents a secondary increase in the demand for A's goods and services and so in A's national income.

The result of this is that the induced inflation in A's national income resulting from a given spontaneous increase in A's domestic expenditure is smaller than otherwise would be the case, and also that there is an increase in the deficit (or decrease in the surplus) on A's balance of trade, since purchasers in A will now be importing more as a result of the increased domestic expenditure.

But this is not, of course, the end of the story. While A's foreign leakage means the avoidance of part of the inflation which would otherwise have occurred in A but causes an unfavourable movement in A's balance of trade, country B (i.e. the rest of the world) now experiences an inflationary pressure and a favourable movement in its balance of trade with A. The increase of imports into A represents an increase in demand for the products of B, and in B it will have the same kind of effect as the primary spontaneous increase in domestic demand had in A. That is to say, it will directly cause an increase in the national income of B whose producers are now selling more exports in A; this will cause a secondary but smaller rise in domestic expenditure in B; this, in turn, will cause a secondary rise in B's national income which will cause a tertiary and still smaller rise in her domestic expenditure; and so on. The final inflation in B will be the smaller the larger is her own home leakage at each round of increase of income and expenditure.

These inflationary developments in B will in turn have repercussions on A. The increased domestic expenditure in B will mean that in B there is an increase in the demand for imports from A. This will exert some inflationary pressure on the demand for A's products and so on A's national income, and at the same time it will prevent the balance of trade from moving quite so unfavourably to A as would otherwise be the case.

In the end A and B, after a series of repercussions upon each other of this kind, will settle down to a new equilibrium[1] in which:

(i) A's national income will be increased as a result of the primary rise in A's domestic expenditure; but this rise will not be as great as would have been the case if A had been a closed economy, since some part of the inflationary pressure will have been exported to B and, because of the home leakage in B, not the whole of this inflationary pressure will be re-exported back by B to A;

(ii) The national income in B will have been increased by reason of the rise in the demand in A for B's exports; and

---

[1] It should be realized that this 'equilibrium', like others discussed in Parts II and III, involves a deficit in A's balance of payments and can, therefore, last only so long as the authorities in A do not run out of reserves of B's currency. When this point is reached, something else must be done. Either the foreign exchange value of A's currency must be allowed to depreciate (see p. 14), or imports must be restricted, or a deflationary domestic financial policy must be adopted in order to reduce the demand for imports. All of these possibilities will be examined in due course, but each of them involves dropping one of the assumptions of the neutral economy.

(iii) The balance of trade will have moved unfavourably to A; the increase in the demand in A for imports resulting from the inflation in A's domestic expenditure will be greater than the increase in demand in B for A's exports because the existence of a home leakage in B will mean that not the whole of the rise in the demand in A for B's goods will find its way back in a rise in the demand in B for A's goods.

We have so far discussed the effect of the spontaneous increase in A's domestic expenditure upon the balance of *trade* between A and B. The effect upon the balance of *payments* may be somewhat different because the variations in the national incomes of A and of B may lead to changes in the transfers between them and in particular in the amount of loans or other capital transfers flowing between them.

The factors which determine the amount of capital transfers from A to B and vice versa are very complex. Among the more important are the following:

(i) When people's incomes rise, they are likely to save a larger amount; and when they save more, they are likely to some extent to increase the amount which they lend abroad as well as the amount which they lend at home.

(ii) When, for one reason or another, the profitability of industry increases abroad without increasing at home, people are likely to be induced to invest a larger proportion of their capital funds abroad.

(iii) When the rate of interest which can be obtained on money loans rises abroad relatively to the rate at home, people are likely to be induced to lend a larger amount abroad instead of at home.

(iv) Changes in taxation may affect the relative attractiveness of investing capital funds in one country or in another. Thus, a reduction of the taxation on profits earned in one country, if it takes place in respect of the profits on capital owned by foreigners as well as on that owned by residents of the country, will increase the relative attractiveness of investment in that country.

(v) When it is expected that the rate of exchange between a country's domestic money and foreign money is likely to depreciate, people are likely to lend more abroad for the time being in order to make an exchange profit on their capital when they bring it back later at the depreciated rate of exchange.

(vi) There are many other risks attaching to the ownership of capital in a particular country which may make investment of funds in one country particularly attractive or unattractive. For example, if it is expected that in any country an exchange control is about to be instituted over the movement of capital funds abroad, or that governmental debt is likely to be repudiated, or that some forms of capital are likely to be nationalized without adequate compensation, owners of capital may immediately remove their funds abroad while the going is good.

(vii) Finally, the direct effect of exchange controls must not be forgotten. The imposition of an exchange control which effectively restricts the movement of capital funds out of a country will obviously diminish the amount of foreign lending from that country.

For our present problem the first two of these factors are relevant. It is probable that, unless A's economy is absolutely considerably larger than that of B which represents the whole of the rest of the world, the proportionate rise in the national income in A, which is the seat of the inflationary influence, will be greater than the proportionate increase in the national income of B which merely experiences the secondary effects of the change in A.

This gives rise to two counteracting forces. On the one hand, the profitability of A's industries would probably have risen more markedly than those of the other countries of the world, and this would be a factor making for a larger flow of capital funds into A for investment in the relatively more profitable country. On the other hand, if A's income has experienced a larger proportionate rise it is probable that A's savings have risen in a larger proportion than savings in other countries; and if savers in both countries are in the habit of lending a certain proportion of their savings at home and a certain proportion abroad, then the movement in relative incomes in A and in the other countries of the world might mean that there was a larger proportionate rise in capital transfers from A to the rest of the world than in the opposite direction; and if the existing flow of capital transfers from A to the rest of the world were not very much smaller in total than the existing flow in the opposite direction, this would represent a factor tending to increase the net flow of capital from A to the rest of the world.

Thus only the particular circumstances of each case can decide whether the spontaneous increase of domestic expenditure in A will induce a net increase or a net decrease in the flow of capital funds into or out of A. Unless there is particular reason to expect a large induced flow of capital into A, we can conclude that the inflation in A will, through its effect upon the balance of trade, cause an unfavourable movement in A's balance of payments and, what is the same thing, a favourable movement in the balance of payments of B, as well as inducing some inflation of domestic expenditure and national income in B.

Now these results are not absolutely certain. There are some possible but improbable conditions, not incompatible with the assumptions of the neutral economy, in which these results would not follow. It is interesting to consider these possibilities as an exercise in our analysis, although it should be clearly borne in mind that the conditions which are about to be discussed are improbable in the extreme.

The first possibility is that the goods and services which are imported into A are 'inferior' goods. Commodities are said to be 'inferior' if they are of a kind which consumers purchase in *smaller* quantities when their incomes *rise*. It is possible, for example, that when people become richer they purchase not more, but less potatoes, because the rise in their incomes means that they can afford a greater amount of the expensive and tasty delicacies and that they need, therefore, to purchase less of the cheaper and less attractive foodstuffs. If the purchasers in a country imported exclusively 'inferior' goods, then an increase in their real incomes, due to the increased employment and output which result from the direct and induced effects of an inflation of domestic expenditure, might cause them to spend less, and not more, on imports. In this case the inflation in A, induced by a spontaneous rise in A's domestic expenditure, would go much further than in the case which we have examined because, far from there being any foreign leakage in A, there would be an opposite effect increasing the successive waves of domestic inflation. If, when income and, as a consequence, domestic expenditure rise, there is a *decline* in the demand for imports, the increase in the demand for home-produced products must be by so much the greater than the total increase in domestic expenditure. At each round of induced inflation a larger rise in the demand for home-produced commodities will occur than can be explained solely by the size of the home leakage. Part of the home leakage will be offset by the fact that there is, as it were, a negative foreign leakage, which means that at each round of inflation some part of the expenditure on imports is diverted from imports and added to the stream of demand for home-produced products.

But in this case not only is the inflation in A increased by more than it would be if A were a closed economy without commercial or financial relations with the other countries; the balance of trade moves in favour of A instead of against A; and the change in A exercises a deflationary instead of an inflationary influence on B, because the inflation of total domestic demand in A now causes a deflation in her demand for the products of the rest of the world. This deflation in B would cause some deflationary repercussion back upon A and would somewhat reduce the improvement in A's balance of trade, since (except in the ultra-improbable case that the rest of the world also imported only inferior goods from A), it would cause some reduction in the demand of the rest of the world for A's exports. But it would not be sufficient to prevent altogether the favourable movement in A's balance of trade and the consequent intensification of the inflation of A's national income.

Let us next consider the case where the goods and services produced in A for consumption in A are all 'inferior' goods. Suppose now that there is some 'spontaneous' increase in domestic expenditure in A, due, for example, to a reduction in the general level of taxation so that consumers in A have larger tax-free incomes to spend on goods and services for personal consumption. If A's home-produced goods are 'inferior', then this increase in the total demand by A's consumers will make them spend *less* on A's goods and thus increase their imports by more than the total increase in their domestic demand. There will thus be a primary *deflationary* influence at work in A; and the primary worsening in A's balance of trade and the primary inflationary influence at work in the other countries of the world will be much more marked than in the normal case.

We cannot conclude from this that if A's products are all inferior from the point of view of A's purchasers, a spontaneous *increase* in A's domestic expenditure will necessarily cause in the end a net *deflation* of A's national income. We have not yet allowed for the repercussions in the other countries of the world. The increased demand in A for imports from the rest of the world will have caused some inflationary tendency of demand in the rest of the world; and unless A's exports are also inferior to the purchasers in the rest of the world this will cause some further increase in the foreign demand for A's products. These foreign repercussions *may* possibly more than offset the decline in the demand in A for A's own goods and *may* mean that in spite of the fact that A's goods are inferior to A's purchasers the spontaneous increase in domestic demand in A does not cause a net deflation of A's national income. But it is most unlikely to do so, particularly when allowance is made for the fact that if A's home products are inferior to A's purchasers A is unlikely to produce for export the sort of goods on which consumers in other countries will spend an exceptionally large part of any increase in their incomes.

But we need not dwell at all on these highly exceptional cases. Inferior goods are not in any case very common; and it would be most exceptional if so large a range of any country's total imports (or total home production) were inferior as to make the *total* demand in that country for imports (or for home products) decline when the demand for goods and services in general increased. We shall proceed with our argument without further consideration of the possibility that any country's total imports or total home produce might be of this inferior character. We shall confine ourselves in what follows to what is undoubtedly the normal case, namely, that when the total demand in any country goes up this (in the absence, of course, of simultaneous separate influences such as changes in the relative prices of imports and of home produce) will cause purchasers in that country to purchase some more imports and some more home produce.

CHAPTER VI

THE PRICE EFFECTS OF A SPONTANEOUS
CHANGE IN DOMESTIC EXPENDITURE

IN the last chapter we considered the effects which a spontaneous increase in domestic expenditure in A might have upon the total demand for A's and B's products (i.e. upon the national incomes and so the levels of employment in A and B) and upon the balance of trade and payments between A and B. We concluded that the normal result would be some inflation of A's and B's national income and some movement in the balance of trade (and probably also in the balance of payments) unfavourable to A. We saw that these conclusions might be modified if A (or B) produced or imported mainly 'inferior' goods, but we observed that such a situation was so improbable that we could entirely ignore it.

But in reaching these conclusions we ignored any repercussions due to the fact that the prices of A's and B's products might change in relation to each other. We must now modify the above conclusions in the light of the fact that the inflationary developments in A and in B (resulting from the direct and induced effects of the spontaneous increase in domestic expenditure in A) may alter the relative prices of A's and B's products. For this change in relative prices may affect the demands for A's and B's products. We are still assuming certain very important price relationships to be constant, namely, rates of interest in all countries, money wage rates in all occupations in all countries, and all rates of foreign exchange between national currencies; and it will be an important part of our task at a later stage to inquire how variations in these price relationships would affect the result. But even while we maintain these rigid assumptions we are not assuming that the prices of finished products in A or B remain unchanged as a result of the inflation of demand in A.

We have already observed (p. 57) that when there is an increase in the demand for a country's products this will increase that country's national income, but that the increase in the national income may take partly the form of an increased output and sale of goods and services to meet the increased demand and partly the form of the sale of a given output of goods and services at a higher price. Now we are assuming for the moment that all money wage rates are constant. In these circumstances costs of production do not rise as more labour is employed and more output produced merely because of an increase in wage rates; but costs may very well rise because, as more and more labour is employed with the given amount of land, capital equipment, and other

resources, it becomes more and more difficult to increase output proportionately to the increase in employment of labour and other variable
factors. If in addition to unemployed labour there is much idle equipment and much more land to be cultivated of not very inferior quality
or position, an increased demand is likely, at constant wage rates, to
cause much increase in output and little rise in price; in such circumstances we will say that the real elasticity of supply is high. If there is
unemployed labour but only little idle equipment or uncultivated land,
or if the only idle equipment or land unused is of much inferior quality
or position, an increased demand, even at constant wage rates, is likely
to cause relatively little increase in output and a considerable rise in
prices; and in such circumstances we will say that the real elasticity
of supply is low.[1]

Now the immediate impact effect of the spontaneous increase in
A's domestic expenditure will be to cause some increase in the demand
for A's products—and provided that the marginal propensity to import
in A is greater than zero—some increase in the demand for B's products.
If the real elasticities of supply in A and B are anything less than
infinite, there will in consequence be some rise in the prices both of
A's products and of B's products even on our assumption that the
wage rate remains unchanged in both countries.

Now unless the real elasticity of supply in A is very markedly greater
than in B, there is some reason to believe that the impact effect of the
increased domestic expenditure in A will be to cause a larger rise in
the prices of A's than in those of B's products. The reason for this is
that a rise in domestic expenditure in A is likely to cause a larger
proportionate increase in the demand for A's products than in the
demand for B's products, and so—if the real elasticities of supply in

---

[1] It is possible that the size of what we have called the 'home leakage' depends
upon the real elasticity of supply in the economy concerned. Where, for example,
the real elasticity of supply is high, a primary increase in demand will cause a
large increase in output and employment; and in consequence a larger proportion of the primary increase in demand will go to increased wages and less to
increased profits than in the case where the real elasticity of supply is small and
there is little increase in output and employment and so in the wage bill paid
at a constant wage rate. If wage-earners save less and pay less in taxes than is
saved or paid in taxes out of a similar increase in profits, and *if not much of the
increased wage merely replaces unemployment benefit*, then the greater the real
elasticity of supply the smaller will be the 'home leakage' and the greater in
consequence will be the final inflation of national income caused by any primary
spontaneous increase in domestic expenditure. In what follows we shall not
pay much regard to this possibility: first, because the smaller marginal savings
and direct tax payments of the wage-earner may very well in large measure be
offset by their larger marginal payments of indirect taxes and by the fact that
increases in the number of wage incomes earned in large measure merely
replaces unemployment benefit; and, secondly, because this consideration, while
it might somewhat modify some of the following conclusions about the effects
of a high or low real elasticity of supply, would be unlikely substantially to alter
their main force.

A and B are the same—a larger proportionate rise in the prices of A's than in those of B's products. Let us suppose that the value of A's total production is $20,000 and of B's is $80,000. Then purchasers in A are likely to spend something less than 80 per cent of A's total domestic expenditure on B's products even though B's output makes up 80 per cent of the total world output; and purchasers in B are likely to spend on A's products something less than 20 per cent of B's total domestic expenditure, even though A's production is 20 per cent of the total world production. Quite apart from import duties or other artificial restrictions on imports, the facts that transport costs will be less in the purchase of her own products and that the purchasers in each country have greater familiarity with the qualities, conditions of sale, supplies, etc. of their own country's products will cause purchasers in each country to have some natural preference for the purchase of home products.[1] Indeed many products, including bulky commodities like houses and perishable services like haircuts, cannot be transported and must be purchased from home production.[2]

The same relationship is likely to hold true in the case of the marginal propensity to import. If there is a small increase in total domestic expenditure in A, something less than 80 per cent of this is likely to be spent on additional imports if B accounts for 80 per cent of total world output, because, for similar reasons to those outlined above, purchasers in A are likely in their additional purchases to show some preference for home products.[3] This is, of course, by no means an absolute necessity. It might so happen that producers in B produced just those things which purchasers in A wanted in greater amount when their incomes went up, in which case the marginal propensity to import in A would be greater than the ratio of B's total output to the world's total output. And it is just conceivable that simultaneously producers in A produced just those things which purchasers in B wanted in greater quantity when incomes in B went up; and in this case the sum of the marginal propensities to import in A and in B would be necessarily greater than one. To take an example, suppose that A is a poor country whose residents obtain their income by

[1] If we define the ratio between total imports and total domestic expenditure as the average propensity to import, we may express the above relationship by saying that in each country the average propensity to import is likely to be less than the ratio between the total production of the rest of the world and the total production of the whole world. It follows that the sum of the average propensities to import in A and in B would be less than unity.

[2] This consideration is undoubtedly an important factor in explaining the fact that propensities to import are lower than might otherwise be expected, but it is not, of course, strictly compatible with the assumption which we are provisionally making (see p. 50) that in each country only one product is produced.

[3] If this were true of B also, then the sum of the marginal propensities to import in A and in B would be less than unity. This is an important relationship of which we shall make much use in the sequel.

producing very inefficiently the luxuries (e.g. spices) which rich people consume; and that B is a rich country whose residents earn their income by producing very efficiently the necessities (e.g. textiles) which poor people consume. When real income in A goes up A's purchasers may spend most of the increase on B's textiles; and when real income in B goes up, B's purchasers may spend most of the increase on A's spices. But we may consider this to be the abnormal case.

Now if the marginal propensity to import in A is less than the ratio between B's output and total world output, the impact effect of a small increase in domestic expenditure in A will be to cause a larger proportionate increase in the demand for A's products than in the demand for B's products. Suppose that A's producers produced a total output of $20,000 and B's producers of $80,000, but that of an increase in domestic expenditure in A of $100 something less than $80 (say, only $40) was spent on imports from B. Then the impact effect would be to increase the demand for B's products by only 40/80,000 or 1/2,000 but to increase the demand for A's products by 60/20,000 or 6/2,000. The proportionate effect upon the demand for A's products would be six times greater than that upon the demand for B's products, and unless the real elasticity of supply in A were much greater than in B, the prices of A's products would rise more than those of B's.[1]

Let us suppose, then, that the effect of the increased domestic expenditure in A is to cause the prices of A's products to rise more than those of B's products. What effect will this change in price relationships itself have upon the analysis of the previous chapter? We can expect a rise in the price of A's products relatively to B's products to cause some shift in the demand of both A's and B's purchasers away from the more expensive products of A on to the less expensive products of B. But what effect this will have on the balance of payments between A and B will depend essentially upon the extent of the shift in demand which follows any given shift in relative prices.

This point is illustrated in Table VIII. In this table we assume (row 1) that to begin with the price of a unit of B's products is four times as high as a unit of A's products,[2] so that four units of A's

---

[1] The argument in the text refers only to the immediate impact effect of the increased demand in A. It does not allow for the repercussions due to the multiplier effects in A and B. But from the formula for v in column 1 of Table I of the separate mathematical supplement it can be seen that, even allowing for all such repercussions, the rise in the prices of A's products will be greater than the rise in the prices of B's products if the real elasticities of supply are the same and if the marginal propensities to import in A and in B are in inverse ratio to the total outputs of A and B but together add up to less than unity.

[2] This does not, of course, mean that the cost of living in A is only one-quarter of that in B. A's products (e.g. apples) are different from B's products (e.g. bicycles). It merely means that we have chosen units so that one unit of B's products (e.g. one dozen bicycles) is four times as expensive as one unit of A's products (e.g. one ton of apples).

products are exchanged for one of B's (column *a*). We assume also that 4,000 units of A's products are being exported from A to B (column *b*) and 1,000 units of B's products are being exported from B to A (column *c*), so that the balance of trade between A and B is zero whether imports and exports are measured in terms of A's products

TABLE VIII

Effect of Changes in Relative Prices on the Balance of Trade between A and B

	B's terms of trade — No. of A's products per unit of B's products	Quantity of A's exports	Quantity of B's exports	Value of B's exports in terms of A's products	A's balance of trade in terms of A's products	Value of A's exports in terms of B's products	A's balance of trade in terms of B's products
	(*a*)	(*b*)	(*c*)	(*d*) (*c*)×(*a*)	(*e*) (*b*)−(*d*)	(*f*) (*b*)÷(*a*)	(*g*) (*f*)−(*c*)
			(i) *Original Position*				
(1)	4·00	4,000	1,000	4,000	Nil	1,000	Nil
		(ii) *Sum of Elasticities of Demand for Imports less than One*					
(2)		(E*b*=0) 4,000	(E*a*=0) 1,000	3,960	+40	1,010	+10
(3)		(E*b*=¼) 3,990	(E*a*=½) 1,005	3,980	+10	1,007½	+2½
		(iii) *Sum of Elasticities of Demand for Imports equal to One*					
(4)	3·96	(E*b*=¼) 3,990	(E*a*=¾) 1,007½	3,990 ⎫	⎫ Nil	1,007½ ⎫	⎫ Nil
(5)		(E*b*=½) 3,980	(E*a*=½) 1,005	3,980 ⎭	⎭	1,005 ⎭	⎭
		(iv) *Sum of Elasticities of Demand for Imports greater than One*					
(6)		(E*b*=1) 3,960	(E*a*=1) 1,010	4,000	−40	1,000	−10
(7)		(E*b*=2) 3,920	(E*a*=4) 1,040	4,118	−198	990	−50

Note.—E*b* = the price elasticity of demand in B for imports from A.

E*a* = the price elasticity of demand in A for imports from B.

(columns *d* and *e*) or of B's products (columns *f* and *g*). Something now happens to alter the relative prices of A's and B's products so that the prices of A's products rise more than the prices of B's products. We suppose that the prices of A's products rise by 1 per cent relatively to the prices of B's products, so that 3·96 units of A's products now exchange for 1 unit of B's products (column *a* rows 2 to 7).

We are not now concerned with the changes in A's demand for B's products and in B's demand for A's products which may have occurred because of the increase of employment and output and so of real purchasing power in A or in B. This we have examined in the last chapter. We are at present concerned solely with any additional shift in the demand for each other's products which may occur simply because A's products have become more expensive relative to B's. In row 2 we consider the case in which the change in relative prices causes no change at all in the amounts of A's products imported by B's purchasers (which remains 4,000 in column *b*) or in the amount of B's products imported by A's purchasers (which remains 1,000 in column *c*).

But if the *amounts* of each country's imports from the other remain unaffected by the change in the price relationship, the *value* of their imports must change. Consider A's balance of trade valued in terms of A's products (columns *d* and *e* of row 2). A's purchasers are importing from B the same amount of B's products (1,000 in column *c*); but they have to pay only 3·96 instead of 4·00 of A's products for each unit of their imports from B. A's purchasers, therefore, spend only 3,960 instead of 4,000 of A's products on their imports from B (column *d*) so that A has a favourable balance of trade, i.e. an excess of actual exports from A over the amount of the exports from A which are needed to purchase A's imports, of 40 (column *e*). This sum can equally well be done if A's imports and exports are valued in terms of B's products, (see columns *f* and *g*). The volume of exports of A's products to B is unchanged at 4,000 (column *b*); but A's products are now worth 1 per cent more of B's products, so A's 4,000 of exports are worth 1,010 instead of 1,000 of B's products (column *f*). But as still only 1,000 of B's products are being imported into A (column *c*), A has an excess of exports over imports worth 10 of B's products (column *g*). In the case, therefore, in which there is no shift of demand in A or in B away from A's more expensive goods on to B's relatively cheaper goods, the fact that A's products are now more expensive relatively to B's products will cause a net shift of total expenditure away from B's and on to A's products, and A's balance of trade will become more favourable as her prices rise relatively to B's prices.

This may happen even if there is some decrease in the quantity of A's products, and some increase in the quantity of B's products, which are bought as a result of A's products becoming more expensive relatively to B's. The greater this shift in demand away from A's and on to B's products the less likely is it that the net total expenditure on A's products will rise and on B's products will fall as a result of the fact that A's goods are more expensive relatively to B's. If a small rise in the relative price of A's products causes a very large shift of demand away from A's more expensive products on to B's less expensive products, then the total expenditure on A's products will decline (in spite of the fact that a higher price must be paid for that amount of A's produce which still continues to be bought) and the total expenditure on B's products will rise (in spite of the fact that a lower price need be paid for that amount of B's produce which was already being purchased before the change); in this case the shift in the quantity demanded will more than offset the shift in the relative price. But if a large shift in price will cause only a small shift in the quantity demanded, then the change in the price which must be paid for the amounts which are bought will more than outweigh the change in the amounts bought, and the total expenditure on the more expensive products will rise and on the less expensive products will fall.

Rows 3 to 7 of Table VIII all illustrate cases in which the 1 per cent rise in the relative price of A's products causes some reduction in the demand in B for A's exports (the figures in column *b* are all less than the original 4,000) and some increase in the demand in A for B's exports (the figures in column *c* are all greater than the original 1,000). But in row 3 these shifts in the quantities demanded are so small that A's balance of trade still becomes favourable as a result of the rise in her prices; the price change still outweighs the quantity change. In rows 4 and 5 the shifts in the quantities demanded are just great enough to balance the shift in the relative prices of A's and B's products, so that there is no change in the balance of trade as a result of the price change. In rows 6 and 7 the shifts in the quantities demanded are great enough in relation to the shift in relative prices to cause a considerable worsening of A's balance of trade as her goods become more expensive.

In order to measure the sensitivity of the quantities demanded to the changes in relative prices which cause them we may make use of the concept of the elasticity of demand for imports in A and B. In row 7, for example, we suppose that when the price of A's exports rises by 1 per cent in relation to the price of B's products, B's purchasers, for that reason, reduce the quantity of A's products which they purchase by 2 per cent from 4,000 to 3,920 (column *b*). If we define the elasticity of demand as the percentage fall in amount bought divided by the percentage rise in the price which causes the fall in demand, we can say that the demand in B for imports from A has an elasticity of 2 in this case. Similarly, (in column c of row 7), we assume A's purchasers to have an elasticity of demand of 4 for their imports of B's products, so that they increase their demand for B's products by 4 per cent from 1,000 to 1,040 when the price of B's produce falls by 1 per cent relatively to the price of her own produce. In columns d and e we see the effect of this on A's balance of trade valued in terms of A's products. Imports into A are now 1,040 units of B's products (column c); but as 3·96 of A's products must be paid for each unit of B's products, 1,040×3·96 or 4,118 units of A's products must be given to finance the imports from B into A. But as the exports from A are only 3,920 (column b), A now has a deficit in her balance of trade of 198 units of A's products (column e). Or in terms of B's products (columns f and g), we can work out the result in the following manner: 3,920 units of A's products are being exported to B (column b); but 3·96 of A's products must be given for each unit of B's products (column a),. so that exports from A to B are worth 3920÷3·96 or 990 units of B's products (column f). But actually 1,040 units of B's products are being imported into A (column c), so that there is an excess of imports of B's products into A over the value of A's exports in terms of B's products, of 50 units (column g).

Now it will be seen from Table VIII that the change in relative prices will itself tend to improve the balance of trade of the country whose products become relatively more expensive if the sum of the elasticities of demand for imports in the two countries is less than one (rows 2 and 3), will have no direct effect upon the balance of trade if the two elasticities add up to one (rows 4 and 5), and will worsen the balance of trade of the country whose products become more expensive if the two elasticities of demand for imports add up to more than one (rows 6 and 7).[1]

In what follows we shall make frequent allusion to this relationship, namely, that a rise in the prices of A's products relatively to B's prod-

---

[1] It is apparent from the table that the increase in the balance-of-trade deficit of a country whose products become 1 per cent. more expensive will, when expressed as a percentage of that country's total trade, be equal to one less than the sum of the two elasticities of demand. This simple result and the simple formula in the text depend upon the assumption that in the original position the imports were equal to exports. If this is not the case, the elasticities of demand for imports and exports must be weighted in the following manner to obtain the formula for the change in the balance of trade:

$$dT = -k\tfrac{1}{q}I_b \ (E_a + qE_b - 1)$$
$$dT' = -kqI_a \ (\tfrac{1}{q}E_a + E_b - 1)$$

In these equations dT = the increase in A's favourable balance of trade measured in units of A's products, dT' = the increase in A's favourable balance of trade measured in units of B's produce, k = a small proportionate movement in the real terms of trade in A's favour, q = the ratio of the value of A's exports to the value of A's imports, I_a = the volume of A's imports, I_b = the volume of A's exports (B's imports), E_a = the elasticity of demand in A for imports and

ucts will tend to cause a net shift of expenditure from B's on to A's products or vice versa according as the sum of the elasticities of demand for imports in the two countries is less than, or greater than, one.

Let us revert now to our consideration of the effects of a spontaneous increase in domestic expenditure in A. We saw in the last chapter that the increased demand for goods and services in A would normally cause some increase in the demand for B's products by A's purchasers, so that (i) an increased deficit (or reduced surplus) would appear in A's balance of trade, and (ii) there would be some internal boom in B since the demand in A for B's products had risen. Now it is possible, though rather improbable, that the result of the changes in relative prices will be such as to reverse these results. The increased domestic expenditure in A will cause a rise in the prices of A's products. If the sum of the elasticity of demand in A for imports from B and of the elasticity of demand in B for imports from A is considerably less than unity, then the rise in A's prices relative to B's will cause a net shift of expenditure away from B's on to A's products. And it is not impossible that this shift of expenditure away from B's and on to A's products which results from the change in the price relationship will more than offset the increased demand in A for imports from B which results from the fact that the total demand for all goods and services has risen in A. In this case the boom in A's domestic expenditure would cause a slump (instead of a boom) in the total expenditure on B's products and a surplus (instead of a deficit) in A's balance of trade.

At least three conditions must be fulfilled for the paradoxical result to be true, that a boom in A should cause a slump in B and an improvement in A's balance of trade. First, the marginal propensity to import in A must be small; there must not be any very marked increase in the demand of A's purchasers for B's products resulting from the initial increase in the demand in A for goods and services in general. Second, the real elasticity of supply in A must be small[1]; the increased

E_b = the elasticity of demand in B for imports. In what follows in the text we shall talk as if the critical point was that $E_a + E_b$ is > 1, whereas it should be $E_a + qE_b$ or $\frac{1}{q}E_a + E_b$ is > 1, according as we are concerned with A's balance of trade in terms of A's products or of B's products. If the balance of trade is very much in surplus or deficit to begin with (q different from 1), then a rise in A's prices might move the balance of trade in one direction when valued in A's products and in the other direction when valued in B's products. Thus if $E_a = \frac{2}{3}$, $E_b = \frac{1}{2}$, and q = 2, a rise in A's prices will cause an unfavourable movement in A's balance of trade valued in A's products $(E_a + qE_b = 1\frac{2}{3})$, but a favourable movement in terms of B's products $(\frac{1}{q}E_a + E_b = \frac{5}{6})$.

[1] We are assuming as one feature of our neutral economy that the money wage rate is constant. For our present purpose, however, all that is necessary is that the prices of A's products should go up relatively to those of B; and this might just as well happen because the increased demand for goods and services, and so for labour, in A caused a marked rise in money wage rates in A as because real costs rose rapidly in A as more was produced.

demand in A must cause a large rise in the prices of A's products rather than a large increase in their output, because it is only if there is a marked rise in the prices of A's products relative to those of B's that the third and decisive factor can work. This third factor is that the sum of the elasticities of demand for imports in the two countries must be markedly less than unity; in other words, when the prices of A's products rise relatively to those of B's, purchasers in A and B must not substitute B's cheaper products for A's more expensive ones, but must continue to purchase A's and B's products in much the same proportions as before; and in order to consume A's and B's products in roughly the same ratio purchasers will have to shift their money expenditure on a large scale from B's cheaper products on to A's more expensive products.

This paradoxical result of a boom in A leading to a slump in B and an improvement in A's balance of trade could not, of course, occur if the sum of the two elasticities of demand for imports were greater than one. In that case any tendency for the prices of A's products to rise more than those of B's, either because the real elasticity of supply in A was less than in B or (as explained in p. 68 above) merely because A is the centre of the general increase in demand, would cause an increase in expenditure on B's products and a decrease in expenditure on A's products. This would be merely an additional factor causing the boom in A to lead to an increased demand for B's products and thus intensifying the boom in B and the deficit in A's balance of trade.[1]

Of course, if the real elasticity of supply in B is much smaller than in A, the prices of B's products may go up more than those of A's. In that case, if the sum of the elasticities of demand for imports in A and in B is greater than one, there will be a tendency to shift total expenditure away from B's products on to A's products. This will mean that the final inflation of the national income in A will be *pro tanto* larger and of the national income in B *pro tanto* smaller; and the deficit on A's balance of trade will increase less than would otherwise be the case. Less of the boom will be exported from A to B.[2]

It is, accordingly, of the greatest importance to know in any particular instance whether the sum of the two elasticities of demand for imports

[1] The shift in expenditure from A's to B's products could not, of course, go so far as to offset entirely the primary increase in demand for A's products and so to cause an absolute fall in A's national income. The shift of expenditure away from A's products is taking place only because the prices of A's products have risen; and the prices of A's products will have risen only because there is some net increase in demand for A's products.

[2] But the shift in expenditure from B's on to A's products could not go so far as to cause an absolute deflation in B's national income. The shift is taking place only because the prices of B's products have gone up, and they will have gone up only if there is a final net increase in the total expenditure on B's products.

is less or greater than one. No *a priori* answer can, of course, be given. The answer must depend upon the particular conditions of the case which is under examination. But there are certain general considerations which suggest that we can take it as the more normal case that if the world is divided into two parts, A and B, the average price elasticity of demand in the one part of the world for the products of the rest of the world is likely to be greater than one half.

In the first place, one must not forget the 'income effect' in the price elasticity of demand itself. If, as in Table VIII, the real terms of international trade turn 1 per cent in favour of A, this in itself will make the purchasers in A better off than before. The same real output of A's products can command 1 per cent more of B's products. Now even if there were no substitutability in A between A's products and B's products—even if purchasers in A had no use at all for B's products unless (like pens and pen-holders or cups and saucers) B's products were purchased in a more or less rigid ratio with A's products—purchasers in A would be better off when the real terms of trade turned in A's favour and for this reason would be likely, with their increased real purchasing power, to purchase a greater quantity of B's products as well as a greater quantity of A's products. Producers in A produce cups and those in B saucers. The price of cups rises and of saucers falls. The total output of cups in A will command more saucers. Purchasers in A use their increased real income partly to keep more of A's cups for themselves but partly to purchase more saucers from B to match the greater number of cups which they are keeping for themselves. There is *some* increase in the quantity of B's products which purchasers in A import, when the relative price of B's products falls, even though B's products cannot be readily substituted for A's; and this effect will be the greater, the higher is the marginal propensity to import in A (i.e. the greater the proportion of any increase in their real power of purchase which purchasers in A allocate to increased demand for imports) because any given improvement in the position of A's purchasers will in these conditions cause a larger increase in the demand for imports in A.

But it would, of course, be most improbable that there was no substitutability between A's and B's products. Normally a large range of products will be imported into A from the rest of the world. Some of these may be goods and services which cannot be substituted at all readily for any of A's own products; but there will most probably be many which, in varying degrees, can be substituted for some of the things which A's producers are selling to A's purchasers.

It must always be remembered that substitution between A's and B's products can take place in consumption or in production and in country A or in the rest of the world. Consider, for example, an import of wheat into A. Now it may well be that, when the price of imported wheat falls relatively to the general level of prices in A, purchasers in A do not wish to switch on a large scale to eating more bread and purchasing less of other commodities, such as home-produced clothes. But if producers in A produce wheat or some other closely substitutable foodstuff, then when the prices of A's other products go up but the price of imported wheat remains low, producers of wheat or its substitutes in A may well shift to the production of the more profitable things. Even though purchasers in A have not consumed more wheat in total, they may still in this way substitute imported wheat for home-produced wheat or other home-produced cereals on a considerable scale. Only if both in production and in consumption in A there is little room for substitution over the whole range of the things which are imported into A and if, at the same time, both in production and in consumption in the rest of the world there is little room for substitution over the whole range of things which are exported from A, will it be true that a rise in A's prices relatively to those in the rest of the world can cause a net shift of expenditure on to A's products and away from those of the rest of the world.

The degree of substitutability between A's and B's products is likely to be much greater if time is allowed for the impact effects of a change in relative prices to work itself out. This is true even in the case of substitutability in consumption. When the prices of imported goods change relatively to those of home-produced goods it takes time for merchants and then for consumers to appreciate the significance of the change and to alter their buying habits. A change in consumption may even require some change in capital equipment. For example, if imported petrol becomes cheaper it will not replace the use of coal for personal transport until sufficient extra motor cars have been produced and distributed to enable people to travel by road rather than by coal-fired railway trains. In the case of substitution in production the time-lags are even more important. If the price of imported wheat falls relatively to that of home-produced textiles, after a time there may be a very significant increase in the home production of textiles at the expense of home-grown wheat, although the immediate effect of the price change might be relatively small. The process of adjustment might continue for as long as a generation, while the sons of farm workers went into the textile industry instead of following their fathers' footsteps in agriculture. But this is, of course, an extreme example. Many substitutions in production could take place much more easily than this, though they might well take a little time before they were fully developed since some reorganizations of equipment etc. might be necessary.

Further, as we shall have occasion to observe at several points in what follows, the substitutability of one country's products for another's in international trade will be much greater in the absence of artificial barriers to international trade than in a world of protection and rigidly controlled trade. The most obvious example of this principle is provided by quantitative import controls. If the quantity of wheat allowed into A is rigidly fixed no matter what happens to prices in A or elsewhere, then the fact that the price at which producers in B offer wheat to purchasers in A falls in relation to the price of A's own products will not occasion any increased import of wheat into A. Such an increased import is simply ruled out by the quantitative control over imports of wheat into A. A similar effect is brought about by high specific import duties. If a unit of imported wheat costs $100 to buy from the producer in B but there is an import duty in A fixed in amount at $200, then the price to the purchaser in A is $300. If now the suppliers in B reduce their price by 50 per cent to $50, the price charged to the purchaser in A will fall to $250 or by $16\frac{2}{3}$ per cent. A 50 per cent reduction in the relative price charged by B's producers will, so far as substitution in A's market is concerned, have the effect only of a $16\frac{2}{3}$ per cent improvement in price.

This last point suggests one reason why, even in the absence of trade barriers, the elasticities of demand in international trade will often be less than the elasticities of demand in domestic trade. Products of B which are imported into A may need to be serviced by merchants or distributors in A before they are sold to the final purchasers in A. Thus suppose that a unit of wheat imported into A costs $100 to buy from the producers in B but that it costs $50 to distribute in A. If the suppliers in B cut their price by 50 per cent to $50, the price to the final purchaser in A will fall from $150 to $100 or by only $33\frac{1}{3}$ per cent. Thus the more important are the services which must be provided in the importing country to make the imported products ready for the final purchaser in that country, the less is the demand for imports likely to respond to a reduction in the price charged by the foreign supplier. This argument should not be exaggerated. It is of importance only in those cases where distributing or similar charges are an important element in price and only to the extent that these distributing or similar services cannot themselves be provided by residents of the exporting country. In the absence of rigid trade barriers and allowing time for adjustments, we can assume that normally the elasticities of demand in foreign trade are reasonably high.

Finally, let us consider the effect upon the elasticities of demand for imports in A and in B of the relative size of A and B. Let us suppose that A is a small country and that B therefore is very large in relation to A. Now the small region A is likely to produce goods and services in competition with a lot of other producers in the rest of the world.

It is only in very special circumstances that A, being a very small part of the whole world, will be the sole producer of the things which she exports to B. The elasticity of demand in B for imports from A is, therefore, likely to be great because A's products are likely to be produced in B as well. But it is quite possible that producers in B may supply many essential things (e.g. tropical raw materials and foodstuffs) which producers in A (if, for example, A is a small country in the temperate regions) cannot possibly produce. Purchasers in A are likely, therefore, to be able to dispense with B's products much less easily than purchasers in B can dispense with A's products; and the elasticity of demand in A for imports from B may be small relatively to the elasticity of demand in B for imports from A. If now we transfer more and more of the world's economy from B to A, the elasticity of demand in B for imports from A is likely to fall and the elasticity of demand in A for imports from B to rise; and, as we have seen above, it is the sum of the two elasticities of demand for imports which is of crucial importance.

When A is very small indeed relatively to B, the elasticity of demand for A's products in B may be nearly infinite; in other words, A's output makes up such a very small part of the world market that variations in the amount supplied by A make no appreciable difference in the market at all and exports from A to B can, therefore, be increased without any appreciable fall in the price which purchasers in B will offer for them. Similarly, at the other extreme, when A is very large indeed relatively to B, the elasticity of demand in A for B's products may be very nearly infinite. In either of these extreme cases, therefore, the sum of the two elasticities of demand is likely to be very great. In the intermediate position in which A and B divide the world approximately in equal halves each elasticity of demand may be substantial but very much less than infinitely large, because an increase in exports from the one half of the world to the other will now have an appreciable effect upon supplies in the importing market. In such an intermediate position, therefore, the sum of the two elasticities of demand is likely to be less than at either of the other two extremes.

So far we have confined our attention to the relations between country A and the rest of the world B, and have come to the conclusion that a boom in A is very unlikely to cause a slump in the rest of the world. But it is rather less unlikely that a boom in A should cause a localized slump in one particular part of the rest of the world; and although, strictly speaking, this topic should be reserved for Part VI of this volume, it may be useful here to outline very briefly the possibility.

Suppose, then, that among the products supplied in country A for export there is one—let us call it wheat—which is produced under conditions of considerable real inelasticity of supply and for which the price elasticity of demand is low. Suppose now that there is an inflation of demand in A. A's consumers buy more wheat and this drives the price of wheat up very considerably, and considerably more than the price of A's other products.[1] The inflation in A may well, by reason of increased purchases in A of imports from other countries, cause a general diffusion of increased purchasing power throughout many other countries, and in all these countries there may be an increased demand for wheat and, because of a real inelasticity of supply, a marked rise in the price of wheat. If, in general, the price elasticity of demand for wheat (though not necessarily for A's other exports) is small, this may well mean that as a result of the inflation in A, A's exporters obtain a larger total value from their exports of wheat (though not necessarily a larger total value from their exports of all commodities together).

Now there might be one other particular country—let us call her B—whose importers for geographical reasons normally purchase the bulk of their wheat from A and do not purchase much else from A. Moreover, let us suppose that B's exporters do not sell much to A, but send the bulk of their exports to the markets of other countries C, D, E, and F. In such circumstances the result of the inflation in A might well be to cause a local deflation in B and to cause B's balance of trade to move unfavourably to her. Purchasers in B have a higher price to pay for wheat from A; and since their price elasticity of demand for wheat is small, they will spend more in total on wheat imports from A and thus less on their own home-produced products. But B's exporters sell their exports to C, D, E, and F and may therefore feel only a slight backwash of the inflation of demand in A so far as the demand for B's exports is concerned. B's importers have to spend

---

[1] It is probable that, in fact, when total demand increases the prices of agricultural products rise much more (and the output less) than the prices (and output) of manufactured products, and that when demand falls the prices of agricultural products fall much more (and their output less) than the prices (and output) of manufactured products. But this is only in part due to a greater real elasticity of supply in the case of manufactured goods than in the case of agricultural products. It is in large measure due to the institutional fact that manufactures are widely produced under conditions involving the employment of well organized wage-labour where the money wage rate is fixed fairly rigidly, whereas a large part of agricultural output is produced either by peasant or other labour working on its own account or by less well organized wage-labour. As a result, when the demand for manufactures falls the first result is likely to be a large reduction in output and employment and a small fall in price, whereas a decline in the demand for agricultural products is likely to result in no great decline in output and employment but a heavy fall in price. These reasons for relative inelasticity of supply of agricultural products reinforce the argument in the text although they rely upon variations in wage rates (in the sense of money earnings per unit of work done) in agriculture and are, therefore, strictly ruled out by our present assumption that money wage rates remain unchanged in all occupations.

much more on imports from A; her exporters experience but a small increase in the demand for their own goods in C, D, E, and F; the balance of trade moves against B; and since her purchasers have to spend so much more on imported wheat they have less to spend on their own home products and there is some deflationary pressure in B's economy. It is thus possible that through the trade in a particular commodity an inflation in A might have a perverse effect upon the balance of trade and the national income of one particular country, B, although it had the normal effect of improving the balance of trade of, and exerting an inflationary pressure in, all the other countries of the world taken together.

We may now attempt to make some summary of the conclusions to be drawn from the extended argument of this and the preceding chapter.

(i) Except in the most improbable case that A's products are inferior goods to A's purchasers (p. 64), a spontaneous increase in domestic expenditure in A will cause an increase in the total demand for A's products and so lead to some rise in national income, employment, and output in A.

(ii) If we rule out the most improbable case that B's products are in general inferior goods to A's purchasers (p. 63), then, unless the sum of the elasticities of demand for imports in A and B is less than one and the marginal propensity to import in A and the real elasticity of supply in A are very small (p. 73), the spontaneous increase in domestic expenditure in A will cause some net increase in the demand for B's products and so in the national income, employment, and output in B.

(iii) In this case the balance of trade will move unfavourably to A, since the demand for B's products will rise in A more than the demand for A's products in B. As far as the balance of payments is concerned it is conceivable that the result of the boom in A might be to cause a net flow of lending from B to A which would offset the unfavourable movement in A's balance of trade. But this is improbable; the flow of lending might just as well be in the opposite direction (p. 62).

(iv) The increased domestic expenditure in A is on the whole likely to cause the prices of A's products to rise more than the prices of B's products, and thus to cause some movement in the real terms of trade in A's favour, because the marginal propensity in A to spend on B's products is likely to be less than the ratio of B's output to total world output (p. 68). But if the real elasticity of supply in B were markedly smaller than the real elasticity of supply in A the real terms of trade might nevertheless move in B's favour.

(v) While a boom in A is thus unlikely to cause a slump in the rest of the world or a favourable movement in A's balance of payments with the rest of the world as a whole, it may in certain special circumstances cause a slump in one particular locality and a favourable movement in A's balance of payments with that particular locality.

These conclusions can, of course, be reversed. A spontaneous decrease in domestic expenditure (i.e. a general depression or slump) in A would thus probably cause a rise in unemployment in A and B, and a growing deficit on B's balance of payments with the terms of trade moving in either direction but probably in B's rather than A's favour.

CHAPTER VII

THE EFFECTS OF OTHER SPONTANEOUS CHANGES

W E can now consider the effects of some other typical spontaneous disturbances. We cannot, of course, examine all the possible forms of spontaneous disturbance; but we shall apply the technique developed at length in the two preceding chapters to one or two representative forms of disturbance. This should give the reader the practice to analyse on similar lines the effects of any other type of disturbance which he may wish to examine. The analysis in this chapter can be carried out much more summarily than the description given in the two preceding chapters of the effects of a spontaneous change in A's domestic expenditure, because much of the analysis there given can be applied to the new cases without detailed repetition.

1. *A Spontaneous Change in Productivity in A*

Let us suppose that because of a series of inventions output per head in all country A's industries increases by, say, 10 per cent. We will suppose that these inventions increase not only the average product of labour in A (i.e. the total output produced by the men already in employment) by 10 per cent, but also the marginal product of labour in A (i.e. the addition to the total output which would be caused by taking on a few more men into employment) by 10 per cent. On the assumptions of our neutral economy (constant governmental demand for goods and services, rates of tax, rates of interest, wage rates, foreign exchange rates, and commercial policy in A and B) what effect will this have on employment in A and B and on the balance of payments and real terms of trade between A and B?

We can best approach this problem by asking what would be the effect of the increased productivity in A if A were a closed economy and had no contacts with the rest of the world. One possible outcome of the increased productivity in A on the assumptions of our neutral economy would be that all commodity prices and the volume of employment would fall by 10 per cent, and that everything else (e.g. total output) should remain unchanged. Since we are assuming that all money wage rates are unchanged, the 10 per cent increase in the productivity of labour would be equivalent to a reduction by 10 per cent in the money cost of production per unit of output. Competition between producers might then cause all money prices to be reduced by 10 per cent. As a result of this all money incomes would be reduced by 10 per cent—in the case of labour because 10 per cent less labour is employed at an unchanged money wage rate and in the case of profits and other incomes because prices and costs had both fallen by 10 per cent. Since, however, the cost of living would also have fallen by 10 per cent, no one would be better or worse off except that the labour still in employment would enjoy a 10 per cent rise in its real income while 10 per cent of those previously employed would now have no wage income at all.

Would this latter change, the only real change in the situation,[1] itself cause any net change in the total real demand for goods and services and so some secondary repercussion upon the total volume of employment? Since the unemployed workers will receive unemployment benefit their expenditure on goods and services will not fall to zero when their wage income falls to zero, and this may represent an additional real demand for goods and services. It will not, however, do so if the money paid out in unemployment benefit is raised by additional taxation on wages and/or profits in such a way that the expenditure of those in receipt of wages and/or profits is reduced by as much as the expenditure of the unemployed is increased through the payment of unemployment benefit.

If we allow for the fact that A is an open economy and has trading relationships with B, the position may be very different. The increased productivity in A will cause the prices of A's products to fall relatively to those of B's products. If the sum of the elasticities of demand for imports in A and in B is greater than one, this in itself will cause a net shift of total expenditure away from the more expensive products of B and on to the cheaper products of A. A surplus will appear on A's balance of trade and a deficit on B's.

This net decrease in expenditure on B's products will cause a reduction in the demand for labour in B and some general slump in B, which will grow larger, (i) the smaller is B's home leakage, and (ii) the smaller is B's marginal propensity to import.

Simultaneously the net increase in expenditure on A's products due to the shift of demand from B's relatively expensive, on to A's relatively cheap, products will cause some increase in the demand for labour in A and a general upward movement of employment and the national income in A, the size of this inflation in A depending upon the size of A's home leakage and marginal propensity to import. And it is possible that if the sum of the elasticities of demand for imports in A and in B is sufficiently great and if the home leakage in A is sufficiently

---

[1] It is to be emphasized that the above result is based upon the assumptions of our neutral economy, namely, that there is no further action, such as a reduction in interest rates or in rates of taxation, taken in order to stimulate demand and absorb the displaced workers.

small, the upward movement in employment in A will actually absorb all of the labour displaced in the first instance by the increased productivity and more besides.[1]

The movements described above will be very much damped down if the real elasticity of supply in B is small. For in that case the prices of B's products will fall quickly as soon as the fall in the prices of A's products causes people to shift their expenditure away from B's and on to A's products. Thus there will not in effect be much change in the ratio between the prices of A's and of B's products; and little change will occur in the balance of trade, in employment in B, or in the secondary stimulus to employment in A.

We can sum up, therefore, by saying that the increased productivity in A will (on the normal assumption that the sum of the elasticities of demand for imports is greater than one) (i) cause a movement in the balance of trade[2] in A's favour, (ii) a depression of employment in B, (iii) a displacement of labour in A which may or may not be offset by the increased demand for labour in A due to the improvement in A's balance of trade, and (iv) some fall in the prices of A's products relatively to the prices of B's products, i.e. some movement in the real terms of trade in B's favour.[3]

2. *A Spontaneous Shift of Demand from B's Goods on to A's Goods*

Suppose next that there is a change of taste among purchasers of a kind which makes them, out of a given amount of total expenditure on goods and services, spend more on country A's goods and less on country B's goods. For our present purpose it makes no difference whether this shift of demand occurs in A or in B or in both of them simultaneously. The point is that there is from world-purchasers as a whole a spontaneous increase in the demand for A's products of a

[1] In the abnormal case in which the sum of the elasticities of demand for imports in A and in B were less than one, the fall in prices in A would cause a net shift of expenditure on to B's products. The balance of trade would move in B's favour; there would be an upward movement in B's income and employment; and in A still more unemployment would be added to those already displaced by the increase in productivity.

[2] And also in the balance of payments, unless the fall in real income in B and rise in real income in A causes such an increase in net lending from A to B as to outweigh the movement in the balance of trade.

[3] While the commodity terms of trade will thus move against A, it is not at all certain that they will move against A by as much as the increased productivity in A. In other words, while a unit of A's products will exchange for a smaller amount of B's products it is not at all certain that a unit of A's labour, which is now more productive than before, will command a smaller amount of B's products. If the real elasticity of supply in B is low, so that the prices of B's products fall quickly when expenditure shifts away from B's products, and if the sum of the two elasticities of demand is very high so that there is a large shift of expenditure away from B's products so long as her prices remain high in relation to A's, the commodity terms of trade will move against A by less than the increased productivity of labour in A.

given net size and a spontaneous decrease in the demand for B's products of the same net magnitude.

With our present assumptions of constant public demand for goods and services, rates of taxation, rates of interest, rates of wages, rates of foreign exchange, and commercial policies, a primary increase in the demand for A's products and decrease in the demand for B's products will start an inflationary upward movement of demand in A and a deflationary downward movement in B. How far the inflation will go in A and the deflation in B will depend *inter alia*, in the way examined in Chapter V, upon the home leakage in A and the home leakage in B. The smaller is each home leakage, the larger will the inflationary or deflationary movement be in the national income of the country concerned.

The shift of expenditure from B's goods on to A's goods will also affect A's and B's balances of trade. The direct effect will, of course, be equal to the shift itself. Thus, suppose there is a spontaneous shift of demand of $100 from B's products on to A's products. If this takes place in A it will represent a $100 decrease in A's imports from B (or decrease in B's exports to A); and if it takes place in B it will represent a $100 increase in B's imports from A (or increase in A's exports to B). Such will be the spontaneous effect on the balance of trade of A and B. But we must also take account of the induced effects which will result from the internal inflation in A and deflation in B. As the national income and the total domestic expenditure rise in A as a result of the induced effects of the increased demand for her products, purchasers in A will be induced to spend more than would otherwise have been the case upon imported goods, the amount of this induced increase in their demand for imports depending upon what we have called the marginal propensity to import in A. If this propensity is high, then as total domestic expenditure rises in A, so will imports into A rise considerably. Conversely, in B the deflation of national income and domestic expenditure will mean that there is an induced decline in the demand for imports in B, the size of which will be greater the greater is the marginal propensity to import in B.

As a result of these developments, A's balance of trade will not improve by as much as the primary shift of demand in favour of her goods for two reasons: first, because the consequent inflation of income and demand in A will induce purchasers in A to spend more on imports; and secondly, because the consequent deflation of income and demand in B will induce purchasers in B to spend less on imports. And the greater are the marginal propensities to import in A and in B, the less will be the final inflation of national income in A and deflation of national income in B (because the foreign leakages in A and B will be so much the bigger) and the less will be the final movement of the balance of trade in A's favour and against B (because the induced increase in imports into A and decrease in imports into B will be by so much the greater).

These changes may have some induced effects upon the amount of lending or other transfers in A's and B's balances of payments, though once again it is not possible to say unequivocally in which direction these induced effects will work. Income will have risen in A and fallen in B. A's residents will therefore have larger incomes from which to save and to lend abroad, and B's residents will have smaller incomes from which to lend abroad. On the other hand, the net increase in the demand for A's products and decrease in the demand for B's products will have made A's industries more profitable and B's less profitable for the investment of foreign funds. If the latter influences predominated, the balance of payments of A would move even more favourably than her balance of trade and of B even more unfavourably; but if the former influences were the more powerful, the final balance of payments would be affected by the primary shift of demand even less than the final balance of trade.

So far we have made no allowance for the price changes which the shift of demand from B's products on to A's products may bring about. As we have seen, the final result of this shift will mean some net increase in the demand for A's products (and so in A's national income) and some net decrease in the demand for B's products (and so in B's national income). There can, therefore, be no doubt about the direction in which the prices of A's and B's products will move as a result of the change; the prices of A's products will rise and those of B's products will fall. The terms of trade will, therefore, move in A's favour. The extent of this movement will, however, depend *inter alia* upon the real elasticity of supply in A and B. If these elasticities are both great, the prices of A's products will not rise much nor those of B's products fall much; there will be little change in the terms of trade; and there will be few further modifications in the balances of trade or the degrees of inflation and deflation to consider as a result of prices changes. If, however, these elasticities of supply are small, there will be a relatively large rise in the prices of A's products and fall in the prices of B's products; the terms of trade will move markedly in A's favour; and there may be important further modifications.

These modifications depend, in the way discussed in the last chapter, upon the size of the elasticities of demand for imports and the real elasticities of supply in A and in B. If the real elasticities of supply are small, then the shift of expenditure away from B's and on to A's products will cause a large rise in the prices of A's products relatively to those of B. If at the same time the sum of the elasticities of demand for imports in A and in B is considerably greater than one, this will cause a large shift of expenditure back from A's more expensive products on to B's less expensive ones; and this will diminish all the changes which we have been examining. It will damp down the net shift in demand from B's on to A's products, so that the inflation of income and employment in A, the deflation of income and employment in B, and the favourable movement in A's balance of trade would all be diminished. In the improbable case of low real elasticities of supply and of very low elasticities of demand for imports, all the changes would be exaggerated by a further shift of expenditure away from B's and on to A's products as a result of the relative rise in A's prices. There are, however, two cases in which the effects of relative price changes upon the national incomes and the balance of trade could be neglected. First, if the real elasticities of supply were very great, there would be no appreciable change in relative prices; and, secondly, if the sum of the elasticities of demand for imports equalled one, there would be no shift in expenditure as a result of price changes, no matter how great those changes were.

To summarize: a spontaneous shift in demand from B's on to A's products will cause an improvement in A's balance of trade, an adverse movement in B's balance of trade, an inflation of national income in A, and a deflation of national income in B. But the final improvement in A's and adverse movement in B's balance of trade will be less than the spontaneous shift of demand because of the induced increase of imports into A and decrease of imports into B. Prices will rise in A and fall in B, and the terms of trade will move in favour of A and against B. If the sum of the elasticities of demand for imports in A and in B is greater than one, this will damp down the ultimate changes in A's and B's balances of trade and national incomes.

3. *A Spontaneous Increase in Foreign Transfers from A to B*

Let us next consider the case of a spontaneous increase in foreign transfers from A to B. An example of this would be where people in A decide to lend more in B; for example, persons with funds to invest on A's capital market decide to purchase securities on B's capital market rather than on A's capital market. Now on our assumption of the neutral economy it is reasonable to assume that the increased transfer from A to B will not be accompanied by any direct or spontaneous change in the demand for A's or for B's products. In the neutral economy banking and monetary policies in A and B are such as to keep the rates of interest on all forms of assets in A and B constant. Since the terms of borrowing remain the same in both markets and nothing has directly happened to alter the profitability of capital development in either country, a decision on the part of operators on A's capital market to purchase securities in B rather than in A might well be accompanied by no change in the demand for real goods and services in either country.

And if that is so, there is no more to be said about this case. A's balance of payments will deteriorate and B's improve by the amount of the increased flow of capital funds from A to B. But there will be no change in the demand for A's or B's products. Neither country's balance of trade, national income, or terms of trade will be in any way affected.

4. *A Reparations Payment from A to B*

Let us suppose that the government of A has to transfer $100 m. in reparations per annum to the government of B. If the government of A raised the money in such a way that it caused no spontaneous reduction in the domestic demand for goods and services in A and if the receipt of the money in B caused no spontaneous increase in domestic expenditure in B, then the case would be exactly like the transfer which we have just examined. Nor is this an impossible case. If the government of A raises the money by borrowing and, as we are assuming, a banking and monetary policy is adopted which prevents this from leading to any change in rates of interest or terms of borrowing in A, then there is no reason why the payment of reparations by A should cause any direct decline in A's domestic expenditure. No consumer will have any motive to buy less for consumption and no entrepreneur will have any motive to borrow less for expenditure on capital development. Similarly, if B's government adds the reparations receipt to its budget surplus and the banking system in B keeps the terms of borrowing unchanged, there will be no reason for any direct change in domestic expenditure in B. The transfer of $100 m. reparations will cause a $100 m. deficit in A's, and surplus in B's, balance of payments; and that will be that so long as the assumptions of the neutral economy can be maintained.

But suppose now that the government of A raises the money for the reparations payment by increased taxation or by economies in public expenditure, while the government of B uses the receipts to finance a reduction in taxation or an increase in public expenditure. These fiscal changes will cause a spontaneous reduction in A's, and a spontaneous increase in B's, domestic expenditure. We have (i) a spontaneous increase in foreign transfers from A to B combined with (ii) a spontaneous decrease in domestic expenditure in A, and (iii) a spontaneous increase in domestic expenditure in B. Change (i) would leave national incomes unchanged but would cause a deficit in A's and surplus in B's balance of payments; change (ii), as we saw in the two preceding chapters, alone would cause deflations in A's and B's national incomes with a surplus in A's and deficit in B's balance of payments; and change (iii) alone would cause inflations in both national incomes and a surplus in A's and deficit in B's balance of payments. To what extent will these changes cancel each other out?

There is one special case in which they will exactly cancel out and there will be no net change in any country's national income or balance of payments. This will be so if the spontaneous decrease in domestic expenditure in A and the spontaneous increase in domestic expenditure in B are both exactly equal to the reparations to be paid, and if purchasers in B increase their expenditure on the products of A and B in exactly the same proportions in which purchasers in A decrease their expenditure on the products of these countries, or in other words if the sum of the marginal propensities to import in A and in B is equal to one.

This possibility is illustrated in case i of Table IX.[1] It is there assumed that in A, as a result of the fiscal measures adopted for raising the extra $100 m. for the payment of reparations, domestic expenditure is reduced by $100 m., of which $60 m. represents a decreased demand for A's products and $40 m. a decreased demand for B's products. These decreases are, however, exactly offset by equal increases in expenditures in B on A's and B's products respectively. In consequence there is no direct net change in the demand for the products of either country and so no direct change in either country's national income. But it is also clear from case i that there is no direct net change in the balance of payments. Country A's exports increase by $60 m.; her imports decrease by $40 m.; and this improvement in her balance of trade of $100 m. just covers the reparations payment of $100 m.

This result will occur only if there is a spontaneous decrease in domestic expenditure in A of as much as the reparations payment and a spontaneous increase in domestic expenditure in B of the same magnitude. But this is not likely to happen, even if the whole of the reparations payment is financed by increased taxation in A and is used to allow a reduction in taxation in B. For some of the increased taxation in A is likely to cause a reduction in the savings and not in the expenditure of the taxpayers, whereas some of the tax reductions in B are likely to cause an increase in the savings and not of the expenditure of the taxpayers in B. Suppose that the reparations payment to be transferred from A to B had been $130 m. instead of $100 m., but that, as in case i of Table IX, the accompanying fiscal changes in A and B had increased domestic expenditure in B by only $100 m. and had reduced domestic expenditure in A by only $100 m. With the sum of the marginal propensities to import in A and B still equal to one, there would still be no direct change in either country's national income. But because

[1] Table IX is constructed on the same principles as Table VII (see p. 36), except that it shows only the changes in imports, exports, expenditure, and income instead of the total quantities involved.

I.E.P.—4*

the spontaneous deflation in A and inflation in B has not been as large as the total reparations to be transferred, there is now an adverse movement of \$30 m. in A's balance of payments. A sum of \$130 m. has to be transferred in reparations to B but the fiscal changes have generated an improved balance of trade of only \$100 m.

TABLE IX

Impact Effect of a Spontaneous Decrease in Domestic Expenditure in A and of an Equal Spontaneous Increase in Domestic Expenditure in B

Case i : *Sum of the Marginal Propensities to Import equal to One*

Marginal propensity to import in A	0·4
,, ,, ,, ,, ,, B	0·6
Sum of propensities	1·0

Receiving Countries	Spending Countries A	B	National Income
A	−60	+60	Nil
B	−40	+40	Nil
Domestic Expenditure	−100	+100	

The balance of trade moves 100 (i.e. 60+40) in A's favour

Case ii : *Sum of the Marginal Propensities to Import greater than One*

Marginal propensity to import in A	0·6
,, ,, ,, ,, ,, B	0·7
Sum of propensities	1·3

Receiving Countries	Spending Countries A	B	National Income
A	−40	+70	+30
B	−60	+30	−30
Domestic Expenditure	−100	+100	

The balance of trade moves 130 (i.e. 70+60) in A's favour

Case iii : Sum of the Marginal Propensities to Import less than One

Marginal propensity to import in A		0·3
,, ,, ,, ,, ,, B		0·2
Sum of propensities		0·5

Receiving Countries	Spending Countries A	B	National Income
A	−70	+20	−50
B	−30	+80	+50
Domestic Expenditure	−100	+100	

The balance of trade moves 50 (i.e. 20+30) in A's favour

Now, it is not impossible that the spontaneous changes in domestic expenditure in A and in B should be less than the reparations to be transferred, but that they should nevertheless lead to direct changes in A's and B's demands for imports sufficiently large to finance the whole reparations transfer. This possibility is represented in case ii of Table IX, where the sum of the marginal propensities to import in A and in B add up to more than one. There are reparations of $130 m. to be transferred from A to B. The fiscal adjustments in A and B are, however, such that there is a decrease of only $100 m. in A's domestic expenditure and an increase of only $100 m. in B's domestic expenditure. But the marginal propensity to import in A is so high that purchasers in A reduce their demand for B's products by no less than $60 m. and the marginal propensity to import in B is also so high that her purchasers increase their demand for imports by no less than $70 m., so that there is an automatic improvement in A's balance of trade of $130 m., which is sufficient to cover the whole reparations payment. But in this case there is a very small reduction by A in her own expenditure on her own goods and, similarly, a very small increase by B in her own expenditure on her own goods. In consequence, while there is no direct effect on the balance of payments of either country, there is a direct net increase in the demand for A's products and so in A's national income and a net decrease in the demand for B's products and in B's national income. Or in other words, if a given spontaneous transfer is associated with a relatively small spontaneous decrease in A's, and increase in B's, domestic expenditure, it could lead to a direct net change in the balance of trade sufficient to finance the transfer only if the decrease in demand in A is concentrated on imports and not on her own products and the increase in demand in B is also concentrated mainly on imports and not on her own produce; and this will mean that there is a net increase in the total demand for A's goods and A's national income and a net decline in the case of B.

Moreover, it must be remembered that Table IX shows only the direct impact effect of the change; it makes no allowance for the induced effects which will result from the changes in the national incomes of the various countries. Now, in case i, since the direct impact effects lead to no changes in national incomes, there will be no induced effects to consider. But in the case ii the net impact effects lead to an increase in national income in A and a decrease in national income in B. As a result of this, depending upon the home leakages and marginal propensities to import in A and B, there will be a further cumulative inflationary movement of income and expenditure in A inducing some secondary increase in imports and there will be a further secondary deflation in B, leading to some fall in the demand for imports. The balance of trade will move somewhat against A and in favour of B. And if the sum of the elasticities of demand for imports in A and in B is greater than one, the price changes which will accompany the inflation in A and deflation in B will accentuate this movement. Or, in other words, if we take into account these induced effects the dispositions on the part of purchasers in A to economize on imports rather than on home products, and on the part of purchasers in B to spend more on imports rather than on home products, must be even more marked than is shown in case ii if the final balances of payments are to remain unaffected by the reparations transfer.

Now we have seen reason to believe (pp. 67–8, above) that normally the sum of the marginal propensities to import in A and in B will be less than one. And we have already stated that the direct fiscal effects of a reparations payment of any given sum from A to B will probably cause a decrease in domestic expenditure in A and an increase in domestic expenditure in B somewhat smaller than the total reparations payment itself.

Case iii of Table IX is meant to represent a more realistic case which takes account of both these points. In it, it is assumed that there is a spontaneous reduction of domestic expenditure in A and increase of domestic expenditure in B of $100 m. (i.e. less than the $130 m. to be transferred in reparations). At the same time it is assumed that a high proportion of the economies of A's purchasers are on A's products ($70 m. out of the $100 m.) and that a high proportion of the increased demand in B is for B's products (namely $80 m. out of the $100 m.). The result is that there is a net decline in the demand for A's products (and so some deflation of income in A) and a net increase in the demand for B's products (and so some inflation in B). But A improves her balance of trade by only $50 m. which is $80 m. too little to finance the reparations transfer of $130 m.[1]

Case iii, as case ii, does not allow for induced effects. The deflation in A and the inflation in B directly set in motion by the impact effects of the change will lead to further induced deflation in the former and inflation in the latter. This will lead to some further fall in imports into A and to some further rise in imports into B. The final effects upon the national incomes of the countries concerned will be more marked, and upon their balances of payments less marked, than those shown in Table IX.

The price changes which are likely to accompany these changes will have further modifying effects upon the changes in incomes and in balances of payments. If the sum of the elasticities of demand for imports in A and in B is greater than one, the fall in prices in A and the rise in prices in B will shift total expenditure away from the goods of B on to those of A. This will cause the balances of payments to come somewhat nearer to equilibrium and at the same time will cause the net income changes to be less marked than they would otherwise be.

We can summarize the final situation, as compared with the situation before the reparations became payable, in the following way, on the assumptions that the spontaneous changes in domestic expenditure are less than the reparations payment and that the sum of the marginal propensities to import is less than one:

In country A there will be a deflation of income, some improvement in the balance of trade, but an adverse movement in the balance of payments; in B an inflation of income, some adverse movement in the balance of trade, but an improvement in the balance of payments; and the terms of trade will move in B's favour.

[1] In terms of the controversy of the inter-war years about the 'transfer problem', we may summarize our conclusions as follows. If in both countries fiscal arrangements are such as to cause a spontaneous change in domestic expenditure equal to the reparations payment and if the sum of the marginal propensities to import is equal to one, then the paying country has a 'budgetary burden', but no additional 'transfer burden' and no 'transfer problem'. If the spontaneous changes in domestic expenditure are less than the reparations payment, there is likely to be a 'transfer problem', since the budgetary changes are unlikely to bring about automatically a sufficient change in the balance of trade. But, if the sum of the marginal propensities to import is equal to one, there is not any additional 'transfer burden', since the further policy deflation in the paying country and inflation in the receiving country which will be required to preserve internal balance in each country will automatically induce the required change in the balance of trade without any change in the terms of trade against the paying country. But if the sum of the marginal propensities to import is less than one, then there is a 'transfer burden' in the paying country; financial policies which preserve internal balance in the two countries will leave a deficit in the balance of payments of the paying country, the removal of which will require a decline in the prices of the products of the paying country relatively to those of the receiving country.

5. *New Investment Opportunities in Country A*

Let us suppose that some inventions or geographical discoveries open up new opportunities for profitable investment in country A. This will cause, at the current rate of interest and terms for borrowing money in A, a spontaneous increase in domestic expenditure on capital development in A. If there were no other change, this would represent a particular example of the spontaneous change which we examined at length in the two preceding chapters. It will cause inflations of income in A and in B and will induce an unfavourable movement in A's balance of trade with B.

But a change of this kind may very well be accompanied by other spontaneous changes. In particular the increased profitability of investment in A may very well cause a spontaneous movement of foreign capital funds into country A to take advantage of the new investment opportunities, quite apart from any induced changes in foreign lending which may result from the changes which take place in the national incomes of A and of B. In a case of this kind, i.e. of a spontaneous increase in domestic expenditure in A combined with a spontaneous increase of net foreign lending to A there is, of course, no presumption one way of the other that the balance of payments will move unfavourably or favourably to A. It depends upon the degrees to which the increased investment opportunities in A tempt foreign capital into A and to which the increased domestic expenditure in A (both the spontaneous and the induced increase) is spent on imports. If the former is great and the latter small, the balance of payments as a whole will move in A's favour.

6. *The Imposition of a Tariff in A*

Suppose now that A imposes a tariff on imports. This will cause a spontaneous reduction in the volume of goods imported into A and will therefore cause a spontaneous reduction in the amount paid by A's purchasers for imports after deduction of the increased import duty. Suppose that a fiscal policy in A is adopted whereby the whole of the additional revenue collected from the import duty is used to increase the expenditure by A's government on goods and services (or to reduce taxation in such a way that private consumers in A increase their expenditure on goods and services) by an amount equal to the increased revenue from the import duty. In this case the imposition of the duty causes no direct net change in the total domestic expenditure on goods and services at factor cost. What is saved net on imports is spent by the government or by private persons on home-produced goods. The case is very similar to the spontaneous shift of demand from B's goods on to A's goods, the effects of which we have examined in the second example in this chapter.

But the case is altered if the government in A does not use the increased customs revenue to spend on goods and services or to remit taxes which will indirectly cause such an increased expenditure on goods and services. In that case the spontaneous shift of demand from B's products on to A's products is accompanied by a spontaneous reduction in domestic expenditure in A equal to the new revenue collected from the import duties.

So far as the effects on the balance of trade and on the national incomes of other countries are concerned these two changes reinforce one another; but so far as the effect on A's national income is concerned they will offset each other. The shift of demand from B's products on to A's products will, as we have seen, cause some inflation in A, deflation in B, and adverse movement in B's balance of trade. The spontaneous decline in domestic expenditure in A will put in motion an offsetting deflationary movement in A, and this (on the lines discussed in the two preceding chapters) will cause a still further decline in the demand for B's products and will thus intensify the deflation of B's income and the adverse movement in her balance of trade.

Which factor will be the more potent so far as A's national income is concerned will depend upon the elasticity of demand for imports in A. If it is very low, then the tariff will not cause much reduction in the quantity of imports into A. This will mean (i) that there is not much diversion of demand away from B's products (i.e. of expenditure on A's imports less duty) and (ii) that there is a relatively large collection of duty, so that the spontaneous reduction in A's domestic expenditure is large. In these circumstances there will be a net fall in A's national income. But if the price elasticity of demand for imports in A is high, there will be a large diversion of expenditure in A away from B's products and a relatively small amount of this diversion will be sucked away in additional revenue. There will be a considerable net increase in the demand for A's products.[1]

[1] If there were no foreign repercussion on A's exports because of the deflation in B, it could be seen that a unitary price elasticity of demand in A for imported goods would mark the dividing line. If the elasticity of demand for imports in A is unity, then consumers in A spend (including the tax) the same amount on imported products after the tax as before; they have, therefore, the same amount to spend on their own products as before; the increased revenue is exactly offset by the reduced amount paid to foreigners for the imports; and if purchasers in B did not reduce their demand for A's exports because of the induced deflation in B, the total amount spent on A's products, and so A's national income, would be unchanged. But since there will be an induced reduction in demand in B for A's exports, the elasticity of demand for imported goods in A must be somewhat greater than unity for there to be no net change in the demand for A's products. In this case there is a net reduction in the amount which purchasers in A spend on imports even including the duty; they have, therefore, more left over to spend on A's products; and this increase in the home demand for A's products is just offset by the reduction in the demand in B for A's exports resulting from deflation of income and expenditure in B which has been set in motion by the reduced demand in A for imports from B.

We have now examined some seven cases of spontaneous change on the assumptions of the neutral economy. Some of these we have examined at length, while others have been only cursorily described. In particular in the last two examples very little reference has been made to the way in which the induced effects will develop as a result of changes in income and prices. But the principles of operation of the neutral economy should now be clear; and it would be tedious to apply the analysis any further by inventing other possible examples of spontaneous changes (though it would be easy to do so) or by working out in detail the direct and induced changes of each example which has been mentioned.

Enough has been said to enable the reader to undertake these developments for himself and to enable us to proceed to the next stage in our analysis, which is to examine the various changes of policy which the authorities in A and B may introduce into the neutral economy in order to offset the disadvantageous effects of these spontaneous changes.

PART III. FINANCIAL POLICY

PART III. FINANCIAL POLICY

CHAPTER VIII

THE MEANING OF FISCAL AND MONETARY POLICY AND OF INTERNAL AND EXTERNAL BALANCE

IN discussing the working of the neutral economy in Part II, we made six institutional assumptions, namely, that the public demand for goods and services, rates of taxation, rates of interest, rates of wages, rates of foreign exchange, and barriers to international trade were all constant. In Part III we shall modify the first three of these assumptions in order to consider how, by a change of financial policy, the authorities in any country can offset those adverse internal or external effects (i.e. the effects upon employment or upon the balance of payments) which various spontaneous disturbances may bring about in the neutral economy.

Let us start by explaining what is meant by a change in financial policy. We shall use the general term 'financial policy' to cover two rather different types of policy, namely, 'fiscal policy' and 'monetary policy'. By 'fiscal policy' we mean a change in tax rates or in the amount of government expenditure which is brought about by the fiscal authorities for the purpose of affecting total domestic expenditure, i.e. the total monetary expenditure on all goods and services in the community. By 'monetary policy' we mean an alteration in the terms on which capital funds can be lent and borrowed (a change which we shall, for short, call a change in the rate of interest) brought about by the banking system through the creation of additional supplies of money in order to ease the terms on which capital funds can be borrowed or through the restriction of monetary supplies in order to harden the terms on which monetary funds can be borrowed.

The processes of 'fiscal policy' and 'monetary policy' for the purpose of influencing the general level of demand for goods and services within any country would have to be an important theme in any Theory of Domestic Economic Policy. In the present context the barest summary must suffice.

Let us start with fiscal policy. A reduction in the rates of direct or indirect taxation (assuming government expenditure and the terms on which money can be borrowed to remain constant) will stimulate the demand for goods and services. A reduction of direct taxes will directly increase the tax-free purchasing power at the disposal of the taxpayer and will thus lead to an increase in his demand for goods and services. A reduction of indirect taxes, by reducing the price which purchasers must pay for a given amount of the taxed commodities, will enable them, out of their unchanged incomes, to purchase increased amounts of the taxed goods or of other goods or services. And this increase of demand will not be offset by a reduced demand from other quarters if (i) the government does not reduce its public expenditure on goods and services *pari passu* with the reduction in its tax revenue, and if (ii) the fact that the government will now have an increased budget deficit to finance by borrowing in the capital market is, through the policy of the banking system, not permitted to lead to any increase in the rate of interest or to any other increased difficulty on the part of other borrowers to obtain funds for expenditure on capital developments of all kinds.

Similarly, an increase in governmental expenditure on goods and services will cause a direct increase in the total demand for goods and services; and an increased government expenditure on such 'transfer payments' as old-age pensions, family allowances, national debt interest, etc. will increase the purchasing power available to the recipients. This will cause a net increase in demand for goods and services provided that (i) the government does not accompany its increased expenditure by raising increased revenue through higher rates of taxation, and (ii) the increased borrowing by the government to finance its increased expenditure is not permitted by the banking system to lead to worsened terms for borrowing new funds by other borrowers. For in these cases no private persons will, as a result of the increased government expenditure, have any incentive themselves to spend less on goods and services either for current consumption or for purposes of capital development.

Let us next consider monetary policy. The authorities may engineer an increase in the total demand for goods and services through the adoption of a monetary policy designed to increase the supply of money and thus to reduce the rate of interest and generally to make it easier and more attractive to borrow money to carry out expenditure on capital developments of all kinds. For this purpose the banks may offer to lend new money directly to their customers at lower rates of interest or otherwise on easier terms; or the banks may engage in 'open market operations' and purchase for new money securities or other assets on the capital market. This will have the effect of raising the price of such assets and thus reducing the rate of yield on them, so that persons who wish to borrow new capital funds by the issue of new securities will be enabled to do so on more favourable terms. In so far as a fall in the rate of interest at which capital funds can be borrowed induces persons or businesses or other corporations to embark on increased capital expenditure, or in so far as a fall in the rate of interest at which new savings can be lent induces people to save less (i.e. to spend a larger proportion of their incomes on goods and services for immediate consumption), there will be a net increase in the demand for goods and services—provided, of course, that it is not offset by a simultaneous increase in rates of taxation (and consequential contraction of the purchasing power in the hands of private consumers) or reduction in governmental expenditure on goods and services.

From our present point of view the main feature of an expansionist fiscal policy or monetary policy is that they will both lead to an increase of domestic expenditure in the country adopting any one of them. This 'policy' increase in domestic expenditure will, in its further repercussions, be equivalent to a 'spontaneous' increase in domestic expenditure, the effects of which we have examined at length in Chapters V and VI above. That is to say, in the normal case it will (i) cause an inflation in the total national income and in the demand for labour in the country concerned, (ii) cause some inflation in the national income and in the demand for labour in the rest of the world as a result of the increased demand for imports in the country initiating the increase of domestic expenditure, (iii) cause an unfavourable movement in the balance of trade of the country concerned, and (iv) thereby probably cause an unfavourable movement in that country's balance of payments.[1] The reader is, however, referred to the analysis of Chapters V and VI for the necessary qualifications of these results which depend, *inter alia*, upon the assumptions (i) that the country concerned does not import only inferior goods which its purchasers buy in smaller quantities when their total domestic demand increases, and (ii) that the real elasticity of supply of goods and services in both countries is great, or that the sum of the elasticities of demand for imports in A and B is greater than one.

As far as most of these results are concerned the effects will be very similar whether domestic expenditure is stimulated by fiscal policy or by monetary policy. But the choice between fiscal policy and monetary policy may make a significant difference to the incentive to lend money abroad.

Of the seven factors enumerated above on pp. 61–2 as determining the amount of foreign lending, the first four may be brought into action through monetary or fiscal policy. But as far as the first two of these four are concerned, there will be no difference between the effects of monetary and of fiscal policy; a given expansion of domestic expenditure and of national income will have the same effect (i) in increasing the supply of savings out of which foreign lending may be made, and (ii) in

---

[1] The opposite effects will, of course, result from a policy reduction in the domestic expenditure of any country.

increasing the relative profitability and attractiveness of home industry, whether the expansion be through monetary or fiscal means. But there may be significant differences between the effects of monetary policy and of fiscal policy so far as the next two factors are concerned, namely, (iii) the effect of a lower rate of interest at home in encouraging foreign lending, and (iv) the effect of changes in tax rates on the yields on, and so on the relative attractiveness of, home and foreign investment.

If fiscal policy is used for the purpose of domestic expansion and if it takes the form of an increase in public expenditure, there will not be any change in rates of interest or in tax rates and these two factors will not operate.

If fiscal policy is used and takes the form of the encouragement of domestic expenditure by reduced tax rates, there will not be any change in the rate of interest. But a reduction in taxation in A may in certain circumstances increase the attraction to residents of B to lend funds in A or reduce the attractiveness of residents of A to lend in B. For example, the tax reduction in A may include a reduction in the tax on the interest or profits to be earned on capital funds and the benefits of this tax reduction may be enjoyed by residents of B as well as by those of A,[1] in which case the investment of funds in A will become relatively more attractive to residents in B. Similarly, if residents of A enjoy the tax reduction on income from property situated in A but not on income from property situated in B, they will have a smaller incentive to lend abroad to B. But, on the other hand, if the reduction of tax rates in A covers the income from property situated in A but accruing to owners in B, there will be so much more tax-free income from property to be transferred from A to B. This will increase the strain on the country's balance of payments, while the attraction of new capital funds will reduce that strain. What the net effect, if any, will be will thus depend not only upon the tax arrangements, but also upon the amount of property income already needing to be transferred from A to B and upon the extent to which a given tax concession attracts new capital.

On the other hand, suppose that the domestic expansion is brought about through monetary policy, i.e. by means of an increase in the domestic supply of money in A leading to an easing of the terms on which new money can be borrowed in A and to a general reduction in the interest yields to be obtained on securities and other assets in A.

---

[1] Whether or not this will be so depends upon the international tax arrangements. If the tax imposed by the government of the taxing country, either by its own decision or by reason of an international agreement for the avoidance of double taxation, relates to the income enjoyed by its own residents and not to the income derived from capital situated in its own territory, a tax reduction will not affect anyone's incentive to lend money in the taxing country rather than in other countries.

This will present an unequivocal additional incentive on the part of B's borrowers to borrow what funds they need in A rather than in B; and it will similarly furnish an additional incentive on the part of existing holders of capital in A to shift their funds from A to B. This tendency for reduced interest rates in A to put an additional strain on A's balance of payments could only be offset to the extent that short-term debt of residents of A to residents of B fell due for repayment and could now be renewed at a somewhat lower rate of interest in spite of the fact that the rates at which B's lenders could place their capital in B's market had not fallen.

In considering monetary policy a distinction must be drawn between the short-run and the long-run effects upon foreign lending of a reduction of interest rates in any one country. Suppose that in country A and country B the long-term rate of interest is 5 per cent and the short-term rate 3 per cent, and that the banking system in A then adopts an internal monetary policy which reduces domestic rates of interest to $4\frac{1}{2}$ and $2\frac{1}{2}$ per cent respectively, the rates in B remaining unchanged at 5 and 3 per cent. There are, broadly speaking, two sources from which an additional demand for B's capital assets on the part of residents of A may arise.

In the first place, owners of capital in A may, as a result of the change, wish to shift a large part of their existing capital funds from A to B, either on long term in order to earn 5 per cent instead of $4\frac{1}{2}$ per cent or on short term in order to earn 3 per cent instead of $2\frac{1}{2}$ per cent. Such a shift of capital may be very large and very short-lived; and this is likely to be particularly true in the case of short-term loans which are likely to be considered as a more mobile fund of capital by their owners than in the case of long-term investments. Once this shift of existing capital funds has taken place the strain on the balance of payments of country A which may have been very great while it was taking place will altogether cease.

But there is a second source from which the demand by residents in A for B's capital assets may proceed, namely, from the annual savings of residents in A who are seeking an outlet for this flow of savings and may be induced to invest a larger part of it in B as a result of the relative fall in yields on capital in A. This source of demand for B's assets is as likely (perhaps, more likely) to be operative in the market for long-term assets as in that for short-term assets; it is not likely to be as great quantitatively as the first source, immediately after the reduction in A's interest rates; but, unlike the first source, it is likely to constitute a continuing additional demand for B's assets. We may, therefore, conclude that when domestic demand is expanded in A by the monetary means of reduced interest rates, the additional strain on her balance of payments due to capital transfers is likely to be large at first (and perhaps concentrated on movements of short-term funds), and then to diminish to a much lower continuing figure (which may be mainly operative in the market for long-term assets).

We may conclude, therefore, that while fiscal and monetary methods of inflating or deflating domestic expenditure will have broadly similar results on the national incomes and balances of trade of the countries concerned, the monetary method of reducing interest rates may cause a significantly larger increase in the transfer of capital funds abroad and thus involve a significantly larger unfavourable movement in its total balance of payments. Moreover, this difference between fiscal and monetary policy is likely to be particularly marked if domestic expenditure is not in fact very sensitive to changes in the rate of interest, i.e. if it needs a very large fall in the rate of interest to induce any required increase in domestic expenditure; for in that case the very large change in interest rates is likely to have a relatively large effect upon foreign lending. The fiscal methods of increased public expenditure and of reduced tax rates will not have these effects, though the method of reduced tax rates, if it covers taxation on income from property and if these tax benefits are extended to foreign property owners but not to resident owners of foreign property, may have some additional effect upon the balance of payments; but in which direction it is impossible to say without detailed knowledge of the particular case.[1]

Let us next consider the objectives which the authorities in a country may hope to attain through an inflation or deflation of domestic expenditure brought about by means of financial policy. Broadly speaking, there are two possible objectives. In the first place, the authorities may bring about a policy change in domestic expenditure in order to offset the secondary effects on *domestic employment* of some other change in the demand for home products, whether this primary change in demand proceeds from some spontaneous change in home demand or from some

---

[1] While the direct effect upon the amount of foreign lending is, for our present purpose the distinguishing feature between fiscal policy and monetary policy, it is not to be implied that on other grounds the choice between them is indifferent. Far from it. Suppose that a deflation of total domestic expenditure is required. The means chosen for the purpose must be considered from at least three other points of view. First, let us compare higher tax rates with higher rates of interest. The former might have worse effects upon the incentives for work and enterprise than the latter. Secondly, compare lower public expenditure on the one hand with higher tax rates or interest rates on the other. The former would involve reducing the field of public expenditure while the latter would involve restricting private expenditure, and the balance between public and private consumption would thus be involved. Thirdly, compare lower public expenditure or higher tax rates on the one hand with higher rates of interest on the other. The former would involve increased saving through an increased budget surplus, i.e. a lower current public or private demand for goods and services, whereas the latter would operate through a reduced demand for capital goods for purposes of capital development. The question of the optimum rate of saving is thus involved. But all these are matters which would be more appropriately considered in a Theory of Domestic Economic Policy.

spontaneous or policy change in the foreign demand for home products. We may call this a policy of 'internal balance'. Secondly, the authorities may bring about a policy change in domestic expenditure in order to offset the secondary effects on the *balance of payments* of any primary change in the foreign demand for home products or in the home demand for foreign products or in the volume of net transfer payments to or from foreign countries. This we may call a policy of 'external balance'.

A simple example may serve to illustrate this difference. Suppose that there is a decline in demand in A for B's products because there is an economic depression (i.e. a spontaneous decline in domestic expenditure) in A. Then there will occur (i) a decline in the demand for B's products and so a reduction in national income and in the level of production and employment in B, and (ii) an unfavourable movement in B's balance of trade, and probably also in B's balance of payments, as the demand in A for B's exports falls off. This was the situation depicted in Chapters V and VI, where it was assumed that the authorities in B did not engineer any policy inflation or deflation of domestic expenditure in order to offset either of these effects, but adopted what we called the neutral policy of letting the repercussions of the depression in A work themselves out on the national income and balance of payments of B.

But the authorities in B might have acted very differently. As the depression in A began to develop and to cause unemployment in B, the authorities in B might (by reducing tax rates, by increasing public expenditure, or by increasing monetary supplies and reducing interest rates) have induced a policy increase in domestic expenditure in B so as to maintain the demand for B's products—a policy which would have avoided the adverse effects upon national income and employment in B only at the expense of adding to the strain on B's balance of payments, since the policy inflation of demand in B would tend to raise the demand in B for imported as well as for home-produced goods and services. Such a policy might be properly called a policy of 'internal balance'.

On the other hand, the authorities in B might have concentrated their attention upon getting rid of the adverse effects of the depression in A upon B's balance of payments. This, so far as financial policy is concerned, would require a deflation of domestic expenditure in B in order to restrict the demand for imports and to reduce the demand for, and so the price of, home-produced products so that they were offered in greater quantity and on cheaper terms in export markets. This would restore B's balance of payments at the expense of making the unemployment problem in B still more acute, since the reduction of domestic expenditure in B would entail a reduction in the demand for B's products as well as in the demand for imports from A. Such a policy would, therefore, be properly called a policy of 'external balance'.

This is not the appropriate place to enter into a detailed discussion of the many domestic problems which a financial policy for internal balance would involve. We shall talk as if the objective of internal balance were simply that of maintaining a level of total demand for all the country's products sufficiently high to maintain full employment, but not so high as to lead to a continuing inflation of money prices and costs.

Broadly speaking, this would be correct if there were (i) complete mobility of labour, and (ii) constant money wage rates. But in the absence of labour mobility it would not be possible to remove all structural unemployment by means of a general inflation of domestic demand by internal financial policy. For example, an inflation of the domestic consumers' demands brought about by a reduction of income tax will not necessarily absorb the particular types of labour in the particular localities which have been hard hit by a reduction in exports to foreign countries, though it will offset the secondary deflationary effects which would otherwise follow from a depression in the purchasing power of those formerly employed in producing the exports.

Moreover, in the absence of constant money wage rates it is not at all certain that both general unemployment and also progressive inflation of domestic money prices and costs can simultaneously be avoided. If the trade unions and similar bodies push money wage rates up progressively as soon as the unemployment percentage falls below, let us say, 10 per cent, then the authorities must choose between a financial policy which keeps the general level of demand so restricted that 10 per cent of the available workers are unemployed but the general level of money wage rates and prices remains stable, and a financial policy which keeps the general level of money demand always high enough to remove all general unemployment, in which case there will be a rapid and continuous upward movement of money prices and costs.

It may be that the best form of financial policy for internal balance would be to maintain total domestic expenditure at such a level as to ensure sufficient demand for home-produced goods and services in general as to maintain constant the general index of prices offered for all home production, and to insist upon sufficient upward and downward adjustments of particular money wage rates against this general background of stability, to avoid general unemployment and—together with other appropriate measures to encourage the mobility of labour and of enterprise between different industries and localities—to reduce structural unemployment to the minimum. But all these matters would more appropriately be discussed in a Theory of Domestic Economic Policy.

For our present purpose we need only say that we define financial policy for internal balance as the control of total domestic expenditure by fiscal or monetary measures for the purpose of achieving whatever is considered *on domestic grounds* to be the best form of stability of demand for home production and for home employment, though for short-hand we shall often talk of this as being synonymous with the maintenance of full employment. And we mean by financial policy for external balance the control of total domestic expenditure for the purpose of preventing a deficit or surplus in the balance of payments, as defined in Chapter I of this volume.

CHAPTER IX

FINANCIAL POLICY FOR INTERNAL AND EXTERNAL BALANCE[1]

I^F we now consider the possible modifications, by means of financial policy, of the neutral economy which we discussed in Part II, it is clear that there are five possible 'policy combinations' which may be pursued in any country as a result of any spontaneous disturbance. The authorities in country A may adopt the neutral policy of Part II; they may seek internal balance through fiscal policy, or internal balance through monetary policy, or external balance through fiscal policy, or external balance through monetary policy. The authorities in B may also choose between any one of five similar 'policy combinations'. And since any one of the five possible policy combinations in A may be chosen against any single one of the five possible policy combinations in B, there are no less than twenty-five possible policy combinations in our two-country world. Each of the seven spontaneous disturbances which in Chapters V, VI, and VII were analysed on the assumption of neutral policies in both countries should at this point be analysed for each of the remaining twenty-four policy combinations which we have now introduced.

It would clearly be out of the question to indulge in the whole of this analysis. All that can be done in this chapter is to take one or two particular examples to illustrate the sort of difference that is made to the analysis of Part II by allowing for financial policies for internal balance or for external balance in the countries concerned. This should familiarize the reader with the technique which he can apply to the other problems which may arise.

We may start with the problem analysed in Chapters V and VI. Suppose that there is a spontaneous increase of domestic expenditure in country A. This would lead to an inflation of national income and employment in A and to an unfavourable movement in her balance of payments and to some inflation of national income and employment in B and to some favourable movement in B's balance of payments.[2] If now the authorities in A adopt either a financial policy for internal

---

[1] The subject matter of this and the following chapter is considered in Section VIII (ii) and (iii) of the separate mathematical supplement.

[2] To illustrate the principles involved we confine ourselves to the normal reactions on incomes and the balances of payments. The reader must work out for himself the analysis for the case where, because A's imports are inferior or because the real elasticity of supply in A is small and the sum of the elasticities of demand for imports in A and in B is very low, the spontaneous increase in domestic expenditure in A causes an unfavourable movement in B's balance of payments and a decline in national income in B.

balance or a financial policy for external balance instead of a neutral policy, all these effects will be offset. In either case a deflationary financial policy would have to be adopted in A; and if the policy reduction of domestic expenditure was exactly the same size as the spontaneous increase in domestic expenditure, then the one would exactly offset the other. It would be as if no change at all had occurred; and both internal and external balance would be preserved in A.[1]

But let us suppose that the authorities in A adopt a neutral policy. Then the authorities in B can adopt a neutral policy (as assumed in Chapters V and VI) or either a financial policy for internal balance or else a financial policy for external balance. If they aim at internal balance, they will deflate domestic expenditure in B as the demand in A for exports from B grows, so that the home demand for B's products falls *pari passu* with the increase in the demand for B's exports in A. But this deflation in B will have a threefold result: first, the favourable movement in B's balance of payments will be increased as a result of the lower demand for imports in B and will therefore be greater than appeared from the analysis of Chapters V and VI; and this will be even more the case if the deflation in B is by means of monetary policy since the higher rates of interest in B will attract additional foreign lending from A to B; secondly, there will, of course, be no net inflation of national income or employment in B; and, thirdly, the inflation of national income in A will go less far than in the conditions envisaged in Chapters V and VI, since the demand for A's products in B will be lower than was there assumed to be the case.

---

[1] This conclusion would need some modification if, as is possible, the import content of the policy decrease of domestic expenditure were not the same as the import content of the spontaneous increase of domestic expenditure. Thus, suppose that the spontaneous increase of domestic expenditure consisted of an increased demand for consumption goods, of which a large proportion was imported, while the policy reduction of domestic expenditure consisted of economies in public investment in capital works, most of which were made at home. Then the spontaneous increase of domestic expenditure of, say, 100 with an import content of 40 would, in order to preserve an internal balance, need to be matched by a policy reduction of domestic expenditure of only 90 with an import content of 30. But this, while preserving the demand for home-produced goods and services constant, would allow an increased demand for foreign goods of 10 (i.e. 40−30), so that external balance would require a larger policy deflation of domestic expenditure. The argument in the text is based on the assumption that the import content of the policy decrease is the same as that of the spontaneous increase. The argument in the text would also need some modification if the authorities in A deflate by means of monetary policy, since the higher rates of interest in A would attract foreign lending from B to A. If the authorities in A deflated sufficiently to preserve internal balance, there would then be a surplus in A's balance of payments due to the flow of capital funds from B. Alternatively, the authorities in A could stop the deflation at a point where they achieved external balance (with their increased flow of funds to A offsetting some deficit in the balance of trade), in which case there would still remain some net inflation of national income in A.

If, on the other hand, the authorities in B adopt a policy of external balance, there will be a policy inflation of domestic expenditure in B so as to increase the demand for imports in B as the demand in A for B's exports increases. This, again, will involve a threefold modification of the analysis of Chapters V and VI: first, there will, of course, in this case be no net movement in B's (or in A's) balance of payments; second, the inflation of national income in B will be greater than in the circumstances assumed in Chapters V and VI, since there will be an increase in demand in B for B's own products (as well as for imports) as a result of the policy of inflation of domestic expenditure in B; and, third, the inflation of national income in A will be intensified by reason of the increased demand for A's exports brought about by the policy inflation of domestic demand in B.[1]

Let us take one more example, namely, that which was examined in section 2 of Chapter VII. Suppose that for some reason or another there is a shift of demand by purchasers either in A or in B or in both from the products of A on to the products of B, there being no spontaneous change in the total of domestic expenditure in either country. In other words, there is a spontaneous increase in the demand for B's products offset by a spontaneous decrease of the same magnitude in the demand for A's products. As has been argued in Chapter VII, if neutral policies were adopted in both A and B, this would lead to a deflation of national income in A and an inflation of national income in B, as a result of which there would be some secondary reduction in the demand for imports in A and some secondary increase in the demand for imports in B so that the final unfavourable change in A's balance of trade would be somewhat less than that caused directly by the primary shift of demand from A's products on to B's products.

Let us consider the difference made in this situation by the adoption of two other possible policy combinations, namely, the case in which financial policies for internal balance are adopted in both A and B and the case in which financial policies for external balance are adopted in both countries, the reader being left to work out for himself the intermediate cases where the authorities in one country aim at internal balance and those in the other at external balance.

If financial policies for internal balance are adopted in both countries, there will, of course, be no net deflation of national income in A or inflation of national income in B as a result of the primary shift of demand away from A's products on to B's products. But the change in

---

[1] The intensifications of the inflations of national incomes in A and in B will be less if the authorities in B operate by monetary policy than if they operate by fiscal policy. For in the former case external balance will in part be restored by the increased flow of capital funds from B to A brought about by the lower interest rates in B, and will not, therefore, need to rely so much upon an inflation in B's demand for imports from A.

the balance of trade between A and B will be even greater than the change caused directly by the shift of demand. A numerical example will serve to show this. Suppose that in A there is (within a constant level of total domestic expenditure in A) a primary shift of demand of $100 m. from A's products on to B's products, thus causing directly a $100 m. increase in A's imports (B's exports), a $100 m. fall in A's income, and a $100 m. rise in B's income. In order to preserve internal balance in A, domestic expenditure in A is by financial policy inflated by, say, $130 m., of which $110 m. represents an increased demand for A's home products and $20 m. represents increased imports from B. Similarly, in order to preserve internal balance in B, domestic expenditure in B is deflated by financial policy by $130 m. of which $120 m. represents a decreased demand for B's home products and $10 m. a decreased demand for imports from A. In these circumstances income will be unchanged in both A and B:

	A	B
	\$ *m.*	
Change in income due to		
(i) primary shift of demand	−100	+100
(ii) changed demand for home products resulting from policy increase of domestic expenditure of $130 m. in A and policy decrease of domestic expenditure of $130 m. in B. . . .	+110	−120
(iii) changed demand for exports due to above policy changes in the other country	−10	+20
	Nil	Nil

But the net favourable movement in the balance of trade of country B will be $130 m. and not merely $100 m., made up of (i) the primary increase in B's exports of $100 m. due to spontaneous shift in demand in A from A's products on to B's products, (ii) the secondary increase of B's exports of $20 m. induced by the policy inflation of domestic expenditure by $130 m. in A, and (iii) the secondary decrease of B's imports of $10 m. induced by the policy deflation of domestic expenditure by $130 m. in B. It is thus clear that, if the authorities in both A and B aim at internal balance and if the policy changes in domestic expenditure in A and B have any import content, the final change in the balance of trade between A and B will be greater than the primary net change in that balance directly caused by the shift of demand from A's products on to B's products. This result is in sharp contrast with the outcome, examined in case ii in Chapter VII, when both countries have neutral policies, in which case, as has already been seen, the final change in the balance of trade is reduced below the primary change brought about by the shift in demand.

Moreover, if the authorities in A and B aim at internal balance by monetary rather than by fiscal policy, the improvement in B's balance of payments will be even more marked. Internal balance in A will require a reduction in interest rates in order to stimulate domestic expenditure in A in order to counteract the reduction in demand for A's products due to the primary shift of demand away from A's on to B's products. For the reverse reason internal balance in B will require a rise in interest rates in B. The fall in interest rates in A and the rise in such rates in B will cause a flow of capital funds from A to B, which will still further improve B's balance of payments.

If, finally, the authorities in both A and B aim at external balance, the result will again be something very different. The authorities in A, instead of inflating, will have to deflate domestic expenditure to the extent necessary to remove totally (and not only partially as in the case of neutral policies) the adverse movement in A's balance of payments due to the primary shift of demand away from A's products on to B's products. Similarly the authorities in B will have to inflate domestic expenditure and national income sufficiently totally to remove B's favourable balance of payments caused by the primary shift of demand. In consequence, there will, of course, finally be no net change in the balance of payments between the two countries; but the deflation of domestic expenditure and national income in A or their inflation in B or both will have to be carried further than in the case of neutral policies. The policy deflation of domestic expenditure in A and inflation in B will not, however, have to be carried quite so far if they are carried out by means of monetary policy rather than fiscal policy, since the balance-of-payments gap will in that case be partially closed by the increased flow of capital funds from B to A brought about by higher interest rates in A and lower interest rates in B.

There is, however, in this case (as in all the cases in which the authorities in both countries adopt policies for external balance) some indeterminacy in the result. Since in this case the authorities in both A and B are simultaneously adjusting domestic expenditures in their own countries to achieve identically the same result—namely, equilibrium in the balance of payments between them[1]—the amount of adjustment which the one must undertake will depend upon the amount of the adjustment which the other happens to make; and vice versa. To revert to our particular example, if the authorities in B inflate rapidly and on a large scale in order to restore external equilibrium to the balance of payments by a large expansion of imports of A's products into B, the authorities in A will not have to deflate much in order to

---

[1] We neglect the possibility that an accommodating payment (or receipt) for one of the countries may be an autonomous receipt (or payment) for the other. Cf. Chapter II.

fill the rest of the balance-of-payments gap by a reduction in the demand in A for B's products; but if the authorities in A have deflated demand in A rapidly and extensively in an attempt to maintain external balance, then the authorities in B will not have to inflate greatly. To what extent the adjustment will be met by inflation in B or by deflation in A will remain a matter of chance unless other considerations are brought into the picture. We shall revert to this problem in due course.

CHAPTER X

CONFLICTS BETWEEN INTERNAL AND EXTERNAL BALANCE

IT will already be clear from the analysis of the preceding chapters that there may often be a conflict between financial policies for internal and for external balance. On the other hand, there are often occasions on which the same financial policy is required for the preservation both of internal and of external balance. The example analysed at some length in Chapters V and VI provides a good illustration of both these possibilities.

There is a spontaneous deflation of domestic expenditure in A which (i) deflates national income in A, (ii) deflates national income in B, and (iii) causes the balance of payments to move favourably to A and unfavourably to B. A policy inflation of domestic expenditure is needed in A both in the interests of internal balance in order to put a stop to the domestic depression and also in the interests of external balance in order to put a stop to the reduction of the demand for imports in A and the movement of the balance of trade in A's favour. There is no conflict of policy so far as A is concerned. But if the authorities in A do not act in this way, the authorities in B are faced with a serious conflict of policy. A policy inflation of domestic expenditure is needed in B in the interests of her internal balance, as a means of offsetting the depression which has been 'exported' to B from A; but in the interests of external balance a policy deflation of domestic expenditure is required in B in order to restrict the demand for imports in B *pari passu* with the decline in the demand for B's exports in A. There is a sharp conflict of policy. The inflationary policy which will stabilize national income will put the balance of payments even more out of equilibrium, while the deflationary policy which will bring the balance of payments into equilibrium will only serve to intensify the depression of national income.

The increase in productivity in A which we examined in section 1 of Chapter VII (pp. 82–4) may also provide an example in which there is no conflict of financial policy for A but a serious conflict for B. Productivity rises in A; at constant money wage rates, costs and prices fall in A; A's products undercut B's products; and if the sum of the elasticities of demand for imports in A and in B is greater than one, this causes a movement in the balance of trade favourable to A and unfavourable to B. This will cause a general deflation and unemployment in B, since the markets for B's products are restricted as a result of the fall in A's competing prices. There may well be some growth of unemployment in A as well, since the increased demand for A's products brought about by A's gain of markets from B may less than offset the displacement of labour by the inventions in A which led to the increased productivity in A.

If this is so, an inflation of domestic expenditure is needed in A, both to expand the demand for labour domestically and also to restore equilibrium to the balance of payments; but, as in our previous example, an expansionist financial policy is needed in B in order to restore the demand for labour in B but a contractionist financial policy is needed in order to restore equilibrium to the balance of payments.

We may take next an example of a spontaneous change which will involve both countries in a conflict of choice between internal and external balance. In section 2 of Chapter VII (pp. 84-7) we assumed that there is a shift of demand from A's products on to B's products within given levels of domestic expenditure in A and B. This will lead to (i) a deflation of national income in A, (ii) an inflation of national income in B, and (iii) an unfavourable movement in A's, and a favourable movement in B's, balance of payments. A policy inflation of domestic expenditure is needed in A in the interests of internal balance to offset the deflation in her national income; but in the interests of external balance a policy deflation of domestic expenditure is needed in A in order to restrain the demand for imports. In B, on the other hand, a policy deflation of domestic expenditure is required in the interest of internal balance and a policy inflation in the interests of external balance. If both countries adopt policies for internal balance, the balance-of-payments problem will be made the more acute. If both adopt policies for external balance, the internal deflation in A and/or inflation in B will become more serious.

We have discussed these possible conflicts on the assumption that there were only two possible criteria to be observed by the authorities of any one country in their choice between possible policies, namely, the effect on that country's national income and employment (internal balance) and the effect on that country's balance of payments (external balance). At our present level of abstraction this is correct, provided that the policy to be chosen by the authorities of any one country is to be judged solely from the point of view of that country's economic position; but if the effects of the policy upon the economy of the other country is to be taken into account, we must introduce a third criterion, namely, the effect of the policy to be adopted by the authorities of any one country upon the internal balance of the other country.

An illustration may serve to explain the point. There is a spontaneous rise in domestic expenditure in A which (i) inflates national income in A, (ii) inflates national income in B, and (iii) causes the balance of payments to move unfavourably to A and favourably to B. If the economy of A was in internal and external balance before the change, then a policy deflation of domestic expenditure will be required in A to offset the effects upon A's national income and balance of payments. But suppose that the economy of B was not in internal balance before the change,[1] but was suffering from heavy unemployment due to a deflated national income which the authorities in B were not finding it easy to offset by a policy inflation of domestic expenditure in B. The inflation of demand for B's exports proceeding from the spontaneous inflation of domestic demand in A might in these circumstances prove a great help in the restoration of internal balance in B.

We have, then, to ask of any policy of inflation or deflation of domestic expenditure in A the three questions: what will be its effect upon internal balance in A? What will be its effect upon internal balance in B? And what will be its effect upon external balance between A and B? There are now a large number of possible conflicts and agreements between these criteria.

These conflicts and agreements are set out schematically in Table X. This table shows in its four rows (numbered on the right-hand side) the four possible situations which may arise by various combinations of the three criteria which have just been mentioned. Thus the first two situations (rows 1 and 2) refer to cases in which the national income of the surplus country is too low and needs to be inflated (column a). Of these the first situation (row 1) refers to the case in which the national income of the surplus country needs to be inflated (column a) and the national income of the deficit country is also too low and needs to be inflated (column b). And so on.

On the assumption made in the table that there is an existing disequilibrium in the balance of payments and in each national income, there is no single situation in the table in which the authorities in both countries have simultaneously an unequivocally clear duty from the standpoint of all three criteria. There are two cases, namely, in rows 1 and 4, in which the authorities in one of the two countries have an unequivocally clear duty from all three points of view. For example, in row 4 the authorities in the deficit country should deflate on all three counts. Let us first consider these two situations.

Row 1 describes a situation of general world depression. The national incomes of both countries need to be inflated. The authorities in the surplus country should in these circumstances engage in a policy of domestic inflation on all counts. Such a policy is required in order to stimulate the demand for the surplus country's products in the interests of internal balance in the surplus country; and in so far as it stimulates

---

[1] If A was in external balance, then B also must be in external balance, if we ignore the possibility (see Chapter II) that an accommodating payment (or receipt) to A (or B) may be an autonomous receipt (or payment) to B (or A). For B's adverse (or favourable) balance must in these circumstances be A's favourable (or adverse) balance.

TABLE X

Conflicts of Criteria for Inflationary and Deflationary Financial Policies.

National income in the surplus country	National income in the deficit country	In the interests of		
		external balance	internal balance in the surplus country	internal balance in the deficit country
is too low (L) or too high (H)		there should be an inflation (S+) or deflation (S−) of domestic expenditure in the surplus country and an inflation (D+) or deflation (D−) of domestic expenditure in the deficit country.		
(a)	(b)	(c)	(d)	(e)
L	L	S+ D−	S+ D+	S+ D+	(1)
	H	S+ D−	S+ D+	S− D−	(2)
H	L	S+ D−	S− D−	S+ D+	(3)
	H	S+ D−	S− D−	S− D−	(4)

the demand in the surplus country for the products of the deficit country
it will help, both to restore equilibrium in the balance of payments and
also to reflate the national income in the deficit country which is suffering from the world depression. The authorities in the deficit country,
on the other hand, suffer from a serious conflict of policies. They desire
to inflate domestic expenditure in order to increase demand in the
interests of the domestic employment policy of the deficit country,
which is also suffering from the general depression of demand. But any
such domestic reflation in the deficit country will also stimulate the
demand in the deficit country for the products of the surplus country;
and while this will be useful in helping to stimulate domestic economic
activity within the surplus country, which is also depressed, it will unfortunately seriously increase the difficulties of the balance of payments.

The first conclusion about policy in such a situation is obvious. In a
period of world depression it is the duty of the authorities in the surplus
country to take the initiative in inflating domestic expenditure, since
this will not only help their own problem of domestic depression but

will help to restore equilibrium to the balances of international payments and also to stimulate economic activity in the deficit country.

It is, of course, just possible that a given degree of such reflationary policy in the surplus country will serve to solve simultaneously all three problems, i.e. to raise both national incomes to the desired level and to restore equilibrium to the balance of payments. But this would, of course, be a pure coincidence. There are three other, and more probable, possibilities: (i) that, while the depressions of both incomes are serious, the balance of payments disequilibrium is slight, so that a given reflation of demand in the surplus country will restore equilibrium to the balance of payments before it has gone far enough to restore internal balance to either economy; (ii) that the internal disequilibrium in the deficit country is very slight, so that the reflation in the surplus country restores internal balance in the deficit country before it has restored external balance or internal balance in the surplus country; and (iii) that the internal disequilibrium in the surplus country is slight, so that internal balance in the surplus country is the first to be restored. Let us consider these three possibilities in turn.

(i) In the first case the situation in row 1 will continue merely with an interchange of countries. The inflation in the surplus country after a certain point will have caused such an increase in the demand in the surplus country for the products of the deficit country that the balance of payments will have become favourable to the previously deficit country at a time when reflation of demand is still required in both countries in the interests of internal balance. What is now required is that the authorities in the new surplus (previously deficit) country should take up the policy of reflation in order to reflate both national incomes and also in order to remove the disequilibrium in the balance of payments. In other words, if the balance-of-payments disequilibrium is not very great in a period of serious world depression of national incomes, the various countries should go ahead with policies of internal reflation as far as possible at a pace which will keep the balance of payments between them in equilibrium.

(ii) But sooner or later the reflation is likely to reach a point at which internal balance is restored in one country before it is restored in the other. We now suppose that, starting from row 1, the inflation in the surplus country proceeds to a point at which a small existing internal depression in the deficit country is removed without, however, removing the considerable depression in the surplus country or the disequilibrium in the balance of payments. If the inflation in the surplus country proceeds further, national income in the deficit country will be over-inflated and row 1 will give place to row 2, where inflation of national income in the surplus country and an improvement in the balance of payments of the deficit country are still required but national income in the deficit country now needs to be deflated. We will deal with this situation when we come to consider the situation in row 2.

(iii) Alternatively, it may be the internal depression in the surplus country which is the first maladjustment to disappear. In this case a continuation of a reflationary policy in the surplus country would cause the national income of the surplus country to become over-inflated, though national income was still depressed in the deficit country, and the balance of payments still in disequilibrium. We should have moved to the situation depicted in row 3, the treatment of which will be considered in due course.

So far, we have considered the situation of row 1—a world-wide depression with a disequilibrium in the balance of payments—on the assumption that the authorities in the surplus country can and will undertake the reflationary policy which is so clearly desirable on all grounds. It may be worth while giving some attention to the position in which the authorities in the deficit country would find themselves if the authorities in the surplus country failed to take such action. It is clear that there would be a straightforward conflict of policies between internal and external balance in the deficit country. If the authorities in the deficit country deflate in order to get rid of the balance-of-payments deficit, they make the internal depression of national income in the deficit country so much the worse; if they inflate in order to restore the home demand in the interests of employment policy, they intensify the deficit in the balance of payments. In this latter case they will, however, incidentally increase the demand for the products of the surplus country and thus help to restore internal economic activity in that country also; and if the failure of the authorities in the surplus country to inflate domestic expenditure to a sufficient degree and sufficiently quickly is due to some political or administrative inability to do so, it may be useful to all concerned that the authorities in the deficit country should adopt a policy of internal inflation in order to induce a restoration of demand for her own products as well as for those of the surplus country, in spite of the fact that this will actually intensify the existing disequilibrium in the balance of payments of the deficit country. But such an arrangement would, of course, depend upon the possibility of the authorities in the deficit country obtaining, if necessary by special arrangements, sufficient accommodating finance on sufficiently favourable terms to carry the cost of the abnormal balance-of-payments deficit during the period while the authorities in the surplus country are preparing themselves for the necessary action for the reflation of their own domestic expenditure.

Row 4 of Table X depicts the second situatoin in which the correct policy for one of the two countries is unequivocally clear. This situation is that of a world-wide boom or inflation in which the national incomes of both countries are excessively high and need to be reduced by policy reductions of domestic expenditure. At the same time there is a balance-of-payments disequilibrium between the two countries. Clearly in such a situation the authorities in the deficit country should deflate in order to restrain the excess demand for goods in both countries and in order to help to restore equilibrium to the balance of payments. As in the case of row 1 which we have just discussed at some length, such action may after a time transform the problem to that of a different type,[1] although the disequilibrium will, of course, be on a smaller scale.

But if the authorities in the deficit country fail to act, how should the authorities in the surplus country behave? Should domestic expenditure in the surplus country be deflated in an attempt to restrain the world inflation even though this will make the balance-of-payments deficit of the other country even greater? Perhaps such a solution would be legitimate and useful all round provided that sufficient accommodating financial help from the surplus to the deficit country could be arranged. Or should domestic expenditure in the surplus country be inflated in order to put the balance of payments right by increasing the demand for the products of the deficit country even though this will intensify the excess inflationary pressure in both countries?[2]

We can next turn our attention to the situation depicted in row 2. In the surplus country there is a depression requiring an inflation of domestic expenditure; and in the deficit country there is an excessively high national income requiring a deflation of domestic expenditure. In this situation the appropriate solution is apparent. The authorities of neither country are faced with any conflict between the policies which they should choose for the restoration of internal and external balance in their own economies. The authorities in the surplus country need to inflate both in the interests of internal balance (i.e. in order to increase the demand for the products of the surplus country) and also in the

---

[1] The type will be of row 3 if the disequilibrium in the national income of the deficit country is the first to disappear; of row 2 if the disequilibrium in the national income of the surplus country is the first to disappear; and will remain of row 4, with the mere interchange of countries, if the balance-of-payments disequilibrium is the first to disappear.

[2] It may not be altogether fanciful to suggest that row 1 represented the position as between the United States and Europe in the depression of the nineteen-thirties, when an inflation in the United States was desirable in order to stimulate the demand for goods and services in both sets of countries and in order to remove the surplus in the United States balance of payments. If so, it might be permissible to suggest that row 4 represented the position as between these same countries in the second half of the nineteen-forties when deflations of domestic expenditure in European countries were required in order to restrain inflationary pressures both in Europe and in the rest of the world and also in order to remove the deficit in Europe's balance of payments. Much mud was slung across the Atlantic from East to West during the former period owing to the failure of the United States to reflate on a sufficient scale sufficiently quickly. Perhaps it was justifiable that some of this mud should have been re-exported in the latter period.

interests of external balance (i.e. in order to increase the demand for imports in the surplus country so as to remove the surplus on the balance of payments). Simultaneously, the authorities in the deficit country need to deflate in the interests both of the internal and of the external balance of the deficit country.

It is, of course, true that the inflation in the surplus country which leads to an increased demand in the surplus country for the products of the deficit country will make it necessary for the authorities in the deficit country to go all the further in their own domestic deflation in order to obtain a net reduction in the total demand for the products of the deficit country; and, similarly, the deflation in the deficit country will make it necessary for the authorities in the surplus country to go all the further in their own domestic inflation in order to achieve the desired net increase in the demand for the products of the surplus country. But this is a relatively unimportant form of conflict of policies, if the authorities in both countries are able and willing to go as far as necessary with their own domestic policies of inflation and deflation respectively; for in this case it will not impede the restoration of full equilibrium, it will merely mean that the authorities in the surplus country must go a little further with their domestic inflation and the authorities in the deficit country with their domestic deflation than would otherwise be the case.

The conflict of policies, however, becomes more marked if the authorities in one of the two countries are, for one reason or another, unable or unwilling to carry out the degree of inflation or deflation required of them. Suppose, for example, that in this situation the authorities in the surplus country fail to adopt a policy of internal reflation. If the authorities in the deficit country, in the interests of the internal and external balance of their own country, embark upon their domestic policy of deflation, this will help to put their national income and balance of payments into equilibrium. But it will make the domestic depression in the surplus country the more intense. It would, however, in such circumstances be altogether too much to expect the authorities in the deficit country to adopt a policy of further domestic inflation merely in order to help the authorities in the surplus country with a policy of internal reflation which they have failed to carry out for themselves. For the cost to the deficit country would be altogether excessive. Not only would such action increase the existing deficit in the balance of payments; even if this difficulty could be overcome by the provision of sufficient accommodating finance from the surplus country, it would also be open to the objection from the point of view of the deficit country that it intensified the existing inflation of her national income. We must conclude that in the row-2 type of disequilibrium the authorities in each country should adopt that financial policy which is required in the interests of their own internal and external balance.

As such policies are adopted to meet a row-2 situation the general disequilibrium will be diminished, but it may at some point turn into a disequilibrium of a different character. (i) If the smallest element of disequilibrium is the excessively high national income in the deficit country, then as the disinflationary policy in the deficit country proceeds the national income in that country may become too low before its balance-of-payments deficit has disappeared or the income of the surplus country been sufficiently reflated. The situation of row 2 will give place to that of row 1 in which, as we have seen, the appropriate action is for the authorities in the surplus country to carry on with their reflation alone. (ii) If the deficiency of national income in the surplus country is the first element of disequilibrium to disappear, the reflationary policy in the surplus country may cause the national income in that country to become excessive before either the surplus in its balance of payments or the deficiency of income in the deficit country has disappeared. The situation of row 2 will give place to that of row 4, in which, as we have seen, the appropriate action is for the authorities in the deficit country to carry on with their policy of disinflation alone. (iii) If it is the balance-of-payments disequilibrium which is the least-marked element of disequilibrium, the reflation in the surplus country may so increase imports into the surplus country and the disinflation in the deficit country may so decrease imports into that country that the surplus on the balance of payments is turned into a deficit before internal balance is fully restored in either country. The situation of row 2 would have turned into that of row 3, to which we must now turn our attention.

It is the row-3 type of disequilibrium which is the most intractable. Indeed this type of disequilibrium is the only one which cannot be handled solely by financial policy even if the authorities in both countries are willing and able to adopt the appropriate reflationary or disinflationary policies. In all the other cases (rows 1, 2, and 4) if the authorities in each country always inflate or deflate when an inflation or deflation is required both for the internal and the external balance of their own country, it will be seen from the preceding analysis that in all cases the disequilibrium will either be totally removed or else will be diminished until it is ultimately turned into a smaller disequilibrium of the row-3 type. Apart from row 3 a conflict of policy can arise for the authorities in one country only if the authorities in the other country fail to adopt the policy which is appropriate to the situation.

But in a row-3 situation there is no combination of inflationary and deflationary financial policies which on our present assumptions of constant wage rates, constant rates of exchange, and constant barriers to international transactions, can deal with the disequilibrium. Row 3 depicts a situation in which there is an excessively high national income in the surplus country which requires deflation and an excessively low national income in the deficit country.[1]

For the authorities in both countries there is now a conflict between financial policies for the internal and external balance of their own countries. If policies for internal balance are adopted in both countries, domestic expenditure will be deflated in the surplus country and inflated in the deficit country; but this will reduce imports into the surplus country still more and increase imports into the deficit country still more and the balance-of-payments problem will become even more acute. For such a situation to continue there would have to be a large flow of accommodating finance from the surplus to the deficit country; and this flow of accommodating finance would have to be permanent.[2]

If the authorities in both countries adopt policies for external balance, domestic expenditure will be inflated in the surplus, and deflated in the deficit, country and this will help in increasing imports into the surplus country and reducing imports into the deficit country and thus removing the disequilibrium in the balance of payments. But this will be done at the expense of intensifying the existing excessive inflation of income in the surplus country and deflation of income in the deficit country.[3]

---

[1] It may be useful to give an example of the way in which such a situation might arise. Suppose that in a situation of full internal and external balance for both countries there is a shift of demand from B's products on to A's products (i.e. the type of spontaneous disturbance discussed in case 2 of Chapter VII). This will inflate A's national income, deflate B's national income, and cause the balance of payments to move in favour of A. We shall find ourselves in a row-3 type of situation with A taking the place of the surplus, and B of the deficit, country.

[2] Unlike the flow of accommodating finance which was suggested (p. 119) in the case of a row-1 situation, if the authorities in the surplus country could not develop a policy of domestic reflation sufficiently quickly. In that case the flow of accommodating finance would merely be a temporary stop-gap until the authorities in the surplus country could achieve the appropriate inflation. In this case, there is no permanently appropriate policy of inflation or deflation for either country.

[3] The whole of the analysis of Table X has been based upon the assumption that we are dealing only with the normal conditions: (i) that the marginal propensity to import in each country lies between zero and one (i.e. neither country imports or produces for itself only inferior goods—see pp.63-4); (ii) that the sum of the marginal propensities to import in the two countries add up to less than one (see p. 67); and (iii) that the sum of the elasticities of demand for imports in the two countries add up to more than one (see p. 72). It may be interesting to note that if the marginal propensities to import in the two countries added up to more than one, it would be row 2 and not row 3 which would present the problem which could not be solved solely by financial policy. In this case row 3 of Table X would require that domestic expenditure in the surplus country should be inflated (in spite of the fact that its national income needs deflating) and that domestic expenditure in the deficit country should be deflated (in spite of the fact that its national income needs inflation); for, as can be seen from case ii of Table IX, where the sum of the marginal propensities to import is greater than one, an inflation of domestic expenditure in one country combined with a deflation of domestic expenditure in the other will cause a deflation of national income in the former and an inflation of national income in the latter as well as an improvement in the balance of trade of the latter.

In such intractable situations of conflict between policies of internal and external balance, what should the authorities concerned do? Should they adopt financial policies for external balance, allowing their national incomes to be excessively inflated or deflated and trusting that this will lead to a rise or fall in their whole wage and cost structures which will thereby restore internal balance as well?[1] Or should they adopt financial policies for internal balance, inflating or deflating their domestic expenditures sufficiently to maintain the desired level of demand for their own products regardless of the immediate effect upon their balances of payments? And if so, should they then let the exchange rate between their currencies change as a means of regaining external balance without sacrificing internal balance?[1] Or should they maintain their fixed exchange rates and adjust their balances of payments by direct controls (by exchange control, import restrictions, tariffs, export subsidies, and the like) over their international transactions so as to restore equilibrium to their balances of payments without disturbing their internal balance?[2]

[1] These possibilities are examined in Part IV, where the assumptions of constant wage rates and constant exchange rates are removed.

[2] This possibility will form the subject matter of Part V, where the assumption of an unchanged commercial policy is abandoned.

SOME EXAMPLES OF INTERNATIONAL-TRADE MULTIPLIERS

IN the separate mathematical supplement, (Section VIII (i), (ii), and (iii)) a mathematical formulation is given of the effects of various spontaneous disturbances combined with financial policies for internal and external balance in either or both or neither of our two countries. It may, perhaps, help some readers who do not wish to cope with that supplement, but who would nevertheless like to go a little farther with the analysis of international-trade multipliers to give some numerical examples of the way in which they operate.

For this purpose we must adopt two simplifying assumptions, with which we are able to dispense in the more general mathematical treatment. First, we assume that there are no changes in the prices of A's or B's products so that shifts of demand between A's and B's products due to changes in relative prices do not occur. Secondly, we assume that there are no 'induced' changes in any transfer items in the balance of payments, so that the balance of payments remains in equilibrium when the change in the balance of trade offsets any 'spontaneous' change in 'transfers' between A and B.

In this note we shall, for purposes of illustration, consider the effects of only three types of spontaneous disturbance, the first being a spontaneous decrease of 100 in domestic expenditure in country A; the second being a spontaneous shift of demand in country A of 100 away from the imported products of B on to the home-produced products of A; and the third being a spontaneous increase of 100 in transfers from A to B.

The object of the numerical examples is to follow out the repercussions of these three spontaneous disturbances as they operate through the following six relationships:

(1) A change in the national income in country A will cause an induced change in domestic expenditure in country A, this induced change in domestic expenditure being in the same direction as, but of a smaller amount than, the change in the national income which causes it. We shall assume in the following examples that in country A the 'home leakage' is $\frac{1}{4}$ of the change in the national income, i.e. that for every unit change in the national income in A there is an induced change of $\frac{3}{4}$ of a unit in domestic expenditure in the same direction.

(2) A change in domestic expenditure in A is assumed to cause an induced change in imports into A, this induced change in imports being in the same direction as, but smaller than, the change in domestic

expenditure which causes it. We assume that the 'marginal propensity to import' in country A is $\frac{1}{5}$, so that for every unit change in domestic expenditure in A there is a change of $\frac{1}{5}$ of a unit in the same direction in imports into A and of $\frac{4}{5}$ of a unit in expenditure by A's purchasers on A's products.

(3) The final change in the national income in A will be equal to the change in the demand by A's purchasers for A's products plus the change in the demand by B's purchasers for imports from A.

(4) In B the 'home leakage' is assumed to be $\frac{1}{3}$, so that for every unit change in the national income in B there is an induced change of domestic expenditure equal to $\frac{2}{3}$ of the change in the national income.

(5) In B the 'marginal propensity to import' is assumed to be $\frac{2}{5}$, so that in B there is an induced change of imports into B equal to $\frac{2}{5}$ of any change in domestic expenditure and an induced change of expenditure by B's purchasers on B's products equal to $\frac{3}{5}$ of the change in domestic expenditure.

(6) The final change in B's national income is equal to the change in the demand by B's purchasers for B's products plus the change in the demand by A's purchasers for imports from B.

In order to express these relationships we shall make use of the type of analysis already employed in Table VII p. 36, except that we shall show in the following tables not the total domestic expenditure, national income, imports, and exports in the countries A and B, but the increases or decreases in these figures which come about as the result of some spontaneous change. Thus, in the following tables the figure entered in the first row of the first column will represent the net increase or decrease in the expenditure by purchasers in A on A's products; the figure entered in the second row of the first column will represent the net

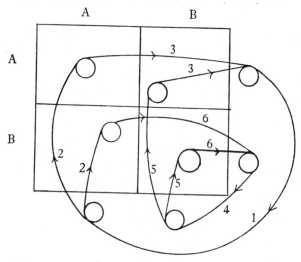

increase or decrease in the expenditure by the purchasers of A on the products of B; and so on. Thus, the figure at the foot of the column marked A will represent the sum of the changes of expenditure by A's purchasers on A's and on B's products, i.e. the total change in domestic expenditure in A. Similarly, the figure at the foot of the column marked B will represent the total change in domestic expenditure in B. At the same time the figure at the right of the row marked A will represent the change in the amount spent by purchasers in A and in B on A's products, i.e. the total change in expenditure on A's products or the total change in A's national income.

The figure in the second column of the first row represents the change in expenditure by purchasers in B on imports of A's products, and the figure in the second row of the first column represents the change in the expenditure by purchasers in A on imports of B's products. The net improvement in A's balance of trade is, therefore, measured by the former figure minus the latter.

The six relationships mentioned on pp. 125–6 will be shown in these tables by arrowed lines. These are numbered in the accompanying sketch so as to correspond with the numbers of these relationships on pp. 125–6, above. Thus the arrowed line marked 1 will lead from a circle enclosing the *total* change in A's national income to a circle enclosing the *induced* change in domestic expenditure in A to which it gives rise; the arrowed lines marked 2 will lead from a circle enclosing the *total* change in domestic expenditure in A to two circles enclosing the *induced* increase in imports and the *induced* increase in expenditure on home products, into which the change in domestic expenditure splits up; the arrowed lines marked 3 will lead from two circles enclosing the *total* change in the expenditure by purchasers in A on A's products and the *total* change in imports of A's products into B and will proceed to the circle enclosing the *total* change in A's national income which must be equal to the sum of these two changes in demand for A's products. The arrowed lines marked 4, 5, and 6 show the similar relationships for B.

In addition to our three spontaneous disturbances (a spontaneous decrease in domestic expenditure in A, a spontaneous shift in demand in A from B's products on to A's products, and a spontaneous increase in transfers from A to B) we shall also allow in some of our examples for the authorities in A or in B to adopt financial policies in order to bring about 'policy' changes in domestic expenditure (i.e. changes which are neither the 'spontaneous' disturbance nor the 'induced' effects of changes in national income) in order to offset the effects of the spontaneous disturbance and of its repercussions upon the internal or external balance of the economy The authorities in either country will be said to achieve internal balance when they thereby avoid any change in the national income of the country concerned, and external balance when they thereby avoid any change in the balance of payments.

We can then proceed to work out the way in which any one of our three spontaneous disturbances will lead to (i) a change in the national income in A (which we will call a), (ii) a change in the national income in B (which we will call b), (iii) a 'policy' increase or decrease in domestic expenditure in A undertaken by the authorities in A for the purpose of preserving internal or external balance (which we will call a'), (iv) a similar 'policy' inflation or deflation in B (which we will call b'), and (v) a change in A's balance of trade (which we will call t).

1. A Spontaneous Decrease of 100 in Domestic Expenditure in A.

Let us start, then, with a spontaneous decrease in domestic expenditure in A of 100. Example 1 shows what would happen if country A were a closed economy and had no relations at all with the outside world, and if the authorities in A did not adopt any financial policy to offset the effects of the depression in A. The final change in the national income in A when all repercussions have taken place is measured by a. Since the home leakage in A is assumed to be $\frac{1}{4}$ we know from relationship 1 above

EXAMPLE 1.

A Spontaneous Decrease in Domestic Expenditure in Country A of 100. A Closed Economy. No Financial Policy in A.

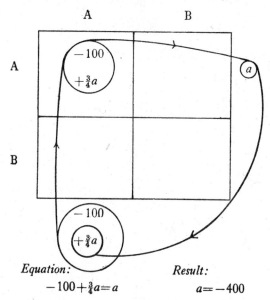

Equation:

$$-100 + \tfrac{3}{4}a = a$$

Result:

$$a = -400$$

that the induced change in domestic expenditure in A will be $\frac{3}{4}a$. The total change in domestic expenditure in A (i.e. the spontaneous change plus the induced change) will therefore be $-100+\frac{3}{4}a$; and since there is no foreign trade the whole of this represents a change in the expenditure by A's purchasers on A's products, which in turn (since there are no exports from A) measures the final change in A's national income. From the first row of the table in Example 1 we see that $-100+\frac{3}{4}a=a$ or $a=-400$. In other words, in our closed economy with a home leakage of $\frac{1}{4}$, any spontaneous change in domestic expenditure will lead to a change in national income of 4 times that amount.

In Example 2 we turn to the case where country A has an open economy, so that we must take into account the marginal propensity to import in A (relationship 2) as well as the home leakage in A (relationship 1); but we assume that there is no foreign repercussion from B, i.e. that for one reason or another the change in demand in A for B's products does not cause any change in demand in B for A's products. Again a represents the final change in the national income in A, so that

EXAMPLE 2.

A Spontaneous Decrease in Domestic Expenditure in Country A of 100. An Open Economy but No Foreign Repercussions. No Financial Policy in A.

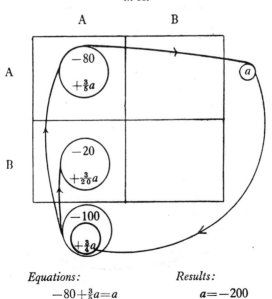

Equations:

$$-80+\tfrac{3}{5}a=a$$
$$20-\tfrac{3}{20}a=t$$

Results:

$$a=-200$$
$$t=+50$$

$-100+\frac{3}{4}a$ represents the final change in domestic expenditure in A (both the spontaneous and the induced change). But in the present case this change in domestic expenditure causes an induced change in the demand for imports into A (relationship 2) which we are assuming to be $\frac{1}{5}$ of the final change in domestic expenditure (i.e. $-20+\frac{3}{20}a$). The remaining $\frac{4}{5}$ of the change in domestic expenditure in A ($-80+\frac{3}{5}a$) represents a change in the demand by A's purchasers for A's products. Since there is no change in exports from A, this sum represents the total change in the demand for A's products and is thus equal to a, the final change in A's national income. Imports into A change by $-20+\frac{3}{20}a$ without any change in exports, so that the improvement in A's balance of trade is equal to minus this sum. From these two equations we can deduce that $a=-200$ and that $t=+50$. The deflation of the national income in A has now been damped down by the fact that some of the reduction in demand in A causes a reduction in the demand for imports and not for home products, and this reduction in the demand for imports has also resulted in a movement in the balance of trade favourable to A.

EXAMPLE 3.

A Spontaneous Decrease in Domestic Expenditure in Country A of 100. An Open Economy with Foreign Repercussion. No Financial Policy in A or B.

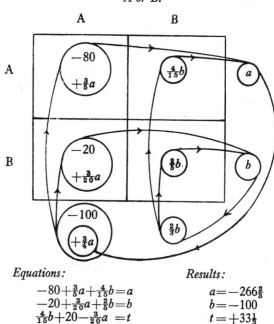

Equations:
$$-80+\tfrac{3}{5}a+\tfrac{4}{15}b=a$$
$$-20+\tfrac{3}{20}a+\tfrac{2}{5}b=b$$
$$\tfrac{4}{15}b+20-\tfrac{3}{20}a=t$$

Results:
$$a=-266\tfrac{2}{3}$$
$$b=-100$$
$$t=+33\tfrac{1}{3}$$

We are now in a position to allow for the foreign repercussion. This is done in Example 3. As in Example 2, the final change in national income in A of a induces a change in domestic expenditure in A of $\frac{3}{4}a$ (relationship 1). The total change in domestic expenditure in A of $-100+\frac{3}{4}a$ induces a change in imports into A of $-20+\frac{3}{20}a$ and of expenditure by A's purchasers on A's products of $-80+\frac{3}{5}a$ (relationship 2). But we must now consider the effect of this in B. The change in imports into A is the same thing as a change in exports from B. As a result of the consequential repercussions in B there will be some final change in national income in B which we call b. This will cause an induced change in domestic expenditure in B of $\frac{2}{3}b$, since we assume the home leakage in B to be $\frac{1}{3}$ (relationship 4); and this in turn will cause an induced change of $\frac{4}{15}b$ in imports into B and of $\frac{2}{5}b$ in purchases by B's purchasers of B's products since we assume that the marginal propensity to import in B is $\frac{2}{5}$ (relationship 5); and this latter sum together with the change in the demand in A for imports from B will make up the final change in B's national income (relationship 6).

We now have two equations from the two rows of the table, one for A which gives $-80+\frac{3}{5}a+\frac{4}{15}b=a$, and one for B which gives $-20+\frac{3}{20}a+\frac{2}{5}b=b$. From these simultaneous equations we can deduce that the national income in A (a) falls by $266\frac{2}{3}$, the national income in B (b) falls by 100, and the balance of trade (t), which is equal to the change in B's imports ($\frac{4}{15}b$) *less* the change in A's imports ($-20+\frac{3}{20}a$), moves in A's favour by $33\frac{1}{3}$. The decline in national income in A is not as great as in Example 1, because some part of the depression in A is still 'exported' from A to B, and, because of the home leakage in B[1], it is not all 're-exported' back to A; but it is greater than in Example 2 because the depression in A does cause a depression in B and therefore some decline in the demand in B for A's products. For the same reason the favourable movement in A's balance of trade in Example 3 is smaller than in Example 2.

We can now allow for the fact that the authorities in B may adopt a financial policy for the preservation either of internal balance in B or of external balance between B and A. Example 4 illustrates the case where the authorities in B adopt a financial policy for internal balance. Relationships 1 and 2 are just the same as in Example 3; but the repercussions in B differ. There is, *ex hypothesi*, no change in national income in B, since a financial policy is adopted in B for the preservation of internal balance. Relationship 4, therefore, does not arise. The policy change in domestic expenditure required to preserve internal balance is

[1] If there were no home leakage in B, the national income and domestic expenditure in B would go on falling until the demand for imports in B had fallen as much as the demand in A for exports from B. There would be no improvement in A's balance of trade and the national income in A would fall as much as in Example 1.

represented by b'. Through relationship 5 this induces a change in imports into B of $\frac{2}{5}b'$ and of expenditure by B's purchasers on B's products of $\frac{3}{5}b'$. From the two rows of the table we can again obtain two equations, expressing relationships 3 and 6: and from these two equations we can calculate the values of a (the change in national income in A) which turns out to be $-133\frac{1}{3}$ and b' (the amount of policy inflation required in B to prevent the spread of depression into B's economy) which turns out to be $+66\frac{2}{3}$. The balance of trade (t) can then be calculated to move by $66\frac{2}{3}$ in A's favour.

The deflation in A is now less and the favourable movement in A's

EXAMPLE 4.

A Spontaneous Decrease in Domestic Expenditure in Country A of 100. No Financial Policy in A. A Financial Policy for Internal Balance in B.

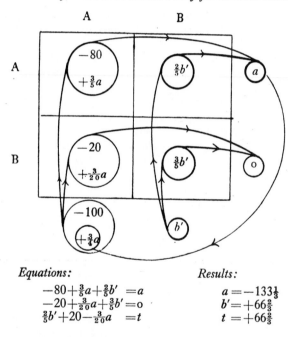

Equations:	Results:
$-80+\frac{3}{5}a+\frac{2}{5}b' =a$	$a=-133\frac{1}{3}$
$-20+\frac{3}{20}a+\frac{3}{5}b'=0$	$b'=+66\frac{2}{3}$
$\frac{2}{5}b'+20-\frac{3}{20}a =t$	$t =+66\frac{2}{3}$

balance of trade is now more than in any previous example. This is so because there is now a net inflation of domestic expenditure in B which is undertaken as an act of policy by B's authorities in order to prevent the decline in demand in A for B's products from causing any decline in national income in B. But this induces a net increase in the demand in B for A's products, thereby helping to maintain the national income in A and also to accentuate the favourable movement in A's balance of trade. It is to be observed that, in order to avoid any change in the national income in B, the authorities in B have to inflate domestic expenditure in B by an amount which is exactly equal to the unfavourable movement in B's balance of trade ($b' = t = +66\frac{2}{3}$).

In Example 4 the authorities in B by adopting an inflationary policy for the preservation of internal balance in B necessarily increased the deficit on B's balance of trade. In Example 5 we consider what will happen if they adopt a deflationary financial policy in order to preserve external balance. Once more relationships 1 and 2 are the same as in

EXAMPLE 5.

A Spontaneous Decrease in Domestic Expenditure in Country A of 100. No Financial Policy in A. A Financial Policy for External Balance in B.

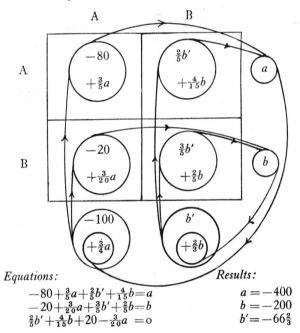

Equations:

$$-80 + \tfrac{3}{5}a + \tfrac{2}{5}b' + \tfrac{4}{15}b = a$$
$$-20 + \tfrac{3}{20}a + \tfrac{3}{5}b' + \tfrac{2}{5}b = b$$
$$\tfrac{2}{5}b' + \tfrac{4}{15}b + 20 - \tfrac{3}{20}a = 0$$

Results:

$$a = -400$$
$$b = -200$$
$$b' = -66\tfrac{2}{3}$$

Examples 3 and 4; but the repercussions in B are different. Internal balance in B is no longer preserved, so that we must allow for a change in the national income in B (b) which will induce a change of $\frac{2}{5}b$ in domestic expenditure in B (relationship 4). But in addition to this induced change in domestic expenditure in B there will also be a policy change (b') which is on a scale sufficient to alter the demand for imports in B in the manner required to keep B's balance of trade in equilibrium. This total change in domestic expenditure in B ($b' + \frac{2}{3}b$) will induce a change in B's imports and in the expenditure by B's purchasers on B's products (relationship 5).

We have once more two equations from the two rows of the table expressing relationships 3 and 6. Moreover, the change in imports must be equal to the change in exports in both countries, because external balance is preserved by means of the financial policy adopted in B. This gives us a third equation expressing the fact that the change in B's imports ($\frac{2}{5}b' + \frac{4}{15}b$) less the change in A's imports ($-20 + \frac{3}{20}a$) must be zero. From these three equations we can obtain values for the three unknowns, namely, a, b, and b'.

We find that the national income has now fallen in A by 400, just as it did in the closed economy illustrated in Example 1. This is as one would expect: as quickly as the demand in A for B's products falls because of the depression in A, the demand in B for A's products is reduced through the deflationary financial policy adopted in B for the preservation of external balance. When, therefore, some part of the decline in demand in A causes a fall in the demand for imports and so an 'export' of the depression to B, the authorities in B, through their deflationary financial policy, 're-export' the whole of the depression back to A. For A, therefore, the position is the same as if A had had no contact with the outside world. But for B the position is very different. The depression in A must be accompanied by a large fall in the national income in B (in fact a fall of 200) if the demand for imports into B is to fall as much as the demand in A for B's exports falls.

In the above examples we have not dealt with the cases in which the authorities in A might adopt a financial policy for the preservation of internal or of external balance. It is unnecessary to do so because the effects of such a policy are too obvious to need any formal analysis. If there is a spontaneous decrease of domestic expenditure in A of 100 and if the authorities in A accompany this with a policy increase of 100 in domestic expenditure in A, there will, of course, be no change in any relevant variable. Public investment would, for example, merely replace private investment, and that would be that. There would be no change in the imports, exports, domestic expenditure, or national income of either country.

2. *A Spontaneous Shift of* 100 *in Demand in* A *from* B's *Products on to* A's *Products.*

But if we turn to the second type of spontaneous disturbance which we intend to study (namely, a spontaneous decrease in the demand for imports in country A out of a given level of domestic expenditure), it is no longer out of place to consider the effects of financial policies in A as well as of financial policies in B. In fact we have now nine possible policy combinations. If we signify by N*a* and N*b* no financial policies in A and B respectively, by I*a* and I*b* financial policies for internal balance in A and B respectively, and by E*a* and E*b* financial policies for external balance in A and B respectively, we have the following possible combinations:

N*a*	N*b*	I*a*	N*b*	E*a*	N*b*
N*a*	I*b*	I*a*	I*b*	E*a*	I*b*
N*a*	E*b*	I*a*	E*b*	E*a*	E*b*

We will proceed to show these nine possibilities in Examples 6 to 14. We will explain the construction of Example 6 in some detail. But the reader should now be able to understand the principles of construction of these examples, and we shall confine ourselves to very brief comments on the remaining examples.

In Example 6 the shift of demand in A from B's on to A's products will cause some change in the national income in A. This change (*a*)

EXAMPLE 6.

A Spontaneous Shift of Demand in A *of* 100 *away from Imports. No Financial Policy in* A *or* B.

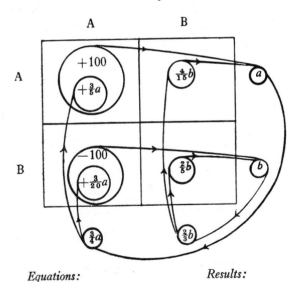

Equations:

$$100 + \tfrac{3}{5}a + \tfrac{4}{15}b = a$$
$$-100 + \tfrac{3}{20}a + \tfrac{2}{5}b = b$$
$$\tfrac{4}{15}b + 100 - \tfrac{3}{20}a = t$$

Results:

$$a = +166\tfrac{2}{3}$$
$$b = -125$$
$$t = +41\tfrac{2}{3}$$

will induce a change of $\frac{3}{4}a$ in domestic expenditure in A (relationship 1), which will induce a change of $\frac{3}{20}a$ in imports into A and of $\frac{3}{5}a$ in expenditure on A's own products (relationship 2).

The total change in imports into A will be $-100+\frac{3}{20}a$, and of expenditure by A's purchasers on A's products will be $+100+\frac{3}{5}a$, i.e. the spontaneous change plus the induced change. In B the national income will be changed by b; this will induce a change in domestic expenditure in B of $\frac{2}{3}b$ (relationship 4), which will induce a change of $\frac{4}{15}b$ in imports into B and of $\frac{2}{5}b$ in expenditure on B's own products (relationship 5). Once again from relationships 3 and 6 we have two equations showing how in each country the final change in the national income is the sum of the change in exports and of the change in expenditure by home purchasers on home products. From these we can find the value of the two unknowns, a and b. From this we can calculate the change in imports and exports and obtain the value of t, the change in A's balance of trade.

Example 7.

A Spontaneous Shift of Demand in A of 100 *away from Imports. No Financial Policy in A. A Financial Policy for Internal Balance in B.*

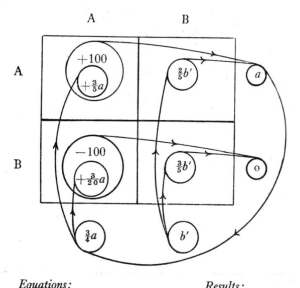

Equations:

$$+100+\tfrac{3}{5}a+\tfrac{2}{5}b' =a$$
$$-100+\tfrac{3}{20}a+\tfrac{3}{5}b'=0$$
$$\tfrac{2}{5}b'+100-\tfrac{3}{20}a =t$$

Results:

$$a=+333\tfrac{1}{3}$$
$$b'=+83\tfrac{1}{3}$$
$$t =+83\tfrac{1}{3}$$

Now the impact effects of the shift of demand in A from B's products on to A's products would be to raise the national income in A by 100, to reduce the national income in B by 100, and to move the balance of trade in A's favour by 100. But the operation of the multiplier has the effect of causing the national income to rise ultimately by $166\frac{2}{3}$ in A and to fall ultimately by 125 in B. The accompanying inflation of domestic expenditure in A and deflation of domestic expenditure in B will cause some induced increase in the demand for imports in A and some induced decrease in the demand for imports in B with the consequence that ultimately the balance of trade moves favourably to A by only $41\frac{2}{3}$, and not by the whole 100.

In Example 7 the adoption of an inflationary financial policy for internal balance in B has meant that the demand in B for A's products has also been inflated. As a result the inflation of the national income in A is larger and the balance of trade has moved more favourably to A than in Example 6. The policy inflation of domestic expenditure in B has to

Example 8.

A Spontaneous Shift of Demand in A of 100 away from Imports. No Financial Policy in A. A Financial Policy for External Balance in B.

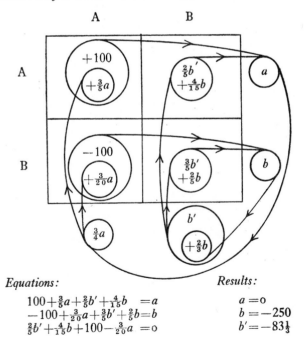

Equations:

$$100+\tfrac{3}{5}a+\tfrac{2}{5}b'+\tfrac{4}{15}b=a$$
$$-100+\tfrac{3}{20}a+\tfrac{3}{5}b'+\tfrac{2}{5}b=b$$
$$\tfrac{2}{5}b'+\tfrac{4}{15}b+100-\tfrac{3}{20}a=0$$

Results:

$$a=0$$
$$b=-250$$
$$b'=-83\tfrac{1}{3}$$

be just as large as the movement of the balance of trade against B in order to offset the deflationary influence of the latter upon the national income in B ($b'=t=+83\frac{1}{3}$).

In Example 8 the authorities adopt a deflationary financial policy ($b'=-83\frac{1}{3}$) which is such as to cause the demand in B for A's products to fall off as much as the demand in A for B's products declines. As a result there is no net change in the balance of trade and no net change in the national income in A, because the shift of demand in A on to A's products and away from B's products is exactly compensated by the decline in the demand in B for A's products. But there has to be a very considerable deflation of the national income in B ($b=-250$) to bring about the necessary decline in the demand in B for imports from A.

In Example 9 the authorities in A adopt a deflationary financial policy ($a'=-62\frac{1}{2}$) which is just sufficient to offset the improvement in A's balance of trade ($t=+62\frac{1}{2}$) so as to prevent any net inflation in the

EXAMPLE 9.

A Spontaneous Shift of Demand in A *of* 100 *away from Imports. A Financial Policy for Internal Balance in* A. *No Financial Policy in* B.

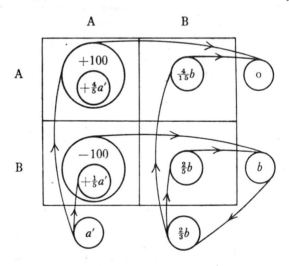

Equations:

$$100+\tfrac{4}{5}a'+\tfrac{4}{15}b =0$$
$$-100+\tfrac{1}{5}a'+\tfrac{2}{5}b=b$$
$$\tfrac{4}{15}b+100-\tfrac{1}{5}a' =t$$

Results:

$$a'=-62\tfrac{1}{2}$$
$$b =-187\tfrac{1}{2}$$
$$t =+62\tfrac{1}{2}$$

national income in A (a=0). The result of this deflationary policy in A is to intensify the deflationary pressure in B (b=$-187\frac{1}{2}$, whereas in Example 6 it equals only -125). The deflation of demand in A also causes the balance of trade to move more in A's favour (In Example 6 t=$+41\frac{2}{3}$, whereas in Example 9 t=$+62\frac{1}{2}$).

In Example 10 the authorities in A continue to adopt a deflationary financial policy in order to prevent the shift in demand on to A's products from causing any inflation of national income in A, and the authorities in B now also adopt an inflationary policy in order to prevent the shift in demand away from B's products from causing any deflation of national income in B. The deflationary policy in A has to be very great (a'=-250) because it has to counteract not only the inflationary repercussions of the spontaneous shift of demand on to A's products but also the inflationary repercussions in A of the inflationary policy adopted in B. Similarly the inflationary policy in B has to be sufficiently

EXAMPLE 10.

A Spontaneous Shift of Demand in A of 100 away from Imports. A Financial Policy for Internal Balance in A and in B.

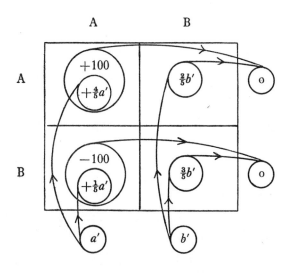

Equations:

$$100 + \tfrac{4}{5}a' + \tfrac{2}{5}b' = 0$$
$$-100 + \tfrac{1}{5}a' + \tfrac{3}{5}b' = 0$$
$$\tfrac{2}{5}b' + 100 - \tfrac{1}{5}a' = t$$

Results:

$$a' = -250$$
$$b' = +250$$
$$t = +250$$

great ($b'=+250$) to offset the deflationary effects in B of the spontaneous shift in demand and of the deflationary policy in A. The result of the deflationary policy in A and of the inflationary policy in B is to cause the balance of trade to move in A's favour by considerably more than the 100 which represents the spontaneous shift in demand in A away from imports ($t=+250$).

In Example 11, since the authorities in B adopt a financial policy for external balance, in each country the change in imports equals the

Example 11.

A Spontaneous Shift of Demand in A of 100 away from Imports. A Financial Policy for Internal Balance in A and for External Balance in B.

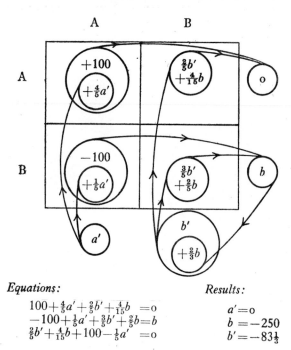

Equations:

$$100+\tfrac{4}{5}a'+\tfrac{2}{5}b'+\tfrac{4}{15}b=0$$
$$-100+\tfrac{1}{5}a'+\tfrac{3}{5}b'+\tfrac{2}{5}b=b$$
$$\tfrac{2}{5}b'+\tfrac{4}{15}b+100-\tfrac{1}{5}a'=0$$

Results:

$$a'=0$$
$$b=-250$$
$$b'=-83\tfrac{1}{3}$$

change in exports and there is no change in the balance of trade. In A this means that the spontaneous shift in demand does not in fact exert any inflationary pressure because the demand for A's products in B is deflated just as quickly as the demand in A shifts away from B's products on to A's products. There is, therefore, no deflationary policy required in A to preserve internal balance ($a'=0$). But there must be a very considerable deflation of national income in B in order to preserve external balance ($b=-250$). The result is thus exactly the same as in Example 8.

In Example 12, the adoption of a financial policy for external balance in A means that the authorities in A adopt so great an inflationary policy ($a=+500$ and $a'=+125$) that the induced increase in imports into A completely offsets the spontaneous decrease in imports into A. There is in consequence no net change in the balance of trade ($t=0$) and no deflationary pressure in B ($b=0$).

EXAMPLE 12.

A Spontaneous Shift of Demand in A of 100 away from Imports. A Financial Policy for External Balance in A. No Financial Policy in B.

A   B

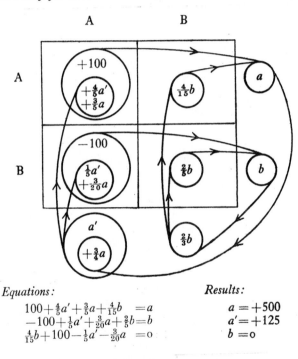

Equations: Results:

$$100+\tfrac{1}{5}a'+\tfrac{3}{5}a+\tfrac{4}{15}b=a \qquad a=+500$$
$$-100+\tfrac{1}{5}a'+\tfrac{3}{20}a+\tfrac{2}{5}b=b \qquad a'=+125$$
$$\tfrac{4}{15}b+100-\tfrac{1}{5}a'-\tfrac{3}{20}a=0 \qquad b=0$$

Example 13 is essentially the same as Example 12. As was shown in connexion with Example 12 the adoption of a financial policy for external balance in A means that there will be no net fall in the demand in A for imports; and therefore there will be no deflationary pressure in B and no inflationary policy will be required in B to prevent a fall in the national income in B ($b'=0$).

EXAMPLE 13.

A Spontaneous Shift of Demand in A *of* 100 *away from Imports. A Financial Policy for External Balance in* A *and for Internal Balance in* B.

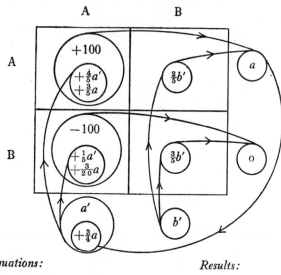

Equations:

$$100 + \tfrac{4}{5}a' + \tfrac{3}{5}a + \tfrac{2}{5}b' = a$$
$$-100 + \tfrac{1}{5}a' + \tfrac{3}{20}a + \tfrac{3}{5}b' = 0$$
$$\tfrac{2}{5}b' + 100 - \tfrac{1}{5}a' - \tfrac{3}{20}a = 0$$

Results:

$$a = +500$$
$$a' = +125$$
$$b' = 0$$

In Example 14 the authorities in A adopt an inflationary policy (a') to expand imports into A so as to help to restore equilibrium to the balance of trade, and at the same time the authorities in B adopt a deflationary policy (b') to contract imports into B for the same reason. The result will be some inflation of the national income in A(a) and some deflation of the national income in B(b). Once again we have two equations expressing relationships 3 and 6 and a third equation expressing the fact that the balance of trade is not allowed to change. But we have four unknowns, a, a', b, and b'.

There is one equation missing. The economic meaning of this is that we have not yet given any indication as to how much of the adjustment for external balance will be carried out in A and how much in B. If the authorities in A adopt a very great inflationary policy, the demand for imports in A will be greatly stimulated and the authorities in B will have to deflate only a little in order to make the remaining contribution to external equilibrium; but if the authorities in A inflate only a little, the authorities in B will have to deflate a lot.

EXAMPLE 14.

A Spontaneous Shift of Demand in A of 100 away from Imports. A Financial Policy for External Balance in both A and B.

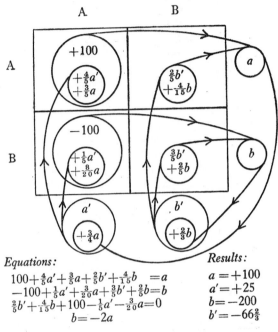

Equations:

$$100 + \tfrac{4}{5}a' + \tfrac{3}{5}a + \tfrac{2}{5}b' + \tfrac{4}{15}b = a$$
$$-100 + \tfrac{1}{5}a' + \tfrac{3}{20}a + \tfrac{3}{5}b' + \tfrac{2}{5}b = b$$
$$\tfrac{2}{5}b' + \tfrac{4}{15}b + 100 - \tfrac{1}{5}a' - \tfrac{3}{20}a = 0$$
$$b = -2a$$

Results:

$$a = +100$$
$$a' = +25$$
$$b = -200$$
$$b' = -66\tfrac{2}{3}$$

Under an orthodox gold standard the flow of international monetary reserves of gold to the surplus country A from the debtor country B would determine the relative sizes of the inflation in A and the deflation in B. The banking and general monetary structures might, for example, be such that a movement of a unit of gold from B to A would have to be accompanied by a decline in the volume of monetary transactions in B which was twice as great as the increase in the volume of monetary transactions which it would finance in A. In this case the missing gold-standard equation would be of the form $b = -2a$. We should then have the following results:—$a = +100$, $a' = +25$, $b = -200$, $b' = -66\tfrac{2}{3}$. The national income in A would have to be allowed to rise by 100 and in B to fall by 200 in order to restore external balance.

3. *A Spontaneous Increase of 100 in Transfers from A to B.*

We suppose now that there is a spontaneous increase in transfers from A to B of 100 which is unaccompanied by any spontaneous change in domestic expenditure in either country; for example, savers in A decide to invest 100 per period of time in securities in B instead of in securities in A, there being no change in interest rates in either country and so no incentive for any change in domestic expenditure in either country.

The impact effect of this will be to put A's balance of payments into deficit by 100; but since there is no impact effect upon expenditure in either country there will be no direct change in the national income of either country or in the balance of trade. If, therefore, the authorities in neither country adopt a financial policy for external balance, there will be no further repercussions. There will be a deficit in A's balance of payments of 100; but no national income will have been changed, so that no action need as yet be taken by the authorities in either country in order to preserve internal balance.

But the picture is changed if the authorities in either or both countries adopt a financial policy for external balance. Suppose, for example, that the authorities in A adopt a deflationary financial policy in order to reduce the demand for imports into A in order to remove the deficit on the balance of payments. Then the demand for B's products will

EXAMPLE 15.

A Spontaneous Transfer of 100 *from* A *to* B. *No Financial Policy in* A. *A Financial Policy for External Balance in* B.

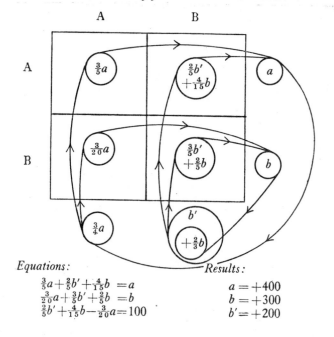

Equations:

$$\tfrac{3}{5}a + \tfrac{2}{5}b' + \tfrac{4}{15}b = a$$
$$\tfrac{3}{20}a + \tfrac{3}{5}b' + \tfrac{2}{5}b = b$$
$$\tfrac{2}{5}b' + \tfrac{4}{15}b - \tfrac{3}{20}a = 100$$

Results:

$$a = +400$$
$$b = +300$$
$$b' = +200$$

decline and a deflation of the national income in B will start to develop. The authorities in B must now decide whether to do nothing about it or whether to adopt an inflationary policy in order to preserve internal balance.

We need, therefore, to examine only those cases in which in either or both countries a financial policy for external balance is adopted. There are five such cases which may be denoted as NaEb, IaEb, EaEb, EaIb, and EaNb where, as before, N, I, and E denote no financial policy, a financial policy for internal balance, and a financial policy for external balance respectively, and where the subscripts a and b refer to the two countries A and B respectively.

We shall illustrate these five cases in Examples 15 to 19. In all these examples no spontaneous change appears in the actual diagram itself. In each case we are concerned in the diagram with the way in which any final change in income will induce a change in domestic expenditure (relationships 1 and 4), and the way in which these induced changes in domestic expenditure plus any policy change in domestic expenditure in either country may lead to changes in the demand for imports and in the

Example 16.

A Spontaneous Transfer of 100 from A to B. A Financial Policy for Internal Balance in A. A Financial Policy for External Balance in B.

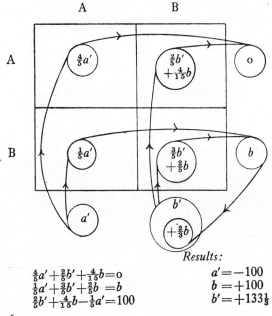

Results:

$$\tfrac{4}{5}a' + \tfrac{2}{5}b' + \tfrac{4}{15}b = 0$$
$$\tfrac{1}{5}a' + \tfrac{3}{5}b' + \tfrac{2}{5}b = b$$
$$\tfrac{2}{5}b' + \tfrac{4}{15}b - \tfrac{1}{5}a' = 100$$

$$a' = -100$$
$$b = +100$$
$$b' = +133\tfrac{1}{3}$$

demand for home-produced products (relationships 2 and 5). From this we shall obtain two equations expressing the fact that the final change in the national income in both countries is made up of the change in the home demand and the change in the foreign demand for the country's products (relationships 3 and 6). Since external balance is being maintained in every case, we shall always have a third equation stating that the increase in A's exports minus the increase in B's exports equals 100, i.e. the spontaneous transfer from A to B whose effect upon the balance of payments has to be offset by an improvement in A's balance of trade.

In Example 15 the authorities in B engineer a policy inflation of domestic expenditure in B ($b'=+200$) in order so to increase the demand for A's products in B that A's balance of trade improves by 100. This inflation in B causes a rise in B's and in A's incomes ($b=+300$, $a=+400$). The inflation in B has to go sufficiently far to cause A's exports to rise sufficiently not only to cover the transfer of 100 but also to cover the increase in the demand in A for imports which results from the inflation of income and of demand in A.

EXAMPLE 17.

A Spontaneous Transfer of 100 from A to B. Financial Policies for External Balance in A and B.

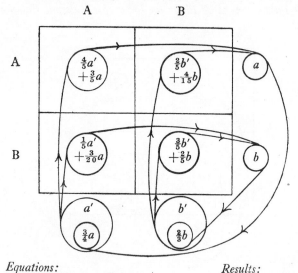

Equations:

$$\tfrac{4}{5}a'+\tfrac{3}{5}a+\tfrac{2}{5}b'+\tfrac{4}{15}b =a$$
$$\tfrac{1}{5}a'+\tfrac{3}{20}a+\tfrac{3}{5}b'+\tfrac{2}{5}b =b$$
$$\tfrac{2}{5}b'+\tfrac{4}{15}b-\tfrac{1}{5}a'-\tfrac{3}{20}a=100$$
$$b=-\tfrac{3}{4}a$$

Results:

$$a =-80$$
$$a'=-120$$
$$b =+60$$
$$b'=+120$$

In Example 16 the inflation in B for the preservation of external balance does not go so far as in Example 15 ($b' = +133\frac{1}{3}$ instead of $+200$, and $b = +100$ instead of $+300$). This is so because the authorities in A instead of allowing an unchecked inflation to develop in A adopt a deflationary financial policy ($a' = -100$) in order to preserve internal balance. Thus, the demand for imports in A instead of being inflated is deflated and external balance is achieved with a much smaller inflationary movement in B.

In Example 17 the authorities in A deflate and those in B inflate to restore external balance; a and a' are therefore negative, and b and b' positive. For these four unknowns we have the two equations expressing relationships 3 and 6, and the equation expressing the fact that the change in A's balance of trade must be 100 in order to restore external balance. We need a fourth equation which is the 'gold-standard' equation which determines how great A's deflation must be in relation to B's inflation. (See Example 14.) If the inflation of B's national income is only $\frac{3}{4}$ of the deflation of A's, then we have $a = -80$, $a' = -120$, $b = +60$, and $b' = +120$.

EXAMPLE 18.

A Spontaneous Transfer of 100 from A to B. A Financial Policy for External Balance in A. A Financial Policy for Internal Balance in B.

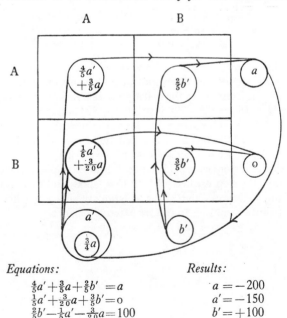

Equations:

$$\tfrac{4}{5}a' + \tfrac{3}{5}a + \tfrac{2}{5}b' = a$$
$$\tfrac{1}{5}a' + \tfrac{3}{20}a + \tfrac{3}{5}b' = 0$$
$$\tfrac{2}{5}b' - \tfrac{1}{5}a' - \tfrac{3}{20}a = 100$$

Results:

$$a = -200$$
$$a' = -150$$
$$b' = +100$$

EXAMPLE 19.

A Spontaneous Transfer of 100 *from* A *to* B. *A Financial Policy for External Balance in* A. *No Financial Policy in* B.

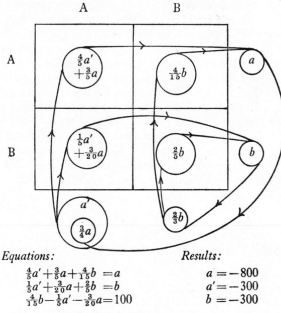

Equations:

$$\tfrac{4}{5}a' + \tfrac{3}{5}a + \tfrac{4}{15}b = a$$
$$\tfrac{1}{5}a' + \tfrac{3}{20}a + \tfrac{2}{5}b = b$$
$$\tfrac{4}{15}b - \tfrac{1}{5}a' - \tfrac{3}{20}a = 100$$

Results:

$$a = -800$$
$$a' = -300$$
$$b = -300$$

Examples 18 and 19 are the reverse of Examples 16 and 15. In Examples 18 and 19 the authorities in A deflate to maintain external balance. But in Example 18 the deflation does not need to be so great as in Example 19 (a is only -200 instead of -800 and a' is -150 instead of -300). This is so because in Example 18 the authorities in B inflate ($b' = +100$) in order to offset the deflationary repercussions on B's income; and thus there is an increase in the demand for imports in B, which helps to restore external balance. But in Example 19 the deflation is allowed to develop unchecked in B ($b = -300$) and this reduces the demand for A's exports, so that the deflationary policy in A has to go so much the farther in order to restore external balance.

PART IV. PRICE ADJUSTMENTS

PART IV. PRICE ADJUSTMENTS

CHAPTER XI
PRICE ADJUSTMENTS AS A MEANS
OF POLICY

In Parts II and III we have already made allowance for the effects which variations in relative prices may in certain circumstances have upon the internal and external balance of our two countries, A and B. In particular in Chapter VI we discussed at length the changes that may take place in the price of A's products relatively to the price of B's products as a result of a general economic boom in A which spreads to B, and the effect which such price changes might have upon the demand for A's products and for B's products and so upon the internal and external balance of A and B. In Chapter VII we took into account both the effect upon relative prices of other spontaneous changes (including a general increase in productivity in one of the two countries which might be expected directly to affect relative costs, and so relative prices, in the two countries) and also the effect of these relative price changes upon the demand for the products of the two countries. Throughout Part III we bore these conclusions tacitly in mind during our discussion of the proper criterion for the use of financial policy.

But all the discussion of relative price changes up to this point has been based upon the assumption that the two most direct regulators of the level of money prices and costs, namely, the level of money wage rates and the rate of exchange between the currencies of the two countries, have remained constant. Up to this point relative prices have changed either as the result of a spontaneous change in productivity or as the result of a change in employment and output leading to an alteration in real labour costs and so, at constant money wage rates, to an alteration in money costs and prices.

We intend now, however, to introduce the possibility of alterations in the general level of prices which are brought about as an act of policy by the authorities of one or other of our two countries expressly in order to exert an influence over the internal or external balance of the country concerned. This involves the modification of two of the assumptions made (p. 48) for the definition of the neutral economy. We shall, in fact, now remove the assumption that the general levels of money wage rates in A and B are kept constant and the assumption that the rate of exchange between A's currency and B's currency is kept fixed,

Now a reduction in money wage rates (and so in money prices) in B, a rise in money wage rates (and so in prices) in A, or a depreciation of B's currency in terms of A's currency (i.e. a rise in the number of units of B's money which have to be given to obtain a unit of A's money) will make the price of B's products fall relatively to the price of A's products when both prices are measured in some common unit of value. We have argued at length in Chapter VI (pp. 68–78) what the direct effects of such a variation in relative prices are likely to be. Here it must suffice briefly to recapitulate the results. If the sum of the price elasticities of demand for imports in A and in B is greater than one, then a fall in the price of B's products relatively to the price of A's products will cause a favourable movement in B's balance of trade whether it be measured in units of B's products or in units of A's products.[1] If the sum of the elasticities of demand for imports in A and in B is less than unity, then a fall in the prices of B's products relatively to those of A's products will cause an unfavourable movement in B's balance of trade whether measured in terms of B's products or of A's products. In other words, if the elasticities of demand for imports are sufficiently high, a fall in the price of B's products relatively to the price of A's products will cause purchasers in both countries to shift so extensively from the purchase of A's products on to the purchase of B's relatively cheaper products that the change in the quantities bought will more than outweigh the fact that one unit of B's exports is now worth less than before in terms of A's products. In consequence the value of B's total exports will rise relatively to the value of B's total imports; B's balance of trade will undergo a favourable movement (and, therefore, A's an unfavourable moevment) whether it is measured in terms of B's products or of A's products. If, however, the volume of B's imports decreases hardly at all, and the volume of A's imports increases hardly at all, when the prices of B's products fall relatively to those of A's products, then the changes in the quantities of imports and exports will not be as marked as the fact that a unit of B's exports is now worth less than before in terms of A's products. In this case the fall in the price of B's products will cause the total value of B's exports to fall relatively to the total value of B's imports, whether measured in terms of B's products or of A's products.

In the rest of this chapter we shall argue on the assumption that the sum of the elasticities of demand for imports in the two countries is

---

[1] It will be remembered that this is strictly true only if there is not much difference between the value of imports and the value of exports to begin with. If the value of B's imports greatly exceeded the value of B's exports, and if the price elasticity of demand for imports in B was less than one, a relative fall in the price of B's products might cause B's balance of trade to move favourably when measured in terms of A's products but unfavourably when measured in terms of B's products (see footnote on p. 72).

greater than one, which (for the reasons given on pp. 75–7 above) we regard as the normal case. If, in these circumstances, the prices of B's products are reduced relatively to those of A's products (either by a fall in money wage rates in B, a rise in money wage rates in A, or a depreciation of B's currency in terms of A's currency), this will cause a net shift of demand (whether measured in terms of B's products or of A's products) away from A's more expensive products on to B's less expensive products. This will have three effects: first, as we have seen, it will cause a favourable movement in B's (i.e. an unfavourable movement in A's) balance of trade; second, it will increase the demand for B's products relatively to their costs of production and thus cause a net inflationary influence domestically in B; and third, it will decrease the demand for A's products relatively to their costs of production and thus exercise a net deflationary influence in A.

Bearing this result in mind, let us now restore the assumptions of the neutral economy which we modified in Part III; that is to say, let us assume once more that the level of expenditure by the public authorities, the rates of taxation, and the rate of interest are all constant. But let us now assume that the relative levels of money prices and costs in A and B can be modified directly either by a 'policy' reduction of wage rates in the one country and increase in the other or by a 'policy' variation in the foreign exchange rate between the currencies of the two countries. Our problem is to determine what price adjustment policies of this kind should be adopted to meet various types of world disequilibrium.

Table XI lays out schematically the four types of situation of world disequilibrium in which the method of price adjustment might be used, just as they were laid out in Table X for the discussion of the use of financial policies. Row 1 of Table XI depicts the case of a world-wide depression in which the national incomes of both countries are suffering from a slump and need to be inflated in the interests of internal balance. Now if the authorities in the deficit country depreciate the exchange value of the currency of the deficit country or bring about a reduction of money wage rates in the deficit country, this will cause a net shift of demand away from the products of the surplus country on to the products of the deficit country. This will help to move the balance of trade in favour of the deficit country and will also help to restore the general level of demand and so to raise the general level of employment in the deficit country (row 1, columns *c* and *e* of Table XI). It will, therefore, have much to recommend it from the point of view of the deficit country. But it will of course intensify the depression and reduce still further the demand for labour in the surplus country. In fact, in so far as the requirements of internal balance are concerned, the authorities in the surplus country (row 1 column *d*) would need to obtain a relative

TABLE XI

Conflicts of Criteria for Price-Adjustment Policies

National income in the surplus country	National income in the deficit country	In the interests of		
		external balance	internal balance in the surplus country	internal balance in the deficit country
is too low (L) or too high (H)		there should be a rise $(S'+)$ or fall $(S'-)$ of money costs in the surplus country and a rise $(D'+)$ or fall $(D'-)$ of money costs in the deficit country.		
(*a*)	(*b*)	(*c*)	(*d*)	(*e*)
L	L	$S'+$ $D'-$	$S'-$ $D'+$	$S'+$ $D'-$	(1)
	H	$S'+$ $D'-$	$S'-$ $D'+$	$S'-$ $D'+$	(2)
H	L	$S'+$ $D'-$	$S'+$ $D'-$	$S'+$ $D'-$	(3)
	H	$S'+$ $D'-$	$S'+$ $D'-$	$S'-$ $D'+$	(4)

reduction in the money wage rates of their own country or to obtain a depreciation of the currency of their own country in order to create a more extensive market for the products of their own unemployed labour by undercutting the products of the deficit country. But this would constitute the most barefaced 'export of unemployment' from the surplus to the deficit country, since it would improve the demand for labour in the former, but at the expense not only of an equal reduction in the demand for labour in the latter but also of a worsening of the disequilibrium in the balance of payments.

Row 4 of Table XI depicts exactly the opposite situation. There is a world boom in progress with the national incomes of both countries requiring some deflation. A rise of money wage rates in the surplus country or an appreciation of the currency of the surplus country in terms of the currency of the deficit country would now help not only to restore a balance to the balance of payments but also, by causing a net reduction in the demand for the products of the surplus country, to restore internal balance in the surplus country (row 4 columns *c* and *d*). But it would, of course, intensify the existing inflationary pressure in the deficit country. On the other hand, a rise in the relative costs and prices of the products of the deficit country, while it would help to restore internal balance in that country (row 4 column *e*) would do so at the cost not only of 'exporting the inflationary pressure' on to the surplus country but also of making the balance-of-payments disequilibrium worse.

Row 2 of Table XI shows the case of the clearest conflict between internal and external balance in so far as the weapon of price adjustment is concerned. In this case there is a domestic slump in the surplus country and boom in the deficit country. In the interests of external balance we want to engineer a shift of demand away from the products of the surplus country on to those of the deficit country, and for this purpose a rise in money wage rates in the surplus country, a fall in money wage rates in the deficit country, or a depreciation of the exchange value of the currency of the deficit country is required (row 2 column *c*). But for the internal balance of both of the countries exactly the opposite is needed (row 2 columns *d* and *e*); we need a relative fall in the price of the products of the surplus country in order to shift demand away from the inflated industries of the deficit country on to the deflated industries of the surplus country.

Row 3 of Table XI, on the other hand, depicts the one case in which there is no conflict at all in the use of the method of price adjustment. Now it is the surplus country which is suffering from a domestic boom and the deficit country which is suffering from a domestic slump. A shift of demand away from the products of the surplus country on to those of the deficit country would now serve the three useful purposes of restoring equilibrium to the balance of payments, of deflating the inflated economy of the surplus country, and of inflating the depressed economy of the deficit country. A reduction in the cost and prices of the products of the deficit country relative to those of the surplus country would achieve this threefold result (row 3 columns *c*, *d*, and *e*).

Now it is interesting to observe that this very case (row 3 of Table XI) in which alone there is no ambiguity about the desirability of price adjustment is the same as the one case (row 3 of Table X) with which financial policies in the two countries, however well devised, could not satisfactorily cope (see p. 122). This suggests that a combination of financial policies and of policies for price adjustment might in all cases be able to achieve satisfactory results—at least so far as, externally, the balance of payments and, internally, the levels of the national incomes are concerned.

Table XII has been constructed in order to show what combinations of financial policies and policies for price adjustment would be sensible for dealing with our four different situations of world disequilibrium. The construction of Table XII is of great simplicity. We have merely copied down from Table X all those cases (but only those cases) in which the authorities of the surplus or deficit country ought to undertake a particular financial policy in the interests both of the internal and also of the external balance of that particular country. At the same time we have copied down from Table XI all those cases (but only those cases) in which the authorities of the surplus or deficit country ought to undertake a particular price adjustment in the interests both of the internal and also of the external balance of that particular country. It is of some interest to comment briefly on the resulting combinations of policy for each of the four situations of world disequilibrium.

In row 1 of Table XII, which shows a situation in which both the

TABLE XII

Reconciliation of Criteria for Financial and Price-Adjustment Policies.

National income in the surplus country	National income in the deficit country	The symbols S+, S′+, S−, S′−, D+, D′+, D− and D′− have the same meanings as in Tables X and XI. Only those instances are marked in this Table in which the authorities in the country concerned should take the action indicated in the interests of both the internal and also the external balance of that country.		
is too low (L) or too high (H)				
(a)	(b)	(c)	(d)	(e)
L	L	S+ D′−	S+	D′− (1)
	H	S+ D−	S+	D− (2)
H	L	S′+ D′−	S′+	D′− (3)
	H	S′+ D−	S′+	D− (4)

surplus and the deficit countries are suffering from a domestic depression, we see that the authorities of the surplus country are enjoined to adopt an inflationary financial policy and the authorities of the deficit country to bring about a downward adjustment of their relative prices (i.e. either by a depreciation of the foreign exchange value of the country's currency or by an internal deflation of money wage rates). This is clearly a sensible set of rules. The reduction in the relative prices of the products of the deficit country will help both to restore external balance and also to give employment in the deficit country; and the domestic inflation in the surplus country will help both to restore external balance and also to give employment in the surplus country.

Row 4 of Table XII depicts the opposite situation of world boom. Here again the rules which are enjoined would seem to be sensible. The authorities in the deficit country by adopting a deflationary financial policy will help to restore external balance and to curb their own internal boom; and a rise in the relative prices of the products of the surplus country by shifting demand away from the products of the surplus country on to those of the deficit country will also help to restore external balance and will curb the inflationary pressures in the surplus country.

In row 2 of Table XII there is a boom in progress in the deficit country and a depression in the surplus country. In this case no price adjustment is called for. An inflation in the surplus country will help to restore external balance by increasing the demand for the products of the deficit country and will also help to offset the deflation in the surplus country by increasing the demand for the products of the surplus country. Simultaneously a deflationary financial policy in the booming deficit country will serve to restore external balance and internal balance in that country.

Row 3 of Table XII shows the case where financial policies are inappropriate but where price adjustment is most called for. There is now a boom in the surplus country and a slump in the deficit country. In this case the shift of expenditure away from the products of the former on to the products of the latter, which will be brought about by a rise in the price of the products of the former and a fall in the price of the products of the latter, will attain all three objectives simultaneously. It will restore equilibrium to the balance of payments, deflate the inflated economy of the surplus country, and inflate the deflated economy of the deficit country.

We must next consider how this desirable combination of financial policies and policies for price adjustment can be brought about. Now there are two ways in which the authorities of a particular country may combine the use of financial policy and of price adjustment. (i) First, financial policy may be used for the preservation of internal balance and price adjustment for the preservation of external balance. (ii) Second, financial policy may be used for the preservation of external balance and price adjustment for the preservation of internal balance. On either of these principles the authorities of any one country can set about the simultaneous preservation of internal and external balance. If the authorities in each of our two countries adopt either of these principles, will their action necessarily result in the desirable combinations of policy outlined in Table XII?

Let us consider in a little more detail what is involved in the two principles mentioned in the last paragraph.

Principle i is that of the use of financial policy for the preservation of internal balance and of price adjustment for the preservation of external balance. This means that if there is a domestic depression, the authorities should bring about (through a reduction of taxes, an increase of public expenditure, or an increase in the supply of money and reduction in interest rates) a net inflation of domestic expenditure; and that if there is a domestic boom they should bring about some policy deflation of domestic expenditure. Simultaneously, if there is a deficit in the country's balance of payments, the authorities (either by a reduction in money wage rates or by a depreciation of the exchange rate) should reduce money prices and costs in their own country relatively to those of the rest of the world; and conversely if there is a surplus on the balance of payments, the authorities should take steps to raise relative prices and costs.

Principle ii involves the use of financial policy for the preservation of external balance and of price adjustment for the preservation of internal balance. If there is a deficit in the balance of payments, the authorities of the country concerned must adopt a financial policy for the deflation of domestic expenditure, or, if there is a surplus in the balance of payments, they must adopt an inflationary financial policy. At the same time steps must be taken (by adjustments of wage rates or of rates of exchange) to raise or to lower the money prices and costs of the country's products relatively to those of the rest of the world according as there is a domestic boom or slump in progress.

Any one country can be in any of four possible disequilibrium situations. It can be (1) a surplus country with a domestic slump, (2) a surplus country with a domestic boom, (3) a deficit country with a domestic slump, or (4) a deficit country with a domestic boom. Let us examine each of these four situations in turn and consider what action would be taken in each situation in conformity with Principle i and Principle ii for the use of financial policy and price adjustment.

(1) The authorities in a *surplus country with a domestic slump* under Principle i will inflate domestic expenditure in order to restore internal balance and will raise prices and costs relatively to those in the rest of the world in order to restore external balance; under Principle ii they will inflate domestic expenditure to restore external balance, but will lower prices and costs relatively to those in the rest of the world in order to restore internal balance.

Consider first their action under Principle i. External balance will be rapidly achieved since both the inflation of domestic expenditure and the rise in relative prices will cause a reduction in the surplus on the country's balance of payments. But internal balance will not be affected, if the financial policy is of just such inflationary strength as to offset the deflationary effect of the shift of demand away from the country's products whose prices have been deliberately raised relatively to those of the rest of the world. The inflationary financial policy must therefore be continued beyond this point in the interests of internal balance, even though external balance is achieved. At this point the country will become a deficit country, since its imports will continue to expand; and Principle i will then enjoin a lowering of its prices and money costs. When it finally reaches internal and external equilibrium, it will be certain that there will have been a substantial domestic inflation through financial policy; but it is quite uncertain whether there will have been finally a net raising or a net lowering of the country's money prices and costs relatively to those of the rest of the world.

Consider next the action that would have been taken under Principle ii. In this case internal balance will be rapidly achieved since both the inflationary financial policy and the lowering of the prices of the country's products relatively to those of the rest of the world will expand the demand for the products of its domestic industries. But external balance will not be affected if the relative stress placed upon financial policy and price adjustment is such that the unfavourable effect of the inflationary financial policy upon the balance of payments is just outweighed by the favourable effect of the relative reduction in the prices of the country's products. At this stage, when the country is in internal balance but is still in surplus in its balance of payments, Principle ii will enjoin a continued inflation of domestic expenditure in order to restore external balance. But this will cause a domestic boom, for the avoidance of which, under Principle ii, the prices and costs of the country must now be raised relatively to those of the rest of the world. Once again in the final position of internal and external equilibrium there will be a substantial net inflation of domestic expenditure through financial policy, but it will be uncertain whether there will be a net rise or fall in relative prices and costs.

From the above it is clear that whether Principle i or Principle ii is adopted, the result is the same. The authorities in a surplus country with a domestic slump will have to concentrate on a financial policy for domestic inflation and will not have to rely upon any substantial net change in the level of their prices and costs relatively to those of the rest of the world. And this is exactly what the authorities of a country in this situation should do in accordance with our earlier argument. (See rows 1 and 2 of Table XII.)

(2) By a similar process of reasoning it can be shown that the authorities of a *surplus country with a domestic boom* will (in accordance with rows 3 and 4 of Table XII) concentrate upon raising prices and costs relatively to those of the rest of the world whether they operate under Principle i or Principle ii.

Under Principle i prices and costs will be raised for the restoration of external balance and domestic expenditure will be deflated for the restoration of internal balance. These two policies will reinforce each other in deflating the national income, but they will have offsetting effects on external balance. Therefore, in the interests of external balance, prices and costs will continue to be raised even after internal balance is achieved; but the resulting unfavourable movement in the balance of trade will have a deflationary effect at home. The financial policy for deflation at home will therefore need to be replaced by a financial policy for the inflation of domestic expenditure. In the end, while it will be certain that prices and costs will be raised relatively to those in the rest of the world, it will be uncertain whether there is any net inflation or deflation of domestic expenditure.

Under Principle ii prices and costs will be raised in the interests of internal balance and domestic expenditure will be inflated in the interests of external balance. External balance will be rapidly achieved; but internal balance will not be affected if the inflationary effects of the financial policy are just offset by the deflationary effects of the reduction in the surplus on the balance of payments. Prices and costs will continue to be raised in the interests of internal balance; but this will produce a deficit on the balance of payments and domestic expenditure must be deflated in the interests of external balance. Once again a marked raising of relative prices and costs is a certain outcome; but the net result may produce either some small net inflation or some small net deflation from financial policy.

(3) Similarly the authorities in a *deficit country with a domestic slump* will concentrate (as rows 1 and 3 of Table XII suggest that they should) upon a lowering of prices and costs whether they operate on Principle i or Principle ii.

On Principle i relative prices will be lowered in the interests of external balance and domestic expenditure will be inflated in the interests of internal balance. Internal balance will be very quickly restored although there is no net change in external balance. Relative prices must, therefore, continue to be lowered, which will tend now to produce a boom at home. The inflationary financial policy must, therefore, be replaced by a deflationary policy. In the end relative prices will be substantially lowered, while there may be a small net inflation or deflation of domestic expenditure by financial policy.

On Principle ii relative prices will be lowered for internal balance and domestic expenditure will be deflated for external balance. External balance will be rapidly achieved. The lowering of prices will continue in order to achieve internal balance. But this will now produce a surplus on the balance of payments, which will call for an inflation instead of a deflation of domestic expenditure in the interests of external balance. Once again there will result a definite lowering of relative prices; but there may be some small net inflation or deflation of domestic expenditure by financial policy.

(4) In the case of a *deficit country with a domestic boom* the application of either Principle i or Principle ii will result in concentration upon a deflationary financial policy in accordance with rows 2 and 4 of Table XII.

Principle i will enjoin a deflationary financial policy for internal balance and a lowering of relative prices and costs for external balance. This will quickly restore external balance without necessarily affecting internal balance. The deflationary financial policy will, therefore, be continued. But this will now produce a surplus on the balance of payments, so that the lowering of relative prices will be replaced by a raising of such prices. In the end there will be a marked deflation of domestic expenditure by financial policy; but there may be a small net raising or lowering of relative prices.

On Principle ii a deflationary policy will be adopted for external balance and a raising of relative prices and costs for internal balance. Internal balance will be rapidly restored. The deflationary financial policy will be continued in order to achieve external balance. This will now cause a slump at home, so that relative prices and costs must now be lowered for internal balance. There will accordingly be a marked and substantial deflation of domestic expenditure by financial policy; but the net movement of relative prices and costs may be somewhat upwards or somewhat downwards.

We may conclude, then, that the adoption in each country of *either* financial policy for internal balance and price adjustment for external balance (Principle i) *or* financial policy for external balance and price adjustment for internal balance (Principle ii) will produce sensible results which, in accordance with the analysis of Table XII, should finally result in internal and external balance for both countries. This should be so even if the authorities in one country adopt Principle i and in the other Principle ii, and whether the method of price adjustment is that of adjustment of levels of wage rates or adjustments of rates of exchange between the national currencies.

We cannot examine in detail all the possible combinations of policy which would arise when we allow that the authorities in the surplus country may adopt Principle i or Principle ii, that the authorities in the deficit country may adopt Principle i or Principle ii, and that under either Principle adopted in either country the method of price adjustment may be by wage-rate adjustment or by exchange-rate adjustment.[1] In fact we shall confine our attention in the remaining chapters of Part IV to two possible combinations of financial policy and

[1] In all, this would give sixteen combinations; and if in each case we distinguished between monetary policy and fiscal policy as separate forms of financial policy we should have no less than sixty-four possible combinations of financial policy and price adjustment for our two countries in ways which would preserve internal and external balance for both countries.

of price adjustment which will simultaneously preserve internal and external balance for both countries.

First, we will examine the case where the authorities in both countries adopt Principle i and where the method of price adjustment is by means of the adjustment of the exchange rate. In this case the authorities in both countries adopt a financial policy for the control of domestic expenditure so as to preserve internal balance; and external balance is preserved by means of variations in the rate of exchange between the currencies of the two countries.

Secondly, we will examine the case where the authorities in both countries adopt Principle ii and where the method of price adjustment is by means of the adjustment of wage rates. In this case the authorities in both countries inflate or deflate their domestic expenditures in order to remove a surplus or a deficit on the balance of payments; but money wage rates are lowered so long as the demand for the country's products, and so for the country's labour, is deficient, and are raised as long as the demand for labour is excessive.

These two systems will be examined and compared in Chapters XIV and XV. But before we consider these two rational 'world' systems for the simultaneous preservation of internal and external equilibrium for both countries, we shall undertake the more limited task of examining the adoption by the authorities of one country of the rules of conduct appropriate to these two systems even though the authorities in the other country may not be adopting either Principle i or Principle ii as described on p. 157. In Chapter XII, accordingly, we shall consider the problems of a country whose authorities adopt a financial policy for internal balance and allow variations in the foreign exchange value of the national currency to preserve external equilibrium; and in Chapter XIII we shall consider the problems of a country whose authorities adopt a financial policy for external balance and in which variations in money wage rates are permitted to take place for the maintenance of full employment, i.e. for the preservation of internal balance.

CHAPTER XII

EXTERNAL BALANCE THROUGH VARIABLE EXCHANGE RATES[1]

IN this chapter we propose to examine in more detail what happens when the authorities in one of our countries decide to resolve a conflict between financial policies for internal and external balance by employing financial policy for the preservation of internal balance and relying upon a variation in the rate of exchange for the simultaneous preservation of external balance.

For example, the authorities in country B have chosen to use financial policy for the maintenance of internal balance, but they then find that there is a deficit on the balance of payments. They will not deflate domestic expenditure in B in order to reduce the consumption in B of imports or of products which might otherwise be exported, because this would mean abandoning the policy of maintaining total demand at the level necessary to preserve full employment. They decide, therefore, to allow equilibrium in the balance of payments to be restored by means of a variation of the rate of exchange between A's and B's currencies in the foreign exchange market.

We can imagine this variation of the exchange rate coming about by either of two institutional mechanisms.

First, there may be a completely free exchange market in which competitive dealers trade in A's and B's currencies. Each such dealer would hold a working balance of A's and of B's currency. He would, for a commission, pay out A's currency in exchange for a receipt of B's currency to anyone in B who had a payment to make in A, and vice versa. When there was a deficit on B's balance of payments, exchange dealers would find that at the current rate of exchange between A's and B's currency they were receiving B's currency from people in B who had payments to make in A in greater amount than they were paying out B's currency to people in A who had payments to make in B. The dealers' balances of B's currency would be rising and their balances of A's currency would be falling. In order to maintain their working balances of A's currency they would demand a higher price in B's currency for the sale by them of A's currency from their depleted stocks of that currency. The deficit in B's balance of payments would have caused B's currency to have depreciated.

Secondly, it is possible that the exchange rate between A's and B's currency is officially pegged, but that by the official decision of the

---

[1] The subject matter of this chapter is considered in Section VIII (iv) of the separate mathematical supplement.

monetary authorities this peg may be altered from time to time.[1] Suppose that the monetary authorities in B undertake to buy and sell in unlimited quantities some asset which we will call 'gold'. It is possible that the 'buying price' at which the monetary authorities in B will purchase gold with newly issued currency notes of B will be a little lower than the 'selling price' which they will demand when they sell gold to persons who want to acquire it in return for the surrender to B's monetary authorities of currency notes of B which have already been issued. By this means the value of B's currency is pegged in terms of gold within limits set by the difference between B's monetary authorities' buying and selling price of gold. The price of gold could not rise in terms of B's currency above the selling price charged for it by B's monetary authorities, because if it did so no one would continue to purchase gold at the high market price but would purchase all they required from B's monetary authorities. Similarly, the price of gold in terms of B's currency could not fall below the buying price offered by B's monetary authorities for it, since no one would continue to sell gold at the low market price but would sell all they wished to dispose of at the price offered by B's monetary authorities.

Thus the value of B's currency is pegged to gold. If A's monetary authorities also set fixed buying and selling prices for gold in terms of A's currency, then the value of A's currency will also be pegged in terms of gold. Thus, indirectly, the value of B's currency will be pegged in terms of A's currency. When B's balance of payments is in deficit under these conditions, B's currency will not automatically depreciate in terms of A's currency except within narrow limits. For a person in B who wants A's currency to make a payment in A can always obtain A's currency for B's currency by purchasing gold from B's monetary authorities at their selling price of gold and then selling the gold for A's currency by offering it to A's monetary authorities at their buying price of gold. Exchange dealers will not, therefore, demand a higher price for A's currency in terms of B's currency than corresponds to the price at which A's currency can be acquired for B's currency indirectly in this way through the monetary authorities. If, because there are more people in B with payments to make to A than there are people in A with payments to make to B, the exchange dealers find that they are piling up working balances of B's currency and are running out of their working balances of A's currency, they will themselves replenish their balances of A's currency by acquiring A's currency in exchange for B's currency indirectly through the monetary authorities in the way described above.

Thus as long as B's peg on gold and A's peg on gold remains unchanged the rate of exchange between B's currency and A's currency

[1] This is, broadly speaking, the institutional arrangement under the Articles of Agreement of the International Monetary Fund.

will remain fixed within narrow limits. But these pegs may themselves be altered from time to time by the action of the monetary authorities themselves. Thus if A's peg remains unchanged, but the monetary authorities in B raise by 20 per cent the prices at which they will buy and sell gold in exchange for B's currency notes, then B's currency will be effectively depreciated by 20 per cent in terms of A's currency. A similar result would, of course, be achieved if B's peg remained unchanged but the monetary authorities in A reduced by 20 per cent the prices at which they would buy and sell gold in return for A's currency notes.

B's currency may thus depreciate in terms of A's currency when B's balance of payments is in deficit for either of two reasons: either because there is a free exchange market or else because the monetary authorities in B deliberately raise their buying and selling prices of gold when B's balance of payments is in deficit (and/or the monetary authorities in A deliberately lower their buying and selling prices of gold when A's balance of payments is in surplus). This latter method we will call the method of the 'adjustable peg'. The choice between these two methods carries with it very important consequences which we shall examine below in Chapter XVII. For the present, however, we shall neglect the points which are there discussed, and shall confine our attention to those matters which are common to all systems of variable exchange rates whether the variations are brought about by a free exchange market or by an adjustable peg.

Let us, then, return to the problem set at the beginning of this chapter. Country B is in internal balance, but there is a deficit on her balance of payments. We suppose now that by the mechanism of a free exchange market or of an adjustable peg, the excess demand for A's currency will cause a depreciation in the foreign exchange value of B's currency. A unit of B's currency (which we will call £1) will purchase a smaller number of units of A's currency (let us say $3·96 instead of $4·00). What will be the effect of this depreciation by 1 per cent of B's currency?

The immediate impact effects of this price change (i.e. abstracting from (i) any consequential change in total domestic expenditure in A or in B in terms of their own currencies, and (ii) any consequential changes in the prices of A's or B's products in terms of their own currency) is as shown in Table VIII (p. 69). If we there define a unit of A's products as the amount of A's products which can be purchased for $1 and a unit of B's products as the amount of B's products which can be purchased for £1, then the impact effect of a 1 per cent depreciation of B's currency from $4·00 to $3·96 will be to cause the number of units of A's products which can be purchased for a unit of B's products to decline from 4 to 3·96. The depreciation of B's currency from $4·00 to $3·96 will cause the price of A's products to rise in terms of B's currency (purchasers in B can obtain only 3·96 instead of 4 units of A's products for £1) and to cause the price of B's products to fall in terms of A's currency (purchasers in A now have to pay only $3·96 instead of $4·00 for a unit of B's products).

In other words, if we assume for the moment that the pound-price of B's products and the dollar-price of A's products remain unchanged, column *a* of Table VIII can now represent the rate of exchange between A's and B's currencies as well as the real terms of trade between A's and B's products. Columns *d* and *e* can then be taken to represent the change in the value of B's exports and in the balance of trade between A and B when valued in dollars (i.e. in A's currency or, at constant domestic prices in A, in A's products). Similarly, columns *f* and *g* of Table VIII can be taken to represent the change in the value of B's imports and of the balance of trade between A and B when valued in pounds sterling (i.e. in B's currency or products).

It is clear from Table VIII and from the previous analysis of Table VIII (pp. 68–72) that a depreciation of B's currency in terms of A's currency, which brings with it a similar reduction in the number of A's products which can be obtained in exchange for a unit of B's products, will cause the value of B's balance of trade to improve provided that the sum of the elasticities of demand for imports in A and B is greater than one (rows 6 and 7 of Table VIII) but will cause the value of B's balance of trade to decline if the sum of these two elasticities is less than one (rows 2 and 3 of Table VIII).[1]

Let us suppose that the sum of A's and B's elasticities of demand for imports is greater than one. What other modifications must we now make in the result if we allow for the fact that there may be consequential effects upon (i) the total level of domestic expenditure in A or B or (ii) the general level of the prices of A's or B's products in terms of their own domestic currencies?

We may start with a consideration of the internal repercussions in B. Now B's balance of trade will have become more favourable as a result of the expansion of her exports and the contraction of her imports due to the depreciation of her currency in terms of A's currency. But since, as we have seen in Chapter III above, the national income=domestic expenditure *plus* the balance of trade, this will tend to cause an inflation of B's national income. The fact that expenditure by purchasers in A (in terms of B's currency) on B's exports has risen and that expenditure by purchasers in B (in terms of B's currency) on imports has fallen— or at any rate has risen less than the rise in the value of B's exports— will have caused a net increase in the money demand for B's products. There will be an inflationary threat to B's internal balance; and since we are assuming that the authorities in B have adopted a financial policy for internal balance, they will contrive a 'policy' deflation of domestic

[1] Subject, of course, to the qualification mentioned in the footnote on p. 72.

expenditure in B sufficient to offset the inflationary effects of the improvement in B's balance of trade.

There is, therefore, likely to be no net change in the general level of prices of B's products in terms of B's own currency, because the upward pressure exercised by the increased demand for B's products resulting from the improvement in B's balance of trade will be more or less exactly offset by the downward pressure of demand for B's products due to the 'policy' deflation of her domestic expenditure. But this 'policy' deflation of domestic expenditure in B will itself cause a reduction in the demand in B for A's products. For we can assume that not the whole of any general reduction in the demand for goods and services in B will represent a decreased demand for B's products, but that some part of it will represent a fall in the demand for imports. For this reason the maintenance of internal balance in B will mean that the final improvement in B's balance of trade resulting from the depreciation of her currency will be greater than is shown in Table VIII.

But we must now take into account the repercussions which are likely to occur in country A. These will be very different according to the policy which is adopted in A. If the authorities in A adopt a financial policy for internal balance, then there are still additional reasons for believing that a depreciation of B's currency will give an even more favourable result from the point of B's balance of trade than is shown in Table VIII; but if the authorities in A adopt a neutral policy, there will be certain factors at work damping down the improvement in B's balance of trade which follows a given depreciation in her currency.[1]

The improvement in B's balance of trade (which as we have seen is the immediate impact effect of a depreciation of B's currency provided that the sum of the elasticities of demand for imports in A and B is greater than one) will represent an unfavourable movement in A's balance of trade. And just as this will tend to increase the demand for B's products and to cause an inflation in the total demand for B's products, so it will exercise a deflationary pressure in A and will tend to reduce the total demand for A's products. Now if the authorities in A adopt a neutral policy, this initial decline in the demand for A's products will start a deflationary spiral of demand in A, whose total national income, and so her total domestic expenditure, will decline as a result. Moreover, the general level of the prices of A's products, expressed in terms of A's currency will decline as the demand for A's products falls, this price decline being larger if the real elasticity of supply in A is small. Both these factors will reduce the improvement in B's balance of trade. The deflation of total domestic expenditure in A which develops as the

[1] We need not consider the possibility of the authorities in A adopting a financial policy for external balance, because in that case there could be no initial deficit in B's balance of payments to occasion the depreciation of B's currency.

depression develops in A will reduce the demand in A for B's exports as well as for A's home products; and the fall in the prices of A's products will mean that the cheapening of B's products in terms of A's products which resulted from the depreciation of B's currency is in part offset by the absolute fall in the level of A's prices in terms of A's currency, so that the shift of demand away from A's on to B's products will not go so far as would otherwise be the case.

But if the authorities in A adopt a financial policy for internal balance, not only will these two adverse effects upon B's balance of trade be avoided, but also a new influence will operate which will positively improve B's balance of trade. In order to offset the internal deflationary effects of the unfavourable movement in A's balance of trade, the authorities in A will now bring about a 'policy' inflation of domestic expenditure in A. But this absolute increase in the demand in A for goods and services in general will mean that purchasers in A increase their demand for imports from B somewhat as well as the demand for A's home products. B's exports will for this reason expand still more than is indicated in Table VIII.

So far we have considered the effect of the depreciation of B's currency only upon B's balance of trade, whereas for external balance we are in fact interested in the balance of payments. If the authorities in countries A and B are both adopting financial policies for internal balance, there are three reasons for believing that the favourable effect of a depreciation of B's currency upon B's balance of payments may be greater than the favourable effect upon the balance of trade.

First, internal balance in B will, as we have seen, involve a financial policy for the deflation of domestic expenditure in B in order to offset the inflationary effects in B of the improvement in the balance of trade. If this deflationary policy is carried out in B by means of monetary policy this will involve a restriction of the supply of money and a rise in interest rates in B. The higher rates of interest in B will induce a larger flow of net lending of capital from A to B, which will still further improve B's balance of payments.

Secondly, in A for the preservation of internal balance an inflationary policy will be required; and if this is carried out by monetary policy it will involve a reduction of interest rates in A, which will still further encourage the flow of capital funds from A to B.

Thirdly, before the change in the exchange rate there may have been some flow of capital from A to B and some flow from B to A.[1] Since

[1] It is not unreasonable to suppose that there may have been some flow in both directions simultaneously. Some of A's investors may have been particularly interested in certain investment opportunities in B, and some of B's investors in investment opportunities in A. And investors in both countries may, on the principle of spreading their risks, have desired to invest some savings in both countries.

internal balance has been preserved in both A and B there is no reason (apart from any changes in interest rates which we have just examined) to believe that there will be any change in the annual flow of savings in B *measured in B's currency* which will be lent to borrowers in A or in the annual flow of savings in A *measured in A's currency* which will be lent to borrowers in B. But the depreciation of B's currency will in these circumstances mean that the gross lending by savers in B to borrowers in A is reduced in value in terms of A's currency (which will further improve B's balance of payments when measured in terms of A's currency).

If, however, the authorities in A adopt a neutral policy these three favourable influences on B's balance of payments will be less marked.

First, it will still be true that, if monetary policy is adopted in B for the preservation of internal balance, the rate of interest will have to be raised in B. But since, as we have seen, with a neutral policy in A, B's balance of trade will enjoy a smaller net improvement, a smaller rise in interest rates will be required in B in order to preserve internal balance. In consequence there will be a *pro tanto* smaller improvement also in the flow of capital funds from A to B as a result of higher interest rates in B.

Secondly, since the authorities in A are no longer adopting a financial policy for internal balance there will be no question of any reduction of interest rates in A to promote still further the flow of capital from A to B.

Thirdly, the fall in the prices of A's products in terms of A's currency combined with the fall in real output in A will mean that the national income of A is reduced and for both reasons there will be a smaller fund of current savings in terms of A's currency out of which savers in A can lend to borrowers in B, and this will probably reduce the flow of capital from A to B. This might conceivably be partially or even wholly offset by the fact that the depression in economic activity in A due to the uncontrolled deflationary effects in A of the improvement in B's balance of trade had so worsened the prospects of profits in A's industries as compared with B's industries as to cause investors in A to invest a larger proportion of their smaller savings in B's industries. But it is unlikely that this consideration would outweigh all the other factors restraining the flow of capital from A to B.

We may conclude from this analysis that if the method of variations in exchange rates is adopted as a means of restoring equilibrium to international balances of payments, then it is important that all the countries taking part in this system should consciously adopt domestic financial policies for internal balance. For the adoption of such policies will not only avoid any unfortunate internal results from those exchange-rate variations which are required to give external balance, but it will positively reinforce the desired effects of the exchange-rate adjustment upon external balance. The preservation of internal balance in A and B will not only cause the improvement in B's balance of trade to be greater than would appear from Table VIII, but it will also cause the most favourable effects upon the balance of capital transfers between A and B.

This conclusion is reinforced when we consider the effects of exchange-rate variation upon the real terms of trade. A depreciation of B's currency is bound somewhat to move the terms of trade unfavourably to B,[1] since its whole *modus operandi* consists in an improvement in B's balance of trade by means of making B's products cheaper in terms of A's products. It is clear from Table VIII that the higher are the elasticities of demand for imports in A and B the less need the terms of trade move against B in order to achieve any needed improvement in B's balance of payments. But, other things being equal, a given improvement in B's balance of trade can be obtained at the cost of a smaller deterioration in B's terms of trade if a financial policy for internal balance rather than a neutral policy is adopted in A.[2] For, in the latter case, as B's products fall in price in terms of A's products and, in consequence, B's balance of trade improves, there will be a general deflation of output and employment in A. And the fall in real income in A will itself (i.e. apart from any change in the terms of trade) cause purchasers in A to import less from B. At any given real terms of trade purchasers in A will purchase more from B if their real income is maintained than if it has been allowed to fall; or, in other words, if internal balance is maintained in A, B's exports at any given real terms of trade will be higher than they would have been if the authorities in A had adopted a neutral policy.

[1] See Chapter XVIII for a possible modification of this conclusion.

[2] This is not inconsistent with the fact that, if a neutral policy instead of a financial policy for internal balance is adopted in A, a given depreciation of B's exchange rate will cause a smaller movement in the terms of trade against B, because in this case it will also cause a smaller improvement in B's balance of trade.

CHAPTER XIII

INTERNAL BALANCE THROUGH WAGE FLEXIBILITY [1]

IN the last chapter we started off from a position in which B's economy was maintained in internal balance through financial policy but in which B's balance of payments was in deficit; and we considered the possibility of removing the deficit on B's balance of payments by means of a depreciation of B's currency in terms of A's currency. Let us now look at the other form of conflict between financial policies for internal and external balance. Let us suppose that the authorities in B now maintain external balance through financial policy but that this results in a loss of internal balance, and that there results a large volume of unemployment in B. At the current level of money wage rates a 'policy' inflation of domestic expenditure would be needed in B in order to achieve internal balance (i.e. full employment), but this will not be undertaken because the increased demand for goods and services in B would put B's balance of payments into deficit.

In these conditions what type of price adjustment might effectively raise the demand for labour domestically without the abandonment by B's authorities of the financial policy for external balance? Let us consider what would be the effect upon the volume of employment in B of a reduction in B's money wage rates, combined with the continuation by the authorities in B of a financial policy for external balance. This method of achieving internal balance we shall call the method of 'wage flexibility'.

We shall say that money wage rates are flexible in a downward direction if there is a decline in money wage rates whenever there is a deficiency of demand for labour in relation to the available supply, so that unemployment[2] exists. And similarly money wage rates may be said to be flexible in an upward direction if wage rates rise whenever there is an excess of demand for, over the supply of, labour so that there are more vacancies than candidates for the vacancies. Flexibility in a downward direction thus implies an organization of the labour market such that in any occupation or region in which there is a deficiency of demand for labour below the available supply of labour, the money wage rate will be reduced. Similarly, flexibility of wage rates in an upward direction

---

[1] The subject matter of this chapter is treated in Section VIII (v) of the separate mathematical supplement.

[2] Over and above unemployment of a 'frictional' character due, not to a general deficiency of demand, but to such causes as the normal movement of men from one job to another. The distinction between the general unemployment with which we are essentially concerned in the text and the various forms of frictional unemployment would need more extensive discussion in a Theory of Domestic Economic Policy.

involves an organization of the labour market of a kind which will cause money wage rates to rise in any occupation or region in which the demand for labour exceeds the available supply.

There are broadly two types of labour-market organization which will bring about this wage flexibility. In the first place, in the absence of monopolistic organizations of workers (trade unions) or employers (employers' federations) or of any governmental agencies fixing wage rates and in the presence of real competition between individual workers and employers, one would expect the forces of competition automatically to drive up the money wage rate offered in any particular labour market in which the demand for labour exceeded the supply, and to depress the money wage rate in any particular labour market in which the supply exceeded the demand. Secondly, wage flexibility of the kind here mentioned could be achieved by a system of public wage boards or similar bodies fixing money wage rates in particular labour markets, provided that such bodies accepted the supply-demand principle of raising wage rates where the demand for labour exceeded the supply and lowering wage rates where the supply exceeded the demand.

Let us consider now the position of country B whose economy is kept in external balance by means of financial policy, but as a result is suffering from heavy unemployment. If there is downward flexibility of wage rates in B, money wage rates will decline in all those labour markets in which there is an excess supply of labour over the demand for labour. As wage rates fall in B, the forces of competition will induce a reduction in the prices at which B's products are offered for sale. For producers in B, being able to get labour more cheaply, will at any given level of prices offered for their products find that production is more profitable. So long as the prices offered for their products exceed the cost of producing more of them at the new and lower wage rate, they will, in competition with each other, take on more labour, expand output, and increase their sales. The increased volume of sales of goods and services, confronting any given level of money demand for them, will result in a lower level of prices for such goods and services.

Assuming for the moment that money prices and costs have not fallen in A, the prices of the goods which are imported into B from A will be unchanged while in B all money incomes and money prices of home-produced goods will have fallen *pari passu* with the fall in money wage rates. The terms of international trade will have moved against B, since residents in B receive a lower money price per unit of B's products but pay an unreduced money price for the goods which they import.

As the money prices of B's products fall, while those of A's products do not fall, there will be a shift of demand in both A and B from A's products on to the less expensive products of B. As can be seen from Table VIII and from the discussion of that table on pp. 68–72 above, this shift of demand from A's products on to B's products will cause a favourable movement in B's balance of trade and an unfavourable movement in A's balance of trade, provided that the sum of the elasticities of demand for imports in A and in B is greater than one. This tendency for B's balance of trade to improve will, however, put B out of external balance. Since the authorities in B are *ex hypothesi* adopting a financial policy for external balance, total domestic expenditure must now be expanded in B by means of a fiscal or monetary inflation of the total demand for goods and services, until the increased demand in B for imported goods and services (and the increased consumption in B of B's home products which B's producers would otherwise have exported to A) has again removed the surplus on B's balance of payments and has put B back into external balance. But both the primary shift of demand in A and B on to B's cheaper products and also the expansion of domestic expenditure in B required to put B back into external balance will have increased the demand for B's products and so have served to restore the level of employment in B.

In considering this mechanism for giving greater employment in B without upsetting B's external balance, we must, however, take into account the repercussions in A of the policy adopted in B; and in doing so we must consider the three possible financial policies with which the authorities in A may react to the changes in B's economy. They may adopt a neutral policy, a financial policy for internal balance, or—like the authorities in B—a financial policy for external balance.

In the absence of any capital movements between A and B, there will in general be no repercussions in A from the wage rate reduction in B if the authorities in A adopt either a neutral policy or a financial policy for internal balance. For as B's products undercut A's products as a result of the reduction of wage rates and as B's balance of trade for that reason improves, so—because of the financial policy for external balance in B—the total demand for goods and services is inflated in B until B's balance of trade is restored to what it was before. There is, therefore, in the end no net change in the demand for A's products or in A's balance of trade; the net reduction in expenditure on A's products which threatened to develop because of the fall in money wage rates and prices in B is exactly counterbalanced by the increased demand for A's products brought about by the 'policy' inflation which is undertaken in B in order to preserve B's external balance.[1]

---

[1] The result would, of course, be quite different if, when wage rates fell in B, the authorities in B adopted a neutral policy instead of a financial policy for external balance. In that case B's products would undercut A's products and this tendency would not be offset by an inflation in demand in B sufficient to restore the total demand for A's products. Unemployment would result in A if the authorities in A adopted a neutral policy; or else the authorities in A would have to contrive a 'policy' increase in domestic expenditure if they adopted a financial policy for internal balance.

This conclusion requires some modification if we allow for the effect which the events in B may have on the flow of capital funds between A and B. We have seen that the tendency for B's balance of trade to improve as a result of the cut in her money costs and prices will cause the authorities in B to adopt an expansionist financial policy in order to preserve external balance. If this is brought about by monetary policy, this will mean that interest rates in B will be reduced, which will cause an increased transfer of capital funds from B to A. This factor may be reinforced by the fact that since B's total employment and output (i.e. her real income) will have increased, residents in B will tend to have more real savings to lend to borrowers in A as well as to invest at home. On the other hand, the improved prospect of profits in B's industries associated with the rise in demand for B's products relatively to the money costs of production in B might encourage lending from A to B; and the fall in the money prices of B's products resulting from the decline in money wage rates in B would be a factor reducing the *money* value of any flow of lending from B to A.

If, as a net result of these changes, there were an increase in capital transfers from B to A, the authorities in B would not need to inflate domestic expenditure so much in order to preserve external balance. Part of B's improved balance of trade which resulted from the under-cutting of A's markets by B's cheaper products would have to be allowed to continue since it would be needed to finance the new flow of capital transfers from B to A. In this case there would be some net deflationary effect in A owing to the permanent improvement in B's balance of trade.

If the authorities in A met this with a neutral policy, then there would be some deflationary decline in A leading to a reduction in the demand in A for imports of B's products and possibly also in lending by A's savers to B's borrowers; this would remove part of B's favourable balance of payments, so that the authorities in B could not go so far with their inflationary financial policy for external balance, and in consequence the net increase in the demand for labour in B following a given decline in money wage rates in B would not be so great as would otherwise be the case. If, however, the authorities in A adopted a financial policy for internal balance, the deflationary effects in A of B's permanently im-proved balance of trade would be offset by a 'policy' inflation of domestic expenditure in A; the demand in A for B's products would *pro tanto* be increased and there would be no decline in the income from which saver's in A could lend to borrowers in B; and in consequence the authorities in B could go farther with their expansionary financial policy for external balance than they could if the authorities in A adopted a neutral policy and in consequence the increase in the demand for labour in B following a reduction of the wage rate in B would be somewhat greater.

But these considerations are but minor modifications of the main theme that if, when money wage rates are reduced in B, the authorities in B simultaneously adopt an expansionist financial policy to offset any consequential improvement in B's balance of payments, then the level of employment in B will grow without any disturbance of the internal or external balance of A.

We can conclude, therefore, in general that a reduction in money wage rates in B will lead to an increase in the volume of employment in B when B adopts a financial policy for external balance, because the reduction in the prices of B's products relative to those of A's products will tend to cause a favourable movement in B's balance of trade which, in turn, will enable the authorities in B to expand domestic demand in B and thus enlarge the market for B's products.

This mechanism will, of course, involve some movement in the real terms of international trade against B, because the whole development rests upon there being some reduction in the price of B's products relatively to A's products. This movement in the terms of trade against B will be small (i) if the elasticities of demand for imports in A and B are great because any given reduction in the price of B's products will in such circumstances cause a large favourable movement in B's balance of trade and will therefore permit a large expansion of domestic demand in B for the purpose of preserving external balance, and (ii) if the marginal propensity to import is small in B because, in that case, a very large expansion in domestic demand in B (and so in the demand for B's products) will be necessary in order to stimulate that increase in the demand for imports in B which is necessary to restore external balance.

So far we have considered the effect of a reduction in money wage rates in B on the volume of employment in B only on the assumptions that the authorities in A adopt a neutral policy or a financial policy for internal balance. We have not considered what may happen if the authorities in A also are adopting a financial policy for external balance.

The important point to realize is that in a case of this kind the outcome will be indeterminate unless we can obtain some other information about the factors which allocate, as between the authorities of A and of B, the contribution which each shall make to the maintenance of external balance. Money wage rates are reduced in B; money costs of production fall in B; B's balance of trade becomes favourable and, at the same time, A's balance of trade becomes unfavourable. In order to preserve external balance the authorities in A must now deflate total domestic expenditure in A just as the authorities in B must inflate domestic expenditure in B. But if domestic expenditure is deflated in A a great deal, then the disequilibrium in the balance of trade between A and B will disappear mainly through a fall in the demand in A for imports from B; from B's point of view there will not in fact be much improvement in the balance of payments and, therefore, not very much call for expansion in domestic expenditure in B and not much rise in employment in B. On the other hand, if domestic expenditure is in fact inflated in B quickly and on a large scale as soon as B's balance of payments with A tends to become favourable, the disequilibrium in the balance of payments between A and B will be removed mainly through an increase in the demand in B for A's products; and the authorities in A will not in fact be confronted with any large or enduring deficit in the balance of payments and will not, therefore, in fact have occasion to restrict demand in A at all extensively in the interests of external balance. In short, if B inflates much then A need deflate little; and if A deflates much B need inflate little. Nothing definite can be said about the outcome until it is known on what principle, if any, the contribution of inflation in B and deflation in A towards removing the external disequilibrium is distributed between the two countries.

Moreover, there is another distinction of real importance which must be borne in mind if a financial policy for external balance is adopted in A as well as in B. Are money wage rates in A more or less rigidly fixed so that a deflation of the level of total monetary demand for A's products will cause a reduction of real output and employment in A? Or is there wage flexibility for the maintenance of internal balance in A as well as in B, so that a deflation of the level of total monetary demand for A's products causes a reduction in the money costs and prices of an unchanged real output and employment rather than a reduction of the level of real production and employment at more or less constant prices and costs? In the first case, any given deflation of domestic expenditure in A undertaken to preserve external balance will operate mainly by a reduction in the demand in A for B's products due to a decline in the real purchasing power of A. But, in the second case, deflation in A will operate mainly through the fall in the prices of A's products relatively to those of B's products and the consequent shift of demand away from B's products back on to A's products.

The question how much contribution to the maintenance of external balance will be made through inflation in B and how much through deflation in A when financial policies for external balance are adopted in both A and B receives a determinate answer if there is in operation a single international monetary system such as that provided by the orthodox gold standard. If, when B's balance of payments with A is in surplus, there is a flow of gold or of some other common international monetary reserve, and if the total amount of domestic inflation in B is in some way tied to the total amount of additional gold reserves received by the monetary authorities in B, and if the total amount of domestic deflation in A is in a similar manner tied to the extent of the loss of this same international monetary unit by A's monetary authorities, then there is a factor at work which will determine in any given situation how much the authorities in B should inflate and how much those in A deflate. We will turn our attention to the working of this type of international monetary system in the next chapter.

CHAPTER XIV

THE GOLD STANDARD

W̶E̶ shall in this chapter speak only of the 'gold' standard. But this should be taken merely as typical of any international monetary standard. What we intend to analyse in this chapter is the way in which external and internal balance can simultaneously be maintained if the authorities in A and B both adhere to a common international monetary standard and at the same time obey certain rules of the game. That the standard should be gold is, of course, not at all essential. The standard might be silver or wheat or a combination of commodities (so much gold plus so much silver plus so much wheat plus so much rubber, etc.). Or it might even be an international unit of account invented expressly for the purpose of providing an international monetary standard. Thus some international authority might issue a given number of notes or claims to notes of one kind or another, each note representing one unit of the international monetary unit (Unitas or Bancor, for example); and the monetary authorities of all the countries concerned could then hold these notes as their international monetary reserves and treat these notes in every respect just as the central monetary authorities treat their gold reserves under a gold standard. All that is necessary for the purpose of this chapter is that we should assume there to be some international monetary standard which, purely for the sake of convenience, we will call 'gold'.

The essential rules of the gold standard which must be observed by all the central monetary authorities which are wishing to operate successfully an international monetary standard are four in number:

(i) The monetary authority of each country must take steps to fix the gold value of its own national currency.

(ii) There must be a free import and export of gold into, and out of, each country which is making up the gold-standard system.

(iii) Each monetary authority must make arrangements for the domestic supply of its own money such that the supplies of that money go up in a more or less automatic manner when there is a persistent inflow of gold into its territory, and such that they go down in a more or less automatic manner when there is a persistent export of gold out of its territory.

These three rules are sufficient to ensure external balance between the countries on the gold standard. But in order to ensure internal balance as well a further rule must be observed:

(iv) In each country there must be wage flexibility of the kind described in the preceding chapter.

The implications of wage flexibility (Rule iv) have already been discussed at some length in the preceding chapter; but we must now say something about the implications of each of Rules i, ii, and iii.

Rule i states that the authorities in each of the countries operating the gold standard must take measures to fix the value of gold, within narrow limits, in terms of their own domestic currency. This can be done through one of three mechanisms:

(*a*) Under the *gold-specie standard* the legal tender money of the country in question takes the form of gold coins of a certain fixed gold content. Thus a certain amount of gold will always be coined by the national mint into a $1 coin, and that amount of gold can always be obtained by melting down a $1 coin. In this way the price of that amount of gold cannot rise above $1, since persons can always obtain that amount of gold by obtaining a $1 gold coin for $1; nor can the price of that amount of gold fall below $1, since people can always obtain $1 for that amount of gold by taking it to the national mint to be turned into a $1 coin.

(*b*) Under the *gold-bullion standard* gold coins are not put into circulation but the authority responsible for issuing the money of the country in question (say, dollar notes) undertakes to purchase a given amount of gold for a new $1 note issued by it and to sell this given amount of gold for a $1 note returned to it. Again the value of this amount of gold cannot rise above or fall below $1, since a seller of gold can always get $1 by selling it to the monetary authority for a new $1 note and a buyer of gold can always get gold for $1 by offering $1 in notes for it to the monetary authority.

(*c*) Under a *gold-exchange standard* gold coins are not put into circulation; nor does the monetary authority of the country in question undertake to buy and sell gold at a fixed price in terms of the notes of the country in question. But it undertakes so to buy and sell the money (e.g. notes) of another country which is itself operating a gold-specie or gold-bullion standard. Thus, suppose that the monetary authority of country B (e.g. the United Kingdom) undertook always to purchase four $1 notes for a £1 note or to sell four $1 notes for a £1 note, and that the monetary authority of country A (e.g. the United States) were operating a gold-specie or a gold-bullion standard, then, since £1 would always be worth $4 and $4 would always be worth a given amount of gold, the price of this amount of gold would always be fixed at £1. A purchaser of gold could always obtain it for £1 by obtaining $4 for his £1 note from the monetary authority of B and obtaining the gold with his $4 from the monetary authority of A, and a seller of gold could always obtain £1 for his gold by selling it for $4 to the authority of A and then selling the $4 for £1 to the authority of B.

If the authorities in two countries, A and B, both fix the value of their currencies in terms of gold in one of these ways and if (Rule ii) there is a free import and export of gold in both countries, the value of A's currency (say, the dollar) will, within narrow limits, be fixed in terms of B's currency (say, the pound). Let us suppose that the same amount of gold is bought and sold by the monetary authorities in B for £1 and in A for $4. Then $4 to £1 is the par rate of exchange. Now let us suppose that there is a deficit in B's and a surplus in A's balance of payments. Persons in B with pounds will be purchasing dollars for payments to their creditors in A in greater amount than the persons in A with dollars who are purchasing pounds in order to make payments to their creditors in B. The value of the 'scarce' dollars in the foreign-exchange market will tend to go up in terms of the 'plentiful' pounds; and a £1 note will exchange for something rather less than $4 notes.

But this change cannot go far since the man in B with a payment to make in A can always obtain his $4 notes by taking £1 to the monetary authority of B, obtaining gold with it, exporting the gold to A, and selling the gold to the authority there for $4. This process is not, however, altogether costless. First, there may be some slight cost in obtaining the gold in B, either a slight cost in melting the gold down from a coin (if B is on a gold-specie standard) or a small service charge by the monetary authority in B for selling gold for the £1 note. Second, there will be the actual costs of sending the gold to A which include the cost of shipping, premium for insurance, and loss of interest on the money while the gold is in actual transit. Thirdly, there may be some small charge for turning the gold into dollars in A, either a cost of coinage or a small service charge for the supply of new notes by the monetary authority in A. Suppose that all these costs amount to 5 cents on $4 worth of gold. Then it will pay to purchase dollar notes with pound notes directly in the foreign-exchange market rather than to send gold from B to A, provided that more than $3·95 notes can be obtained directly in exchange for a £1 note. If less dollars than this can be so obtained, it will pay to ship £1 worth of gold to A. In these conditions $3·95 to £1 is said to mark B's gold-export point and A's gold-import point.

Similarly, if it costs 5 cents to send $4 worth of gold from A to B, it will pay anyone in A who has a payment to make in B to give anything up to $4·05 notes directly for £1 note rather than to ship gold to B. But if he has to give more than $4·05 for £1, it will pay him rather to ship gold to B. For this reason $4·05 to £1 is called A's gold-export point and B's gold-import point. Thus the pound can appreciate in value in the foreign-exchange market from its par value of $4·0 for £1 up to $4·05 for £1, or depreciate down to $3·95 for £1. Outside these narrow limits there will be no variation in the exchange rate, but gold will flow to accommodate any deficit or surplus in the balance of payments.

The operation of Rules i and ii will thus bring it about that the rate of exchange between the currencies of the countries on the gold standard is fixed within narrow limits set by the gold-import and gold-export points, and that a deficit country will lose gold while a surplus country will gain gold.

We must turn next to a consideration of Rule iii, which states that domestic monetary arrangements must be such that when gold flows into a country there must be a more or less automatic increase in the domestic supply of money, and vice versa when gold flows out.

The simplest mechanism for ensuring that this relationship holds good is when the domestic circulation of money has a 100-per-cent gold backing. An example of this would be a gold-specie standard where gold was freely minted into coins and where gold coins constituted the only form of money in the community. But other forms of 100-per-cent money can be imagined. The country might be on a gold-bullion standard without any internal circulation of gold coins; but if the banking system would always buy and sell gold freely against notes or bank deposits and if it kept 100 per cent of the notes issued and of its deposit liabilities covered by gold, there would once again be an exact equality between the domestic supply of money and the total amount of gold reserves.

But such 100-per-cent money is most uncommon. In all modern communities only a fraction of the total domestic supply of money is backed by reserves of gold or of other internationally acceptable means of payment. In such cases we must distinguish between two possible cases.

In the first case, which we will call the 'fiduciary-issue principle', only a fraction of the total domestic supply of money is backed by gold, but it remains true that any increase or decrease in the gold reserve will lead to an exactly equal absolute increase or decrease in the domestic supply of money. Thus suppose that in any country the banking system issues $1,000 m. in notes against the backing of loans to producers or in purchase of government securities, but over and above this fixed 'fiduciary issue' will issue notes only dollar for dollar against gold. Then if there is a reserve of gold of $500 m. in the country, the domestic supply of notes will be $1,500 m., so that only one-third is covered by gold. But the loss or gain of $1 in gold will nevertheless cause a decrease or increase of $1 in the domestic monetary supply.

This system can work indefinitely so long as gold is being imported. Every additional $1 of gold imported can be matched by a $1 increase in the domestic supply of money. But there are strict limits to its operation in the case of a loss of gold. Thus suppose that, in the example given in the previous paragraph, external equilibrium demands a reduction in the domestic supply of money from $1,500 m. to $900 m., and it is considered unsafe to allow the gold reserve to drop below $200 m. Then a loss of $300 m. of reserves will have to be accompanied by a reduction of $600 m. in the domestic supply of money. The only safe way to operate the 'fiduciary-issue principle' of a one-to-one ratio between changes in the gold reserve and changes in the domestic supply of money is to have 100-per-cent money.

In the second case, which may be called the 'percentage-reserve principle', once again only a fraction of the total domestic monetary supply is backed by gold, but in this case it is also true that only a percentage of any marginal increase or decrease in the domestic supply of money is backed by gold. Thus, suppose a banking system to work to the simple rule that one-third of any increase or decrease in the domestic supply of money should be backed by gold; then, as before, against a domestic supply of money of $1,500 m. there will be held a gold reserve of $500 m., but if the gold reserve went up or down by $1 the domestic supply of money would go up or down by $3.

In fact the structures of banking systems, even if they work automatically, are likely to be much more complicated than this.[1] Reserves of gold may be held by the central bank on different principles against the note liabilities and the deposit liabilities of the central bank; the commercial banks may hold their reserves partly in notes and partly in deposits with the central bank, and they may have different principles for backing their own deposit liabilities with these reserves; and finally the public may elect to hold little or much of its money in the form of notes (which has one form of gold backing) or in the form of deposits with the commercial banks (which have quite a different indirect gold backing). But all systems will fall into one of three possible categories:

(i) Where the gold reserve is always equal to the domestic supply of money, which we will call the 100-per-cent-money principle;

(ii) where the gold reserve is less than the domestic supply of money, but changes in the gold reserve give rise to equal absolute changes in the domestic supply of money, which we will call the fiduciary-issue principle; and

(iii) where the gold reserve is less than the domestic supply of money, and changes in the gold reserve are also less than the consequential changes in the domestic supply of money, which we will call the percentage-reserve principle.

In fact the percentage-reserve principle is the normal principle, particularly if allowance is made for the point made on p. 181 above. In what follows we shall concentrate attention on this principle, but shall compare its effects from time to time with those of 100-per-cent money.

[1] See my article, 'The Amount of Money and the Banking System', in the *Economic Journal*, March 1934.

In fact, percentage-reserve systems may be of very different types, and it is not our purpose here to go into the various possibilities in any detail, which is a task more appropriate to a Theory of Domestic Economic Policy. But it may suffice to give two examples.

Suppose (i) that the central bank in B operates a fiduciary-issue system as far as notes are concerned under which for every £1 of gold which it receives it issues only £1 more in notes; (ii) that the commercial banks in B keep all their monetary reserves in notes and maintain 1/8 of their deposit liabilities covered by a reserve of notes; and (iii) that the public in B always elect to hold an amount of cash (i.e. notes) equal to 1/20 of the money which they hold on deposit with the commercial banks. Then the total supply of money in B would increase (or decrease) by six times any increase (or decrease) in the gold reserves held by B's central bank. For example, suppose that the central bank in B received an additional £70 m. of gold reserves. The total supply of notes in B would go up by £70 m. because B's central bank is operating a fixed fiduciary-issue system of this kind. Suppose that £20 m. of these additional notes were held by the public and, therefore, £50 m. by the commercial banks as additions to their monetary reserves against which these banks increased their deposit liabilities to the public by £400 m. The amount of money held by the public would go up by £420 m. (£20 m. in the form of additional notes held and £400 m. in the form of additional sums on deposit with the commercial banks) or by six times the receipts of £70 m. of additional gold reserves by the central bank. And all the other monetary conditions in our system would be satisfied: (i) the total amount of notes issued by B's central bank (£20 m. to the public and £50 m. to the commercial banks) would have gone up by the same amount as B's import of gold; (ii) the commercial banks would be keeping 1/8 of their additional deposit liabilities (£400 m.) covered by their additional holdings of notes (£50 m.); and (iii) the public would be holding an additional amount of cash (£20 m. in notes) equal to 1/20 of their additional holdings of money on deposit with the commercial banks (£400 m.).

Suppose at the same time that (i) the central bank in A operates a fixed proportionate-reserve system and always keeps 1/2 of its total notes issued covered by gold reserves; (ii) that the commercial banks in A keep all their monetary reserves in the form of notes issued by A's central bank but keep only 1/16 of their deposit liabilities so covered; and (iii) that the public in A always hold in notes an amount equal to only 1/44 of their total holdings of money on deposit with their commercial banks. Then the total increase in the supply of money in A (i.e. the public's holding of notes and of deposits with the commercial banks) would be equal to no less than 24 times any increase in its gold reserves. For example, suppose that the central bank in A received $15 m. in gold. Then the total increase in monetary supplies in A would be 24 times this, or $360 m., of which $352 m. would be held by the public in the form of deposits with the commercial banks and the remaining $8 m. (or 1/44 of $352 m.) in the form of notes. Against the additional deposit liabilities of $352 m. the commercial banks would hold an additional reserve of notes of $22 m. (or 1/16 of $352 m.) so that the increase in the total note issue would be $30 m. ($8 m. to be held by the public and $22 m. by the commercial banks); and against its increased note issue of $30 m. the central bank would be holding $15 m. in additional gold, i.e. a reserve ratio of 1/2.

We have in the above example a case in which a flow of gold from B to A would cause the supply of money in B to contract by 6 times that amount and the supply of money in A to expand by 24 times that amount. We have spoken in this example as if the reactions of the banking systems in A and B were purely automatic. This may, of course, not be the case. The actual reserve ratios which the various parts of the banking system observe may be in large part discretionary. The banking authorities may 'offset' a gold loss by reducing the existing reserve ratios so that the domestic supply of money is kept above its normal relationship to the gold reserve, or it may 'sterilize' a gold gain by raising the existing reserve ratios and thereby keeping the domestic supply of money abnormally low in relation to the gold reserve.[1]

But in any case, in order that the gold standard should work effectively Rule iii must be observed in some form; there must be a reduction (or increase) in the domestic supply of money when gold is lost out of (or gained into) the reserve. It is clear from what has been said that, even when allowance has been made for an element of discretion in management, in modern gold-standard systems (i) the total supply of money is likely to change by many times the change in the gold reserves, and (ii) the reaction of the domestic supply of money to a given change in the gold reserve may be much greater in one country than in another. Both these facts have important implications.

The fact that the reaction of the domestic supply of money to a change in gold reserves may differ in our two countries, A and B, means that in order to remove a disequilibrium in the balance of payments between them, one of them may have to carry out much more of the adjustment than the other. Thus, in the numerical example which we have just given a flow of gold reserves from B to A of, say, £100 m. (or $400 m.) would cause the total supply of money in B to go down by £600 m. and in A to go up by $9,600 m. (or £2,400 m.). Because of the differences in the various banking and monetary ratios in the two countries four times as great an absolute domestic adjustment of the supply of money would fall upon A as upon B. In other words, the authorities in the country

[1] See pp. 204–5, below.

with the lowest marginal ratio of gold reserves to domestic monetary supplies will have to undertake an unduly large share of the adjustment, by deflation if it is the deficit country and by inflation if it is the surplus country.[1]

But there is a more important disadvantage of the percentage-reserve system, which would still remain even if both countries maintained the same ratio between changes in gold reserves and changes in the domestic supplies of money. Suppose that B has a balance-of-payments deficit with A. Then with a percentage-reserve system the deflation of the supply of money each year in B and the inflation in the supply of money each year in A will have to be many times as great as the annual flow of gold from B to A, which will be equal to the annual deficit in B's balance of payments with A. But with a 100-per-cent-money system the deflation in the supply of money each year in B and the inflation in A need be only equal to this annual flow of gold. In other words, with the former system any necessary adjustments in the domestic supplies of money must be carried out much more quickly than with the latter system.

The final adjustment of relative prices, money incomes, total domestic supplies of money, etc., in A and B required to get rid of a given deficit in the balance of payments between B to A may be the same under both systems. But with the system of 100-per-cent money the necessary adjustment will be much more easy to attain than with the percentage-reserve system, since in the former case both countries will have much more time in which to carry out the required adjustment. If, therefore, a common international monetary standard is to be adopted, there are strong arguments for having a single common money which constitutes 100 per cent of the actual domestic monetary circulation in both countries rather than an international reserve held by each central bank in small quantities which represent only a small percentage reserve against the total domestic monetary supplies of each country.

From the point of view of Rule iii, certain special problems arise in the case of the gold-exchange standard. In this case the central bank of, say, B, instead of holding a reserve of gold, holds a reserve of the money of A (e.g. A's currency notes or deposit liabilities of A's banks), and pays out these holdings of A's money to anyone in B who wishes to purchase them at a predetermined price. (See p. 179.) If B has an

---

[1] The strain involved in any adjustment does not, of course, depend upon the absolute size of the adjustment so much as upon its size relatively to the size of the country's total economy. Thus suppose that a flow of reserves from B to A involves a reduction in the national income in B by £100 m. and a rise in the national income in A by the same amount; but suppose that B's economy were only half as large as A's, B having a national income of £1,000 m. and A of £2,000 m. Then the same absolute adjustment of £100 m. in the money national income of each country will involve a 10-per-cent deflation of income in B but only a 5-per-cent inflation in A.

annual deficit of £100 m. (or $400 m.) with A, then the central bank in B will be paying out $400 m. of its holdings of A's money each year to people in B who have these payments to make in A. The banking system in B will then have to reduce the total supply of money in B in exactly the same way as it would have done if B had lost £100 m. of an ordinary gold reserve.

But how will the banking system in A react to the change? There are at least two possibilities.

The monetary authorities in A may treat the dollar notes and deposits which B's central bank holds instead of gold reserves just as it treats the dollar notes and deposits which ordinary persons and businesses in A hold. In this case, when the central bank of B loses part of its holdings of A's dollar notes and deposits there will be no repercussion upon the total supply of dollar notes and deposits by A's banking system. The domestic circulation of notes and deposits in A will go up by an amount exactly equal to the reduction in the amount of A's notes and deposits held by the central bank of B. From the point of view of the readjustment in A it will be exactly as if A were operating an ordinary gold standard with a one-to-one ratio between changes in gold reserves and changes in the domestic supply of money; the supply of money in A will go up by an amount exactly equal to A's balance-of-payments surplus with B. But this will, of course, mean that the greater part of the monetary adjustment will have to fall on B. If the banking and monetary ratios in B are such that the total supply of money in B changes by six times any change in B's central-bank holding of gold reserves or of gold-exchange reserves, then the deflation in B will be six times as great as the inflation in A.

The monetary authorities in A may, however, regard the dollar notes and deposits held by B's central bank in a different light from the dollar notes and deposits held by the ordinary residents of A. The dollar notes and deposits held by B's central bank constitute an international monetary reserve which may be used at any time for the making of payments by residents in B to residents in other countries. In a world in which A and B were the only countries this would be of little importance to A's monetary authorities since the central bank in B could use its holdings of A's currency only to finance a payment to a resident in A. But if we allow for the existence of other countries (whom we will call C), the position is very different. In that case B's monetary authorities may at any time wish to use their holding of A's currency to finance a deficit which B has with C.

At this point we must distinguish between (i) the case in which C is also on the gold-exchange standard with C's central-bank reserves being held in the form of holdings of A's money and (ii) the case in which C is on a gold-specie standard, a gold-bullion standard, or a gold-exchange standard with C's central-bank reserves being held in the form of holdings of another country's (say, D's) money.

If, in case i, country B is in deficit and country C in surplus, the excess payment from B to C will be financed by a transfer of some of A's money from B's central-bank reserve to C's central-bank reserve. The adjustment between the deficit country B and the surplus country C will take place just as if both had been on the gold-bullion standard with A's money taking the place of gold bullion. An excess payment from B to C financed in this way will have no effect upon A to whose authorities it is presumably a matter of indifference whether A's money is held by the central bank of B or of C. In other words, if all the countries of the world are on a gold-exchange standard except one which constitutes the 'parent' country in whose money the central-bank reserves of all the others are held, then a payment from one ordinary member of the system to another (e.g. B to C) will have the normal gold-bullion-standard effect of deflating the central-bank reserve in the paying country and inflating it in the receiving country. A payment from a member country to the parent country (B to A) will also have the normal gold-bullion-standard effect of deflating the central-bank reserve in the paying country; but it will not directly affect the central-bank reserve in the parent country, whose domestic monetary supply will be increased only by the actual release of its money from the central-bank reserves of the member country.

But in case ii above (in which country C is not on a gold-exchange standard with its central-bank reserves held in A's money) the reaction of a payment from B to C upon A's monetary situation will be very different. When B transfers the payment to C, the central bank in C withdraws gold from A's central-bank reserves in order to add to C's own domestic gold circulation (if C is on a gold-specie standard) or to add to C's own central-bank reserves of gold (if C is on a gold-bullion standard) or to pay over to D's banking system (if C is on a gold-exchange standard with its reserves held in D's money). In any case the central bank of the 'parent' country A will lose gold reserves if a member country B has to finance a deficit with a non-member country C.[1]

In view of this possibility the monetary authorities in A may well decide to count as their own free gold reserves only their holding of gold less the amount of A's currency which B's central bank is holding as its monetary reserves. In this case the operation of the gold-exchange standard will differ in no essential from the operation of the gold-bullion standard even in the case of payments between A and B. If, for example, B has a deficit with A, then B's central bank will lose reserves

[1] It should be noted that this analysis of a gold-exchange standard is applicable to any foreign-exchange standard, e.g. to a sterling standard where the central banks of certain 'sterling-area' countries keep their reserves in the form of balances of sterling on deposit in London banks.

to that extent and A's central bank will also add to its own free gold reserves to the same extent and will expand the supply of money in A accordingly.

Now the gold-exchange standard was in historical fact developed largely for the purpose of economizing gold. It was hoped that B's central bank could operate a gold standard without increasing the demand for gold if, instead of holding an actual gold reserve, it held a reserve of the notes or deposit liabilities of A's banks, A being itself on a gold-bullion standard. But in view of the above analysis we may conclude that *either* the gold-exchange standard does not economize gold,[1] *or* the gold-exchange standard imposes upon the country which is operating the gold-exchange standard a quite undue part of the burden of any readjustment which may be necessary between a country operating a gold-exchange standard and the country in whose money the gold-exchange reserves of the former are held.[2]

We have now examined at some length the way in which, and the extent to which, under different banking systems a variation in the gold reserves will affect the domestic supply of money. We may now briefly indicate the main effect of this Rule iii of the gold standard, whereby the total domestic supply of money varies more or less automatically in the same direction as the country's gold reserves.

Now there are, broadly speaking, two factors which determine the demand for money in any country: first, the total volume of monetary transactions to be financed per period of time; and, second, the rate of return which could be obtained by investing any holdings of money in securities or in other non-monetary assets. These matters cannot be examined at length here; their detailed consideration would be more appropriate to a Theory of Domestic Economic Policy. Here it must suffice to say that it is always convenient to hold one's wealth in the liquid form of money which gives ready and instantaneous purchasing power over goods and services, but that some loss is involved in so doing, since a return (in the form of interest on money loaned to other persons, or profits on shares held in business enterprises, or a capital profit on commodities or other real assets whose price is expected to go up) could be expected on the capital if it were invested in non-monetary assets instead of being held in a liquid monetary form. A man is, therefore, more likely to hold more money (i) the higher is the total volume of monetary transactions which he may be called upon to finance, since in this case there is great convenience in holding money, and (ii) the lower is the rate of interest or other form of return expected to be gained

[1] This will be so in our example if A's central bank counts as its own 'free' gold reserves only its holding of gold over and above the holding of A's currency by B's central bank.

[2] This will be so in our example if A's central bank does not increase the total supply of money in A when B's central bank loses reserves to A.

on other non-monetary capital assets, since in this case he sacrifices a smaller extra return by holding additional money in a liquid form instead of investing it in non-monetary assets. Thus the demand for money to hold in liquid form in any country will be greater (i) the higher is that country's money national income, and (ii) the lower is the rate of interest in that country.

Rule iii implies that when a deficit country loses gold something will happen more or less automatically to reduce the supply of money in that country; and this implies that, unless something else has simultaneously occurred to reduce the demand for goods and services and so the volume of transactions to be financed in that country, the rate of interest will rise as monetary funds become scarcer until people are willing to reduce their demands for money in line with the reduced supplies of money. And this (in our terminology) is equivalent to the pursuit by the authorities in the deficit country of an automatic deflationary monetary policy for the restoration of external balance. Thus, the effect of Rule iii in a deficit country is that, one way or another, there will be a deflation of the money demand for goods and services so long as the deficit on the balance of payments continues.

Similarly, Rule iii implies that in any surplus country which is gaining gold the domestic supply of money shall be increased and thus, unless something else has simultaneously occurred to increase the volume of transactions to be financed in that country, that the rate of interest should fall until people are willing to hold the increased supply of money. But this is the same as the adoption by the authorities in the surplus country of an inflationary monetary policy for the restoration of external balance. Thus, for one reason or another, there will be an inflation of the demand for goods and services so long as the surplus on the balance of payments continues.

CHAPTER XV

THE OPERATION OF THE GOLD STANDARD AND OF VARIABLE EXCHANGE RATES COMPARED[1]

IT is our purpose in this chapter to consider and to compare the operation of two out of the many possible world systems for combining financial policies and price adjustments in such a way as to preserve internal and external balance in all countries.

The first system is that of the gold standard which we have just described and which in effect means the automatic use in all countries of monetary policy for the maintenance of external balance and of wage flexibility for the maintenance of internal balance. The second system is that in which financial policy is employed in all countries for the maintenance of internal balance and variable exchange rates are used for maintaining external balance.

It will be a chief object of this chapter to show that both these mechanisms are essentially of the same nature in 'real' terms. Both operate to maintain the two objectives of internal and external balance by the combined use of the two means, first, of a financial policy of expansion or contraction of total domestic expenditure and, second, of an alteration in the relative prices of the products of the two countries making up our international system. This last change is brought about under the gold standard mechanism by a reduction in the domestic level of money wage rates and prices in the deficit country and by a rise in money wage rates and prices in the surplus country: in the case of variable exchange rates it is achieved by a depreciation of the value of the currency of the deficit country in terms of the currency of the surplus country. But if we abstract for the moment from certain complicating factors (such as the existence of debts fixed in terms of the currency of one or the other country; or the effect of variations in exchange rates upon speculative capital movements; or the differences that may exist in the ease of adjustment of wage rates on the one hand and of exchange rates on the other), the two mechanisms bring about fundamentally the same 'real' adjustments to any given spontaneous disturbance.

Let us, then, assume that both A and B start in internal and external balance and that some spontaneous disturbance then occurs to upset this equilibrium. We will then examine how internal and external balance is restored on two assumptions. Our first assumption will be that the authorities in both A and B follow the four rules of the gold

---

[1] The subject matter of this chapter is treated in Section VIII (vi) of the separate mathematical supplement.

standard: by fixing the value of their currencies in terms of gold; by permitting the free import and export of gold; by inflating or deflating the domestic supplies of money in a more or less automatic way as they receive or lose gold; and by institutional arrangements which mean that money wage rates continue to rise (or to fall) as long as there is an excess demand for (or supply of) labour on the labour market. Our second assumption will be that the authorities in both A and B maintain internal balance by means of a financial policy for the expansion (or contraction) of their general levels of domestic expenditure so long as there is an excess supply of (or demand for) labour in their labour markets and that they preserve external balance between them by allowing the currency of the deficit country to depreciate in terms of the currency of the surplus country.

Let us start, then, by considering the effect on these two sets of assumptions of a spontaneous increase in foreign lending from A to B which is unaccompanied by any spontaneous change in demand for A's or B's products. Savers in A simply decide to invest their money on B's rather than on A's stock exchange. The operation of the gold-standard mechanism and of the mechanism of variable exchange rates in view of this disturbance is set out schematically in Table XIII.

Let us consider the left-hand half of this table which outlines the operation of the gold-standard mechanism.

The increased flow of capital transfers from A to B causes A to have a deficit and B a surplus in the balance of payments; A's exchange rate depreciates slightly to A's gold-export point; gold flows from A to B; as a result of the movement of gold reserves there is a contraction in the domestic supply of money in A and an expansion in B. So far there has been no change in the level of output, employment, prices, imports, or exports in either country, so that the demand for money to finance business transactions will be so far unchanged in both countries. But since the supply of money has been reduced in A and increased in B, there will be a scarcity of funds on A's capital market and an excess on B's. Interest rates will rise in A and will fall in B. This will itself reduce the incentive for capital transfers from A to B and increase the incentive for capital transfers from B to A; and this will be the first factor at work restoring equilibrium to the balance of payments between A and B.

But the higher rates of interest in A will lead to some reduction in total domestic expenditure in A; and, similarly, the lower rates of interest in B will lead to some expansion of domestic expenditure in B. Now if there is any marginal propensity to import in A and any marginal propensity to import in B, the reduction in domestic expenditure in A will involve some reduction in the demand in A for imports from B and the increase in domestic expenditure in B will involve some

TABLE XIII

The Operation of the Gold Standard and of Variable Exchange Rates with a Spontaneous Increase in Foreign Lending from A to B

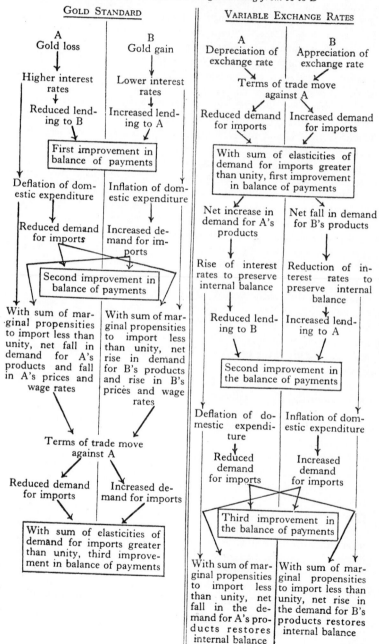

GOLD STANDARD | VARIABLE EXCHANGE RATES

A
Gold loss

B
Gold gain

A
Depreciation of exchange rate

B
Appreciation of exchange rate

Higher interest rates

Lower interest rates

Terms of trade move against A

Reduced lending to B

Increased lending to A

Reduced demand for imports

Increased demand for imports

First improvement in balance of payments

With sum of elasticities of demand for imports greater than unity, first improvement in balance of payments

Deflation of domestic expenditure

Inflation of domestic expenditure

Net increase in demand for A's products

Net fall in demand for B's products

Reduced demand for imports

Increased demand for imports

Rise of interest rates to preserve internal balance

Reduction of interest rates to preserve internal balance

Second improvement in balance of payments

Reduced lending to B

Increased lending to A

With sum of marginal propensities to import less than unity, net fall in demand for A's products and fall in A's prices and wage rates

With sum of marginal propensities to import less than unity, net rise in demand for B's products and rise in B's prices and wage rates

Second improvement in the balance of payments

Deflation of domestic expenditure

Inflation of domestic expenditure

Terms of trade move against A

Reduced demand for imports

Increased demand for imports

Reduced demand for imports

Increased demand for imports

Third improvement in the balance of payments

With sum of elasticities of demand for imports greater than unity, third improvement in balance of payments

With sum of marginal propensities to import less than unity, net fall in the demand for A's products restores internal balance

With sum of marginal propensities to import less than unity, net rise in the demand for B's products restores internal balance increase in the demand in B for imports from A. Because of these changes in total demand in the two countries the value of A's exports will rise and of A's imports will fall; and this is a second main factor restoring equilibrium to the balance of payments. A's balance of trade will have become more favourable, and this will help to cover the spontaneous increase in capital transfers from A to B.

If the sum of the marginal propensities to import in A and in B were equal to unity, these changes would not have any net effect upon the total demand for B's products or for A's products. Suppose, for example, that the rise in interest rates in A and the fall in interest rates in B had caused domestic expenditure in A to fall by $100 m. and in B to rise by $100 m.; then, as can be seen from case i of Table IX (p. 90), with the sum of the marginal propensities to import in A and in B equal to unity there would be an improvement in A's balance of trade also equal to $100 m. But there would be no net change in the total demand for A's or for B's products and no disturbance of their internal balance. The two factors which we have described above—namely the encouragement of a capital transfer from B to A as a result of the higher interest rates in A and lower interest rates in B, and the reduced demand for imports in A and increased demand for imports in B resulting from the deflation of domestic expenditure in A and inflation of domestic expenditure in B, which were themselves due to the rise in interest rates in A and the fall in B—would in this case have to deal with the whole of the disturbance to external balance brought about by the spontaneous increase in foreign lending from A to B. In fact, gold would flow from A to B until interest rates had fallen in B and risen in A to the extent necessary to bring this result about; and there would be no disturbance to internal balance in the process.

But if the sum of the marginal propensities to import in A and in B is less than unity (which is the normal case), then—as can be seen from case iii of Table IX (p. 91)—a fall in domestic expenditure in A brought about by the higher interest rates in A combined with a rise in domestic expenditure in B brought about by lower interest rates in B will cause a net fall in the demand for A's products and a net rise in the demand for B's products. As a result of this the total national income in A will decline and in B will rise. But we are assuming that both countries start in internal balance and that there is also wage flexibility in both. In this case there will be no net change in employment in A or B, but the money wage rate will fall in A and will rise in B. The money costs and prices of B's products will rise in relation to those of A's products; the terms of trade will move against A; and, as a result, if the sum of the elasticities of demand for imports in A and in B is greater than unity (see Table VIII on p. 69), the balance of payments will move still further in A's favour. This is the third factor which will be at work restoring external balance. The movement of gold from A to B will continue until these three factors are all operating on such a scale that they completely offset the primary unfavourable movement in A's balance of payments due to the spontaneous increase of foreign lending from A to B. At this point a new external balance will be achieved; and internal balance will still be maintained, although the money wage and price levels in A and B will have changed.

We may now consider how the mechanism of variable exchange rates would have worked when confronted with this same spontaneous increase in foreign lending from A to B. This is shown schematically on the right-hand half of Table XIII, where it will be seen that the same three influences are at work restoring external balance, although in a different order and by rather different means.

With variable exchange rates, the immediate effect of the increased transfer of capital funds from A to B is to increase the demand of A's residents for B's currency so that the value of A's currency in terms of B's currency depreciates. This depreciation of A's currency will make A's products cheaper relatively to B's products; and, provided that the sum of the elasticities of demand for imports in A and in B is greater than one (see Table VIII on p. 69) this will cause A's balance of trade to become more favourable. This is the first factor restoring external balance between the two countries.

This improvement in A's balance of trade will, however, upset internal balance in A and B. It will represent a net increase in expenditure on A's products and a net decrease in expenditure on B's products. In order to preserve internal balance the authorities in A must, therefore, adopt a deflationary financial policy and those in B an inflationary financial policy. If the authorities in both A and B adopt monetary policies for this purpose, this will involve some rise in interest rates in A and some fall in interest rates in B with the result that the incentive to lend from A to B will be reduced. The change in capital transfers between A and B induced by this change in interest rates will thus constitute a second influence restoring external balance between A and B.

As we have just seen, the rise in interest rates in A is brought about by monetary policy in order to reduce domestic expenditure in A, in order to reduce the demand for A's products, in order to preserve internal balance in A. But, provided that there is any marginal propensity to import in A, this reduction in domestic expenditure in A will cause a reduction in the demand in A for imports from B. At the same time the fall in interest rates in B which has been brought about by monetary policy in B in order to increase the total demand for B's products in the interests of B's internal balance, will cause an increase in domestic expenditure in B and so some increase in the demand in

B for imports from A. This change in the balance of payments between A and B will be the third factor restoring external balance between A and B.

Now if the sum of the marginal propensities to import in A and in B are less than unity these factors will effectively restore internal balance in the two countries. A reduction of domestic· expenditure in A by, say, $100 m. combined with a simultaneous increase in domestic expenditure in B by the same amount will improve A's balance of trade by something less than $100 m. but will also cause a net decrease in the demand for A's products and increase in the demand for B's products. (See case iii of Table IX on p. 91.) And this is what is wanted in order to restore internal balance in the two countries.

But if the sum of the marginal propensities to import were equal to unity then (see case i of Table IX) a reduction of domestic expenditure in A by $100 m. combined with an increase of domestic expenditure in B by $100 m. would cause an improvement of $100 m. in A's balance of trade but it would not in fact help to restore internal balance at all, since it would not cause any net change in the total demand either for A's or for B's products. The deflation by monetary policy in A and the inflation by monetary policy in B would apparently have to go on more or less indefinitely in a vain attempt to reduce the excess demand for A's products and to increase the deficient demand for B's products.

But in fact internal balance would be achieved by a different route. As the deflation of domestic expenditure proceeded in A and the inflation in B, so imports into A from B would be reduced and imports into B from A increased. Simultaneously the higher and higher interest rates in A and the lower and lower interest rates in B would induce a larger and larger movement of capital funds from B to A. These two factors would together do more and more to cope with the whole of the primary deficit in A's balance of payments due to the spontaneous increase in foreign lending from A to B. There would, therefore, be less and less need for any depreciation in A's currency which resulted only from A's net balance of payments deficit. There would, therefore, be a smaller and smaller improvement in A's balance of trade resulting from any shift of demand away from B's products on to A's products as a result of the movement in the terms of trade against A. But this shift of demand was (see p. 194 above) the only thing which had upset internal balance in A and B by causing a net increase in the demand for A's products and decrease in the demand for B's products. If the sum of the marginal propensities to import were in fact as high as unity, in the end there would be no depreciation of A's currency and no upset of internal balance; and external balance would (as in the case of the gold standard) be achieved by two factors: first, the increased flow of capital from B to A induced by the rise of interest rates in A and their fall in B and, second, the increased demand for imports in B and the reduced demand for imports in A due to the inflation of domestic expenditure in B and its deflation in A. No change in the terms of trade would be necessary.

It must suffice to give only two further illustrations, and that in much less detail, in order to complete our comparison between the workings of the gold standard and of variable exchange rates. The two other spontaneous disturbances which we will consider for purposes of illustration are (i) a spontaneous increase in domestic expenditure in country A, and (ii) a spontaneous shift of demand away from country B's products on to country A's products.

Let us suppose, then, that there is an improvement in business expectations in country A as a result of which producers in A decide, at the current rate of interest, to borrow more capital funds for domestic expenditure on goods and services for extensions of capital equipment of all kinds. The stage is set for a regular economic boom in A.

Under the mechanism of the gold standard the process of adjustment will be as follows. In A the increased demand for goods and services will cause an increased demand for A's products and thus in conditions of wage flexibility an increase in the general level of money wages and prices. There will result an increase in the rate of interest in A because there will be an increased demand for money to finance the greater volume of monetary transactions which results from the general rise in money prices and costs.

There will be a further factor causing the rate of interest to rise in A. The rise in the money prices and costs of A's products will tend to move the terms of trade against B, and thus, if the sum of the elasticities of demand for imports in A and in B is greater than unity, to cause a deficit in A's balance of trade. Gold will move from A to B, and for this reason the rate of interest will rise still further in A. The rise in the rate of interest in A will in itself be a factor keeping down the total real demand for goods and services in A and will thus help to offset the effects of the spontaneous increase in A's domestic expenditure.

In B two things will be happening. There will have been a net increase in the demand for B's products because of the increase in the demand in A for B's products. Since there is wage flexibility in B the general level of money wages and prices will rise in B. This will cause the demand for money in B to rise; but there is no reason to expect a rise in the rate of interest in B because at the same time the supply of money in B will be rising because of the import of gold into B.

Let us suppose for the moment that the rise in the rate of interest in A has no effect in encouraging a flow of capital transfers from B

to A. In that case we shall settle down to a new equilibrium in which
(i) money prices and wage rates have risen equally in A and B, the
increased demand for money which this will cause being met by the
reduced demand for money in A due to the higher rate of interest in
A, (ii) the rate of interest in A will have risen to an extent sufficient to
offset the whole of the spontaneous increase in domestic expenditure
so that the total demand for goods and services in A has remained
unchanged except for the increase in their money prices, and (iii)
there is no change in the real terms of trade or in the balance of trade
between A and B. In fact all that has happened is that the rate of
interest has risen in A sufficiently to preserve internal balance in A by
restraining the spontaneous increase in domestic expenditure in A, but
this rise in interest rates in A has reduced the demand for money to
some extent which has allowed some overall equal rise in all money
prices in A and B. No real change of any kind except the higher interest
rate in A has occurred.

But if the rise in the rate of interest in A should cause some flow
of capital funds from B to A, then some modification of the above
analysis is required. In this case, in the new equilibrium there must
be some deficit in A's balance of trade by which the induced flow of
capital from B to A can be covered. This will be achieved in the
following way. As the rise in interest rates in A causes some flow of
lending from B to A less gold will flow from A to B; the inflation can,
therefore, go rather further in A and less far in B; money wage rates
and prices will rise more in A than in B; the terms of trade will move
in A's favour; this (if the sum of the elasticities of demand is greater
than one) will cause some net shift of expenditure from A's on to B's
products which will give rise to the required balance of trade surplus
for B; interest rates will go up rather less in A and they will rise in
B; this will mean that domestic expenditure is rather higher in A and
lower in B than would otherwise have been the case; and this in turn
will preserve internal balance in A and in B, offsetting the deflationary
effects in A of A's balance of trade deficit and the inflationary effects
in B of B's balance of trade surplus.

The mechanism of these changes is essentially the same, although
considerably easier to follow, under a system of variable exchange
rates. In this case the spontaneous increase in domestic expenditure
in A will threaten to disturb A's internal balance by increasing the
total demand for A's products. Since we are assuming a monetary
policy in A expressly devised to maintain internal balance in A, the
monetary authorities in A will now restrict the total supply of money
in A and raise interest rates in A until the incentive to increase domestic
expenditure in A has been wholly removed by the higher cost of
borrowing new capital funds in A.

This would be the end of the matter if the rise in interest rates in A did not give rise to any increased lending from B to A. If, however, it does do so, B's currency will depreciate in terms of A's currency; the terms of trade will move against B; with the sum of the elasticities of demand for imports in A and in B greater than unity there will be a net shift of demand from A's products on to B's products and a deficit in A's balance of trade which will cover the increased lending from B to A; but to preserve internal balance in the face of this shift of demand from A's on to B's products a lower rate of interest and so a higher level of domestic expenditure will now be required in A than would otherwise have been the case and some increase in the rate of interest and a consequential reduction in domestic expenditure will be needed in B.

Let us finally consider the effects under the gold standard and under a system of variable exchange rates of a spontaneous shift of demand from B's on to A's products.

Under the gold standard, gold will immediately move from B to A as B's balance of payments will be put into deficit by the increased demand in B for imports from A or by the reduced demand in A for imports from B. But there is no reason to expect any change in interest rates in A or B. For while the domestic supply of money in B is falling as gold flows from B to A, at the same time the demand for money in B for the finance of business transactions will also be falling. The shift of demand away from B's products will have reduced the total demand for labour in B and with wage flexibility the general level of money wage rates and prices in B will be falling.

At the same time in A the supply of money will be rising as gold is received from B, but the demand for money will also be rising as the general level of money wage rates and prices rises in A because of the increased demand for A's products due to the shift of demand on to A's goods and services.

The terms of trade will thus be moving against B as the prices of B's products fall and of A's products rise. This will cause a shift of expenditure back again from A's products on to B's cheaper products, provided that the sum of the elasticities of demand for imports is greater than unity. This process of change in relative prices will go on until there has been a shift of expenditure back again from A's products on to B's products sufficient to offset the primary spontaneous shift in the opposite direction. A new equilibrium will be found without any change in interest rates in either country but with the terms of trade having moved against B. How much of this movement in the terms of trade against B will have been brought about by a fall in the prices of B's products and how much by a rise in the prices of A's products will depend upon the extent to which the total supply of money in each country responds to a change in its gold reserves and upon the relative size of the total national incomes of the two countries in the way described in the last chapter.

The above analysis may need some modification if there is already any considerable flow of capital transfers from A to B and from B to A before the disturbance took place. The fact that money prices and money income in B will be lower after the change than before may mean that, measured in terms of money, less is lent from B to A than before the change. Similarly, the rise in money income and prices in A may mean that more is lent from A to B than before the change. In this case there will be some net increase in the flow of capital funds from A to B. This will mean that not quite so much gold is lost from B to A; and that wage rates do not fall so much in B nor rise so much in A, so that the terms of trade are not quite so unfavourable to B. In consequence B's balance of trade deficit with A will not completely disappear, but in part will be financed by the net flow of capital from A to B. Interest rates will in this case fall slightly in B and rise slightly in A as a result of the fact that B has somewhat more gold and A somewhat less; and this will mean that domestic expenditure is somewhat greater in B and less in A than would otherwise be the case, which serves to preserve internal balance in both countries in spite of the fact that there is now a deficit on B's and a surplus on A's balance of trade.

With variable exchange rates the process of adjustment is very easy to follow. The spontaneous shift of demand from B's products on to A's products will cause B's currency to depreciate; this will turn the terms of trade against B; with the sum of the elasticities of demand for imports greater than unity, this will cause a shift of expenditure back from A's products on to B's products; and when this process has gone sufficiently far to offset the primary spontaneous shift of expenditure away from B's products the new equilibrium will be fully restored without any other change.

But if there has been a considerable flow of capital from A to B and from B to A before the change, the depreciation of B's currency will mean that a flow of lending from A to B of a constant amount in A's currency will be worth more of B's currency, or, alternatively, that a flow of capital from B to A of a constant amount in terms of B's currency will be worth less of A's currency. For this reason the depreciation of B's currency may cause the appearance of an increase in the net flow of capital from A to B. This will mean that B's currency need not depreciate quite so much; the terms of trade will not move quite so far against B; B's balance of trade deficit will not be entirely removed but will be covered in part by this increase in the net flow of capital from A to B; there will, however, have to be a deflationary monetary policy and rise in interest rates in A in order to reduce domestic expenditure in A to offset the inflationary effects of A's balance of trade surplus; and, conversely, to preserve internal balance in B in spite of B's balance of trade deficit there will be somewhat lower interest rates and higher domestic expenditure in B.[1]

[1] It is interesting to observe the difference in the process of adjustment when the disturbing factor is (i) a transfer from one country to another and (ii) a shift of demand from the products of one country on to those of another. In case ii, if full employment is to be maintained, equilibrium depends essentially upon the 'classical' mechanism of price adjustment through a reduction of money prices and costs in the deficit country relatively to those in the surplus country. But in case i there are two other equilibrating forces. First, interest rates will permanently rise in the deficit, and fall in the surplus country, thereby inducing some capital movements from the latter to the former. Secondly, domestic expenditure in real terms will be permanently reduced in the deficit and raised in the surplus country; and this change in real demand will help to restore equilibrium in the absence of price changes. Indeed, if the sum of the marginal propensities to import is equal to one, equilibrium will be restored without any price changes. This may help to explain why in some cases it has been found that equilibrium has been restored without unemployment but with surprisingly little of the 'classical' mechanism of price adjustment.

CHAPTER XVI

THE CONDITIONS NECESSARY FOR
EFFECTIVE PRICE ADJUSTMENTS

W E have described in some detail the way in which mechanisms for price adjustment such as those of wage flexibility or of variable exchange rates may be expected to operate. We can now proceed to deduce from this discussion what conditions must be fulfilled if these methods are to prove effective for the preservation of internal and external balance. We shall consider these conditions under five main heads.

Condition 1. *Flexibility of Real Wage Rates*

We have already seen that for the gold-standard mechanism to operate in such a way as to preserve internal as well as external balance, there must be a sufficient degree of wage flexibility in the sense that the general level of money wage rates must continuously fall (or rise) so long as there is an excess supply of (or demand for) labour in the economy.

Such wage flexibility is a matter of degree. In some economies the labour market may be so organized that money wage rates are extremely flexible; for example, the existence of an overall unemployment percentage of 5 per cent might (where there was great labour mobility, little monopoly organization of workers or employers for fixing wage rates, and no State fixation of money wage rates) be sufficient to cause the general level of money wage rates to fall by, say, 5 per cent per annum so long as it lasted. Where the institutional factors in the labour market are such that large pressures of unemployment will cause only small and slow adjustments of wage rates the opposite might be true; a 20 per cent level of unemployment might cause a decline in money wage rates of less than 5 per cent per annum.

There is thus no absolute criterion by which it can be decided whether there is sufficient wage flexibility to operate the gold-standard mechanism successfully. It depends upon the degree of wage rate adjustment which it is expected that the adoption of this mechanism will demand; and that depends upon other factors which will be discussed later in this chapter under Conditions 2, 3, 4, and 5. If it were judged that there were insufficient flexibility of *money* wage rates to meet the demands which were likely to be put upon a gold-standard system, then some other mechanism of adjustment (such as variable exchange rates) would have to be chosen in its place.[1]

But it would be useless to turn to the mechanism of variable exchange rates unless there were sufficient flexibility of *real* wage rates, because any spontaneous disturbance which, if a new equilibrium is to be found, requires a change in the real terms of trade between A and B is likely to require some change in real wage rates in A and B. For example, a shift of demand away from B's products on to A's products will (if external balance is to be achieved through price adjustment and without disturbance of internal balance) require a movement in the terms of trade against B sufficient to shift demand back again from A's products on to B's products (see p. 199). And this movement of the terms of trade against B means that a unit of B's goods can exchange for a smaller amount of A's goods; and, therefore, in so far as imported products are consumed by wage earners it involves a fall in the real wage rate in B.

Under the gold standard the necessary reduction in the real wage rate of labour will be brought about partly by the reduced demand for labour in B causing a reduction in the money wage rate in B,[2] and partly by the increased demand for A's products leading to a rise in the money prices of A's products and so in the money cost of imported products in B. With variable exchange rates the decline in the real wage rate in B will be brought about by the depreciation of B's cur-

---

[1] But it should not be imagined that wage flexibility is a matter of indifference if some other suitable mechanism of general international adjustment can be found which does not depend upon it. On the contrary, flexibility of money wage rates is much needed in the interests of purely domestic economic problems. The flexibility of the *general* level of money wage rates with which we have been chiefly concerned in the last three chapters can be attained only as the sum of flexibilities of *particular* wage rates. That is to say, the general level of money wage rates will decline (rise) when there is an excess of supply (demand) in the labour market as a whole, only if this is true of the various particular labour markets in different regions and occupations. But it is this flexibility of particular wage rates which is needed for the solution of many domestic economic problems. If, for example, within any country the demand shifts from product X to product Y, in the absence of changes in money wage rates this will lead to a shortage of labour in the industry producing Y and a surplus of labour and so unemployment in the industry producing X. Unless this unsatisfactory state of affairs with localized unemployment in X is to be allowed to continue or authoritarian direction of labour or of demand is to be introduced, the method of inducing a shift of labour (and of demand) through some rise of wage rates (and so of costs and prices) in Y and fall of wage rates, costs, and prices in X must be adopted; and this implies some wage flexibility in each of the particular labour markets for X and Y. Some degree of wage flexibility is, therefore, highly to be desired on grounds which would more appropriately form the subject matter of a Theory of Domestic Economic Policy.

[2] This decline in the money wage rate in B will, of course, be accompanied by an equal decline in the price of B's products and so in the money cost of living in B in so far as B's workers purchase B's products. The fall in real wage rates is due only to the movement of the real terms of international trade against B, i.e. is confined to the relative movements between the money wage rate in B and the money price of A's products.

rency which will make A's products more expensive in terms of B's money. Money wage rates in B and the money prices of B's products will remain unchanged, but imports from A will be higher in price.

Now if the mechanism of variable exchange rates is to operate effectively this decline in real wage rates in B must be accepted. Any offsetting rise in money wage rates in B (due, for example, to a tie between money wage rates in B and the cost of living in B) would prevent the terms of international trade from moving against B and would therefore remove the whole inducement to shift demand back again from A's more expensive products on to B's relatively cheaper products. The whole mechanism of adjustment would be frustrated.

We may conclude, therefore, that for the gold-standard mechanism to work effectively there must be 'sufficient' flexibility of money wage rates; and for the variable-exchange-rate mechanism to work effectively there must be 'sufficient' divorce between movements in the cost of living and movements in money wage rates. How much and how quickly real wage rates must be allowed to change in order to achieve 'sufficient' adjustment will depend upon the other conditions in which the adjustments are taking place. We shall now turn to an examination of these other conditions, all of which can be regarded as conditions which minimize the amount of price adjustment which will be required per unit of time in order to cope with any given disequilibrium.

Condition 2. *The Sharing of Price Adjustments between Deficit and Surplus Countries*

Let us suppose. that some spontaneous disturbance takes place (e.g. a shift of demand from B's on to A's products) which requires a 10 per cent movement of the terms of trade against B for the restoration of internal and external balance. With the gold-standard mechanism, if money prices and wage rates in A remain unchanged, money wage rates will have to be reduced by 10 per cent in B; or alternatively, if money prices and wage rates remain unchanged in B, money wage rates will have to be raised by 10 per cent in A. But if money wage rates are raised by 5 per cent in A, money wage rates will only have to be reduced by 5 per cent in B.

If the price adjustment is shared between the two countries, the absolute amount of price adjustment which will be required in any one country will be much reduced. We may conclude, therefore, that a second condition which will make it easier to operate an effective gold-standard system is that all countries, surplus as well as deficit, should make a contribution towards the necessary price adjustment. What does this involve?

In the first place, it means that *both* countries must enjoy wage flexibility. An increase in the total money demand for A's products must cause a rise in the money wage rate in A just as a decrease in the total money demand for B's products must lead to a fall in the money wage rate in B.

Secondly, *both* countries must obey Rule iii of the gold standard (see p. 178). The authorities in the surplus country which receives gold must allow the increase in the gold reserve to have its full effect in inflating the domestic supply of money and so in causing a general inflation of domestic expenditure. And the authorities in the deficit country which is losing gold must allow this loss of gold to have its full effect in deflating domestic expenditure. There must be no 'off-setting' of gold losses or 'sterilizing' of gold gains in the interests of internal balance.

It is always possible for the monetary authorities in a surplus country which is receiving gold to take action, in the interests of the internal balance of that country, to 'sterilize' the new gold, i.e. to prevent it from having its full effect in adding to the domestic supply of money in the country. For example, suppose that there has been a shift of demand away from B's products on to A's products. This will be causing a net increase in the total demand for A's products and so an upward tendency of output, employment, prices, and money wage rates in A. Suppose that the monetary authorities in A decide that they wish to avoid these boom conditions in A. They can take action to restrict the supplies of money in A in spite of the fact that gold is flowing into A. This they can do, for example, if the banks in A sell securities or other assets which they hold in return for notes or deposits held by the public in A and then cancel these notes or deposits. By such means[1] the monetary authorities could 'sterilize' the gold which is flowing into A and could prevent the upward movement of money prices and costs from developing in A. But if they did this, so much the more downward reduction of money prices and costs would be required in B in order to restore equilibrium.

Conversely, the banking system in B could attempt, in the interests of internal balance, to 'offset' the deflationary effects by expanding the supply of money in B (e.g. by the purchase of securities or other assets with newly created notes or deposit money) in order to expand total domestic expenditure in B and to offset the downward deflationary pressure of the reduced demand for B's products. It would, of course, be more difficult for the authorities in the deficit country to carry on indefinitely such a policy of offsetting the internal deflationary effects of its gold loss than it would for the authorities in the surplus country to carry on a policy of preventing the internal inflationary effects of a gold gain, because the authorities in the deficit country may actually

---

[1] Which would need detailed discussion in any Theory of Domestic Economic Policy.

run out of gold reserves if the loss continues whereas the authorities in the surplus country have merely to face the continued piling up of additional gold reserves.[1] But in so far as the authorities in one country do offset a gold loss or sterilize a gold gain, so much more of the price adjustment is ultimately thrown on to the other.

The above remarks should not, of course, be taken to imply that the monetary authority in any country which is operating a gold standard must never take any positive steps to expand or contract the total domestic supply of money. Consider the case of country A when there is a surplus on country A's balance of payments due, for example, to a spontaneous increase in capital transfers from B to A, and at the same time there happens to be a spontaneous decrease in domestic expenditure in A. If the authorities in A allow the depression in domestic expenditure to develop, this will exert a deflationary pressure on prices and money wage rates in both A and B.[2] If there is a universal deflationary pressure on prices and, at the same time, money wage rates and prices must be reduced in B relatively to money wage rates and prices in A in order to generate a favourable balance of trade for B to cover the increased capital transfers from B to A, the deflationary effect in B may be very severe.

Suppose that, in order to generate the favourable trade balance required to finance the capital transfer from B to A, the prices of B's products must fall by 10 per cent relatively to those of A's. If the prices of A's products could be simultaneously raised by 5 per cent, only a 5 per cent deflation in B would be required. But if, because of the simultaneous domestic slump in A, the prices of A's products are falling by, say, 10 per cent, then the prices of B's products must fall by no less than 20 per cent to obtain the required adjustment.

The condition which we require for an easy price adjustment under the gold standard is that the surplus countries should permit, or if necessary take positive steps to induce, an upward movement of their domestic monetary supplies and of their money wage rates and prices, while the deficit countries should permit or should take positive steps to induce a domestic deflation.

With the mechanism of variable exchange rates some of these same conditions remain important. Thus it is important that the authorities in a surplus country should adopt an internal financial policy which does effectively prevent a domestic slump in money wage rates, incomes,

[1] Indeed, if a 'fiduciary issue principle' were being operated in a deficit country, the authorities, far from being able to offset a gold loss, might have to take special measures to reduce the domestic supply of money even more extensively than the fiduciary issue principle would demand. See pp. 181–2.

[2] See the argument on pp. 196–7, above, where it was shown that a spontaneous increase in domestic expenditure in a country will, under the gold standard, cause an upward movement in money wages and prices in it and in other countries.

and prices. Suppose again that there is a spontaneous increase in capital transfers from B to A and that a 10 per cent fall in the prices of B's products relatively to the prices of A's products is needed in order to generate the required favourable movement in B's trade balance. If internal balance is maintained in A and B (i.e. constant prices in A and B in terms of their own currencies), then this can be achieved by means of a 10 per cent depreciation of B's currency in terms of A's. But if at the same time a domestic depression is allowed to develop in A which causes the prices of A's products to fall by 10 per cent, then a 20 per cent depreciation of B's currency will be needed to reduce the prices of B's products 10 per cent relatively to those of A's. And, as will be argued in Chapter XVII, it is important to keep the necessary adjustments of exchange rates within as narrow limits as possible. For this reason it is important with a system of variable exchange rates that the authorities in the surplus country should effectively adopt a domestic financial policy which prevents any decline in the total demand for its products in terms of its own currency; and for similar reasons, the authorities in the deficit country should effectively prevent any rise in the total demand for its own products in terms of its own currency.

If the system of variable exchange rates is carried out by means of a free-exchange market there is little or nothing more to be said of the principle that surplus and deficit countries should share in the price adjustment. Given the domestic financial policies for internal balance in the various countries, the rates of exchange between the currencies of the various countries will adjust themselves automatically so as to equate the supply of and the demand for each currency. There will be no meaning in saying that the surplus country should share the adjustment by appreciating its currency as well as the deficit country by depreciating its currency.

If, however, a system of variable exchange rates is carried out by means of an adjustable peg (see p. 165, above), there is some meaning to be attached to this condition. The monetary authority of the surplus country which is receiving gold can lower the official buying and selling price of gold in terms of its own currency (i.e. appreciate the gold value of its currency) just as much as the monetary authority of the deficit country can raise its official buying and selling price of gold. But it might appear at first sight that it made no difference whether a necessary depreciation of B's currency in terms of A's currency were achieved solely by a depreciation of B's currency in terms of gold, solely by an appreciation of A's currency in terms of gold, or partly by the one and partly by the other. Broadly speaking, this is true on our present assumption that there are only two countries, A and B; but if there are more than two countries it becomes very important that the surplus countries should move their adjustable pegs in an upward direction as well as the deficit countries in a downward direction. The reason for this will become clear when we discuss the mechanism of price adjustment in a many-country world in Chapter XXVII.

Condition 3. The Need for Adequate Reserves of International Means of Payment

Any given price adjustment will be more easily carried out if the speed at which it is required to be effected is not too great. In our present connexion this means that the authorities in each deficit country must have sufficiently large reserves of gold or of other means of making payment to the surplus countries for it to be possible for them to finance a continuing deficit in the balance of payments for a considerable time while the necessary price adjustments are being made and are becoming effective.

As far as the gold-standard mechanism is concerned, this point is closely connected with the distinction drawn in Chapter XIV (pp. 181–185) between the working of a 100-per-cent money system and a percentage-reserve system. As we saw there, in the former case a deficit in the balance of payments of, say, £100 m. per annum will cause a loss of £100 m. gold per annum and in consequence the domestic supplies of money will be reduced by only £100 m. But if only a 10 per cent reserve of gold is held against total domestic monetary supplies, for every £100 m. gold which is lost in order to finance a balance-of-payments deficit the total domestic supplies of money must be reduced by £1,000 m. if the same ratio of gold reserves to domestic supplies of money is to be preserved. In the first case the domestic deflation of prices and money wage rates need not be anything like as quick as in the second.

Suppose that in country B there is a total domestic supply of money of £10,000 m. and a balance of payments deficit of £100 m. per annum, and that to regain external balance B's total supply of money (and so her money wage rates and prices) must be reduced by 20 per cent or from £10,000 m. to £8,000 m. If £10,000 m. in gold is held against the £10,000 m. of domestic money in B, £100 m. of gold can be exported annually for twenty years from B who will then be in a new external balance with domestic monetary supplies of £8,000 m. and gold reserves of £8,000 m., monetary supplies in B having fallen by £100 m. per annum or about 1 per cent per annum.[1]

---

[1] In fact the adjustment would be even slower than this. The numerical example assumes that B's balance of payments deficit remains unchanged at £100 m. per annum until the twentieth year when the 20 per cent deflation in B is fully achieved and the deficit completely disappears. In fact the deficit would throughout these years be becoming gradually smaller and smaller as the deflation proceeded.

But if only £1,000 m. of gold reserves are held against B's total monetary supplies of £10,000 m., the adjustment cannot proceed at this leisurely pace. If gold reserves continued to be lost at the rate of £100 m. a year and domestic monetary supplies to be deflated only by £100 m. a year, by the end of the tenth year literally no gold reserves would be left, although domestic monetary supplies in B would have been reduced to only £9,000 m. instead of the necessary £8,000 m. The authorities in B would be compelled to deflate much more quickly. In fact they would have to deflate ten times as quickly if they wished to keep a 10 per cent ratio of gold reserves to total monetary supplies. For during each year they would have to reduce total monetary supplies in B by an amount equal to ten times the loss of gold in that year (i.e. by an amount equal to ten times the balance of payments deficit of that year). A 20 per cent deflation of money wage rates might be bearable if it were spread over twenty years but quite impossible if it were necessary to carry it out in two years. Indeed, the contrast may be even more marked than this. Suppose that through continuous annual increases in productivity in B the general level of money wage rates could be expected to rise by 2 per cent per annum in B. To get rid of the deficit in B's balance of payments requires a cut in money wage rates in B 20 per cent below what they would otherwise be. Spread over twenty years this means that money wage rates for twenty years should go up in B by only 1 per cent instead of 2 per cent per annum. Spread over two years the adjustment means that money wage rates should be reduced in B by 8 per cent instead of rising by 2 per cent in each of the two years.

The larger, then, is the proportion of the total domestic monetary supply which is covered by gold or by other acceptable international means of payment, the more leisurely is the pace at which the authorities in any country can make any necessary domestic price adjustments under the gold-standard mechanism. And since very rapid price adjustments may be impossible, whereas the same price adjustment spread over a longer period may be quite feasible, the successful operation of the gold standard depends upon the potentially deficit countries starting with an adequate supply of gold reserves or their equivalent.

A rather similar point arises in the case of the mechanism of variable exchange rates. Suppose an adjustment is required which involves a 20 per cent depreciation in B's currency. If this has to take place instantaneously in one movement of the exchange rate, it may involve a very great and sharp reduction in real wage rates in B because of the very great rise in the price of imports from A. If it could be spread over twenty years by a 1 per cent depreciation of B's currency each year, the effect in B might be merely that real wage rates rose by only 1 per cent per annum instead of by 2 per cent per annum as they would have done if there had been no depreciation of B's currency. But such a spreading of the exchange-rate variation over a longish period of time would, of course, mean that B's balance of payments deficit continued for a much longer period of time. This would need financing by means of gold or other acceptable international means of payment by B's monetary authorities. Or, to put the same matter in another way, the deficit in B's balance of payments would alone cause such an excess demand in the foreign exchange market for A's currency for the making of payments to A that B's currency would immediately depreciate by a full 20 per cent. If B's monetary authorities wish to prevent this, they must have at their disposal a reserve of A's currency (or of gold or of something else which A's monetary authorities will accept in payment for A's currency) which they can sell in the foreign exchange market to persons in B who wish to purchase A's currency. The sale of these international monetary reserves in the foreign exchange market by the monetary authorities of B at an appropriate rate will provide the means for financing some of B's deficit and for restraining the depreciation in B's currency.[1]

There is one more feature of the mechanism of price adjustment which makes it necessary for the authorities of the deficit countries to hold sufficient reserves of international means of payment. We have seen reason to believe (p. 76, above) that the responsiveness of the demand for imports in A and B to changes in the relative prices of A's and B's products will be much greater after some period of time has been allowed to elapse for demand and supply conditions to adjust themselves to the new relationships than immediately after the change. When the prices of B's products fall and those of A's products rise, purchasers will shift from A's to B's products on a larger and larger scale as they become more and more fully aware of the price change, as they learn more and more about the possibility of substituting B's products for A's products, and as they have more and more time for making those long-run changes in their productive equipment, which may be necessary if they are to rely upon the products of B rather than those of A.

It is even possible that in the very short run the sum of the elasticities of demand for imports in A and in B might be less than unity, though in the longer run it was very considerably greater than unity. This would mean that the immediate effect of a reduction in B's wage rates relatively to A's, or of a depreciation of B's currency in terms of A's, would be to make B's balance of trade more unfavourable, although in the longer run it would make B's balance of trade much more favour-able. In such a case it would be essential that the authorities in the

---

[1] This spreading of the exchange rate adjustment over time may be brought about by speculation in the foreign exchange market. See Chapter XVII.

deficit country should possess an adequate reserve of gold, of the currency of the surplus country, or of some other acceptable international means of payment to tide over the period during which the price adjustment was working out its effect. There would be some period during which the mechanism of price adjustment alone just could not prove effective.

Condition 4. A Commercial Policy which Permits an Easy Change in the Channels of Trade

For the reasons which we have already examined at length the methods of price adjustment will work much more easily if the elasticities of demand for imports in A and in B are high. Indeed, as we have seen, price adjustment cannot be expected to work at all unless the sum of these elasticities of demand is greater than unity. And the greater these elasticities are, the smaller is the movement in the terms of trade (and thus the changes of wage rates or of exchange rates) required to remove any given deficit in B's balance of payments by inducing a shift of expenditure away from A's products on to B's cheaper products.

But, as we have seen on p. 77, above, one of the factors which will most intimately affect the size of these elasticities of demand is the commercial policy followed in A and B. These elasticities may be greatly reduced by the existence of barriers to international commerce which impede the shift of demand from the products of one country to those of another. For example, control of trade through rigid import restrictions which prevent the importers in country A from buying more from country B whatever may happen to the price of the commodity; or a heavy specific import duty on the purchase of the commodity in A which prevents the fall in B's cost of production from having an equivalent effect upon the price charged to consumers of the commodity in A; or an international commodity agreement which lays down a quota limiting the amount of the commodity which producers in country B may export regardless of what happens to the cost of production of the commodity in B; or a cartel agreement among the producers of a commodity which effectively prevents producers in B from expanding their exports of that commodity; or State-trading arrangements in A which fix the quantities to be imported or the sources from which those quantities are to be obtained, without full regard to changes in price; or laws in A which require goods to be shipped in the vessels of A regardless of cost; or subsidies to production or to export in A; or duties on import in A, which are constantly adjusted to offset any price and cost changes unfavourable to the domestic production of A—all these things effectively prevent a shift of demand away from A's more expensive products on to the cheaper products of B. The mechanism of adjustment through internal price and cost adjustments or through

variations of exchange rates will work the more smoothly, the fewer are
the restrictions on the flow of international trade in goods and services.

Condition 5. The Absence of Fixed Money Debts

A final condition which is favourable to the effective operation of
systems which rely upon price adjustment is the absence of too heavy
a structure of debts fixed in terms of money.

As far as the method of variable exchange rates is concerned, internal
indebtedness of A or B is not of any great importance. Under this
system the authorities in both countries can preserve internal balance
by a financial policy designed to maintain the total monetary demand for
their products, and so the level of their own money prices and costs,
more or less stable. Internal debts fixed in terms of their own currencies
will thus not change in their real value.

But the position is very different with the method of the gold standard.
In this case the maintenance of equilibrium may involve, let us say, a
10 per cent absolute deflation of the general level of money prices and
costs in B in terms of B's own currency. The effect of this in B will be
much affected by the existence of a large structure of debts, the principal
and interest of which is fixed in terms of money. If the debt is an
internal national debt, the fixed interest payable out of the national
budget will not decline even though prices and the money national
income, and in consequence government tax revenue and other forms
of government expenditure, all fall more or less equally in money terms.
Higher and higher rates of direct and indirect taxation will be required
to pay a national debt interest which, being fixed in money terms,
becomes worth more and more in real terms as prices fall.

If there is a large volume of private debt, a similar phenomenon will
appear in private industry or commerce. Consider the position of a
business concern which has financed a considerable part of the installation of its capital equipment by means of fixed interest debt. Out of its
gross profits it has to pay a considerable amount in fixed interest on its
debt before obtaining the net profits for distribution to its shareholders
or for further extensions of the business. If the prices which it has to
pay for its labour and materials and the prices which it receives for its
product all now fall in the same ratio as a result of a general monetary
deflation, its gross profits will fall in the same ratio. But because the
fixed interest payable out of its gross profits does not decline, its net
profits will fall in a much greater proportion. This will, in any case,
greatly increase the riskiness of the business, since, after the general
deflation, any given percentage decline in the demand for its product
will cause a much greater percentage decline in its net profit than
before, as is shown in the table on p. 212. And if the general deflation
of demand has gone far enough, any remaining net profit may easily be

turned into a net loss and the business be driven into bankruptcy because of the combined effect of the monetary deflation and the fixed debt.

For these reasons, absence of large-scale fixed debt, whether public or private, as well as wage flexibility, is desirable for the successful adoption of the gold standard; and the presence of a large structure of

Effect on a Business Concern's Profit of a General Monetary Deflation

	Before deflation	*After 20 per cent deflation of all Prices*	*Percentage change*
	$		
Total receipts	1,000	800	−20
Running expenses	800	640	−20
Gross profit	200	160	−20
Fixed interest	150	150	Nil
Net profit	50	10	−80
	Two per cent decline in total receipts ($20), with expenses unchanged, would now cause net profits to fall from $50 to $30	Two per cent decline in total receipts ($16), with expenses unchanged, would now turn net profit of $10 to net loss of $6	

domestic debt may be an important reason for preferring variation in exchange rates to the gold-standard mechanism.

The existence of international debts fixed in terms of money affects the operation of both the gold standard and also of variable exchange rates. As has been explained in Chapter I, we treat the interest or dividends payable from A to B on capital previously invested by residents of B as a current payment by residents of A for the current use of the services of some of B's capital. What we have, therefore, to ask is what is the size of the elasticity of demand in A for the import of this service into A from B and what is the size of the elasticity of demand in B for the imported service of A's capital, in so far as residents of B also have interest or similar payments to make to A. The larger are these elasticities of demand the easier will it be to use the method of price adjustment for preservation of equilibrium in the balance of payments between A and B.

Now the size of these elasticities of demand depends upon whether the payment for the service of the other country's capital is in respect of a debt fixed in terms of the money of the borrowing country, or a debt fixed in terms of the money of the lending country, or an equity holding in respect of which the debtor pays only a certain proportion of whatever profits the capital investment happens to earn from time to time. These differences are set out schematically in Table XIV.

Let us suppose that B is in deficit and that the restoration of equilibrium demands that the terms of international trade must turn 10 per cent against B. Let us suppose further that under the gold-standard mechanism this adjustment takes place by a fall of 7½ per cent in all money wage rates, money prices, and money incomes in B (including, of course, all money profits made in B's industries), and by a simultaneous rise of 2½ per cent in all money wage rates, money prices, and money incomes in A. In other words, conditions are such that the deflation in B accounts for ¾ of the necessary change while the inflation in A accounts for ¼ of the necessary change. Finally, let us suppose that, with the mechanism of variable exchange rates, all money wage rates, prices, and incomes remain constant in A and B, but that B's currency depreciates by 10 per cent in terms of A's.

TABLE XIV

Effect of Service of International Debts upon the Balance of Payments

	Payment of interest or dividends from	Equivalent to import of service	
		by	with elasticity of demand of
Section (i) Dividends on Equity Capital			
Gold standard	A to B	A	1
	B to A	B	1
Variable exchange rates	A to B	A	1
	B to A	B	1
Section (ii) Interest on Debt Fixed in Terms of A's currency			
Gold standard	A to B	A	¾[1]
	B to A	B	¼[1]
Variable exchange rates	A to B	A	1
	B to A	B	0
Section (iii) Interest on Debt Fixed in Terms of B's currency			
Gold standard	A to B	A	¾[1]
	B to A	B	¼[1]
Variable exchange rates	A to B	A	0
	B to A	B	1

[1] On the assumption that A bears ¼ and B ¾ of the necessary adjustment of domestic prices.

We can now go through the various sections of Table XIV. In section i we deal with equity capital. Under the gold standard a payment of dividends on equity capital from A to B will be equivalent to the import by residents of A of a service from B for which the elasticity of demand in A is equal to unity. The reason for this is clear. When the adjustment takes place money prices and money incomes in A rise by $2\frac{1}{2}$ per cent. Residents in A therefore pay in dividends to residents in B $2\frac{1}{2}$ per cent more than before because the profits of A's industries are up by $2\frac{1}{2}$ per cent. But the prices of A's products are also up $2\frac{1}{2}$ per cent so that an amount is being paid in dividends from A to B which has the same purchasing power over A's products as before. This is equivalent to an elasticity of demand of unity. The prices of B's products have fallen relatively to those of A's by 10 per cent; a purchaser in A can get 10 per cent more of B's products for a unit of A's products; but so far as the payment from A to B for the equity capital which residents in A have borrowed from residents in B is concerned, the same amount is paid in terms of A's own products. It is as if, when the prices of B's products had fallen relatively to those of A by 10 per cent, importers in A had then purchased 10 per cent more of B's products so that the total amount payable by importers in A in terms of A's own products was unchanged.

Similarly with any payment of dividends on equity capital from B to A. Money incomes (including profits) have fallen by $7\frac{1}{2}$ per cent in B; $7\frac{1}{2}$ per cent less in money is, therefore, paid in dividends to A; but the prices of B's products have also fallen by $7\frac{1}{2}$ per cent, so that the same amount is being paid from B to A in terms of B's products in spite of the 10 per cent rise in the relative price of A's products. And this again is equivalent to an elasticity of demand for imports in B of unity.

With the mechanism of variable exchange rates it is equally clear that dividends payable on equity capital will be equivalent to a demand for imports with an elasticity of unity. Suppose that dividend payments are to be made from A to B; then since money prices and incomes are now stabilized in A, the same amount of money dividends is paid from A to B with the same real purchasing power over A's products regardless of what happens to the rate of exchange between A's and B's currency and so to the price of B's products in A. This is equivalent to a demand in A for imports from B with an elasticity of demand of unity, because when the price of B's products in terms of A's products falls by 10 per cent importers of the services of B's capital into A continue to spend the same total amount in terms of A's products on the purchase of the services of B's capital. Similarly, businesses in B will continue to pay to residents in A, in respect of any dividends on B's equity capital owned by residents in A, the same amount of B's money with the same real purchasing power over B's products, even though the prices of A's products have risen in B by 10 per cent. This is equivalent to an elasticity of demand in B for imports of capital services of unity.

If we turn now to debts fixed in terms of money, the position is very different. If we are considering the gold-standard mechanism it makes no difference whether the debts are fixed in A's or B's currency because the value of A's currency in terms of B's currency is also fixed. We can then deal with these two cases (first half of section ii and first half of section iii of Table XIV) together. Let us consider first the payment of a fixed money sum for interest payable from A to B. Now the prices of all B's products have fallen in terms of money by $7\frac{1}{2}$ per cent, so that the fixed money payment from A to B represents a purchasing power over $7\frac{1}{2}$ per cent more of B's products. In other words, when the price of B's products falls by 10 per cent relatively to the price of A's products, residents in A have paid to residents in B, in interest on debt owed to B, an amount which will purchase $7\frac{1}{2}$ per cent more of B's products. This is equivalent to an elasticity of demand for imports in A of $\frac{3}{4}$; for it is only if a 1 per cent fall in the price of B's products would lead to a $\frac{3}{4}$ per cent increase in the amount of B's products which were bought by residents in A that a 10 per cent fall in their price would lead to a $7\frac{1}{2}$ per cent increase in the amount bought.

Conversely, if fixed interest is being paid from B to A, and the prices of A's products all rise by $2\frac{1}{2}$ per cent in terms of money, debtors in B will be paying to creditors in A an amount in interest which will purchase $2\frac{1}{2}$ per cent less of A's products. It is as if importers in B purchased $2\frac{1}{2}$ per cent less of A's products when the prices of A's products rise by 10 per cent in terms of B's products; and this is the equivalent of an elasticity of demand of $\frac{1}{4}$. The principle is clear. A payment of fixed interest from A to B will represent a demand for imported services in the debtor country A with an elasticity of demand equal to the proportion of the total price adjustment which falls on the creditor country B.

In the case of the mechanism of variable exchange rates it does, of course, make a great difference in which currency the debt is fixed. Let us consider first a debt fixed in terms of A's currency (second half of section ii of Table XIV). Since the prices of A's products are constant in terms of A's currency and the debt interest is fixed in terms of A's currency, the interest payment will have a constant purchasing power over A's products. If it is an interest payment from A to B, this is equivalent to an elasticity of demand for imported services in A of unity, because debtors in A pay over to creditors in B the same total amount in terms of A's products although the price of B's products in terms of A's products has fallen by 10 per cent. If, however, the interest payment is from B to A, this is equivalent to an elasticity of demand for imported services in B of zero, because debtors in B pay to creditors in A an amount of money which will purchase the same amount of A's products even though the prices of A's products have risen by 10 per cent in terms of those of B's.

By a similar reasoning it can be seen (second half of section iii of Table XIV) that if an interest payment is fixed in terms of B's currency this will have a constant purchasing power over B's products; and it will, therefore, be equivalent to an elasticity of demand for imports in A of zero if it is a fixed payment from A to B and to an elasticity of demand for imports in B of unity if it is a fixed payment from B to A.

Now it is clear from Table XIV that, if international investment takes the form of equity capital on which dividends are payable according to the actual money profit which happens to be earned, the payment of dividends from one country to another will be equivalent in effect to a demand for imports in the paying country with an elasticity of demand equal to unity. And this is the case whether the mechanism of adjustment is that of the gold standard or of variable exchange rates and whether the payment is from the deficit or the surplus country. Such payments will always help the process of equilibrium rather than hinder it, because—as we have seen—the essential condition for the operation of any system of price adjustment is that the sum of the elasticities of demand for imports in the *two* countries should be greater than unity; and here is a case in which this particular portion of *one* country's demand for imports will have an elasticity equal to unity.

From Table XIV it can be seen that no other form of international investment is preferable to this from our present point of view. There are, however, two other special cases in which the position might be as good.

First, if the system of variable exchange rates is in operation and if the interest payment is fixed in terms of the currency of the country which has to make the interest payment, this again will represent an elasticity of demand for imports of unity by the debtor country. But the elasticity of demand falls to zero if the payment is fixed in terms of the currency of the creditor country; and with a system of variable exchange rates this is the more probable case, because the creditors will wish to protect themselves against a possible depreciation of the debtors' currency—a depreciation which may, of course, go to quite unpredictable lengths if the debtor country were ever to adopt a domestic policy of unbridled internal inflation.

Second, if the gold-standard mechanism is in operation and if the whole of the domestic price adjustment is made to fall on the creditor country, then again this will represent an elasticity of demand for imports of unity by the debtor country. But this is clearly a most exceptional case. In the equally likely case that the whole of the domestic price adjustment had to fall on the debtor country the elasticity of demand for imported capital services would be reduced to zero.

We may safely conclude, therefore, that from the point of view of facilitating the operation of the methods of price adjustment for the preservation of external balance as much international investment as possible should take the form of equity capital rather than of fixed money debts.

CHAPTER XVII

THE RÔLE OF SPECULATION[1]

IN a free exchange market important purchases and sales of foreign exchange may be undertaken for speculative reasons. These transactions represent elements in the balance of payments for which, up to this point, we have not made proper allowance.

Suppose that the value of the pound (the currency of country B) is expected to appreciate significantly in the near future in terms of the dollar (the currency of country A). The current rate is $2 = £1; the rate next year is expected to be $3 = £1. For every $200 which an owner of dollars changes into pounds he can at present obtain £100 and he expects next year to be able to get back $300 with £100. If his expectations are correct he will make $100 on his $200 by buying pounds with them now and exchanging the pounds back into dollars later. If he has to hold his money in pounds for one year before the anticipated appreciation of the pound materializes, he will make 50 per cent on his money in one year, i.e. he will earn a rate of 50 per cent per annum on the capital used for speculation. If he has to hold his money in pounds for only four months before changing it back into dollars at the appreciated value of the pound, he will earn 50 per cent on his money in one-third of a year, i.e. the equivalent of a rate of interest of no less than 150 per cent per annum.

Such speculation may take many forms. It may be undertaken by more or less professional speculators in the foreign exchange market, that is to say, by persons who hold a certain amount of capital which they deliberately shift from one currency to another in the search for profits from changes in exchange rates. It may, on the other hand, be undertaken rather indirectly by traders. An importer in A who has a payment to make in B, or an exporter in B who has received payment in A's currency for his goods, may be much quicker than usual in selling A's currency in order to acquire B's currency if he thinks that an appreciation of B's currency is about to take place. At the same time an exporter in A who has received B's currency for his goods, or an importer in B who has to acquire A's currency to pay for his purchases, may delay as long as possible these normal purchases of A's currency with B's currency, if he expects a serious appreciation of B's currency in the foreign exchange market. Anticipations and delays in normal foreign exchange transactions have the same effect as, and are due to the same

---

[1] Some part of the argument of this chapter is based on propositions contained in my article on 'Degrees of Competitive Speculation' in the *Review of Economic Studies*, Vol. 17 (3), in the preparation of which I received great help from Professor A. Henderson and Mr. Lomax of Manchester University.

causes as, straightforward speculative movement of capital funds from one currency to another.

There are three factors which may restrain the volume of such speculative movements.

In the first place, if the rate of interest which must be paid by a borrower in A is much higher than the rate of interest which can be obtained by a lender of funds in B, then this will discourage capital movements, including speculative capital movements, from A to B. As the example which we have given above makes clear, this factor is not likely to be of any great practical importance if a really substantial exchange depreciation is expected to occur in a very short period of time. The fact that a speculator may have to pay, say, 5 per cent per annum to borrow in dollars the funds with which to speculate on a rise in the exchange value of the pound and that he can recoup himself only, say, at 2 per cent per annum when he lends these funds in B's currency on B's money market while he waits for B's currency to appreciate will constitute a negligible deterrent when he anticipates a profit on the depreciation at the rate of 50 or even 150 per cent per annum. But where the speculative motive in capital movements is much less marked because expected variations in exchange rates are much more moderate and gradual, the comparison between the anticipated exchange profit and the net rate of interest payable on the speculative funds may be of some importance.

The second factor which sets a limit to the volume of speculative funds is the essential uncertainty of such speculation. The speculator expects an appreciation of the pound; but he does not know at all precisely how much it will appreciate nor how soon; and he realizes that his anticipation may turn out to be quite incorrect; the pound may in fact depreciate, in which case he will make a substantial loss on his speculative venture. At any given time, for this reason, the extent to which speculators will speculate in any one direction is limited; they will not commit all their resources on one venture which may prove a loss.

There is a third factor which sets a limit to speculation and which is of essential importance for our analysis. Suppose the present rate of exchange to be $2 = £1 and that it is expected to move to $3 = £1. As we have seen this will give rise to a speculative movement of capital funds from dollars into pounds, with the intention that the pounds should be changed back into dollars at a later date when the appreciation of the pound has actually occurred. But the speculative purchase of pounds with dollars now will cause the exchange value of the pound to appreciate immediately since it will represent an additional element of autonomous purchases of pounds in the current balance of payments. And as speculators realize that they and other speculators are getting into a position in which they hold abnormally large amounts of pounds which they all intend to change back into dollars when the appreciation has occurred, they will change their expectations about the future value of the pound. They will realize that the future bringing back of the speculative pounds from pounds into dollars will help to reduce the future demand for pounds so that the appreciation will not in fact go so far as would otherwise be the case. The immediate appreciation of the pound combined with the worsened prospects for the pound in the future will reduce the incentive to speculate. Speculators will pay now, say, $2·25 (instead of only $2·0) for £1 and will expect next year to obtain only $2·75 (instead of $3·0) for £1. Half the incentive to speculate is removed by the results of a given speculative movement itself.[1]

This closing of the margin between the current rate of exchange and the anticipated rate of exchange which, as we have seen, speculation will itself tend to bring about has three important results.

First, it tends to remove the profit of speculators. Indeed, if there are sufficient speculators willing and able to speculate, and if the change in the exchange rate is correctly anticipated, the competition among speculators will completely remove any abnormal profit from speculation. In the absence of all speculation this year's exchange rate would have been $2 = £1 and next year's would have been $3 = £1, and a speculative profit of 50 per cent per annum would have been available. But if new speculators can always come in so long as any abnormal profit is available, the speculation will be carried on until all speculators are having to pay such a high price for pounds purchased now and will have to pay such a high price for dollars purchased next year that they are not in fact making abnormally large profits on their speculation. It is too little, not too much, speculation which produces large speculative profits.

Second, speculation of the kind described above helps to iron out large price movements. In the absence of speculation this year's exchange rate would have been $2 = £1 and next year's rate would have jumped to $3 = £1. But as a result of speculation this year's rate is raised to, say, $2·25 = £1 and next year's rate is lowered to, say, $2·75 = £1. The rate of exchange is thus more stable. It varies less in extent and less quickly.

This may be of considerable institutional importance. Suppose, for

[1] This closing of the speculative price margin may also be associated with an intensification of the interest cost of speculation. Speculation takes place and raises the current value of the pound from $2·00 to $2·25; if this has the effect of improving A's current balance of trade (the sum of the elasticities of demand for imports being greater than one), this will exercise an inflationary pressure on A's and a deflationary pressure on B's economy; if the authorities in both countries adopt monetary policies for internal balance, interest rates in A will rise and in B will fall; the interest cost of a speculative movement of funds from A to B will thus be raised as an indirect result of a given speculative movement of funds in that direction.

example, that the cost of living in country A depends to a significant extent upon the price of imports. Then a sudden jump in the exchange rate from \$2 to \$3 = £1 will cause a sudden jump in the price in dollars of A's imports from B and thus a sudden jump in the cost of living in A. A smaller and more gradual exchange-rate variation will lead to a smaller and more gradual adjustment of the cost of living, which may greatly simplify the problem of wage policy in A.

Third, speculation of the kind which we have analysed above will directly ease the mechanism of price adjustment in restoring equilibrium to a disordered balance of payments.

Let us take an example. Suppose that A and B are in internal and external balance at a rate of exchange of \$4 = £1; suppose that there is then some unexpected spontaneous disturbance (e.g. a shift of demand away from B's products on to A's products) which would make necessary a depreciation of B's exchange rate in order to restore equilibrium. Now it may be that in the long run a depreciation of B's exchange rate to \$3 = £1 would be sufficient to restore equilibrium by making B's products cheaper relatively to A's products and thus causing a shift of demand back again on to B's products. But, as we have already seen, (p. 76), the elasticities of demand for imports in A and B, on which this shift depends, are likely to be smaller in the short run than in the long run, when producers and consumers have had time to adjust themselves to the lower relative price of B's products. The temporary depreciation of B's currency required to fill the balance-of-payments gap immediately after the spontaneous deterioration of B's external position might be much greater, say, \$2 = £1. In the absence of speculation we should, therefore, have an initial period in which \$4 = £1, a very difficult balance-of-payments period immediately after the worsening of B's position in which \$2 = £1, and ultimately a new long-run equilibrium in which \$3 = £1.

Speculation of the kind which we have been examining might materially ease the problems of the difficult middle period. When the unexpected deterioration in B's external position occurs, the exchange rate threatens to deteriorate to \$2 = £1. But at some point it is realized that the value of the pound is abnormally low and that it will recover towards \$3 = £1 when the forces of readjustment have had time to operate. Speculators will now have an incentive to move speculative funds temporarily from dollars into pounds which will prevent the pound from going below, say, \$2·80 = £1. Later, when the forces of readjustment have worked themselves out, the pound will recover still further and the speculators will take their funds back into dollars. During this period the rate of exchange would, in the absence of the movement of speculative funds, have been \$3 = £1; but the return of speculative funds from pounds into dollars will reduce it to, say,

$2·90 = £1. Only when the speculative funds have been moved back will the rate of exchange settle down at the new equilibrium rate of $3 = £1.

Now this development has once again helped to moderate the fluctuations in exchange rates. Without speculation, they would have been $4 = £1 in year 1, $2 = £1 in year 2 and $3 = £1 in year 3 and subsequent years. With speculation, they are $4 = £1 in year 1, $2·80 = £1 in year 2, $2·90 = £1 in year 3 and a few following years, and $3 = £1 in all subsequent years. But it has done more than this. It has greatly eased the balance-of-payments problem of B. Capital funds have been temporarily lent from A to B during the period when there was the maximum strain on B's balance of payments, so that B did not need in that period to generate so favourable a balance of trade as would have been necessary in the absence of speculation. This loan has been repaid at a later date when the mechanism of price adjustment has had time to operate and when it is, therefore, easier for B to develop the necessary favourable balance of trade.

The above analysis has been carried out on the assumption that speculators have anticipated more or less correctly the future course of the movements in exchange rates. In these circumstances, as we have shown, unhindered competitive speculation brings with it many important social advantages. But it is by no means always certain that speculators will correctly anticipate the future, and where serious mistakes in anticipation are made the difficulties of adjustment of the balance of payments may be intensified instead of mitigated by speculation.

There are two sorts of speculation, based on wrong anticipations of price changes, which may make the position worse than if there had been no speculation at all. The first type, which we may call 'perverse' speculation, occurs when speculators expect the rate of exchange to appreciate when it does in fact depreciate or to depreciate when it does in fact appreciate. In this case they speculate in the wrong direction. The second type which we may call 'grossly excessive' speculation, occurs when they expect an alteration of the exchange rate in the correct direction but on a much larger scale than in fact turns out to be the case.

Let us illustrate from our previous example the evil effects which speculation of these kinds have. A spontaneous disturbance worsens B's external position; the exchange rate in the absence of speculation would depreciate from $4 = £1 to $2 = £1 in the first year, but later would appreciate again to $3 = £1 when the price adjustments had had their full effect. Now if the initial depreciation from $4 = £1 to $2=£1 makes people so pessimistic that they think that the external position of country B is going to get worse and worse instead of subsequently improving to $3 = £1, speculators instead of moving speculative funds from dollars to pounds at $2 = £1 will move speculative funds from pounds into dollars at this rate. The exchange rate will be temporarily driven down to, say, $1·5 = £1. It will recover finally to $3 = £1 when the speculators have learnt their mistake, and when the forces of readjustment have fully worked themselves out. But the speculation will (i) have increased the extent and speed of the exchange-rate fluctuation instead of diminishing it, and (ii) have increased instead of diminishing the difficulty of the balance-of-payments adjustment by causing an extra speculative movement of capital from B to A precisely during the period of the maximum strain on B's balance of payments.

Grossly excessive speculation may produce a similar evil effect in a different way. Suppose, again, that a spontaneous disturbance weakening B's external position would, in the absence of all speculation, cause a depreciation from $4 = £1 to $2 = £1 at first and then a recovery to $3 = £1 as the forces of readjustment asserted themselves. Suppose, however, that when the first depreciation threatens to occur speculators are so excessively optimistic about the future value of the pound that speculative funds are shifted from dollars into pounds on such a scale that the rate of exchange, far from depreciating to $2 = £1, is allowed to depreciate only to the insignificant extent of $3·9 = £1. Then for a period funds move in from dollars to pounds on a scale which alone practically entirely fills the balance-of-payments gap caused by the spontaneous disturbance. The mechanism of price adjustment scarcely operates at all. None of the required extensive readjustments of consumption and production are initiated. At some time the speculators find out their error because the exchange rate of $3·9 = £1 can be maintained only by a continual flow of speculative funds from dollars into pounds. At this point the speculative flow ceases. The rate of exchange falls at once to about $2 = £1, the rate which is temporarily needed to initiate substantial price adjustments. But this is not all. This rate is achieved when the main corpus of speculative funds has already been moved from dollars into pounds; and instead of there being speculative support of the pound at this rate, it is probable that the depreciation will be further intensified at this point (perhaps to $1·75 = £1) by the moving back of some speculative funds from pounds into dollars. Once again the price fluctuation has been intensified and an additional burden placed upon B's balance of payments at the moment of maximum weakness.

How can these dangers of ill-informed speculation be met without preventing[1] useful as well as anti-social forms of speculation?

The most straightforward way to achieve this end is for the monetary authorities of one or the other country or of both in combination to

[1] e.g. by the exchange control over capital movements which will be discussed in Chapter XXII.

offset undesirable private speculative movements from one currency to another by movements of governmental funds in the opposite direction. Thus, in our case of perverse speculation given above, speculators were moving funds from pounds into dollars when they should have moved from dollars into pounds. The monetary authorities could have met this position by simultaneously themselves moving funds from dollars into pounds on a scale sufficient not only to offset the speculative movement in the wrong direction but also to achieve a net movement of the right amount in the right direction. Or, in our case of grossly excessive speculation, private speculators were moving funds in the right direction from dollars into pounds but were doing so on much too large a scale. In this case the authorities could have attempted to move funds from pounds into dollars on a scale sufficient to offset merely the excessive part of the private movement in the other direction.

By such means the monetary authorities can attempt to make the market for foreign exchange approximate towards what it would have been if there had been free competitive speculation with correct fore-sight of future movements. In this case all that the authorities have to attempt to do is to anticipate more correctly than private speculators the future course of exchange rates. And in so far as they do so they will make a profit at the expense of the private speculator.[1]

The monetary authorities might, however, attempt to introduce even more stability into the exchange rate then would be achieved by per-fectly competitive private speculation even with perfect foresight. To revert to our example. Suppose (see pp. 221–2, above) that such speculation would have replaced a temporary depreciation of the value of the pound from $4 to $2 and a subsequent recovery to $3 by a depreciation in the first instance from $4 to $2·8 and a subsequent recovery first to $2·9 and later to $3. The monetary authorities might attempt to prevent any depreciation below $3 = £1 by purchasing pounds with dollars at this rate on a sufficient scale and for a sufficient period to enable the new equilibrium to be re-established at once at this rate.[2] This would achieve a still greater measure of exchange-rate stability; and additional price stability might have some institutional advantages. But if the movement of funds from one currency to the

---

[1] In our first example of perverse speculation the monetary authorities could have entered the market to buy pounds with dollars from the private speculators as the value of the pound fell towards $1·5 in order to resell pounds to speculators later at about $3·0 = £1. In our second example of grossly excessive speculation they could have entered the market to sell pounds for dollars to the private speculators as the value of the pound rose towards $3·9 and could have rebought the pounds subsequently at around $3·0 = £1.

[2] The rate chosen would in fact have to be a little lower than $3 = £1 (say $2·95 = £1) in order to generate ultimately a sufficiently favourable balance of payments for B to enable the monetary authorities to move back their funds into dollars over a period of time.

other had any interest or other cost it would not in fact be profitable.[1]

In order that a monetary authority can undertake speculative movements of this kind it must operate an exchange equalization fund. Such a fund must possess balances of both A's and B's money, so that when the authority wishes, for example, to support B's exchange rate it can sell some of its holdings of A's currency for B's currency in the foreign exchange market and thus add to its holdings of B's currency at the cost of some decline in its holdings of A's currency, and vice versa.

Such an exchange equalization fund may be a national fund; that is to say, it may be held and operated by A's or by B's national authority separately. Or it may be international in character; that is to say, it may be held and operated by some body which represents both A's and B's authorities or which in some way stands above the national authorities.[2] There are at least two important advantages which an international exchange equalization fund, if it could be operated effectively, would possess over separate national funds.

In the first place, a national fund may run out of its holding of a foreign currency, but there is no technical limit to the extent to which, for example, B's national exchange equalization fund could support A's exchange rate. It is always technically possible for the banking system in B to create additional supplies of B's money and to use it to purchase in the foreign exchange market additional holdings of A's currency. Thus, if the authority in charge of B's fund wishes to support A's currency, there is no technical limit to the extent of the operations. But the authority in charge of B's fund can support B's currency only by selling part of the existing holding of A's currency in order to acquire the funds for the purchase of B's currency. When B's fund has run out of A's currency these operations must stop unless the authority in charge of B's fund can borrow more of A's currency in A's market; the banking system in B cannot create additional supplies of A's currency. But a truly international exchange equalization fund which had the full backing of A's and B's authorities would be subject to no such technical limits. The banking system in B could always produce without limit the supplies of B's currency required to support A's exchange rate, and the banking system in A could always produce without limit the supplies of A's currency required to support B's exchange rate. If the two authorities once agreed upon the rate which it was wise to support there could be no technical difficulty in supporting that rate.

[1] As we shall see in Volume II, the unprofitability of the operation may well express a real cost to society.

[2] For our purposes we are not interested so much in the legal ownership of the fund as in the way in which it is in fact operated. If the national authorities of A and B both held legally separate national exchange equalization funds but in fact always reached joint decisions on when, in what direction, and to what extent each fund should operate, this would, for our present purposes, constitute a single international exchange equalization fund.

In the second place, a national exchange equalization fund is liable to misuse. As we have seen above (p. 154) it is always possible for the authorities in one country to attempt to cure a domestic unemployment problem by inducing an unnaturally large favourable balance of trade, i.e. to give employment at home not by a financial policy for internal balance but by an 'unnatural' invasion of the other country's markets. Such a policy, in so far as it is successful, will achieve an increased demand for the one country's products and labour only at the expense of the demand for those of the other country; and in a period of general world depression this will cause increased unemployment in the second. A national exchange equalization fund is an instrument which could be misused for purposes of this kind. Thus the authority in charge of A's fund might purchase B's currency with A's currency, not because it was thought that private speculators were unduly pessimistic about the future value of B's currency and were thus causing A's currency to have a value in the foreign exchange market which was too high in relation to what was needed for external balance, but merely in order to expand the market for A's products at the expense of B's markets so as to give greater employment to A's labour regardless of any consequent surplus in A's balance of payments. The very fact that an international exchange equalization fund would have to use its resources to support exchange rates which were agreed to be 'normal' either by the monetary authorities of both countries or by some supranational body would avoid misuses of the fund for this kind of illegitimate purpose.

In addition to the increased stability which can be brought about by the proper use of national or international exchange equalization funds, there is another device which will help to remove some of the dangers of the excessive fluctuations in exchange rates which might be occasioned by misguided speculation. This is the device of the forward-exchange market. This mechanism cannot itself remove the main disadvantages of ill-judged speculative movements; it can merely remove the uncertainties of exchange-rate variations to which such movements may submit traders. But, on the other hand, it can remove those uncertainties not only when they are due to ill-judged speculation, but also when they arise from the necessary and unavoidable adjustments of the method of exchange-rate adjustment.

In any free exchange market traders must often be presented with serious risks from possible exchange-rate variations. For example, a producer in B sells goods in A for a promise on the importer's part to pay him a certain sum in A's currency (dollars) at a certain future date. The producer in B has with this sum to cover costs which are contracted mainly in terms of B's currency (pounds). If, in the interval between the sale of the goods in A and the receipt of A's money and its exchange into B's money, the exchange value of A's currency should depreciate, the exporter in B will make a serious loss on his production.

This exchange risk may be eliminated by means of a market in forward exchange. The B-exporter knows that he will receive, say, $200 next year. He wishes to fix now the rate at which he can exchange $200 into pounds next year. He goes to an exchange dealer and fixes a bargain with him to give the exchange dealer $200 for £100 in a year's time. In this operation the exchange dealer is said to purchase dollars 'one year forward' and the trader to sell dollars 'one year forward'. This rate of $2 = £1 which is fixed now to operate in a transaction which is to take place in a year's time is called the 'forward' rate of exchange, as opposed to the 'spot' rate which refers to the rate fixed now for a transaction which is completed now.

The exchange dealer, if he wishes, can also cover himself against any exchange risk, because when he purchases dollars one-year forward (e.g. undertakes to give £100 for $200 next year) he can always himself simultaneously purchase pounds spot (i.e. purchase now with dollars the £100 which he has undertaken to make available to the trader next year). In this case he knows exactly where he stands. He has acquired £100 for a given amount of dollars now, and knows that he will get exactly $200 in return for the £100 next year.

The relation between the spot rate and the forward rate of exchange will depend in very large measure upon the relation between the short-term rate of interest on money loans in A and B. Suppose the exchange dealer borrows $200 now at, say, 1 per cent in order to purchase pounds spot at a spot rate of $2 for £1, thus acquiring £100 immediately. And suppose that he can obtain 10 per cent on money lent for one year in pounds in B. Then at the end of the year he will have £110 to change back into dollars. This he must do at a rate of exchange which will provide him with at least the $202 which is necessary to enable him to repay the $200 which he borrowed plus the interest of 1 per cent (i.e. $2) on it. If the forward rate of exchange were now the same as the spot rate of $2 = £1, he would next year obtain $220 from traders for £110 and would make a profit of $18. With a spot rate of $2 = £1 and with rates of interest as high as 10 per cent per annum in B and as low as 1 per cent per annum in A, the exchange dealer can afford to charge the trader a forward rate for pounds as low as only $1·84 per £1 (i.e. $202/£110) without making a loss.

It follows that with a well-organized forward-exchange market a trader can always fix now the rate at which he can change pounds into dollars or dollars into pounds in the future, so as to avoid exchange risks. And the forward rate will be cheap in terms of the spot rate in the case of that currency in whose money market the rate of interest is relatively high. The exchange dealer, that is to say, will like to buy spot and to sell forward that currency on which he can earn a high rate of interest, so that he will offer that currency to traders at a relatively cheap forward rate.

So much for the problem of speculation in a free exchange market. The matter takes on a quite different aspect if exchange-rate variations are used as the means of restoring equilibrium, but if the market mechanism is carried out, not by a free exchange market, but by means of an adjustable peg. (See p. 165 above).

Suppose, once again, that there is some spontaneous deterioration in B's external position which ultimately requires a depreciation of B's exchange from $4 = £1 to $3 = £1. Until the change in the peg is actually made, speculators will have a strong incentive to move funds from pounds into dollars. They will see the continuing deficit in B's balance of payments and will therefore realize that sooner or later a movement in the peg will be inevitable. But as the speculators move speculative funds from B to A this will not in itself cause any immediate depreciation of B's currency, which will not take place until the peg is itself adjusted; nor will the prospect of a future move of speculative funds back from A to B cause speculators to anticipate that B's currency will appreciate above what it would otherwise be after the necessary adjustment of the peg to the new long-run equilibrium level has taken place. In other words, the profit from the anticipated exchange-rate adjustment is not only certain, but there is also no limit to the amount of speculative capital on which this profit is obtainable. In the result a very large speculative movement of funds from B to A can be anticipated on which this profit will be earned.

Now this speculation serves no useful purpose. Because of the exchange-rate peg, it is not permitted to affect the exchange rate. It merely means that the speculators can make a certain profit on an almost unlimited scale at the expense of the monetary authorities. In order to maintain the value of B's currency when speculators are moving funds from B to A before the change in the peg, the monetary authorities will have to purchase B's currency at its previous value in terms of A's currency; and later, in order to maintain the value of A's currency when speculators are bringing funds back from A to B after the change in the peg, they will have to resell their previous purchases of B's currency at its new and lower value in terms of A's currency.

For this reason an adjustable-peg mechanism can be successfully operated only if there is some direct control over speculative capital movements between the currencies concerned. And as we shall see below (pp. 301–2), this involves the maintenance of the apparatus of exchange control over all transactions and raises difficult problems in the decision as to what are, and what are not, speculative capital movements. This is undoubtedly a grave disadvantage of this mechanism of adjustment.

There remains the question of the rôle of speculation in the conditions of the gold standard. With the gold standard the rate of exchange is rigidly fixed except for fluctuations within the gold points. For the reasons explained above (p. 180) with a par rate of exchange of, say, $4 = £1, the actual rate of exchange can vary between the limits of, say, $4·05 = £1 and $3·95 = £1. Within these narrow limits there is some scope for speculation of the type which we have discussed above. Let us suppose that B's external position deteriorates. The value of B's currency then depreciates to B's gold export point of $3·95 = £1. At this point speculators know that the pound cannot depreciate any further, but that, when the necessary readjustments are made and external balance has been restored, there may be some appreciation of the pound as far as, but no farther than, B's gold import point of $4·05 = £1. At any rate over the range of $3·95 to $4·05 = £1 there is the possibility of an exchange profit and no possibility of loss. Speculative funds may, therefore, be moved on a modest scale from dollars to pounds during the process of adjustment, and this may help to fill part of B's balance-of-payments gap during the most difficult period of readjustment to the new conditions.

But in this case the final readjustment has got to be brought about, not by an alteration in the exchange rate, but by an absolute fall in money wage rates and prices in B and an absolute rise in such prices in A. Here there is theoretically the same possibility of useful speculative movements as in the case of a free exchange market, but in practice the scope for such speculation is likely to be limited in the extreme.

Since the sensitivity of international demand to relative price changes is likely to be much smaller in the short-run than in the long-run, the prices of B's products immediately after the change ought to fall (and of A's products to rise) much more than is necessary in the long-run to achieve the necessary readjustment of demand. Speculators would then expect a long-run fall in the price of A's products and rise in the price of B's. They could then sell A's products from stock, use the money to purchase B's currency and use B's currency to purchase B's products for stock, thus changing a holding of A's products (whose prices will fall in the future) for a holding of B's products (whose prices will rise).

But for a number of reasons this development is not at all likely to occur on any very considerable scale.

In the first place, it rests on the assumption that the domestic prices and wage rates in A and in B are as flexible under the gold standard as is the rate of exchange in a free market. But money wage rates are notoriously sticky. While the value of B's currency in a free market may fall from $4 to $2 for a year and then recover to $3, it is most improbable that the wage rate in B would fall from £4 to £2 a week for a year and then recover to £3; and while it is probable that the prices of finished products are rather more flexible than wage rates it is improbable that they are anything like as flexible as the rate of exchange in a free market.

What is much more likely to happen is that after the first spontaneous disturbance prices will go on gradually falling in B as the pressure of unemployment in B causes a gradual decline in money wages, and prices will gradually rise in A as the pressure of increased money demand in A causes an upward change. But if this happens, speculators may for a considerable period after the change actually speculate for a continued decline in the prices of B's products and rise in the prices of A's products and thus move from B's products into A's products. This could only intensify the difficulties of the process of adjustment, leading to even more serious temporary unemployment in B's industries and loss of gold from B to A.

But it is doubtful whether much speculation as between B's products and A's products will in fact take place. In any case it will certainly be on a much smaller scale than the speculation which is likely as between A's and B's currencies in a free exchange market. Speculation between A's and B's currencies involves relatively little cost other than the possible exchange loss if the speculation is misjudged. But quite apart from the possibility of losses due to misguided anticipations, speculation between A's and B's products involves the real cost of storage of the products of the country whose prices are likely to go up, which may be very high in the case of many commodities which are bulky or perishable, and the real inconvenience of running down the holding of normal trading stocks of the products of the country in which prices are expected to fall.

One may conclude that with the gold standard the scope for speculation whether for the good or the ill of society is comparatively limited. With the mechanism of the adjustable peg the scope for speculation is very wide; but private speculation is likely to bring no gain to society and merely to involve the monetary authorities in the prospect of serious loss to the benefit only of the speculators themselves. Indeed, the system would seem difficult to maintain without an efficient exchange control which could simply eliminate speculation. With the free exchange market there is wide scope for speculation in which the speculators' interest will, on the whole, coincide with that of society. But ill-informed speculation can bring serious loss to society. From the point of view of the service which, if properly controlled, speculation can confer on society, there would seem to be much to be said for a free exchange market combined with a well-organized market in forward exchange and an internationally controlled exchange equalization fund.[1]

[1] If it is desired to control capital transfers for reasons other than those connected with the avoidance of noxious speculative movements, certain further issues arise in the choice between the mechanisms of the gold standard, an adjustable peg, and a free exchange market. These are discussed in Chapter XXII below.

CHAPTER XVIII

FOREIGN-TRADE AND HOME-TRADE PRODUCTS [1]

UP to this point we have considered the mechanisms for the adjust-ment of the balance of payments between A and B on the assumption that we can treat A's products as a single homogeneous group of goods and B's products as another single homogeneous group of goods (see pp. 49–50). For this reason, in our consideration of the effects of exchange-rate adjustment or of wage-rate adjustments we have asked only to what extent the resulting price adjustments will cause A's prod-ucts as a single group to be substituted for B's products as a single group.

This is not, of course, altogether realistic. Many different products will be produced in A and many different products in B. Some prod-ucts will be produced in A and consumed in A but will not compete at all directly with B's products. These products will not be in direct competition with B's products because they can be transported between A and B only with extreme difficulty and at a very high cost. They may be perishable (like milk) or too bulky and heavy (like houses) or requiring direct contact between the actual producer and the ultimate consumer (like the services of a hairdresser). In reality, this is, of course, only a matter of degree. Products range with almost continuous variation between those for which the cost of transport is negligibly low in rela-tion to their value and those for which the costs of transport are so high as to be in all imaginable circumstances prohibitive. We shall, however, proceed with our analysis on the simplifying assumption that the prod-ucts of each of our two countries can be divided into two groups: its 'home-trade' products in the case of which the costs of international transport are prohibitively high and its 'foreign-trade' products in the case of which the costs of international transport are negligibly low.

This divides each country's products into two groups: its 'home-trade' products and its 'foreign-trade' products. For certain purposes we shall need to subdivide its 'foreign-trade' products into two sub-groups: its 'export products' and its 'import-competing' products, thus:

Total Production

Home-trade products   Foreign-trade products

Export   Import-competing
products   products

[1] The subject matter of this chapter is treated in Sections IX and X (i) of the separate mathematical supplement.

A country's export products are those which it exports to other countries as well as consuming at home, and its import-competing products are those which it consumes at home without exporting, but which are very similar to the products which it imports. Moreover, when we wish to distinguish between a country's export products on the one hand and its home-trade and import-competing products on the other, we shall talk of its 'export' products and its 'non-export' products; and when we wish to distinguish between its import-competing products on the one hand and its home-trade and export products on the other hand, we shall talk of its 'import-competing' and 'non-import-competing' products.

The producers in each of our two countries thus produce three sets of products: home-trade, export, and import-competing; and the purchasers in each of our countries purchase four sets of commodities: all three of the products produced in their own country and the export products of the other country.

Let us now reconsider on these more realistic assumptions the problem raised in Chapter XII. We assume that country B's exchange rate is depreciated by a given amount; and we ask what effect this will have on B's balance of trade and upon the real terms of trade between A and B on the assumption that money wage rates are constant in both countries and that the authorities in both countries adopt domestic financial policies for internal balance.

This is, of course, only one special problem out of the many which we could select for discussion on the basis of our new assumptions. But it is a central question and in one sense can be regarded as covering the whole ground. For if we suppose that, whatever disturbances may occur, the authorities in both A and B adopt domestic financial policies for internal balance, the only problem which remains is the problem of external balance. Accordingly we ask: what effect will a depreciation of a country's currency have upon a country's balance of payments and upon its real terms of trade with the rest of the world, on the assumption that both inside its territory and in the rest of the world money wage rates are constant and there are financial policies for internal balance? If the depreciation of the currency of the deficit country will improve its balance of payments without an intolerable movement of the terms of trade against it, then this method of adjustment—namely, domestic financial policies for internal balance combined with variations in exchange rates for external balance—will still work effectively in face of all types of spontaneous disturbance.

Now a depreciation of B's currency in terms of A's will increase the price in B of a unit of A's money and will thus tend to raise the price in B of A's products. Similarly, it will lower the price of B's money in A and will thus tend to lower the price of B's products in A.

The consequence of this will be that the price in B of all B's foreign-trade products will tend to rise relatively to the price of B's home-trade products. The price of B's import-competing products will rise because the rise in the price of A's exports in B's currency will cause a rise in the demand for, and so in the price of, the products of B which compete closely with these imports; and the price of B's export products will rise in terms of B's currency because the fall in their price in A's currency will increase the demand for them in A and will thus drive up the price offered for them in B's currency. Similarly in A, the price of all foreign-trade products will tend to fall relatively to that of home trade products because the imports from B will be cheaper in terms of A's currency and will thus depress the price of A's import-competing products, and the demand in B for A's exports (whose price will have risen in B's currency) will have fallen off so that the price in A's currency for A's export products will decline.

The process of readjustment of the balance of trade between A and B can now be regarded as essentially a matter of the consequential shift of demand and supply between foreign-trade and home-trade products in A and in B. In B, for example, the price of foreign-trade products has gone up relatively to that of home-trade products. Demand will, therefore, shift away from the more expensive foreign-trade products; and this will involve a reduction in the demand in B for imports and for products of B which might otherwise be exported to A. Productive resources will at the same time be shifted so as to increase the supply of foreign-trade products, and this will increase the supply of exports to A and also of products which enable purchasers in B to dispense with imports from A.

Similarly in A the fall in the price of foreign-trade relatively to that of home-trade products will cause a shift of demand away from the latter on to the former. This will involve an increased demand in A for imports and for the products of A which might otherwise be exported to B. Simultaneously in A producers will shift from the production of foreign-trade to that of home-trade products; and this will involve a reduction in the supply of the products which are exported from A and in the supply of those products which enable purchasers in A to dispense with imports.

Thus the shift of demand in B from foreign-trade to home-trade products and of supply in the reverse direction will diminish imports into B and increase exports from B, while the shift of demand in A from home-trade to foreign-trade products and the shift of supply in A in the opposite direction will increase imports into A and reduce exports from A. By this mechanism the depreciation of B's currency will cause a favourable movement in B's balance of trade provided that there is sufficient substitutability either in consumption or in production in A or in B between foreign-trade products on the one hand and home-trade products on the other.

The above mechanism involves some rise in the price of foreign-trade relatively to that of home-trade products in B and some fall in the price of foreign-trade relatively to that of home-trade products in A. It is the change in these price relationships which, if there is sufficient substitutability in consumption or production between these two broad classes, will bring about the adjustment of the balance of trade. But the real terms of trade (i.e. the ratio between the price of B's exports and A's exports) may move in either direction so far as the above analysis is concerned.

We have seen in Chapter XII that in the case in which each country's products can be treated as a single homogeneous group whose prices all move up and down more or less together, a depreciation of B's currency will always turn the real terms of trade against B, but will improve B's balance of trade if the sum of the elasticities of demand for imports in the two countries is greater than one. But now that we are distinguishing between the home-trade and foreign-trade products of each country it is *possible* that a depreciation of B's currency, in addition to improving B's balance of trade, will also move the terms of trade in B's favour.

In what conditions is this likely to happen? Let us suppose that the immediate effect of a depreciation of B's currency is to cause the price of B's imports to go up by the same percentage as the price of B's exports in terms of B's currency. It would, of course, follow that the price of A's exports would have gone down by the same percentage as the price of A's imports in terms of A's currency. Since the prices of all foreign-trade products have moved in the same way, the real terms of trade are so far unchanged; but they will ultimately move in B's favour if the subsequent shifts of demand and supply between foreign-trade and home-trade products in A and in B are such as to maintain the price of B's exports and to lower the price of A's exports.

Two conditions must be fulfilled in B for the adjustments of demand and supply in B to tend to lower the price of B's imports relatively to that of her exports.

First, when the shift in demand in B takes place from foreign-trade to home-trade products, this must take the form of a shift of demand away from imports and import-competing products in B, rather than a shift of demand away from B's export products. Otherwise the price of B's exports would tend to fall as quickly as that of her imports.

Secondly, when the shift in supply in B takes place from home-trade to foreign-trade products, this must take the form of an increase in the supply of B's import-competing products rather than an increase in the supply of B's export products. Otherwise the price of B's exports would tend to fall again as quickly as the price of B's imports.

Similarly, two conditions must be fulfilled in A for the price of A's exports to be kept low relatively to the price of A's imports.

First, the shift in demand in A from home-trade on to foreign-trade products must be on to imports and import-competing products in A rather than on to A's export products. Otherwise the price of A's exports would tend to be kept up as much as the price of her imports.

Second, for the same reason, the shift in supply in A from foreign-trade to home-trade products must be from import-competing products rather than from export products.

These changes in relative prices are illustrated in Table XV. B's exchange rate is depreciated in terms of A's currency. The impact effect of this is, as we have shown, to cause the prices of foreign-trade products in A to fall relatively to those of home-trade products; and vice versa in B. This is shown in the first line of plus and minus signs in Table XV. There has as yet been no reason for the price of imports and import-competing products to change relatively to that of export products either in A or B.

We now turn to case i of Table XV which shows the conditions in which the terms of trade are most likely to move in B's favour. In A the rise in the price of home-trade products relatively to that of foreign-trade products causes a shift of demand on to the cheaper foreign-trade products and of supply away from the less profitable foreign-trade products. But the shift of demand is mainly on to, and that of supply mainly away from, imports and import-competing products rather than export products. The price of imports thus tends to rise relatively to that of exports. Simultaneously in B the rise in the price of foreign-trade products causes a shift of demand away from, and of supply towards, foreign-trade products; but this shift of demand is mainly on to, and of supply is mainly away from, imports and import-competing products rather than export products. The result is a tendency in B for the price of imports to fall relatively to exports. The terms of trade will, therefore, be moved in B's favour by forces operating both in A and in B.

Case ii of Table XV shows the opposite possibility. Once again the relative rise in the price of home-trade products in A and of foreign-trade products in B causes demand to shift on to foreign-trade products in A and away from them in B; and for the same reason the relative supply of foreign-trade products falls in A and rises in B. But this time the shift of demand in A is mainly on to, and of supply mainly away from, export products, so that A's exports rise in price relatively to A's imports; and in B the shift of demand is mainly away from, and of supply mainly on to, export products, so that B's exports fall in price

TABLE XV

The Effect of a Depreciation of B's Exchange Rate upon the Terms of Trade.

Note: Relative Price Changes are shown by Plus and Minus Signs in joined Circles.

COUNTRY A   COUNTRY B

| Home-trade products | Foreign-trade products | | Home-trade products | Foreign-trade products | |

Export products | Import-competing products   Export products | Import-competing products

Case i. Terms of Trade move in B's Favour.

Demand Shift   Demand Shift

Supply Shift   Supply Shift

Case ii. Terms of Trade move in A's Favour.

Demand Shift   Demand Shift

Supply Shift   Supply Shift

relatively to B's imports. In this case the terms of trade will obviously move against B.

Now, in case i the shift of demand in B away from foreign-trade products is mainly from import-competing products and the shift of supply on to foreign-trade products is mainly on to import-competing products. But this combination of shifts is merely another way of saying that the elasticity of supply of exports from B to A will be small, i.e. that a rise in the price in terms of B's currency offered by A's importers for B's exports will not cause much increase in the supply of B's exports to A. This will be so (i) because when their price goes up in B additional economic resources cannot easily be shifted into their production from the production of non-export products so that their total supply is very little increased, and (ii) because the rise of their price in B does not cause much shift in purchases in B away from these relatively expensive export products on to the now relatively cheap home-trade products, so that of the constant total supply of export products not much more is available for export to A.[1]

Similarly in case i of Table XV the shift of demand in A on to foreign-trade products is mainly on to import-competing products and the shift of supply is mainly away from import-competing products. But this combination of shifts is merely another way of saying that the elasticity of supply of exports from A to B will be small. When the price offered by purchasers in B for A's exports falls in terms of A's currency, then the supply sent to B will not fall much because (i) there will not be much shift of resources in A out of the industries producing for export, and (ii) there will not be much increased consumption in A of these products merely because their price is lower in A.

A country's elasticity of supply of exports will, therefore, be low if both in production and in consumption there is little substitutability between its export products on the one hand and its non-export products on the other hand. If either in production or in consumption such substitutability were high, the elasticity of supply of exports would be high and we should in fact reach the same conclusions as we reached in Chapter XII in the case in which we were able to treat each country's products as making up one single homogeneous group.

Thus, suppose that there is an easy substitution between a country's export and non-export products in so far as the *consumption* of these commodities in the country in question is concerned. Let us take an example. Suppose that country B's exchange rate is depreciated. This lowers the price of B's export products in A's currency. More of them are bought in A. This increases the demand for them and their price in B's currency rises. Since the authorities in B are adopting a financial policy for internal balance the probability is that the price offered for B's non-export products will have fallen as a result of the reduced domestic expenditure in B (which will involve reductions in expenditure on B's non-export products as well as on export products and on other commodities) brought about as an act of policy in order to prevent the increased demand in A for B's exports from causing an inflation in B.

[1] A small elasticity of supply of *exports* from B to A must thus be carefully distinguished from a small elasticity of supply of *export products* in B. This latter elasticity of supply would be low if a rise in the price of such products in B caused a very small increase in the total production of such products in B. But the elasticity of supply of exports to A would, nevertheless, be high, if the rise in the price of B's export products caused purchasers in B to buy much less of them, thus releasing a much larger part of the given output for export to A.

The price of B's export products thus tends to rise relatively to the price offered in B for B's non-export products. But if purchasers in B shift very readily from the consumption of B's export products to the consumption of B's non-export products when the price of the former goes up relatively to the price of the latter, the demand for B's export products will be reduced again and the demand for her non-export products will be increased. As a result there will be only a small net rise in the price of B's export products relatively to that of her non-export products. This easy shiftability of consumption in B between export and non-export products will mean that the prices of all B's products in B's currency will rise and fall more or less in line; and for this reason we can treat B's products as forming a single group. If the same is true of A also, then once again we need consider only the extent to which A's products (as a single group) can be substituted for B's products (as a single group). For, since B's export and non-export products are easily substitutable in B's consumption and since A's export and non-export products are easily substitutable in A's consumption, we need now consider only the extent to which B's export products and A's export products are substitutable for each other in A's and B's consumption— i.e. what is the sum of the elasticities of demand in A and B for imports of each other's products.

The second case in which we can treat each country's products as forming one homogeneous group is when the producers in each country can shift easily from the *production* of its export to that of its non-export products. Let us take the same example as before. B's exchange rate is depreciated. As a result the demand in A for B's export products is increased. The price of B's export products in terms of B's currency rises. The price of B's non-export products will not have risen in the same way, and may indeed have fallen as a result of the policy deflation of domestic expenditure in B which is undertaken in order to prevent the increased demand in A for B's products from causing a general inflation in B. If in these circumstances the producers of B's non-export products can readily shift to the production of her now more profitable export products, the price of the non-export products will rise as their supply is reduced and the price of her export products will fall again as their supply is increased. If the shiftability of productive resources between the two sets of industry is great, then in the end the price of B's export products will not rise much in relation to that of her non-export products. If the same is true in A also, we have again reduced our problem to the former simple terms. For, since B's export and non-export products can easily be exchanged for each other through shifts of production in B and since A's export and non-export products can easily be exchanged for each other through shifts of production in A, we need now consider only the extent to which A's and B's export products can be substituted for each other in A's and B's consumption—i.e. the sum of the elasticities of demand in A and in B for each other's exports.[1]

In these cases (where in both countries the prices of non-export products keep more or less in line with those of export products because of the shiftability of consumption or of production or of both between the two groups of products) the analysis of Chapter XII needs no modification. The terms of trade will move against B more or less in proportion to the depreciation of her exchange rate; for, since the adoption of financial policies for internal balance will keep the prices of each country's products more or less constant in terms of its own currency, the amount of B's products which must be given for a unit of A's products will rise in a proportion equal to the rise in the amount of B's money which must be given for a unit of A's money. Moreover, if the sum of the elasticities of demand in A and in B for each other's products is greater than unity this movement of the terms of trade against B will be associated with a favourable movement in B's balance of trade.

The result may, however, be quite different if the elasticity of supply of exports is low.

Let us first consider what happens to the price of B's exports, when B's currency is depreciated by 10 per cent. The depreciation will tend to make B's products cheaper in terms of A's currency; the demand in A for B's exports will go up; this will cause some rise in the price offered for them in B's currency. In the end there will be some fall in their price in A's currency and some rise in B's currency. One extreme limit is a 10 per cent fall in their price in terms of A's currency; and in this case there would be no significant change in their price in terms of B's currency, since exporters in B obtain 10 per cent less of A's currency for a unit of B's exports but obtain 10 per cent more of B's currency for a given amount of A's currency. The other extreme limit is no fall in the price of B's exports in terms of A's currency; and in this case there would be a 10 per cent rise in their price in terms of B's currency, since exporters in B can get the same amount of A's currency for a unit of B's exports but can get 10 per cent more of B's currency for a given amount of A's currency. In fact a 10 per cent depreciation of B's currency causes a 10 per cent gap between the prices of B's exports in B's currency and in A's currency; if the price in A's currency goes

[1] It is, of course, the combined effect of the factors discussed in this and in the previous paragraph which matters, namely, the substitutability between export and non-export products in production and consumption. When the price of B's export products rises relatively to that of B's non-export products, the price ratio will be restored partly by the increased supply of export products and reduced supply of non-export products which results from the shift of productive resources to the more profitable lines of production and partly by the reduced demand in B for the relatively expensive export products and the increased demand for the relatively cheap non-export products.

down by 3 per cent, then the price in B's currency must go up by approximately 7 per cent; and so on.

In the case in which the elasticity of supply of exports from B is very small the price adjustment will take the form mainly of a rise in the price in terms of B's currency. The 10 per cent depreciation of B's currency will tend to cause some decline in the price at which B's exports are offered to purchasers in A in terms of A's currency; this will increase the demand in A for B's exports and cause some rise in the price offered for them in B's currency. But because their elasticity of supply in B is low not much more of them will be exported to A. The increased demand for them in A will, therefore, lead to a very considerable rise in their price in terms of B's currency and to little increase in the supply of B's exports on A's markets and so to little decline in their price in terms of A's currency. In the limit, if there is no increase at all in the supply of B's exports to A, the price of these products will not decline at all in terms of A's currency, since purchasers in A will buy the same amount at the same price in terms of A's currency. The result of the 10 per cent depreciation of B's currency would be merely a rise by 10 per cent in the price of B's exports in terms of her own currency, the amount supplied to A being unchanged.[1]

If at the same time the elasticity of supply of exports from A is also small, the depreciation of B's currency will take the form mainly of a fall in the price of A's exports in terms of A's currency rather than of a rise in their price in terms of B's currency. Once again a 10 per cent depreciation of B's currency will tend to make A's exports more expensive in B's currency; purchasers in B will demand less of them; but as purchasers in B buy less of them, their price in terms of A's currency falls heavily since the supply from A to B is very little reduced. Again in the limit, in which there is no reduction at all in the supply of A's exports to B, the price of A's exports in terms of B's currency will not rise at all (because the amount put on to B's market is unchanged), so that their price in A's currency will fall by the full 10 per cent of the depreciation of B's currency.[2]

---

[1] On our assumption that a financial policy for internal balance is being adopted in B, the price of B's non-export products will be kept constant by any degree of internal policy deflation or inflation of domestic expenditure in B which may be necessary for this purpose. Since there is zero real elasticity of supply of B's export products the rise in the price of such products will not provide any increased employment in the export industries. Internal balance in B, therefore, means unchanged employment in the industries producing non-export products. But since the money wage rate is constant, this requires a constant money expenditure on (and so money demand price for) non-export products.

[2] A financial policy for internal balance in A will in these circumstances involve an adjustment of total demand in A such as to keep constant the total expenditure on (and so the price in A's currency offered for) A's non-export products.

In these conditions of very low elasticities of supply of exports in both countries, a depreciation of B's currency will cause (i) a favourable movement in B's balance of trade, even though the sum of the elasticities of demand for imports in A and in B is less than unity, and (ii) a simultaneous improvement in B's terms of trade. We have seen above that, in the limiting case in which there is a zero elasticity of supply of exports in both countries, the price of B's exports in B's currency will rise by the full amount of the exchange depreciation while the price of A's exports in B's currency will not rise at all. In other words, the depreciation of B's currency will have caused a movement in the terms of trade favourable to B and equal to the depreciation of the exchange rate. Moreover, in this limiting case the balance of trade will have moved favourably to B, since exporters in B will be selling an unchanged volume of their exports to purchasers in A at a price in B's currency which is higher by the depreciation of her currency, and importers in B will be purchasing an unchanged volume of A's exports at a price which is unchanged in terms of B's currency. In other words, there will be a gain on B's balance of trade, because the value of B's imports will have remained unchanged and the value of B's exports will have increased in the same proportion as the depreciation of her exchange rate.

This situation of zero elasticities of supply of exports is, of course, merely a limiting case. In fact the elasticity of supply of exports in each country is likely to be something greater than zero and something less than infinity. Moreover, these various elasticities of supply of exports in each country may be combined with various elasticities of demand for imports in each country.[1] Let us consider briefly four possible combinations. (i) Elasticities of demand for imports and of supply of exports are high in both countries. (ii) Elasticities of demand for imports are high but elasticities of supply of exports are low. (iii) Elasticities of demand for imports are low but elasticities of supply of exports are high. (iv) Elasticities of demand for imports and of supply of exports are both low. The reader must work out for himself the cases where the demand or supply elasticity is high in the one country but low in the other.

(i) The most favourable condition for obtaining an extensive adjustment of the balance of trade between A and B with comparatively little strain on the terms of trade is that high elasticities of demand for imports in each country should be combined with high elasticities of supply of exports in each country. A depreciation of B's currency will

---

[1] We have seen that the elasticity of supply of exports from a country is likely to be low if, and only if, there is little substitutability both in production and consumption between that country's export and non-export products. Similarly, the elasticity of demand for imports is likely to be low if, and only if, there is little substitutability both in production and consumption between that country's imports and import-competing products on the one hand, and its non-import-competing products on the other hand.

always tend to make B's exports cheaper in A's currency and A's exports dearer in B's currency. If the sum of the elasticities of demand for imports in A and in B is greater than unity, this will always lead to an improvement in B's balance of trade. If the elasticity of demand for imports in A is very high, then the depreciation will lead to a very large increase in the demand in A for B's products; and if the elasticity of supply of exports in B is very high, the increased demand will not lead to any considerable rise in the price of B's exports in terms of B's currency, with the result that their price in A's currency will remain low as a result of the depreciation and the demand in A will, therefore, remain much increased. The value of B's exports will, therefore, increase most where the elasticity of demand in A for these products is high and where the elasticity of supply of exports from B to A is also high.

Similarly, if the elasticity of demand in B for A's exports is high, the rise in the price of A's exports in B's currency resulting from the depreciation of B's currency will cause a large decline in the demand in B for A's exports and thus a considerable decline in expenditure by B's purchasers on imports; and if the elasticity of supply of exports from A to B is also great, this reduction in the demand for A's exports will not cause much fall in the price of A's exports in A's currency, so that their price in B's currency will remain relatively high and the decline in the demand in B will, therefore, remain great. B's imports will thus fall most in value if the elasticity of demand in B for A's exports is high and the elasticity of supply of exports from A to B is also high.

In this case, while there will be a large favourable movement in B's balance of trade as a result of the depreciation of B's currency, there will at the same time be a moderate movement of the terms of trade against B. The high elasticity of supply of exports in B will mean that the price of B's exports does not rise much in terms of B's currency when the demand for B's exports rises; and the high elasticity of supply of exports in A will mean that the price of A's exports does not fall much in terms of A's currency when the demand for A's exports falls. In consequence a unit of B's exports will command less of A's exports when, as a result of the depreciation, a unit of B's currency commands less of A's currency.

(ii) We may consider next the case in which the elasticities of demand for imports remain large, but the elasticities of supply of exports are low. The fact that the elasticities of demand for imports are still large means that the depreciation of B's currency will necessarily lead to an improvement in B's balance of trade. A 10 per cent depreciation of B's currency is bound to cause some fall in the price of B's export products in A's currency; and if the elasticity of demand in A for B's exports is high, the value of B's exports will in consequence go up in terms of A's currency. The value of B's exports in B's currency will go up by 10 per cent more than their value in A's currency because of the 10 per cent depreciation of B's currency. A low elasticity of supply of exports from B will mean merely that the price of B's exports tends to rise rather more in terms of A's currency, than would otherwise have been the case. With a high elasticity of demand in A this means that the increase in the value of A's imports in terms of A's currency is less than would otherwise have been the case, so that the improvement in the value of B's exports in terms of B's currency is also less than would have been the case with a high elasticity of supply in B.

Similarly, it can be seen that the depreciation of B's currency will cause some rise in the price of A's exports in B's currency; if the demand in B is elastic, the total expenditure by B's purchasers on imports in terms of B's currency will fall when the price of B's imports rises. But if the elasticity of supply of exports from A to B is small, the price of A's exports will fall heavily in terms of A's currency, and will not, therefore, rise very much in terms of B's currency. In this case, since the demand in B for A's exports has a high elasticity, expenditure by B's purchasers on imports from A will not decline as much as it would have done if the elasticity of supply of exports from A to B had been great and the price of A's exports in B's currency had, therefore, been higher.

Thus, since the elasticities of demand for imports are high, the balance of trade will in any case move in B's favour when B's currency is depreciated; but since the elasticities of supply of exports are low the improvement in B's balance of trade which will follow any given depreciation of B's currency will not be as great as in the previous case where the elasticities of supply as well as the elasticities of demand were large.

On the other hand, the improvement in the balance of trade of the depreciating country will be brought about with a very small adverse movement in the terms of trade. Indeed, if the elasticities of supply are sufficiently small, the improvement in the balance of trade will be combined with an improvement in the real terms of trade. The price of B's exports in B's currency will go up by the greater part of the 10 per cent depreciation in the exchange rate if the elasticity of that supply is sufficiently small. And the price of A's exports in A's currency will go down by the greater part of the 10 per cent depreciation of B's exchange rate if the elasticities of their supply in A is sufficiently low, so that there will be little rise in their price in B's currency. With the price of B's exports up by the greater part of 10 per cent in B's currency and with the price of A's exports very little raised in B's currency, there would be a marked improvement in B's terms of trade.

(iii) We now come to a case where the depreciation of B's currency will cause a deterioration instead of an improvement in B's balance of trade. In this case the elasticities of supply of exports are high, but the elasticities of demand for imports are low. If in any country the elasticity of supply of exports is high and if a financial policy for internal balance is maintained in that country, then the price of that country's exports cannot be much changed in terms of that country's currency. The elasticity of supply of exports will be great if, in that country, there is considerable shiftability either of production or of consumption between its export and non-export products; in this case, as we have seen above (pp. 238-9), the price of export products cannot move very differently from that of non-export products; and a financial policy for internal balance will mean that the general level of prices of its products is stabilized in terms of the home currency. If it is true of each country that the price of its export products is stabilized in terms of its own currency, then the terms of trade will move against B by the full amount of the depreciation of B's currency. In this case if the sum of the elasticities of demand for imports is less than unity, the balance of trade will also move unfavourably to B (see Table VIII). We are, in fact, back in terms of the analysis of Chapter XII.

(iv) There remains the case where all the elasticities—both of supply and of demand—are small. In this case a depreciation of B's currency will lead to an adverse movement in B's balance of trade if the elasticities of demand are small relatively to the elasticities of supply and to an improvement in B's balance of trade if the elasticities of supply are small relatively to the elasticities of demand.

Let us first consider the case where, while the elasticities of supply are low, the elasticities of demand are very much lower. In this case when B's currency is depreciated, the price of B's exports will fall very heavily in terms of A's currency (because of the extremely low elasticity of demand for imports in A), so that the rise in price of B's exports in terms of B's currency will be small even though the elasticity of supply in B is rather low. There will, in fact, not be a sufficient increase in demand in A to cause any appreciable rise in the price of B's exports in terms of B's currency. The price of B's exports in terms of B's currency. will, therefore, rise very little; the volume of B's exports will be practically unchanged; and, in consequence, the value of B's exports in terms of B's currency will rise very little. At the same time, if the elasticity of demand in B for A's exports is very low, the depreciation of B's currency will cause a large rise in the price of A's exports in terms of B's currency, because purchasers in B will reduce their purchases of imports very little when their price goes up. Suppliers of exports in A will, therefore, be faced by an almost unchanged demand in B, so that the price of A's exports in terms of A's currency will hardly fall at all even though the elasticity of their supply is rather low. In consequence, the price and the total value of B's exports will go up very little and the price and the total value of B's imports will go up very much in terms of B's currency. The terms of trade and the balance of trade will move unfavourably to B as a result of the depreciation of B's currency.

But it may be that, while the elasticities of demand are low and add up to less than unity, the elasticities of supply are even lower. In this case when the price of B's exports falls in A's currency as a result of the depreciation of B's currency there is sufficient increase in demand in A to cause an appreciable strain on the supply of B's exports. But the supply of B's exports is so inelastic that their price goes up very much in B's currency and, in consequence, goes down very little in A's currency. At the same time when the price of A's exports rise in B's currency as a result of the depreciation of B's currency, there is sufficient reduction in demand in B to cause an appreciable excess supply of A's exports. But the supply of A's exports is so inelastic that their price goes down very much in A's currency and, in consequence, rises very little in B's currency.

The value of B's imports in B's currency goes up a little because the demand in B is inelastic and there is some increase in that price in B's currency; but it goes up only very little because there is only a very little rise in their price in terms of B's currency. The value of B's exports in A's currency goes down a little because the demand in A is inelastic and there is some fall in their price in A's currency; but it goes down very little because there is only a very small decline in their price in terms of A's currency. The value of B's exports in B's currency will, therefore, have risen by almost as much as the percentage depreciation of B's exchange rate. In consequence the value of B's exports will have risen more than the value of B's imports and the balance of trade will have moved in B's favour.

Moreover, in this case if the elasticities of supply are sufficiently low, the improvement in B's balance of trade will be combined with an improvement in her real terms of trade. The price of B's exports in B's currency will have gone up by the greater part of the 10 per cent depreciation of B's currency because of the very low elasticity of supply of exports in B. At the same time the price of A's exports in A's currency will have fallen by the greater part of the 10 per cent depreciation of B's currency because of the very low elasticity of their supply in A, and will, therefore, have risen only a very small amount in B's depreciated currency. As a result the price of B's exports has risen more than the price of A's exports in terms of B's currency, and the terms of trade will have moved in B's favour.

To summarize: (i) High elasticities of demand for imports combined with high elasticities of supply of exports will produce a large favourable movement in the balance of trade of a country whose currency is depreciated with the terms of trade moving somewhat against the depreciating country. (ii) If the elasticities of demand remain high but the elasticities of supply are low, there will still be a favourable response of the balance of trade to an exchange depreciation; but it will not be so favourable as before, because the low elasticities of supply will remove some of the effectiveness of the high elasticities of demand. But the movement of the terms of trade will not be so adverse to the depreciating country and may actually be favourable to it. (iii) If the elasticities of demand add up to less than one and are also sufficiently small relatively to the elasticities of supply, we have the perverse case in which a depreciation will lead to an unfavourable movement of the balance of trade; and this unfavourable movement in the balance of trade will be combined with an unfavourable movement of the terms of trade. (iv) If, however, the elasticities of supply are sufficiently small, relatively to the elasticities of demand, a depreciation will lead to a favourable movement of the balance of trade even though the sum of the elasticities of demand is less than one; and if the elasticities of supply are sufficiently small this will be combined with an improvement in the terms of trade of the depreciating country.

It still, therefore, remains true, as was argued in Chapter XII, that a depreciation of a country's currency will improve its balance of trade provided that the sum of the elasticities of demand for imports in it and in the rest of the world is greater than unity. Moreover, if the elasticities of supply of exports are high, then we can add, as we did in Chapter XII, that if the sum of the elasticities of demand is less than unity, a depreciation of a country's currency will worsen its balance of trade. But if the elasticities of supply of exports are low relative to the elasticities of demand, an exchange depreciation will cause an improvement in the balance of trade even though the sum of the elasticities of demand for imports is less than one; and with low elasticities of supply an improvement in the balance of trade will require a smaller adverse movement in the real terms of trade and may actually be combined with an improvement in the real terms of trade.

We have seen in the above analysis how the 'price' effects of low elasticities of supply may cause a depreciation of a country's currency to bring about an improvement in that country's balance of trade combined with an improvement in its terms of trade. We may conclude this chapter by considering one way in which the 'income' effects of financial policies for internal balance in the two countries might also help to bring about this happy combination.

Suppose, then, that a depreciation of B's currency has caused an improvement in B's balance of trade. Internal balance now requires that domestic expenditure should be deflated in order to offset the domestic inflationary effects of the improvement in B's balance of trade.

Conversely, in A there must now be a policy inflation of domestic expenditure.

Now in so far as the decreased domestic expenditure in B causes a reduced demand for imports and the increased domestic expenditure in A causes an increased demand for imports, this will reduce the demand in B for A's exports and increase the demand in A for B's exports, and will thus move the balance of trade still more in B's favour. It will also be a factor tending to improve B's terms of trade, since the price of B's exports will be somewhat raised above what it would otherwise be, and that of A's exports somewhat lowered below what it would otherwise be, by these changes of demand.

But this factor will, of course, do nothing to restore internal balance in the two countries. On the contrary, the increased demand for B's exports in A will merely intensify the inflationary movement in B and the decreased demand for A's exports in B will merely intensify the deflationary movement in A. It is only in so far as the policy deflation of domestic expenditure in B causes a reduction in the demand for B's products and only in so far as the policy inflation of domestic expenditure in A causes an increase in the demand for A's products, that internal balance will be restored in the two countries. In other words, it is only in so far as the decreased domestic expenditure in B and the increased domestic expenditure in A causes a net decrease in the demand for B's products and a net increase in the demand for A's products that internal balance will be restored.[1]

When a country's export and non-export products are more or less interchangeable and form a more or less homogeneous group (because they are close substitutes either in production or consumption) these policy inflations and deflations, if they are successful in restoring internal balance, will tend to move the terms of trade against B, though they may help to improve the balance of trade for B. There is a net decrease in the demand for B's products, because the deflation of domestic expenditure in B causes a larger decline in the demand for B's products by B's purchasers than the increase in the demand for B's products by A's purchasers which is brought about by the policy inflation in A; as a result there is some decline in the price of B's products and the price of B's export products falls more or less *pari passu* with the price of B's non-export products. Simultaneously, there is a net increase in the demand for A's products as a result of the policy inflation in A having a more marked effect upon the demand for A's products than the policy deflation in B; the price of A's export products rises with the general level of A's product prices. Thus the prices of B's export products tend to fall and the prices of A's export products to rise

[1] i.e. the sum of the two marginal propensities to import must be less than unity (see p. 195).

as a result of the policy changes in domestic expenditure required to preserve internal balance; and this tends to turn the terms of trade against B. At the same time, of course, these shifts of demand tend also to improve B's balance of trade, because the deflation of domestic expenditure in B causes purchasers in B to spend somewhat less on imports from A and the inflation of domestic expenditure in A causes purchasers in A to spend somewhat more on imports from B.

But if there is little interchangeability either in consumption or in production between a country's export products and its non-export products, the financial policies for internal balance will in certain very special circumstances tend to move the terms of trade as well as the balance of trade in B's favour. This will be so if in each country there is a very small marginal propensity to consume its own export products. Suppose, for example, that when there is a policy deflation of domestic expenditure in B for the purpose of maintaining internal balance, some part of the decreased demand represents a reduced demand for imports from A, that practically the whole of the rest represents a reduced demand for B's non-export products, and that practically none of it represents a decline in the demand for B's export products. Suppose further that, in so far as the reduced demand in B for B's non-export products causes a fall in the price of such products (because their real elasticity of supply is not infinitely great), this causes purchasers in B to shift their purchases from imports of A's products on to B's relatively cheap non-export products, but it does not cause any significant shift of demand in B away from her own export products.

Similarly, let us suppose that in A the 'policy' increase in domestic expenditure causes some increase in demand for B's exports, some increase in demand for A's non-export products, but little or no increase in demand for A's export products. Let us suppose further that any consequential increase in the price of A's non-export products causes purchasers in A to shift to the purchase of imports from B but not to the purchase of A's export products.

In these special circumstances the deflation of domestic expenditure in B and its inflation in A will: (i) restore internal balance in the two countries because it will cause both a larger decline of demand in B for B's non-export products than an increase in A for B's export products and also a larger increase of demand in A for A's non-export products than a decrease in demand in B for A's export products; (ii) cause a further improvement in B's balance of trade, because it will cause a net decrease in expenditure in B on imports as a result both of the reduction of domestic expenditure in B and also of the fall in price of B's non-export products which will cause a shift of demand in B away from imports, and because for similar reasons it will cause a net increase in A's expenditure on imports; and (iii) cause some tendency for B's terms of trade to improve because the price of B's exports will rise since the demand for them has increased in A without its having diminished in B, and because the price of A's exports will fall since the demand for them has fallen in B without its having increased in A.

These conclusions, however, also rest upon the assumption that there is not much substitutability in either production or consumption between a country's export and non-export products. In some cases this may be true. But if time is given for currents of demand and of supply to adapt themselves to new price ratios—for consumers to learn about the new possibilities of substituting cheaper for more expensive products and to adjust their habits accordingly and for producers to learn about the new possibilities of making better profits in other lines of production and to make the necessary adjustments in their capital equipment—in the long run there may in most cases be considerable opportunities for substitution either in production or consumption. And in so far as this is the case, the analysis approximates again to the more simple analysis carried out in Chapter XII where each country's products were treated as forming a single homogeneous group.

CHAPTER XIX

INTER-REGIONAL AND INTERNATIONAL ADJUSTMENTS COMPARED [1]

I T is often asked whether, and if so in what way, the problems connected with the balance of payments between two regions of the
same country differ from those connected with the balance of payments
between two countries of the same world.

We have in fact already covered three important factors which may
cause these problems to differ.

(i) In the first place, two regions of a single country are likely to
share a common monetary and banking system. There will at any time
be a given total supply of money (coins, notes, and bank deposits) in the
country, which can be used equally well in any region of the country.
For this reason, a payment when it is made from one region to another
of the same country causes the total supply of money to be reduced in
the paying region by the amount of the payment and to be increased
in the receiving region by the same amount. If £100 is paid from a
man in Dorset to a man in Yorkshire, or $100 from a man in California
to a man in Massachusetts, or 100 francs from a man in Normandy to
a man in Provence, the total supply of money in the United Kingdom, the United States, or France is likely to remain unchanged;
there will, however, be a fall in the supply of money in the paying
region and a rise in the receiving region equal to the sum which is
transferred.

In this respect the mechanism of payments between two regions of
the same country corresponds to that of 100-per-cent money (see pp.
207-8, above). As was there argued, such a mechanism makes the
process of adjustment more gradual and therefore easier than is the
case with a percentage-reserve system, under which each country's
reserves of international means of payment are only a small proportion
of its total domestic means of payment. Thus, if in countries A and B
only 10 per cent of the domestic supplies of money are covered by gold
(or other assets which are acceptable as a means of payment to the other)
and if B has a balance-of-payments deficit with A of $100 m. per year,
then in order to maintain a constant ratio of reserves to her total domestic supply of money the banking system in B must deflate the total
domestic supply of money at the rate of $1,000 m. per annum. The
inhabitants of one region of a single country cannot run out of supplies
of means of payment acceptable to another region until they have lost

[1] The subject matter of this chapter is treated in Section VIII (vii) of
the separate mathematical supplement.

all their existing stock of money to that other region; but the residents of a country which has a domestic supply of money of $10,000 m. against which a gold reserve of only $1,000 m. is held, will run out of reserves of international means of payment when they have paid $1,000 m. to another country, at which point the domestic stock of money will still be $9,000 m., unless the banking system has taken steps to deflate the domestic supply of money nine times as quickly as the loss of gold.

The fact that two regions of the same country will share a common money means, therefore, that when there is a balance-of-payments disequilibrium between them, the necessary readjustments can be made in a more leisurely and gradual manner, though it does not in itself do anything to reduce the size of the ultimate readjustments of relative prices and incomes which will be necessary to restore equilibrium.

(ii) But there is a second difference between inter-regional and international adjustments which will affect the ultimate adjustment of relative prices and incomes which is necessary. Because national governments are likely to adopt protective policies the movement of goods and services in international trade is likely to be more restricted than in inter-regional trade.

Now we have already observed (p. 210) that the existence of barriers to imports is likely to reduce the elasticity of demand for imports in any country; a reduction in the price at which producers in B offer their products to purchasers in A will not lead to so great an increase in the demand in A for B's products if there is a quantitative import restriction in A which simply prevents A's purchasers from buying more of B's products or if there is a heavy specific import duty in A on B's products so that the price of B's products to A's purchasers does not fall by as large a proportion as the price at which B's producers are offering their products.

It has been a constant theme of Part IV that, if B's balance of payments is in deficit, the method of price adjustment (either through a depreciation of B's currency or through an internal deflation of B's money wage rates and costs relatively to those of A) normally requires that the prices of B's products should be reduced relatively to those of A's in order to tempt purchasers in A and B to shift from the purchase of A's to that of B's products. Such a shift will be more readily obtained if the elasticities of demand for imports in A and in B are high; and this is more likely to be the case if A and B are different regions of a single country between which there are no trade restrictions than if A and B are two separate countries with trade barriers between them.

On the other hand, the absence of trade barriers would, of course, prevent the use of commercial policy for the express purpose of restoring equilibrium to a disordered balance of payments. This possibility will be considered in Part V, where we shall discuss, for example, the possibility that a deficit in B's balance of payments might be removed by an increase in restrictions on imports into B, expressly carried out for the purpose of restoring equilibrium to the balance of payments. Such commercial policy arrangements would be impossible between two regions of a country within which there was free trade, though they would be possible between two separate countries each with a commercial policy towards the other.

(iii) There is a third special feature of the mechanism of adjustment between two separate countries, which we have already noticed. In different countries there are more likely to be different financial policies or different institutional arrangements in other important economic respects than in different regions of the same country. It is not possible here to recapitulate all that has already been said on this point; but a single example may help. It may be, for example, that in country B there is what we have called a neutral economy (including institutional arrangements in the labour market which lead to more or less rigidly fixed money wage rates), whereas the authorities in country A may be operating a gold standard of the type described in Chapter XIV. In this case a spontaneous disturbance (e.g. a shift of demand in B from B's on to A's products) might lead to unemployment at constant wage rates in B (where the demand for labour falls) but to unchanged employment at higher money wage rates in A (where the demand for labour rises). If A and B were merely different regions of the same country it would be unlikely that there would be such marked differences in their institutional arrangements.

There remains, however, a further difference between the processes of international and of inter-regional adjustment of which we have as yet said nothing, due to differences in the degree of freedom with which factors of production such as labour and capital move between different regions of the same country and between different countries of the same world. The classical economists in fact distinguished between the theory of international trade and the theory of domestic trade on this single ground. They assumed, broadly speaking, that there was complete mobility of labour and capital between different occupations and regions within a single country but that there was no mobility of these factors between one country and another.

It is, of course, normally true that labour and capital will move more easily from a region of low earnings to a region of high earnings within one country than that they will move from one country of low earnings to another country of high earnings. As far as the migration of labour is concerned, movement from one country to another often involves longer distances and therefore greater expense than movement within a country; it is more likely to involve movement to a place where a foreign language is spoken; and, more broadly still, it is likely to involve greater 'patriotic' or other sentimental resistances.

Similarly, a movement of capital from one country to another will often involve the investment of funds in enterprises and concerns of which the investor is less familiar than he is with those in his own country. It may involve risks of exchange-rate adjustments, since it involves the investment of funds in a foreign currency. Moreover, a lender may be more confident of obtaining legal redress for any breach of contract by the borrower if the loan is made within his own country; and, more broadly, an investor may in general expect to obtain more favourable treatment from the authorities of his own country than from those of a foreign country.

For all these reasons, quite apart from governmental restrictions on international movements, labour and capital may move more readily within a country than between two countries in response to any given increase in the wage rate or in the rate of interest (or other return on capital) which they may hope to obtain by the move.

So far we have been concerned solely with the degree to which factors of production will move in response to an increase in the reward offered to them in an alternative employment in another place. But the net reward offered to any given factor in any given place may, of course, diverge very considerably from the true productivity of that factor in that place; and such divergences are likely to be much more marked from country to country than from region to region within one country. For example, suppose that in country B there is a very heavy tax on profits and on other incomes from property, the proceeds of which are used to pay unemployment benefit, children's allowances, sickness benefits, old age pensions, etc., to all residents in the country; but that in country A there is no such fiscal arrangement. Then owners of capital will have an incentive to move their funds from B to A to avoid the tax in B (even though its true productivity in A may be somewhat lower than in B); and labour will have a strong incentive to move from A to B to obtain the benefits of the advanced social security offered in B (even though the true productivity of labour may be somewhat higher in A). For reasons of this kind it may be desirable to impede the movement of capital from B to A in order to prevent a large and uneconomic transfer of capital funds from B from imposing a heavy strain on B's balance of payments, and this is a point which we shall have to bear in mind in Part V of this volume. Moreover, in the interests of maximizing the total of world production it may be desirable to impede the movement of labour from A to B and of capital from B to A, since these are both movements to places of lower real productivity for each factor of production.

But these matters are not strictly relevant to our present problem. We are not at the moment inquiring whether greater mobility of labour and capital between countries would lead to a more productive use of these resources. We are asking whether a greater mobility of labour and capital from a place in which there has been a relative deterioration in the reward offered to them to a place in which there has been a relative improvement in the reward offered to them would make easier or more difficult the process of adjustment of the balance of payments to any given disturbance.

Let us suppose, then, that there is free trade in commodities between A and B, that internal balance is preserved in both A and B by means of appropriate monetary policies so as to avoid unemployment in either country, and that external balance is preserved between them by means of variable exchange rates in a free exchange market.[1]

In these conditions we will examine the effect of various spontaneous disturbances of the balance of payments between A and B, in order to inquire whether (i) a greater mobility of capital from the place in which the rate of interest has fallen to that in which it has risen, and (ii) a greater mobility of labour from the place in which real wage rates have fallen to that in which they have risen, would ease the process of readjustment of the balance of payments.

We may concentrate our attention upon movements in the real terms of trade as the best single indicator of the ease of adjustment. If there is some spontaneous disturbance which causes a balance-of-payments disequilibrium between A and B, then, as we have seen, the method of price adjustment will normally mean that the real terms of trade must move against the deficit country. Under the gold-standard mechanism the deficit country will lose gold; it will have to deflate its internal money prices, money costs, and money incomes and the surplus country will have to inflate its money prices, money costs, and money incomes until the fall in the prices of the products of the deficit country relatively to those of the surplus country causes a sufficient shift of demand away from the products of the surplus country on to those of the deficit country. If the readjustment is difficult, there will be a greater shift in the terms of trade unfavourably to the deficit country. And similarly with the mechanism of variable exchange rates. The exchange value of the currency of the deficit country will depreciate; the products of the deficit country will become cheaper relatively to those of the surplus country; if the adjustment is difficult there will be a large depreciation of the currency of the deficit country and a large movement of the real terms of trade against it.

[1] The mechanism of the gold standard would in fact lead to the same conclusions as those which follow in the text. The reader is left to himself with the aid of the analysis of Chapter XV and of Section VIII (vii) of the mathematical supplement to establish the fact that the effect of mobility of labour and capital upon the ease of adjustment is similar for both the gold-standard and the variable-exchange-rate mechanisms of price adjustment.

Let us first consider the mobility of capital. It is not, in fact, possible to say that a greater mobility of capital will invariably make the process of adjustment of the balance of payments between A and B easier or more difficult. The answer will depend upon the nature of the spontaneous disturbance to meet which the adjustment has become necessary. It may suffice to take as illustrations three possible spontaneous disturbances, in the case of the first of which a high mobility of capital will make the process of readjustment more difficult, in the case of the second of which the mobility of capital will have no effect, and in the case of the third of which a high mobility of capital will ease the process of adjustment.

Suppose, then, that there is some spontaneous decrease in domestic expenditure in country A. This tends to cause a deflation of the total demand for goods and services in A, and A's internal balance is disturbed. In order to restore internal balance the banking system in A increases the supply of money and lowers the rate of interest so as to re-stimulate domestic expenditure in A. If there were complete immobility of capital between A and B, the fall in interest rates in A would not cause any increased foreign lending from A to B. Interest rates would go on falling in A until they had reached a sufficiently low level to increase domestic expenditure in A to the previous equilibrium level. And at this point there would be no further change required. Since domestic expenditure in A is in the end no smaller than before the change, there is no net decrease in the demand for imports in A. There is thus no change at all in B. The prices of A's products and of B's products are unchanged, and the terms of trade and the balance of trade between A and B are unaltered. The only thing that is different is that interest rates are lower in A than before the change.

But if there is some mobility of capital between A and B, the result will be different. The lower rates of interest in A will cause property owners in A to lend more to borrowers in B and owners in B to lend less to borrowers in A. B's balance of payments will now become favourable; B's currency will appreciate in terms of A's currency; if the sum of the elasticities of demand for imports in A and B is greater than unity, there will be a shift of demand from B's on to A's products which will help to restore equilibrium to the balance of payments. But this unfavourable movement in B's balance of trade will disturb B's internal balance since the smaller net demand for B's products will tend to cause some deflationary pressure in B's economy; and conversely, A's favourable balance of trade will cause an inflationary pressure in A. To preserve internal balance the banking system in B will have to lower interest rates somewhat and the banking system in A will have to raise them above the level to which they would have fallen in the absence of any lending from A to B. The consequential increase in domestic expenditure in B will itself somewhat increase the demand in B for imports and the decreased domestic expenditure in A will somewhat decrease the demand in A for imports, and this will help to generate the favourable balance of trade for A which is necessary to match the capital transfer from A to B. But, on the assumption that the sum of the marginal propensities to import in A and in B is less than unity, this improvement in A's balance of trade will not in itself be sufficient to cover the capital transfer from A to B. In other words, if there is some movement of capital from A to B in order to take advantage of the relatively higher interest rates in B, the terms of trade will have to move somewhat against A in order that the necessary balance of trade surplus may be generated to cover the capital transfer from A to B. There will be a balance-of-payments problem requiring some deterioration of A's terms of trade, whereas if capital had been completely immobile there would have been no balance-of-payments adjustment necessary at all.[1]

Let us next consider a case in which the mobility of capital will make no difference to the process of adjustment. Suppose that there is a spontaneous shift of demand away from country A's products on to country B's products. This will cause the value of A's currency to depreciate in terms of B's currency until the price of B's products has risen so far in terms of A's products that consumers' expenditure shifts back again to the same extent away from B's products on to A's products. The balance of payments will be restored to equilibrium by this shift of demand back from B's on to A's products. The balance of trade of each country will thus be undisturbed. There will be no net inflationary or deflationary factor at work within A or B. There will, therefore, be no reason why the banking systems in A or B should alter the rate of interest in either country, so that there will be no occasion for a capital movement. Thus the terms of trade will have to move against A in order to restore equilibrium; but this movement will be just the same whether capital is mobile or immobile between the two places.

Finally, let us take an example where the mobility of capital will definitely ease the process of adjustment. Suppose that there is some unrequited transfer of funds from A to B. For example, the government of A pays an indemnity to the government of B; but in the interests of the preservation of internal balance in both countries fiscal policies are such that the raising of the funds by the government of A is not allowed to lead to any net reduction in domestic expenditure in A nor is the use of the funds by the government of B allowed to lead to any net increase in domestic expenditure in B. There will be a deficit in A's balance of

[1] This is not, of course, to suggest that capital movements should for this reason be stopped. The movement of capital to the place of highest yield will increase the total world production and this must, of course, be set against the fact that the immobility of capital might in this case make the adjustment of the balance of payments easier.

payments equal to the unrequited transfer, but otherwise everything will be unchanged.

The deficit in A's balance of payments will cause the value of A's currency to depreciate in terms of B's currency; this will cause a movement in the terms of trade against A; provided that the sum of the elasticities to import in A and B is greater than unity purchasers will shift their expenditure away from B's products on to A's products and this will cause a favourable movement in A's balance of trade which will cover the unrequited transfer from A to B. The favourable movement in A's balance of trade will, however, exert an inflationary pressure in A's economy, and the corresponding unfavourable movement in B's balance of trade will exert a deflationary pressure in B. To preserve internal balance the banking system in A will have to restrict monetary supplies and raise interest rates in order to restrain domestic expenditure, and the banking system in B, for the opposite reasons, will have to adopt a policy of monetary expansion and lower interest rates.[1] In the absence of any mobility of capital funds between A and B this change in interest rates will not itself directly help the external adjustment. But in so far as the higher interest rates in A and the lower interest rates in B cause capital to flow from B to A, this will itself help to finance the unrequited transfer from A to B. There will be less of the unrequited transfer to be matched by a surplus in A's balance of trade, so that the depreciation of A's currency and the movement of the terms of trade against A need be less marked. The mobility of capital will have eased the process of readjustment of the balance of payments.

In all the three cases examined above—namely, a spontaneous decrease in domestic expenditure in A, a spontaneous shift of demand away from A's on to B's products, and a spontaneous unrequited transfer from A to B—there is some movement of the terms of trade against A.[2] There is some difficulty of adjustment of the balance of payments which shows itself in this movement of the terms of trade against A. In all these cases the terms of trade would need to turn less unfavourably to A if labour were mobile between A and B.

[1] The consequential deflation of domestic expenditure in A will cause purchasers in A to purchase somewhat less imports and the consequential inflation of domestic expenditure in B will cause the purchasers in B to purchase somewhat more imports. This in itself will help to generate a favourable balance of trade for A to match the unrequited transfer from A to B. But if the sum of the marginal propensities to import in A and in B is less than unity, this will not be sufficient in itself to generate a favourable balance of trade for A sufficient to cover the unrequited transfer from A to B. Some fall in the price of A's products relative to that of B's will be necessary in order to shift demand from B's on to A's products, so as to generate a large enough favourable balance of trade by A.

[2] This will be so unless, in the case of a spontaneous decrease in domestic expenditure in A, there is complete immobility of capital and unless, in the case of a spontaneous unrequited transfer from A to B, there is perfect mobility of capital. In these two cases no change in the terms of trade would be necessary.

The movement of the real terms of trade against A's products will mean that the real wage rate has fallen in A compared with the real wage rate in B. Since internal balance has been maintained in A and B, employment and output will be unchanged in A and B; and since employment and output are unchanged, the marginal physical product of labour[1] will be unchanged in A and B. Labour in A will, therefore, be paid a real wage which, in terms of A's products, is unchanged; and labour in B will be paid a real wage which, in terms of B's products, is unchanged. But since less of B's products can now be obtained for a unit of A's products, the cost of imports will have risen in A and fallen in B. The real wage rate in A will thus have fallen relatively to the real wage rate in B.

If labour is mobile, workers will now move from A to B. In order to preserve internal balance in A there must now be some decrease in domestic expenditure in A since employment has to be found for a smaller number of workers in A. Conversely, in order to preserve internal balance in B, there must be some increase in domestic expenditure in B in order to absorb more workers into employment. But the reduction in domestic expenditure in A will to some extent reduce the demand for imports in A and the increase in domestic expenditure in B will increase the demand for imports in B. The movement of labour from A to B will thus itself cause a favourable movement in A's balance of trade. There will, therefore, be less need for the real terms of trade to move against A in order to remove the deficit in A's balance of payments which, in each of the three cases examined above (pp. 256–8), was the primary cause of the unfavourable movement in A's terms of trade.

The mobility of labour will by this mechanism in all cases ease the process of adjustment in the balance of payments. Indeed, if the mobility of labour were perfect—if, that is to say, labour would continue to move from A to B until relative real wage rates in A and B were restored to their previous level—it might appear that no other mechanism would be required to adjust the balance of payments. So long as A's terms of trade were at all unfavourable the real wage in A would be low relatively to the real wage in B; labour would, therefore, continue to move from A to B; the demand for imports would continue to rise in B and fall in A as a result of the expansion of output and demand in B and their contraction in A; and this would go on until any required change in the balance of payments had been brought about at an unchanged real terms of trade merely by the expansion of total demand in B and its contraction in A as the population of B grew and of A fell.

[1] That is to say, the addition to the output of the country's products which would be caused by employing one more unit of labour in that country's industries. This will be unchanged in each country because in each country the total employment of labour and the total output is unchanged.

This conclusion would be correct if the real elasticities of supply of output in A and B were infinitely great; that is to say, if the expansion of employment in B did not lead to any reduction in the marginal physical product of labour in B and if the contraction of employment in A did not lead to any rise in the marginal physical product of labour in A. But as the working population of A is reduced in size, each member of the population will be able to work with a larger amount of natural resources and of other forms of physical capital equipment. For example, agricultural work need take place only on the more fertile or better situated land. The marginal physical product of labour will thus be increased in A. For converse reasons, it will fall in B, as the working population of B which requires to be employed with B's natural resources and capital equipment increases.

For this reason, as labour moves from A to B it will be possible to pay labour in A a higher real wage rate in terms of A's products; and, conversely, the real wage rate paid in B will fall in terms of B's products. This, from the point of view of the standard of living of the workers in A and B, will offset some movement of the real terms of trade unfavourable to A's products in terms of B's products. The remaining workers in A will be paid more in terms of A's products, and the workers in B will be paid less in terms of B's products; but simultaneously a unit of A's products will be worth less than before in terms of B's products. When these two changes just balance each other, there will be no more incentive for labour to move from A to B.

We may conclude that mobility of labour from A to B will always ease the process of readjustment in the balance of payments. If the real elasticities of supply in A and B are large, this easement of the readjustment will take the form of a large movement of labour from A to B, leading to a large increase in B's and decrease in A's demand for imports, thus bringing about the required improvement in A's balance of payments with little or no movement in the terms of trade against A. If, on the other hand, the real elasticities of supply are small there will not be so large a movement of labour and not so large an increase in the demand for imports in B or decrease in A, so that a considerable part of the required improvement in A's balance of payments will have to take the form of a shift of demand from B's products on to A's products caused by a fall in the price of A's products relatively to that of B's. But this movement in the terms of trade unfavourable to A's products will not cause an unfavourable movement in the real wages of A's workers, because the movement of labour out of A's industries would cause a marked increase in the physical productivity of A's workers as each worker can be equipped with more capital and more natural resources and thus a marked increase in real wage rates in A in terms of A's products; and vice versa in B.

PART V. DIRECT CONTROLS

PART V. DIRECT CONTROLS

CHAPTER XX

TYPES OF DIRECT CONTROL:
FINANCIAL CONTROLS

IN Parts III and IV we examined certain policies for influencing a country's balance of payments, namely, domestic financial policies for affecting the general level of demand and so the demand for imports and the supply of exportable products (Part III) and adjustments of one country's prices and costs relatively to those of another by means of a general domestic inflation or deflation of money costs or by means of an alteration in the foreign exchange rates (Part IV). All these measures have one feature in common. They constitute broad acts of policy which will alter the general relationships between the economies of one country and another. Their effect on the balance of payments depends upon the indirect influence which the general mechanism of money prices and money incomes will exercise upon the demand and supply of imports and exports and upon transfer payments.

We turn now to those policies which aim directly at controlling particular elements in the balance of payments. The class of control with which we shall be concerned is thus a very broad and comprehensive one. Any measure of governmental intervention which is directly aimed at increasing or decreasing some particular group of payments or receipts in the balance of payments we shall include in our category of 'direct controls' for the purpose of Part V.

In some cases the distinction between these 'direct controls' and the more general measures discussed in Parts III and IV is very clear. For example, compare, as a means of improving a country's balance of payments, the complete prohibition of certain luxury imports into that country and a general deflationary financial policy designed to reduce the general level of money incomes and prices in that country. The former is a direct intervention in one small item of the balance of payments; the latter exerts its influence less directly through its influence on the general economic situation. The former is a quantitative control which pays no regard to the price mechanism; the latter works through its effect upon relative money prices and money incomes.

But, at the other extreme, compare a 10 per cent depreciation of a country's currency on the one hand with a 10 per cent *ad valorem* tariff on all imports combined with a 10 per cent *ad valorem* subsidy on all exports on the other hand. As far as commodity trade is concerned it makes no significant difference to the United Kingdom trader whether the pound will purchase 10 per cent less dollars in the foreign exchange market or whether, the exchange rate remaining unchanged, he has to pay a 10 per cent *ad valorem* tax on everything which he purchases from the United States and receives a 10 per cent subsidy on everything which he sells to the United States. But import and export duties and subsidies on particular products are certainly examples of the 'direct controls' which we wish to examine in this Part. Moreover, a general 10 per cent *ad valorem* import duty alone or a general 10 per cent *ad valorem* export subsidy alone would constitute a 'direct control'; these devices are not examples of the truly general price adjustments discussed in Part IV, since they would directly affect the price of imports without affecting that of exports or vice versa. Yet the combination of these two 'direct controls' would approximate very closely to the general price mechanism adjustment of an alteration in the exchange rate.

We have, therefore, to recognize that the class of 'direct controls' is a very wide and rather vague one, containing, at the one extreme, quantitative interventions with particular items of the balance of payments and, at the other extreme, tax or subsidy arrangements which affect in a non-discriminatory manner very broad groups of foreign payments or receipts. In fact Part V ought to cover all those remedial measures which are not already covered in Parts III and IV, though we cannot, of course, hope to do more than discuss some important examples of different types of direct control.

In this and the following chapter we shall enumerate the main administrative mechanisms which can be used to enforce direct controls, leaving to later chapters the more strictly economic analysis of the results achieved by operating directly upon one or other element in the balance of payments by means of whatever type of direct control may be administratively most convenient. As administrative devices we shall divide direct controls into 'financial controls', which comprise 'monetary' and 'fiscal controls', and 'commercial controls'. 'Monetary controls' we shall take to cover exchange controls and multiple exchange rates, while 'fiscal controls' cover all ordinary taxes and subsidies on particular items in the balance of payments. By 'commercial controls' we shall mean the use of quantitative regulations and State trading as methods of affecting the flow of a country's imports or exports.

Let us start, then, by considering the various types of financial control.

1. *Exchange Control.*

An important means by which the authorities in a deficit country may attempt to restore equilibrium to the balance of payments is the restriction of payments to other countries by means of exchange control. For a system of exchange control to operate effectively it is necessary that the purchase and sale of foreign exchange by the residents of the exchange-control country should be made illegal except through the agency of a central authority, which for this purpose we shall call the 'exchange-control authority'. Every resident in the country concerned who desires to make a payment in foreign currency must purchase that foreign currency (at the official exchange rate) from the exchange-control authority (or an authorized agent of that authority) and from no other source. And every resident in the country who has acquired foreign currency (e.g. as a receipt from goods which he has exported to the rest of the world) must sell that foreign currency at the official exchange rate to the exchange-control authority or to its authorized agent and must dispose of the foreign currency in no other way.

If this monopolization of foreign exchange dealings by the exchange-control authority and its authorized agents can be effectively enforced, then the authorities of the country concerned can effectively maintain equilibrium in the country's balance of payments with the rest of the world by rationing foreign currency to those who wish to make payments abroad and thereby restricting the demand for foreign currency to the amount currently received from the country's exports and other sources of receipt of foreign money. All these receipts will be surrendered at the official rate of exchange to the exchange-control authority; applications for the purchase of foreign exchange for the purchase of imports and other payments will be coming in to the exchange-control authority; if these applications amount to a greater sum than the foreign exchange which is being currently surrendered to the exchange-control authority, then that authority must decide in a more or less arbitrary fashion which applications should be granted and to what extent. By this means there is a direct control which restricts quantitatively the total of foreign payments to an amount necessary to keep the balance of payments in equilibrium.

It is not our purpose to discuss in detail the technical problems involved in making effective any system of exchange control. Such a system to be effective does, however, require a very extensive apparatus of bureaucratic regulation. It must suffice here to give four illustrations of the problems which are encountered and of the sort of regulation which their solution involves. For the purposes of these illustrations we will suppose that country B, whose currency is the pound, is a deficit country whose authorities are unwilling to allow the exchange value of the pound to depreciate and have instituted a system of exchange control in order to limit, at the given rate of exchange, payments to A which represents the rest of the world and whose currency is the dollar.

(i) It is necessary to prevent residents in B from acquiring A's currency other than by a licensed purchase through the exchange-control authority of B. For example, a resident in B who wishes to import goods from A must not be allowed to send B's currency notes by post to a resident of A. Otherwise an importer in B who was not allowed by B's exchange-control authority to purchase the particular imports which he desired might send B's currency notes by post to someone in A who wished to purchase some of B's products and obtain in return the currency notes of A with which he (the importer in B) could acquire the imports from A which he is not legally permitted to acquire. Such a 'black-market' purchase of A's currency notes by a resident in B would almost certainly take place at a depreciated exchange value for B's currency; because the importer in B is not allowed to obtain the desired imports through the official channels at the official rate, he is probably prepared to offer a higher price in the black market in terms of B's currency for the currency notes of A which he desires to obtain. This will mean that it is profitable for importers in A to deal in the 'black market' rather than at the official rate with B's exchange-control authority, because they can obtain B's currency more cheaply in terms of A's currency that way. B's exchange-control authority will thus find that it is not in fact acquiring at the official exchange rate all the foreign currency which might be obtained from the sale of B's exports; for a part of B's exports are being purchased by A's importers with the currency notes of B which A's importers have acquired by post from B's black-market importers.

In order to prevent transactions of this kind it is necessary to institute a postal control which prevents the sending of B's or of A's currency notes between A and B. And it is necessary to make sure that travellers between A and B do not carry A's or B's currency notes between A and B (except in very limited amounts). For as soon as a direct exchange of A's currency notes for B's currency notes can be organized in either country, residents in B can make a black-market purchase of foreign currency for making payments in A which are not permitted by B's exchange-control authority.

(ii) But the apparatus of regulation must, of course, go much farther than this. Suppose that a resident in B wishes to obtain imports from A for the payment of which B's exchange-control authority will not give permission and that he is willing in fact to pay a price for A's currency which is higher in terms of B's currency than the official exchange rate. If the importer in B can find an importer in A who intends to purchase some of B's products, he can make the following proposition: 'If you in A will purchase $300 worth of the A-products which I want and will ship them to me, I here in B will purchase £100

worth of the B-products which you want and will ship them to you.'
In effect, the importer in A is acquiring for $300 the £100 he requires
to purchase the imports he desires from B, and the importer in B is
acquiring for £100 the $300 which he wants for the purchase of the
imports for which his exchange control authority will not permit him
to pay. The official rate of exchange may be, say, $4 to £1; but the
importer in B has acquired $300 at a depreciated black-market rate of
$3 to £1 for an illegal purpose. And all this has happened without
any actual deal in any foreign currency at all. Extensive bureaucratic
inquiry at the ports into the way in which each parcel of imports or
exports has been financed will be necessary to prevent this sort of
'barter' development.

(iii) A detailed regulation of actual trade movements is required for
another reason. Suppose that an importer in B has been permitted by
the exchange-control authority to purchase a given amount of A's
currency for the purchase of certain specified necessities from A. It is
necessary then to ensure that the funds are in fact used for this purpose
and not for the purchase of some disallowed luxuries from A or for
some other illegal purpose (such as the purchase of securities on A's
stock exchange). This means that the actual provision of the foreign
exchange to B's importer must depend upon evidence that the
specified goods have been or will be actually imported.

But it involves more than this. The importer in B may in fact import
the goods for which he obtained the foreign currency, but he may have
overstated the price which he has to pay for the goods to the foreign
exporter. The importer in B obtains $400 of foreign exchange to pur-
chase 100 units of A's products at a price of $4 a unit; but the price
which he has to pay in fact is only $3 a unit, so that the importer in B
has $100 which he can use for illegal purposes in A. It is necessary,
therefore, for the exchange-control authority to ensure not only that
the goods are actually imported into B but also that the price at which
they are stated to have been bought is not an artificially high one.

And similarly with B's exports. If an exporter of 100 units of B's
products sells them in A at $4 a unit but states that he obtained only
$3 a unit for them, he will have obtained $100 which he will not be
required to surrender to B's exchange-control authority and which he
can use for illegal purposes in A. When any parcel of goods is exported
from B to A it is necessary to ensure not only that the foreign exchange
corresponding to their stated value is handed over to the exchange-
control authority but also that their value as declared to the authorities
is not an artificially low one.

(iv) Merchants in A may normally hold a certain amount of money
on deposit with banks in B and the import and export trade of A and
B may be conducted largely in terms of B's currency. This is likely

to be true if B's currency is an important currency in world trade, like the pound sterling; and B will receive a certain amount on the balance of payments from the banking and other similar commissions which are obtained by those persons and institutions in B which are concerned with the business of the finance of international trade. But such a business is unlikely to prosper under a régime of exchange control in B if the residents of A have to obtain the uncertain permission of B's exchange-control authority whenever they wish to turn into their own currency any part of the balances which they hold on deposit with B's banks. In such circumstances it will be necessary for B's exchange control authority to treat these 'non-resident' balances at B's banks as being readily convertible at the official rate into A's currency for any purpose at any time.

But this means that the transfer of funds within B's banking system from accounts held by residents of B ('resident' accounts) to those held by residents of A ('non-resident' accounts) must be controlled. An exporter of B's products may not acquire any of A's currency from his sales; he may be paid in pounds out of a 'non-resident' account. An exporter of B's products must, therefore, satisfy the exchange-control authority of B that he has either surrendered the foreign currency which he received from his exports or that payment for his exports has been effected by a transfer of B's currency from a 'non-resident' to his 'resident' account within B's banking system. An importer in B of A's products may not have to acquire any of A's currency in order to purchase the goods he wants; the exporter in A may wish merely to receive from the importer in B some of B's currency to add to the 'non-resident' account which he (the exporter in A) holds in B's banks and which he is free to use as he likes. In this case, however, the transfer of funds from a 'resident' to a 'non-resident' account within B's banking system must be subject to the same rigid control by B's exchange-control authority as is the purchase of an actual foreign currency by a resident in B.

2. *Multiple Exchange Rates*

If an exchange-control authority in B has effectively monopolized the purchase and sale of foreign exchange, it can, as we have seen, proceed to use its control for the straightforward rationing of the available foreign exchange at a single official rate of exchange. It can simply decide how much of the available foreign currency may be used for this purpose and how much for that purpose, and dole it out accordingly.

But the exchange-control authority may use its monopoly power in a rather different way. It may no longer operate on the basis of one single official rate of exchange. It may charge a higher price for A's currency in terms of B's currency when A's currency is required for certain purposes than when it is required for certain other purposes.

Let us take a simple example. Suppose that all foreign currency (dollars) which B's residents receive for the sale of their exports or from other sources must be surrendered to B's exchange-control authority for B's currency (pounds) at $4 for £1. Suppose, further, that for the import of necessities from A (wheat) B's exchange-control authority is willing to sell dollars to B's importers at this same rate of $4 for £1. But suppose that for the import of luxuries from A (motor-cars) B's exchange-control authority is willing to sell dollars to B's importers only at a higher price in terms of pounds so that B's importers obtain only $3 for £1 for the import of motor-cars.

Such an arrangement is in fact equivalent to the imposition of an import duty of 33⅓ per cent *ad valorem* on the import of motor-cars into B. Essentially the same result would be achieved if all purchases and sales of dollars by B's exchange-control authority were carried out at the single rate of exchange of $4 to £1, while on the import of motor-cars an import duty of 33⅓ per cent *ad valorem* was imposed. In this case $400 worth of A's motor-cars would cost an importer in B £133⅓, of which £100 would represent the cost at $4 to £1 of buying the necessary foreign exchange and £33⅓ would represent the import duty of 33⅓ per cent *ad valorem* on the £100 worth of motor-car imports. But £133⅓ is the cost of $400 at an exchange rate of $3 to £1, so that a price for dollars at this rate charged by the exchange-control authority for this purpose would be the equivalent of a foreign exchange rate of $4 to £1 combined with an *ad valorem* import duty of 33⅓ per cent. In the one case the authorities in B would obtain a revenue from the import duty and in the other case they would obtain a revenue from selling dollars at $3 to £1 which they had acquired at $4 to £1.

This arrangement might be combined with a continued rationing of the available foreign exchange by the exchange-control authority to the various importers in B. On the other hand, it might be used as a complete substitute for the rationing of foreign exchange. The exchange-control authority having paid £1 for every $4 received by residents in country B from exports, etc., might then allow all importers in B who wished to import wheat to have all the dollars which they wanted for this purpose at $4 to £1. There might still be some dollars over which the exchange-control authority might then sell to those residents in B who wished to purchase motor-cars from A, at a sufficiently high price to equate the demand for, to the supply of, the remaining dollars. If it so happened that at a rate of $3 to £1 the demand for dollars to finance motor-car imports was equal to the remaining supply of dollars, this rate (the equivalent of an *ad valorem* import duty of 33⅓ per cent) would just serve to clear the market. There would be no quantitative limitation on the amount of wheat or the amount of motor-cars which any importer in B might import nor on the amount of dollars which any importer in B might acquire (if he was willing to pay the price) for the import of wheat or of motor-cars. It would be just as if an import duty had been imposed on the import of motor-cars and as if this duty had been gradually adjusted upwards until it reached that level (namely 33⅓ per cent *ad valorem*) at which it happened to restrict the demand in B for imported motor-cars just to the extent necessary to put B's balance of payments into equilibrium.

We have so far considered only the most simple case where all dealings in foreign exchange take place at $4 to £1 except that in the case of dollars required for the import of a single class of commodity (motor-cars) the exchange-control authority charges $3 to £1. This we have seen is equivalent to the imposition of a duty on the import of motor-cars.

But the exchange-control authority may dispose of the profit which it makes on the sale of dollars at a high price to importers of motor-cars by giving a rather better price in pounds for the dollars which it acquires from B's exporters to A. Suppose that B's exchange-control authority sells dollars at $4 to £1 for the finance of imports of wheat into B, sells dollars at $3 to £1 for the finance of motor-cars into B, but buys dollars from B's residents (obtained from B's exports and other sources of receipt of foreign currency) at $3½ to £1. If the value of B's wheat imports is equal in pounds to the value of her motor-car imports, the flow of dollars into the exchange control at $3½ for £1 will just finance the sale of one half of these dollars (for wheat imports) at $4 to £1 and the other half of these dollars (for motor-car imports) at $3 to £1. This system will be equivalent to the maintenance of the exchange rate at $4 to £1 combined with an import duty of 33⅓ per cent *ad valorem* on motor-car imports, the revenue from which is used to pay an export subsidy of 12½ per cent[1] *ad valorem* on all exports.

But there is no reason why B's exchange-control authority should wish to subsidize all B's exports at an equal rate. As we shall argue in Chapter XXIII, it may be desired to reduce the price in foreign exchange of those exports of B for which the demand in A is very elastic (so that a small reduction in price would cause a large increase in the amount imported into A and thus a large increase in B's total receipts of A's currency) and not to reduce the price in foreign currency, and even to raise it, in the case of those exports of B for which the demand

---

[1] B's exports costing £100 would cost A's importer $400 at $4 to £1 and without a subsidy. A change of the rate of exchange to $3½ to £1 would reduce the cost to A's importers by $50 from $400 to $350. This is equivalent to a subsidy of 50 on a cost price of 400, i.e. a subsidy of 12½ per cent *ad valorem*.

in A is very inelastic (so that a considerable rise in the price charged to A would cause a very small decline in the amount imported into A with the consequence that B's total receipts from these exports would rise when their price was increased). To meet such a situation the exchange-control authority in B might offer different rates of exchange for the foreign currency which was surrendered to it, according to the way in which the foreign exchange was earned.

Thus, suppose that B's exports to A consisted of rubber (for which the demand in A was considered to be inelastic) and machines (for which the demand in A was considered to be elastic). The exchange-control authority in B might sell dollars for pounds at $4 to £1 for the import of wheat into B, sell dollars for pounds at $3 to £1 for the import of motor-cars into B, (the equivalent of an *ad valorem* import duty of 33⅓ per cent), buy dollars for pounds at $5 for £1 from the exporters of rubber to A (the equivalent of an export tax of 25 per cent *ad valorem*), and buy dollars for pounds at $3½ to £1 from the exporters of machinery to A (the equivalent of an export subsidy of 12½ per cent *ad valorem*).

Clearly, an innumerable range of combinations of export and import duties and subsidies can be arranged by such multiple exchange rates. If they are so arranged as to cause decreases in the dollar value of imports into B and increases in the dollar value of exports from B on such a scale as to remove the deficit in B's balance of payments, then external balance will have been achieved without any quantitative limitation of imports or payments. And if the absolute rates of duties and subsidies are arranged so that the total cost of the subsidies equals the total revenue from the duties, the arrangement will not have any net effect upon B's budgetary position.

Such, in essence, is the nature of a system of multiple exchange rates. There are, however, a great many ways of administering such a system. The system may be of the straightforward type which we have outlined above, where the exchange-control authority monopolizes all foreign exchange dealings but sets different rates at which it will sell foreign exchange for different uses and different rates at which it will purchase foreign exchange acquired from different sources. But it may be operated in other ways. For example, all exporters may be permitted to sell a given proportion of the foreign-exchange proceeds of their exports in a free exchange market, or the exporters of particular products may be permitted to do so.[1] Importers of certain products (e.g. necessities) may be enabled to purchase their foreign currencies

---

[1] Or, what becomes important when we allow for more than two countries in our world, so that B may be exporting to a 'hard currency' and a 'soft currency' market, exporters to certain markets may be permitted to sell the whole or part of the proceeds of their exports in a free exchange market. These matters will be a main subject of discussion in Part VI.

at the official rate from the exchange-control authority, whereas others who wish to obtain foreign currencies for any purpose may be allowed to acquire what they want in the free exchange market.

Provided that the official rate of exchange sets too high a value on B's currency in terms of A's currency to enable the ordinary price mechanism to remove the deficit on B's balance of payments, the value of B's currency in the free exchange market will be lower than in the official market. Such a system will, therefore, represent a combination of (i) an export subsidy to those exporters who are permitted to sell a part or the whole of the foreign-currency proceeds of their exports in the free exchange market with (ii) an import duty on those importers who have to purchase their foreign currencies in the free exchange market. Since this latter is a *free* exchange market, the rate of import duty on such imports will automatically adjust itself so that the demand for foreign currency for such imports is equal to the supply of foreign currency which is made available after the exchange-control authority has compulsorily taken over from exporters at the official rate those amounts of foreign currency which are necessary to meet the demand for foreign currency at this official rate for the favoured class of imports of necessities.

The above is only one illustration of the infinite variety of schemes for multiple exchange rates which might be devised. All, however, are of this general type: each is the equivalent of a system of duties and subsidies for particular classes of payments and receipts in the balance of payments, grafted on to some single rate of exchange.

3. *Fiscal Controls*

By 'fiscal controls' we mean the use of taxes and subsidies for the purpose of influencing the various items in a country's balance of payments. The clearest examples of such fiscal controls are the imposition of import duties in order to reduce the amount of foreign products purchased and so to decrease the total expenditure in foreign currency upon them, and the imposition of an export duty (where the foreign elasticity of demand is thought to be less than unity) or of an export subsidy (where the foreign elasticity of demand is thought to be greater than unity), in order to increase the total receipts of foreign exchange from the exports concerned.

It should be clear from what has been said above that the 'fiscal controls' of import and export duties and subsidies and the 'monetary controls' of multiple exchange rates are two different administrative devices for attaining the same economic results. Some of the main considerations which must govern the choice between the one or the other device are as follows.

It is impossible to operate a system of multiple exchange rates without an extensive and effective system of exchange control which monopolizes dealings in foreign exchange into the hands of a single exchange-control authority and its agents. Otherwise there will be arbitrage dealings in which people will purchase foreign exchange in the market in which foreign exchange is cheap only to resell it in that particular market in which foreign exchange is dear.[1] But it is, of course, possible to impose duties on particular imports and exports—and in particular on visible imports and exports—without any extensive system of exchange control. Ordinary import and export duties and subsidies will therefore alone be feasible in a system without an extensive exchange control.

There are, however, some items in the balance of payments which it is extremely difficult administratively to tax or to subsidize by an ordinary fiscal device. Tourists' expenditures in foreign countries may be taken as an example. Suppose that it is wished to impose a 10 per cent *ad valorem* tax on all expenditures by residents of B on holidays in A. For this purpose it is essential to know how much each tourist in fact spends abroad. But this can only be known at all accurately when there is a complete exchange control which allots to the tourist a certain amount for expenditure in A and which can be sure that the tourist has no other source for obtaining funds for expenditure in A. A 10 per cent *ad valorem* duty on the foreign exchange allocated for tourists' expenditure abroad is in fact a multiple exchange rate; this amount of foreign exchange is sold at a price 10 per cent higher than

---

[1] In fact, in order that a system of multiple exchange rates should be feasible it is not only necessary that there should be a complete system of exchange control. It is necessary also that this system should be of a particular kind. Consider a resident of B who wishes to make a payment to a resident of A. The foreign exchange which he requires will be provided at one rate by the exchange-control authority if it is for one purpose and at another rate if it is for another purpose. This system will work all right if the resident in A does not hold a balance of B's currency with the banks of B but always asks to be paid in his own currency. In this case the exchange-control authority will provide A's currency to the resident of B at the rate appropriate for the particular payment. But suppose that B's currency is widely accepted in international transactions; that the residents of A hold balances of B's money on deposit with B's bank; and that in the way described on p. 268 above B's exchange-control authority exercises its control not only by regulating the purchase of foreign currencies by the residents of B, but also by regulating the payment of funds from a 'resident account' in B to a 'non-resident account' in B (i.e. from an account in B's currency held with B's banks by a resident of B to a similar account held by a resident of A). If in this case a system of multiple exchange rates were to be operated it would be necessary to levy a tax at the appropriate rate on any such transfer within B's banking system from a 'resident' to a 'non-resident account' if the transfer was made in respect of a payment for which the price of foreign currency was above the normal rate or to pay a subsidy if the transfer was in respect of a payment for which the price of foreign currency was fixed below the normal rate. This would clearly complicate the workings of a multiple exchange rate system.

that at which foreign exchange is sold to other purchasers by the exchange-control authority.

'Visible' commodity imports and exports are the things which lend themselves most readily to a simple fiscal tax or subsidy. They can be seen and taxed or subsidized as they pass over the frontier into or out of the country concerned. Some 'invisible' items, such as tourists' expenditures, would, as we have seen, be very difficult to cover by means of an ordinary fiscal device. Other 'invisible' items, such as the sale of shipping services to foreigners or the purchase of foreign shipping services by residents of the country concerned, might fall into an intermediate position. The fact that foreign ships must come to the country's ports if they are to fetch its exports or bring its imports, and that the ships of the home country will normally operate from its ports, may provide a point at which they can be controlled for the purpose of enforcing a tax or subsidy system. But it might be possible to enforce such a system more effectively and completely if it relied upon an exchange control which effectively regulated all payments for and receipts from shipping services.

A case in which a fiscal device of taxation or subsidy would completely break down unless it was reinforced by an effective exchange control would be that of capital movements. Suppose, for example, that B's authorities desired to tax all capital transfers from B to A and/or to subsidize all capital transfers from A to B. Fiscal devices might be able to cover some elements in this field. Thus a company in A which set up a branch plant in B might qualify for a subsidy, the fiscal authority in B being able fairly easily to verify the facts in such a case. Or, conversely, a company in B which set up a branch plant in A might be taxed, and such a special tax might not be much more difficult to enforce than the ordinary taxation of the company's profits which must in any case be based upon an extensive knowledge of its accounts. Or it might be possible to discourage capital transfers to A by levying a special tax on all interest, dividends, rents, etc., earned by residents of B from property situated in A. Such devices might not be much more difficult to enforce than a normal income tax, for the enforcement of which income from all sources must be checked by the tax authorities. But all such fiscal devices would, in the absence of a complete exchange control, leave many devious ways whereby capital funds could be transferred from B to A or A to B without falling into these more obviously taxable categories.[1] A general tax on capital transfers out of B could only be enforced through a system which approximated very closely to that of an exchange-control authority which charged a specially high price for foreign exchange purchased

[1] For example, an exporter from B could leave the proceeds of his sales in A's market on deposit in a bank in A.

by residents of B for all purposes other than current (i.e. non-capital) transactions. A general subsidy on capital transfers into B could be enforced only by a system which approximated very closely to that of an exchange-control authority which paid a specially high price for all foreign exchange surrendered to it by residents of A for all capital payments to B.[1] We should be driven to something corresponding more closely to a monetary system of multiple exchange rates than to a fiscal system of taxes and subsidies.

[1] The problem of distinguishing between capital and current transactions is considered below (p. 302).

CHAPTER XXI

TYPES OF DIRECT CONTROL:
COMMERCIAL CONTROLS

LET us turn now to the consideration of commercial controls.

1. *Quantitative Restrictions*

The total payments or receipts in a country's balance of payments may be influenced by commercial measures which set a limitation upon the amount (or the value) of a particular product which may be imported or exported. Such a form of direct control is most likely to be applied to 'visible' commodity imports and exports, since it can be readily enforced as the commodity in question passes over the country's frontier.

Let us start by considering a quantitative restriction on the imports of a particular commodity into B. This quantitative import restriction may limit the *volume* of the commodity which may be imported into B (e.g. not more than four foreign motor-cars to be brought in this year) or the *value* of the commodity which may be imported (e.g. not more than $400 worth of motor-cars to be imported this year which can cover a larger number of cheap cars or a smaller number of expensive cars). It may be administered through an 'open' or 'global quota' (e.g. as soon as four motor-cars have crossed the frontier into B the frontier will be closed to the import of cars for the rest of the year) or it may be administered by the grant of licences or permits to individual persons to import motor-cars (e.g. Messrs W, X, Y, and Z are each given a licence to import one motor-car this year) and in this latter case the licences may or may not specify from what source the commodity is to be procured (e.g. Messrs W, X, and Y each have a permit to import one motor-car from the United States and Mr Z has a permit to import one from France).

The purpose of this quantitative import restriction will be to reduce the value of the country's import of this commodity by a certain amount. This it will certainly do, if it takes the form of limiting the total value of the class of imports in question. But if it takes the form of a limitation on the volume of the commodity which may be imported it is not certain that it will achieve this objective even if it is effectively enforced.

Let us revert to our previous example. Motor-cars cost $100 each to produce in A.[1] At this price consumers in B would purchase five

---

[1] Since throughout this chapter we shall be assuming a fixed rate of exchange we shall give all values in terms of A's currency (dollars) and will not translate them at the fixed rate of exchange into B's currency (pounds).

cars, making a total expenditure of $500 on motor-car imports. The number which is allowed to enter B is reduced by administrative action to four. Consumers in A would now be willing to pay a scarcity price of $133⅓ a car when only four are available, making a total expenditure of $533⅓ for four cars. But the producers in A would be prepared to provide the four cars at $100 apiece, i.e. for $400 in all. There is a gap of $133⅓ in all or of $33⅓ per car between the price which the home consumer will be prepared to pay for the four cars and the price which the foreign supplier would be prepared to accept for them.

When imports are restricted by the fiscal means of an import tax or by the monetary means of a multiple exchange rate, this problem of the 'margin' between demand and supply price does not arise. The restriction of imports always leads to a rise in the price which consumers are willing to pay above the price at which the foreign exporter is willing to offer the commodity. But this 'margin' automatically accrues to the authorities of the importing country in the form of a revenue from the import duty in the case of the tax and in the form of a profit on the dealings of the exchange-control authority in the case of a multiple exchange rate.

But with an exchange control which merely restricts the amount of money which may be spent on the particular imports or with a quantitative import restriction which limits a particular import by value or by quantity, this problem of the margin between demand and supply price arises. Suppose the import of cars is restricted, by exchange control or by a value quota, to $400 in value (for which the producers in A would be willing to supply four cars) or, by a quantitative quota, to four in number (which will cost the producers in A $400 to produce). Then the consumers in B will pay $133⅓ for each car which costs the producers $100 a car to produce. To whom does this margin of $33⅓ per car accrue?

We must consider at least five possibilities.

(i) In those cases in which licences to import the permitted number of cars or to pay for the permitted value of cars are issued to individual dealers, part of this $33⅓ may accrue as a bribe to the official who has to decide whether to grant the application of Mr X or Mr Y, both of whom seek either an exchange-control permit to acquire $100 for the purchase of a motor-car or else an import licence to import one car or $100 worth of cars from A. Each such permit or licence is itself commercially worth $33⅓; it will enable Mr X or Mr Y, if he obtains it, to purchase for $100 a car which can be sold for $133⅓. Mr X and Mr Y may be prepared to use some part of this difference to help the official to decide to whom he shall hand out the valuable permit.

(ii) Where there is no issue of individual permits or licences or where the administrative machine is sufficiently honest and competent, this will not occur. But the margin between the supply price and the demand price of the restricted amount of imports will still exist. The margin may accrue to the lucky middlemen who happen to have received the necessary permits or licences or, for some other reason, happen to deal with the restricted amount of car imports. They purchase an imported car at \$100 and sell it in the home market at \$133$\frac{1}{3}$.[1]

(iii) Administrative arrangements may, however, be made to prevent the middlemen from raising the price of imported motor-cars to the final consumer, apart from a reasonable merchant's margin of profit. This will necessitate a system of price control. It will also mean that the demand of the final consumers cannot all be fulfilled at the controlled price. In our example, at a controlled price of \$100 per imported car consumers will want to buy five such cars while only four are available. Either an official system of rationing or allocating the supplies to the final consumers must be adopted or else there will be shop shortages, queues, under-the-counter sales, etc. Moreover, it will be difficult, if not impossible, to prevent final consumers from re-selling the product; the customer at the head of the queue may purchase the car at the controlled price of \$100 and re-sell it for \$133$\frac{1}{3}$ to the customer at the end of the queue.

(iv) In certain circumstances the exporters in A may be able to appropriate to themselves the margin between the high demand price at which the restricted number of cars can be sold in B and the lower price at which they would in normal competitive conditions be prepared to supply these cars.

(v) There remains the possibility that while the value or the volume of cars to be imported into B will be fixed quantitatively by an administrative order of an exchange-control or import-licensing authority, measures will be taken at the same time, by the imposition of an import fee by the fiscal authorities in the importing country, to·ensure that the margin between the demand and supply prices for the limited quantity of imports accrues to the government of the importing country.

[1] Some part of this margin of \$33$\frac{1}{3}$ between the new supply price and demand price may be absorbed by increased costs of distribution. If the import restrictions are administered on a basis which reduces the turnover of each individual trader (e.g. by allocating licences to each individual importer so as to reduce his imports by a given percentage), each merchant's business may become uneconomically small. In this case it is conceivable that the increased costs of handling each unit of trade would absorb the whole of the margin between the new supply price and demand price. But this is unlikely. Moreover, if the import restrictions are administered on a basis which still permits more economic trading units to drive out the less economic (e.g. by the auctioning of licences to import—see p. 286, below), the rise in distribution costs is much less likely to occur. In what follows we shall continue to talk simply of the margin between the new supply price and demand price. This must be interpreted as the net margin, i.e. after making allowance for any rise in the cost of handling each unit of trade. But we shall assume that in all cases the rise in distribution costs is not so great as to reduce this net margin to zero.

We need not discuss at any great length cases i and iii above. As far as case i is concerned, if the governmental machine is not strong enough to resist bribery, then when permits or licences are issued, some of the additional profits which would thereby accrue to the lucky licensees may, in fact, be shared with the government officials who are responsible for allocating the licences. So long as we remember this fact in our future discussion of the special profits to be made from the receipt of such licences or permits, we need not make any further special analysis of this possibility.

Case iii may be equally shortly discussed. If a system of price control is adopted so that some privileged final consumers of the product obtain the special advantage of obtaining the supplies at a price lower than the free market price, it is as if licences to import had been issued to these specially privileged consumers. If we remember that the issue of licences to importers may take this special form, the following discussion will cover this case as well.

We are left, then, with three possibilities. The government of the importing country may itself appropriate the margin between demand and supply price by means of the simultaneous imposition of some special import duty or fee (case v). But in the absence of such action the margin must accrue *either* to the producers and exporters in A (case iv) *or* to the importers in B (case ii). Which of these two latter will obtain the margin is of crucial importance from the point of view of the effect of the import restriction upon the balance of payments and the terms of trade of the importing country B.

Let us consider a quantitative import restriction on the number of cars which may be imported. Previously five cars were imported and sold at $100 a car (or $500 for the five cars) and this represented a receipt to the producers in A which just covered their costs. Only four cars may now be imported. The consumers in B would now be willing to pay $133\frac{1}{3}$ a car or $533\frac{1}{3}$ for the four cars, whereas producers in A would be prepared to take $100 a car or $400 for the four cars. If the margin between the demand and selling price accrues to the importers in B, the value of B's imports and so B's deficit will have been reduced from $500 to $400. But if the margin accrues to the exporters in A, the value of B's imports will have risen from $500 (i.e. five cars at $100 a car) to $533\frac{1}{3}$ (i.e. four cars at $133\frac{1}{3}$ a car). Because the elasticity of demand for cars in B is less than unity, the total amount which consumers in B will pay for the smaller number of cars is greater than before; and because the whole of the margin between buying and selling price accrues to the exporters in A, B's deficit is worse than before. Moreover, B's real terms of trade were unchanged when the margin accrued to B's importers, since B's importers paid A's exporters the same price of $100 per car; but when the margin accrued to A's exporters, B's terms of trade became less favourable than before, since A's exporters now received the higher price of $133\frac{1}{3}$ per car. In short, if the margin accrues to B's importers the terms of trade will be unchanged[1] but B's deficit will be reduced; whereas if the margin accrues to A's exporters the terms of trade will move unfavourably to B and the deficit in B's balance of payments will be reduced less than in the first case and, if the elasticity of demand for the imports in B is less than unity, it will actually be increased.

So much for a restriction by quantity. We must now consider the case of a restriction of imports by value. If the margin accrues to the importers in B, there is nothing to add to the above analysis. But if the margin accrues to the exporters in A, the case is rather different. In this case, if the imports into B are effectively restricted by value, the result must be to reduce the value of B's imports, even if the demand for imports in B is inelastic. But there may still be a very considerable movement in the terms of trade against B.

To revert to our example. Exporters of motor-cars in A find that they may export only $400 instead of $500 of their motor-cars to B. As they reduce their supplies to B, the price per car in B's market goes up. In consequence they must reduce the supplies in B's market still further since they must keep their total sales down to $400. Suppose that the elasticity of demand in B for imported motor-cars is so small that when the supply is reduced from five to two the price will rise from $100 a car to $200 a car. At this price a total of $400 will be paid for the import of only two cars. It is true that the value of B's imports have effectively been reduced from $500 (i.e. five cars at $100 a car) to $400 (i.e. two cars at $200 a car). But the terms of trade have moved very markedly against B, since B's imports have doubled in price (from $100 to $200 a car). The improvement in B's balance of trade has been achieved at the cost of a very great movement of the real terms of trade against B; and the foreign supplier can now obtain a special margin of no less than $100 per car. His receipts from purchasers in B are twice as great as is necessary to cover his costs of producing the cars exported to B.

It is, therefore, of the greatest importance to determine whether it is the importers in B or the exporters in A who will enjoy the margin between the buying and selling price. The result will depend upon two main factors: the methods of administering the import restrictions and the organization of the market to which they are applied. We must consider each of these factors in turn.

Table XVI describes in schematic form twelve different ways in which import restrictions may be organized.

---

[1] In fact the terms of trade might well move somewhat in B's favour since the reduced demand for cars in B might make A's producers willing to supply at a somewhat lower price than before.

TABLE XVI

The Administration of Quantitative Import Restrictions

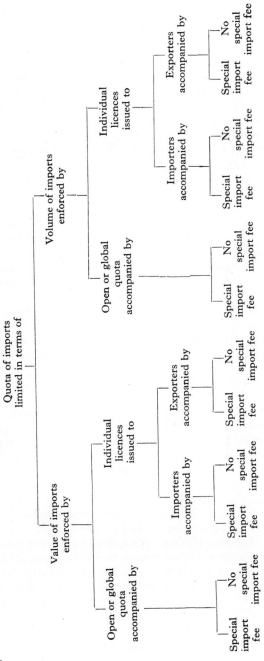

In the first place, as we have already seen, the restrictions may be fixed in terms of a maximum value of imports or in terms of a maximum volume of imports which are to be permitted into the country.

In the second place, the import restriction may be enforced by means of an open or global quota or by means of the issue of import licences to individual traders. With the open or global quota, imports are allowed into the importing country on the principle of 'first come, first served' until the permitted amount or value of the import has entered. The frontier is then closed to all further imports of the commodity concerned for the rest of the quota period. With such a system it is not possible to say who will obtain the benefit of the margin between the buying and selling price. Since anyone is free to import the commodity until the quota has been filled, there will be a rush to the frontier with the goods. Some dealers will be lucky and will reach the frontier before others. Those who are lucky will enjoy the abnormal profit; but there is no *a priori* reason to believe that they will be the exporters of A rather than the importers of B or vice versa.

The margin might, of course, be appropriated to the government of the importing country, even under an open or global quota, if a special import duty or other import fee were simultaneously imposed upon the importation of the commodity. And in so far as this special import fee were nicely adjusted to absorb neither more nor less than the margin between selling and buying price, the chaotic rush to the frontier to fill the quota would also be avoided. The special import duty would just serve to restrict the demand to the supply permitted under the quota, and the result would be that the exporters as a whole would no longer find it profitable to supply more than the market could absorb. In fact, the quota would become in large measure inoperative, and the restriction of imports would be achieved by the import tax.

In order to avoid the chaos of an open or global quota it is normal to issue import licences to individuals which permit them to import given quantities or values of the commodity, the sum of all the individual licences adding up to the total quantity or value which is to be permitted to enter the country.

At this point we must consider the organization of the market into which these licences are introduced. The market may be competitive or it may be monopolistic in organization. Let us first consider the case in which the market is competitive before the introduction of the import restriction, and in which it remains competitive after the introduction of the import restriction. This is perfectly possible if the import licences are issued in small amounts to a large number of separate individual traders. In this case no single trader can by refraining from using the import licence which has been allotted to him influence either the price at which he can purchase the product from the producer or the price at which he can sell it to the consumer. But each trader will be restricted to import less than he would like to have imported at this price margin. The outcome is simple. The margin will accrue to the traders to whom the import licences have been granted, and the margin will accrue to the importers in B if the licences have been issued to the importers in B and it will accrue to the exporters in A if the licences have been issued to the exporters in A.[1]

A very similar analysis applies where the market for the commodity is already monopolized in the hands of one or two very large traders, who already fix their prices more or less in agreement to obtain the maximum profit. The import restriction will clearly have no effect unless it is fixed below the level which the monopoly was already importing. Since this level is already the one which maximizes the monopolist's profit, the monopolist will lose in profit by the further restriction which his licence imposes upon him. But this restriction will cause some further rise in the price which he can charge the consumers and, perhaps some further fall in the price which he must pay to obtain the supplies from the producer. This increased margin per unit of the product will accrue to the monopolist licensee. It will, therefore, accrue to the exporting or the importing country according as the monopolistic trader is an exporter or importer. If he is an exporter, the terms of trade will move against the importing country; but the balance of trade cannot move against the importing country. That could happen only if the elasticity of demand for the imports in the importing country were less than unity, so that the total value of the imports would be increased by putting less of them on the market of the importing country. But if this were the case, the monopolistic exporter would already have had an incentive to restrict his exports farther without being compelled to do so through the import restriction.

So far we have dealt with the cases where the market was competitive and remained competitive, and where it was already monopolistic and remained monopolistic. But in fact a licensing system may turn a competitive market into a monopolistic market. This would be the obvious outcome if all the licences to import were given to a single trader. It may also occur where there were previously a number of traders who did not try to get together to form a monopoly in order to exploit the

[1] The only complication is where the licences are for fixed values for imports and are issued to the exporters in A. In this case, since each exporter is not allowed to obtain from B a greater total value of payments than his licence permits, he will export to B the minimum volume of the commodity which will sell for the total permitted value. We shall in fact obtain the result mentioned on p. 278 above. The value of B's imports will be duly restricted; but the terms of trade will move against B because the restriction in the volume of the imports will be continued until it is so small that, even at the much higher demand price offered in B, the total value of exports from A is restricted to the value permitted by the quota.

consumers (and possibly also the producers) of the commodity, because they knew that any monopoly which they formed would be open to the competition of newcomers to the trade. But if they are protected by being the only persons with licences giving a right to import, they may now come together to form an effective monopoly.

In this case the total volume (or value) of imports may be restricted by the import restriction to a lower level than that actually permitted by the import licences which are issued. Suppose that the allotment of the import licences to certain traders enables an impregnable monopoly to be formed by them, but that the total amount of imports specified on the licences is greater than the amount which would maximize the monopolist's profit. Then the traders may, in concert, restrict the imports below the amount stated on the licences. The margin between the buying and selling price of the imports (both per unit of imports and in total) will be greater than would otherwise be the case. If, on the other hand, the amount stated in the licences is equal to, or less than, the amount which will maximize the monopolist's profit, restriction will be merely to the amount specified on the licence. But in either case the margin between the buying and selling price will accrue to the monopoly trader, i.e. to the exporting or importing country according as the monopoly trader is an exporter in A or an importer in B.[1]

In fact the result of any given issue of licences upon the monopolization of the trade is not likely to be as clear-cut as the above argument suggests. The outcome depends not only upon the persons to whom the import licences are granted but also upon the conditions upon which they are granted. For example, the licences may be issued to importers (Messrs W, X, Y, and Z, residents in the United Kingdom, may receive a licence to import one car each into the United Kingdom) but they may be issued on condition that certain amounts of the commodity are purchased from certain specified sources (thus, Messrs W, X, and Y may have to import an American car and Mr Z a French car in order to ensure that the quota is allocated as to three cars to the United States and as to one car to France.)[2] This condition breaks the exporters up into watertight areas of supply. French exporters of motor-cars can no longer drive out the American producers by undercutting them, nor vice versa. The French are guaranteed a market for one car and the Americans for three. Whereas previously when competition between American and French suppliers was feasible, it would have needed an

---

[1] Again, if the restriction to import is by value and the monopoly trader is an exporter in A, the value of A's exports will be restricted to the permitted level by as great a restriction of volume as is compatible with the earning of this value in B's markets. This may mean a very small volume of exports from A and a very large change in the terms of trade against B.

[2] This kind of arrangement has often been made to ensure non-discrimination between the exporting countries; but on this see the discussion in Chapter XXVIII below.

international cartel of French and American car exporters to exploit the United Kingdom market, now a separate French cartel and a separate United States cartel can have the same effect. There are in any case only going to be four imported cars on the United Kingdom market, one French and three American. A French cartel can then withhold its supplies until it obtains a price for the French car which corresponds to the scarcity price of cars in the United Kingdom market; the United Kingdom importer cannot threaten to transfer his custom to the American supplier. And similarly with a separate American export cartel.

Now where a monopoly of purchasers of a particular commodity is faced with a monopoly of sellers of that commodity, the division of the margin between buying and selling price is indeterminate economically. It depends upon such things as bluff. One can, therefore, merely say that with a system of licences the margin between the buying and selling price is more likely to accrue to the importing country if the licences are issued to residents of the importing country on conditions which do not tie them as between their sources of supply. The opposite conditions will make it more probable that the margin accrues to the exporting country, with the consequences upon the balance of trade and the real terms of trade which we have examined above.

We may summarize this discussion by saying that the margin between the demand and supply price due to import restriction is less likely to go to residents in the exporting country, (i) if the import licences are granted to the traders or consumers in the importing country and not to the traders or producers in the exporting country, (ii) if the importers who receive the licences are not restricted in the use which they can make of them, and (iii) if the exporters are in any case highly competitive with each other. The opposite conditions will increase the risk that the margin will accrue to residents in the exporting country.

The margin between the buying and selling price can, of course, be appropriated by the government of the importing country if it charges some import duty or licensing fee equal to this margin at the same time that it issues the import licence.[1] It can attempt to adjust this charge so

---

[1] It is interesting to observe that where the licensed traders are competitive it does not make any difference to the outcome whether the fee is a fee per unit of import equal to the margin per unit of import beween the buying and selling price or a lump sum licence fee equal to the total abnormal profit which each trader can make on the turnover which he is licensed to conduct. But if the trader is a monopolist and can affect the price per unit which the consumer will offer or the price per unit which he has to offer to the producer by varying his own turnover, he may be induced to restrict his turnover further below his permitted import quota if the fee is a charge per unit of turnover and not a lump sum charge regardless of his actual turnover. For the monopolist, unlike the competitive trader, the margin between the buying and the selling price may be greater than the margin between his marginal revenue and his marginal cost, so that a tax per unit equal to the margin between buying and selling price of the product may cause him to restrict his sales.

that it just accounts for the margin between buying and selling price, in which case the import restriction has essentially the same effect as that brought about by a tariff.

One way of adjusting the import fee to the correct height and, at the same time, of ensuring an equitable and efficient distribution of the import licences among the competing importers would be to sell the import licences by auction to the highest bidders.[1] This would enable more efficient dealers with lower costs of merchanting to outbid the less efficient and to expand their business at the expense of the less efficient; it would thus minimize the risk that import licensing would encourage monopolization of the trade. Exporters in the exporting country, final consumers in the importing country, wholesalers in the importing country—all could bid in the auction without discrimination as between countries of origin of the goods or as between individuals within an country. The State would obtain the whole of the 'margin' due to the scarcity prices. In fact the device would be the equivalent of an import duty which was automatically so adjusted as to reduce the demand for imports to the predetermined fixed volume or value which might be permitted to enter.

This device of auctioning import licences could be used so as progressively to transform a system of rigid quantitative control over particular imports into a generally flexible fiscal mechanism for the restriction of imports to the degree required to put the balance of payments into equilibrium. Suppose we start with a large number of separate schemes for restricting by volume the imports of a lot of individual commodities. We can then turn these into value quotas instead of volume quotas. We then hold separate auctions to sell the rights to import the permitted value of each particular import. The licence fee which results in each case will show what *ad valorem* import duty would be required in each case to keep the import value down to the permitted level. We can then broaden the classes; for example, instead of holding two separate auctions for rights to import $200 worth

---

[1] The import licensing authority would state in advance the total amount of the commodity which might be imported in a future period. It would then invite bids for this limited right to import. All potential importers would be invited to send in to a central office a statement of the number of import licences which the purchaser would wish to purchase at different specified prices of import licences, thus: Mr X will purchase licences for the import of 1,000 cars if the import licence fee is $100 a car, licences for the import of only 800 cars if the import licence fee is $150 a car, and so on. The central office would add up all the licences demanded at each licence fee and would then fix a fee at which the total licences demanded was equal to the predetermined fixed quantity of imports which were to be admitted in the period in question. Each individual importer would then receive the import licences for which he had asked at that price. To discourage the monopolistic 'cornering' of the licences penalties might be imposed for the failure to make use of licences once they had been acquired. The licences should, of course, be freely marketable, subject to this condition.

of raw cotton and to import $100 worth of raw wool, we can hold a single auction of the rights to import $300 of raw wool or raw cotton. These broadenings of classes could go on successively until all imports were in one single class, and we were in fact holding a single auction of the foreign exchange available to purchase all imports. Alternatively, the same result could be obtained by a different means without merging all the imports into a single class. We could gradually increase the permitted level of imports in those cases in which the auction results in a licence fee which was abnormally high in relation to the value of the imports, and could gradually diminish the permitted level of imports in those cases in which the auction resulted in an import licence fee which was low in relation to the value of the imports. We should by either means end up with a general non-discriminatory restriction of all imports by what is essentially the same degree of severity. The import licence fee taken in relation to the value of imports would be the same on all commodities and would indicate what rate of *ad valorem* import duty or of exchange depreciation would be necessary to restrict imports by the same amount. Nor would it be essential to go the whole way in this course. A halt could be called when any desired degree of use of the price mechanism had by these means been introduced into the original arbitrary system of quantitative controls.

So far we have considered only import restrictions. It is also possible, of course, to limit the amount (or value) of exports by restricting by licence the quantity (or value) of a particular commodity which may be exported. If the export permits are issued to the country's exporters and are not tied to particular import markets, the price of the restricted exports should rise in the foreign markets. The total value of the exports in terms of foreign currency will rise or fall according as the foreign elasticity of demand is less or greater than unity. A price margin on the exports will now appear as a result of the rise of the price of the restricted supplies in the foreign markets above the price at which the suppliers are prepared to supply it in the exporting country; and this 'margin' may accrue in bribes to the licensing authorities, in abnormal profits to the middle-men exporters, in abnormal profits to the producers of the product, in low prices to the purchasers of the product in the importing country, or to the government of the exporting country if it charges some form of export licence fee (fixed by means of an auction or otherwise) to absorb the margin between supply and demand price. The actual outcome depends upon considerations analogous to those which we have examined in the case of import restrictions.

2. The Tariff Quota

Results similar to those of an ordinary quantitative import restriction can be obtained by means of a 'tariff quota', by which device a certain restricted quantity of the commodity may be imported without duty or on the payment of only a low import duty, while additional quantities can be imported but only on payment of a much higher import duty. The import duty on additional imports may be so high that traders do not find it profitable to import beyond the low-tariff quota, because the then still existing margin between the buying and selling price of the commodity is lower than the duty on additional imports. In this case the problems connected with the tariff quota are in no way different from those which arise in the case of ordinary quantitative import restriction. Indeed, an ordinary quantitative import restriction is merely a tariff quota in which the duty on additional imports is prohibitively high.

If the duty on additional imports is less than the margin between the buying and selling price to which the quota restriction gives rise, then some additional imports will be brought in. The additional supplies on the importing market will cause the price offered by consumers on that market to fall; and the additional purchases of the product from the exporting producers may cause some rise in the price which they obtain. In any case the margin between the buying and selling price will be closed by the sale of more of the commodity in the importing market, until it no longer exceeds the duty on additional imports.

At this point the restriction is exactly similar to that caused by a duty equal to this duty on additional imports, with the only exception that we have to decide who gets the benefit of the abnormal profits to be made on the 'quota' part of the imports on which a lower or no duty is levied. The issues raised here are exactly the same as those discussed in the previous section on ordinary quantitative import restrictions. Who in fact is responsible for the import of these preferential quantities? Is there an open or global quota for these low-duty imports, or are import licences issued for them? If so, to whom and in what sort of market conditions? The result will, as before, depend upon the answers to these questions.

3. *State Trading Monopolies*

Similar results to those obtained by quantitative restrictions through the issue of a limited quantity of import or export licences can also be obtained through a State trading monopoly. Suppose that all private imports of a particular product are prohibited and a State trading organization is set up to import the commodity in question. The State trading organization can now restrict the total quantity of the product which it imports as a means of reducing the value of the country's commodity imports and so diminishing the deficit on the balance of payments. In this case, again, a margin will appear between the relatively low price at which the foreign suppliers are prepared to supply the product and the relatively high price which the reduced supplies will fetch in the domestic market of the importing country. But in this case the margin will accrue directly to the government of the importing country in the form of an abnormal profit made by the State trading organization.

And similarly with a State export monopoly, which can purchase a restricted amount of the product for export and dispose of it at a scarcity price to the foreign country, itself absorbing the margin between the relatively low home supply price and the relatively high foreign demand price in the form of an abnormally high profit made on the State trading organization's dealings.

In this way State trading monopolies, by restricting the volume of imports and exports and by themselves absorbing the monopoly profits on such restricted trade, can have substantially the same effects in reducing the volume of trade as can be achieved by a system of import and export licences sold to private traders or by a system of import or export taxes which are so adjusted in height as to have a similar effect upon the volume of import or export trade.

State trading organizations (in this case even if they are not legal monopolies) can also be used for the purpose of expanding import or export trade in a way which would result from the payment of import or export subsidies.[1] A State export organization can, for example, purchase larger quantities of the home produce for sale abroad than would be exported by private traders. If the elasticity of the foreign demand for the exports is greater than unity, the total amount of foreign currency obtained for the exports will be increased because the price in the foreign market will fall less than in proportion to the increase in the amount exported. But the price in the foreign market will in any case fall somewhat as a result of the increase in the amount put on to the foreign market, and the State export organization will make a loss on its exports. This loss will correspond to the export subsidy which in a régime of private trade would have been necessary to promote this increase in exports.

Similarly with a State import organization. It could purchase larger quantities of imports than the ordinary competitive amounts and put these on sale on the home market at a loss. This loss would correspond to the import subsidy which would be necessary to promote this increased quantity of imports.[2]

[1] This result cannot, of course, be achieved by import and export licences issued to private traders, which can be used only to restrict and not to expand trade.
[2] In the above paragraphs we have tacitly assumed that the State import monopoly was purchasing, and the State export monopoly selling, in fairly free competitive world markets. In these cases we can assume that any abnormal margin between buying and selling price accrues to the State trading organization. But where a State import monopoly in B has to deal with a State export monopoly in A it cannot, of course, be assumed that the 'margin' is more likely to accrue to the authorities in B than to the authorities in A.

CHAPTER XXII

THE CONTROL OF CAPITAL MOVEMENTS

WE have now considered the various controls by means of which the authorities of a country may exert a direct influence upon particular items in the balance of payments. We must now consider in what conditions and for what purposes, if any, it is desirable to exert a direct control over various elements in the balance of payments. In this chapter we shall consider the arguments for and against direct control over capital movements; and in the next chapter we shall consider the arguments for and against direct controls over current transactions.

Let us start, then, with the question of the control of capital movements. Are there any special reasons why, if country B is in deficit and country A in surplus, the authorities in either or both countries should take special measures to limit net capital payments from B to A or to encourage net capital payments from A to B?

Before we can analyse this question we must limit its scope somewhat. In the first place, the effect of a capital movement between A and B will differ very much according to the other policies which are being adopted in A and B. The authorities in A may adopt a neutral policy (see Chapter IV); they may modify this neutral policy only with a financial policy for internal balance or with a financial policy for external balance (see Chapter IX); there may or may not simultaneously be wage flexibility in A (see Chapter XIII); or the authorities in A may or may not simultaneously adopt a system of variable exchange rates (see Chapter XII). Simultaneously the authorities in B may adopt any one of the many possible policy combinations which can be built out of these separate bricks. And any particular policy combination in A may be combined with any other particular policy combination in B, so that a world of only two countries may take a very large number of forms, so far as its principles of policy are concerned.

The effect of a transfer of capital between A and B will depend upon the particular economic policies through which the authorities in both countries react to a change in economic conditions. In order to consider fully whether there are any special reasons for controlling capital movements as a means of achieving a smooth adjustment of the balance of payments between A and B, we should be obliged to consider the problem separately for each of the many possible policy combinations.

Such a task is clearly impossible. We shall, therefore, restrict ourselves to a consideration of the problem on two alternative assumptions. We shall consider the problem first on the assumption that in both A and B there is in operation what we have described in Chapter XIV as the mechanism of the gold standard. Broadly speaking, by that we mean that if there is a deficit in B's balance of payments, (i) the exchange rate is maintained, (ii) total domestic expenditure is deflated in B and inflated in A, and (iii) sooner or later as a result of a deficient demand for labour in B and an excess demand for labour in A the general level of money wage rates, costs, and prices falls in B and rises in A so that, with the sum of the elasticities of demand for imports greater than unity, B's balance of trade is improved.

The second set of assumptions on which we shall examine the problem of the control of capital transfer between A and B is that the authorities in both A and B are adopting the type of policy outlined in Chapter XII above. That is to say, the authorities in both A and B adopt financial policies for internal balance, so that whatever disturbance takes place the total demand for each country's products is kept constant in terms of the currency of that country. And with this domestic background disequilibria in the balance of payments between A and B are removed by variations in the exchange rates. If B's balance of payments is in deficit, B's exchange rate is depreciated, thus making B's products relatively cheaper in terms of A's so that—again with the sum of the elasticities of demand for imports greater than unity—B's balance of trade is improved.

Both the above systems are 'complete' in the sense that by price and income adjustments they permit both internal and external balance to be maintained simultaneously in both countries. We shall now proceed to inquire whether the operation of such systems should be modified by the introduction of direct controls over capital movements. It must, however, be carefully remembered that this does not cover the arguments for and against the use of direct controls over capital movements in the case of 'incomplete' systems (such, for example, as the neutral economy modified only by a financial policy for internal balance, see Chapter IX) where, in the absence of some direct interventions, it may be impossible simultaneously to maintain internal balance in both countries and external balance between them.

For example, suppose that the authorities in both A and B adopt neutral economies with the addition only of financial policies for internal balance and that as a result there is full employment in both A and B but a serious balance-of-payments deficit for B. B is continually losing gold reserves to A. This cannot go on indefinitely; and the authorities in B may be obliged to abandon their expansionist financial policy for internal balance and to adopt a deflationary financial policy for external balance, causing a sufficient fall in employment and income and so a sufficient decline in the demand for imports to stop the drain on the gold reserves. If in these conditions the authorities in B by introducing a direct control over capital movements from B to A can stop the drain on the reserves, this may well be preferable to the adoption of a deflationary financial policy for external balance and the consequent unemployment and deflation in B.

But this is not the issue which we intend to discuss in this chapter. The authorities in B can always attempt to restore external balance through price adjustments, either through wage flexibility (in which case as the deflationary policy in B took effect in reducing domestic expenditure in B the general level of money wage rates and money costs in B would fall and B's exports to A would expand and imports from A contract) or else through variable exchange rates (in which case the financial policy for internal balance in B need not be abandoned but B's exchange rate would be allowed to depreciate in order to enable B's products to undercut A's products and so put a stop to the loss of gold reserves). The question which we intend to discuss in this chapter is whether the method of direct control of capital movements is preferable to these methods of price adjustment.

Before we embark upon this analysis there is one more preliminary matter to be cleared out of the way. A transfer of capital from B to A may or may not be directly associated with, or directly cause, a reduction in domestic expenditure in B and an increase in domestic expenditure in A. For example, private capitalists in B may decide not to spend £100 on building a productive plant in B but to change this sum into $400 and to spend it on building a productive plant in A instead; and this is a decision simultaneously (i) to reduce domestic expenditure in B by a given amount, (ii) to increase domestic expenditure in A by the same amount, and (iii) to transfer the same amount of capital funds across the foreign exchanges from B's currency into A's currency. Or, to take a very different example, suppose that someone who holds idle money in B's currency decides now to hold the same idle sum in A's money instead; with £100 of deposits at B's banks he purchases $400 to deposit with A's banks; there is again a decision to transfer £100 of capital funds across the foreign exchanges, but there is no simultaneous decision to alter domestic expenditure in either A and B; and any change in domestic expenditures would only occur very indirectly— for example, by reason of the fact that the loss of gold reserves by B's banking system and the gain of such reserves by A's banking system might lead to a rise in interest rates in B and a fall in interest rates in A and so to some influence on domestic expenditure in the two countries.

A capital transfer from B to A may therefore be directly associated with a fall in domestic expenditure in B ranging from 0 to 100 per cent of the total transfer and it may be directly associated with a rise in domestic expenditure in A ranging again from 0 to 100 per cent of the total transfer, these two percentages being quite independently determined.

In many conditions the effect of the transfer of capital may depend very much upon the extent to which it directly causes variations in domestic expenditure in the two countries. But we need only consider the relevance of this point to the two particular 'policy combinations' which we are proposing to study; and luckily in these two cases this consideration is not of importance.

A continuing transfer of funds from B to A, occurring in a position of equilibrium under the gold standard, will cause B to lose gold to A.[1] To put a stop to this drain of gold there must be a deflation of domestic expenditure in B and an inflation of domestic expenditure in A so as to cause a decline in B's money wage rates and costs relatively to A's.[2] If the transfer of capital from B to A is not directly associated with any change in domestic expenditure in B or A, then the necessary deflation in B and inflation in A must be induced *either* by the discouragement to new capital development in B which will result from higher interest rates in B which will result from the loss of reserves and scarcity of money in B (and vice versa in A), or *else* by a consciously designed fiscal policy for the deflation of domestic expenditure in B and its inflation in A. But if the transfer of capital from B to A is directly associated with a deflation of domestic expenditure in B and an inflation in A, then some of the necessary deflation in B and inflation in A will automatically occur so that less deflation in B and inflation in A need be brought about as a secondary induced effect of the loss of gold reserves from B to A. In both cases the total deflation in B and inflation in A required to restore equilibrium will be the same.

In the case in which the authorities in both A and B adopt domestic financial policies for internal balance, it will make equally little difference whether the transfer of capital from B to A is or is not directly associated with a deflation of domestic expenditure in B and an inflation of domestic expenditure in A. In either case a certain level of domestic expenditure in each country will be required to maintain internal balance; and whatever 'spontaneous' change may occur in association with the capital transfer will simply be combined with a different 'policy' change in order to achieve that level of domestic expenditure which is necessary to avoid changes in the national income.

[1] Save in the very exceptional case in which it is directly associated with a considerable fall in domestic expenditure in B and rise in domestic expenditure in A and the sum of the marginal propensities to import is not less than unity. (See case ii of Table IX above). We shall ignore this possibility.

[2] Assuming that the sum of the marginal propensities to import is less than one.

In what follows we shall, therefore, neglect the question whether or not spontaneous changes in domestic expenditure in A or B are directly associated with the transfer of capital funds from B to A. We assume merely that with the gold standard there is a sufficient deflation of domestic expenditure in B and inflation in A to restore external balance, whether this change in domestic expenditure is itself a 'spontaneous' accompaniment of the capital transfer or is a 'policy' change designed to restore equilibrium. And we assume that with variable exchange rates total domestic expenditure in both countries is so adjusted as to leave the national income unchanged, i.e. that any 'spontaneous' changes of domestic expenditure which may be associated with the capital transfer have been offset by such 'policy' changes of domestic expenditure as are necessary to keep the national income constant.

Let us, then, turn to the question whether there is any reason to interfere with the mechanisms of price adjustment by means of a direct control of capital movements. Let us start by examining the case of sudden and large-scale movements of short-term funds from one currency to another—what is often known as the problem of 'hot money'.

Persons or private institutions, whether residents of A or of B, who hold considerable sums of money on deposit in B's currency with the banks of B,[1] may decide for one reason or another to move these sums from B's currency into A's currency suddenly and on a large scale. There are many reasons which may cause such a flight from B's currency into A's currency. Fears that B's currency is to be depreciated, or that there will be social unrest in B, or that there will be a capital levy in B, or that there will be a war between A and B in which A will prevail— such expectations which will thrive in a world of political instability may cause more or less panic movements of funds from B's currency into A's currency.

Let us first consider the matter under the operation of the gold standard. The flight of funds from B to A will cause a loss of gold reserves from B to A. This cannot continue unchecked.[2] One of three policies must be adopted to put a stop to it:

[1] Or invested in short-term assets in B (such as Treasury Bills issued by B's government) which are repayable at short notice in cash in B's currency.

[2] If the flight of funds was merely from holding idle money in B's currency to holding it in A's currency and if both A and B were on a 100 per cent money standard (see Chapter XIV, above), the movement could continue unchecked. The supply of money in B would be reduced by no more than the movement of idle money from B to A. Since B's supply of domestic money is backed as to 100 per cent by gold which is also the actual money of A, there would be no fall in the ratio of gold reserves to money in B nor any rise in this ratio in A. There would simply be a movement of idle money from B to A. There would be no scarcity of money in B nor excess supply of money in A and no fall in reserve ratios in B nor rise in A. This once again illustrates the great virtues of a system of 100 per cent money as opposed to a percentage-reserve system.

(i) The gold-standard mechanism can be allowed to work itself out with a deflation of demand and so of money wage rates, costs, and incomes in B and with a similar inflation in A, until B's products undercut A's products in price on a scale sufficient to generate a surplus in B's balance of trade sufficient to finance the continuing flight of funds from B to A.

(ii) The authorities in B can institute a system of exchange control in order to put a stop to the movement of funds from B to A.

(iii) The authorities in B (and perhaps in A as well) can offset the private flight of funds from B to A by selling supplies of A's currency to be held by those who are moving funds into A's currency and by buying up in exchange the supplies of B's currency which these private operators are selling in order to acquire A's currency.

Method i has two serious disadvantages. Since the flight of funds is sudden and only temporary it involves undertaking a sharp deflation in B (and inflation in A) which may well need to be reversed again in the near future. Wage flexibility is always a matter of degree; and in reality a sharp and sudden deflation will always cause some considerable unemployment before the necessary downward adjustments of money prices and costs have been made in B.

But even if the necessary adjustments could be carried out instantaneously and without any social friction, this method of meeting the flight of 'hot money' would have serious disadvantages. It will in any case take some time before the fall in the price of B's products in terms of A's products, consequent upon the internal deflation in B and inflation in A, will cause any very large shift of demand in A or in B away from A's products on to B's products. For this reason the immediate deflation of prices and income in B might have to be very large indeed in order to generate a sufficiently favourable movement in B's balance of trade to finance immediately a sudden, large-scale, and insistent panic flight of 'hot money' from B's into A's currency. This might cause a temporarily catastrophic movement in the real terms of trade against B which would very seriously and very sharply diminish the standard of living in B for the purpose of financing an economically useless movement of capital from B to A.

Method ii, the method of exchange control, would avoid this evil. It would, however, involve the institution of an extensive administrative apparatus for the regulation of all payments between A and B on the lines described in Chapter XX.

Method iii would avoid the evils of both methods i and ii. The unnecessary deflation in B and inflation in A could be avoided without an extensive apparatus of bureaucratic control if the authorities in A or B, or both, offset the private exchange of funds from B's into A's currency by a public exchange of funds in the opposite direction. The authorities who acted in this way would, of course, stand to lose thereby if the fears that B's currency would be depreciated or that funds in B would be confiscated from their owners in A (or whatever fear had caused the flight) proved well grounded. But since the fear which causes the flight of capital is often a fear concerning the future action of the authorities themselves, there may be many cases in which the authorities can take a more reasonable view than private owners. Effective action under method iii will often require the full co-operation of the authorities in A; for it may involve the sale to private operators who are flying from B's currency of amounts of A's currency which are greater than the amounts which can be provided out of B's monetary reserves alone. On the other hand, as we have seen on p. 225, while the authorities in B may run out of reserves of A's currency it is always technically possible for the authorities in A to create and provide unlimited amounts of A's currency to be held by the private operators on the foreign exchanges.

So far we have considered the flight of 'hot money' from B to A on the assumption that the mechanism of the gold standard is in operation. We must now consider the problem on our alternative assumption, namely, that the authorities in both A and B adopt financial policies for internal balance and that there is a system of variable exchange rates between their currencies. Here again there are three methods by which the flight of funds from B to A can be met:

(i) The mechanism of price adjustment can be allowed to work itself out without interference. In this case the movement of funds from B to A must be allowed to cause a depreciation in B's exchange rate sufficient either to generate such a surplus in B's balance of trade as to finance the flight of funds from B to A or to cause so great an expectation that B's currency is now seriously undervalued and will soon appreciate as to cause a speculative movement of funds from A to B which will help to offset the flight of funds in the opposite direction.

(ii) As in the previous case, the flight of funds might be stopped by the imposition of exchange control in B.

(iii) As in the previous case, the flight of funds might be offset by counterbalancing movement of funds from A to B by the authorities of A and B.

In order to compare the relative merits of these solutions we must distinguish between the case in which the exchange rate variation is brought about through an adjustable peg and the case in which it is brought about by means of a free exchange market with the possible intervention of national or international exchange equalization funds (see Chapter XVII).

In the case of an adjustable peg it is difficult to avoid strict exchange control in order to cope with flights of 'hot money'. Suppose that a flight of 'hot money' is proceeding from B to A because speculators foresee correctly that a depreciation of B's currency is necessary in order to preserve external balance between B and A. Or suppose that a movement of funds from B to A has started for some other reason, but that speculators see correctly that the necessary reserves of A's funds are not forthcoming to enable the authorities to deal with it by a counter-balancing movement of funds from A to B. In these conditions, in the absence of exchange control, some future movement of the adjustable peg which will depreciate B's exchange rate is seen to be inevitable.

Now, we have already seen (p. 228, above) that where an adjustable peg is in operation in the foreign exchange market between A's and B's currency, speculators who correctly foresee an alteration in that peg will be able to make large and certain profits at the expense of the monetary authorities of A or B without their speculation serving any useful function. The monetary authorities would, of course, have the technical power of avoiding an exchange control to prevent the flight of 'hot money' from B to A, if they were willing to provide all the amounts of A's currency which those who were flying from B's currency wished to hold. But this would be a very expensive form of solution if the speculative flight from B's currency was based upon a virtual certainty that the adjustable peg would eventually be altered, because in this case the speculators would make a gain, and the monetary authorities a loss, on the whole amount of B's currency which the speculators had sold to the monetary authorities in exchange for A's currency.

This particular difficulty does not arise in a free exchange market. Method i could now operate immediately. The flight of 'hot money' from B's currency to A's currency would cause an immediate depreciation of B's currency which, when it had gone far enough, would make speculators begin to anticipate a future appreciation of B's currency and, therefore, cease to wish to move their funds from B to A.

But this raises another problem. If the speculators are very pessimistic about the future value of B's currency a great immediate depreciation of B's currency may be caused by the heavy and sudden withdrawal of 'hot money' from B's currency for exchange into A's currency. Since it will take some time for the consequent fall in the price of B's products relatively to A's products to cause any large shift of demand in A or B away from A's products on to B's products, the immediate depreciation of B's currency may have to be very great in order to generate a sufficiently favourable movement in B's balance of trade to enable the flight of 'hot money' from B's currency into A's currency to be financed. This may cause a temporary but catastrophic movement in the real terms of trade against B which would seriously and sharply diminish the standard of living in B.

The imposition of exchange control would, of course, avoid this evil. But it would bring with it the need for an extensive system of bureaucratic regulation of all payments between A and B.

For these reasons the method of official 'counter-speculation' might once again provide the best solution. For this to be so the authorities in A or B or both must be willing to provide the private speculators with as much of A's currency as they wish to hold at a rate of exchange which is not catastrophically unfavourable to B's currency.[1] And, up to a point at least, this may be a reasonable and economic thing for the monetary authorities to do. If the flight of hot money from B's currency is due to an over-pessimistic view of the future course of events by the private speculators, the authorities can gain at the expense of these speculators by selling A's currency to, and purchasing B's currency from, them at a rate of exchange at which the speculators (wrongly) consider B's currency to be still over-valued in relation to its future value and at which the authorities (rightly) consider B's currency to be already under-valued.

So far we have confined our attention to the control of flights of 'hot money'. But there may, of course, be important movements of capital of a quite different kind. There may be a continuing and steady flow of long-term capital from B to A due to the fact that a higher net yield can be earned on capital investment in A than on capital investment in B.

Such a steady movement of capital from B to A may impose a continuing strain on B's balance of payments; and the question arises whether it should be stopped by means of exchange control. It should be possible to remove the deficit on B's balance of payments caused by this continuing capital movement by means of a price adjustment. If B is on the gold standard a deflation of money wage rates, costs, and prices in B, or if there is a system of variable exchange rates a depreciation of B's currency, would serve to reduce the price of B's products relatively to that of A's. This in turn would serve to improve B's balance of payments, provided that the sum of the elasticities of demand for imports in A and in B was greater than one. On the other hand, if the flow of capital from B to A were stopped by means of a direct control, the fall in the price of B's products relatively to that

---

[1] As we have seen on p. 225, while the authorities in B may run out of their reserves of A's currency it is always technically possible for the authorities in A to provide unlimited amounts of A's currency to be held by the private speculators. If the necessary co-operation by the authorities in A is not forthcoming, the authorities in B may be driven back to the method of exchange control.

of A's, i.e. the movement of the real terms of trade against B which the mechanism of price adjustment would normally involve, would be avoided.

There is, of course, one reason why the argument for the restriction of capital transfers by exchange control or for their offsetting by the use of exchange equalization funds carries more weight in the case of large and sudden panic flights of 'hot money' than in the case of more steady and continuous long-term capital movements. The former type of capital movement is likely to give occasion for very abrupt and very large-scale readjustments which may then need to be as sharply reversed some time in the future. A steady and continuous movement of capital, on the other hand, allows time for a more moderate price adjustment to work out its full effects upon the balance of trade. For this reason the case against carrying out a price adjustment to meet a change which occurs more gradually and is likely to last longer is a great deal less strong.

Nevertheless it remains true that, if the authorities in B impose an exchange control in order to put a stop to a capital transfer from B to A, external balance can be maintained without the movement of the terms of trade against B which would be necessary if the capital transfer were allowed to occur unchecked and external balance were to be maintained by price adjustment.

This conclusion is, however, subject to certain qualifications. There are at least three reasons why it does not at once follow that the direct control of capital movements is advantageous even from the point of view of country B alone.

In the first place, the argument is, of course, unsound if there is a simultaneous transfer of capital funds from A to B and the authorities in country A cannot be relied upon not to retaliate by imposing a control on such capital transfers from A to B. In fact there may at any one time be a considerable flow of capital funds from B to A and a simultaneous considerable flow from A to B with a moderate net flow in the one direction or the other.[1] If the authorities in B, by an exchange control, reduce gross lending from B to A by £100 m. per annum, this will help B's balance of payments and terms of trade only if the authorities in A do not retaliate by imposing an exchange control which reduces gross lending from A to B by £100 m. or more.

Secondly, whereas the lending of a capital sum from B to A will put a strain on B's balance of payments and terms of trade, the future payment of interest on the capital and repayment of the capital sum from

---

[1] With a perfect capital market there would presumably be a flow of funds predominantly in the one direction or the other. But even so, since risks differ in different investments in different regions, the principle of spreading risks would mean that owners in A were investing some funds in B at the same time that owners in B were investing some funds in A.

A to B will put a strain on A's balance of payments and terms of trade. It is therefore possible that if the authorities in B allow the capital transfer now they will make up in an improvement of B's terms of trade when the loan and interest are repaid as much as (and possibly even more than) they lose now.[1] This is not, of course, to deny that the restriction of capital export now will ease B's present balance of payments problem, but merely to point out that B may get back in the future as much alleviation to the terms of trade as the burden which must now be endured.

Thirdly, it must not, of course, be forgotten that if capital is moving from B to A the rate of interest which lenders in B can obtain in A may well be higher than the real productivity of capital invested in B, so that even some net loss to B on the terms of trade might well be more than offset by the higher yield obtainable in A.

In spite of these three qualifications it may, of course, remain to the national interest of B that capital transfers from B should be restricted

---

[1] The outcome will depend upon (i) the extent to which the capital transfer is concentrated on one year and the repayment is spread out over many or, on the other hand, the extent to which the transfer of the capital is spread over many years and the repayment concentrated in a few, and (ii) the extent to which a large payment has a more marked effect upon the real terms of trade than a small one. For example, suppose that a capital sum equal to C in terms of B's products is lent from B to A in year 1, that the loan is never repaid but that interest equal to i in terms of B's products is received every year after year 1. Suppose that the transfer of C from B to A causes B's real terms of trade to deteriorate by an amount t_1 on a turnover of trade (total imports or total exports) equal to T in terms of B's products. Suppose further that when the interest is paid from A to B, the terms of trade turn in B's favour by t_2. Then in year 1 B gives up $C + t_1 T$ and in every subsequent year gains $i + t_2 T$. Now $\frac{i}{C}$ is the nominal return on the loan, whereas $\frac{i + t_2 T}{C + t_1 T}$ is the real yield to B allowing for the terms of trade effect. Now $\frac{i + t_2 T}{C + t_1 T}$ is $\lessgtr \frac{i}{C}$ according as $\frac{t_2}{t_1} \lessgtr \frac{i}{C}$. Suppose that the generation in a single year of a trade surplus sufficient to cover a large single transfer C requires a movement in the terms of trade which is proportionately larger than the movement in the terms of trade required later to generate a small trade deficit in order to finance the relatively small annual payment of interest i (i.e. $\frac{t_2}{t_1} < \frac{i}{C}$). Then the adverse movement in the terms of trade when the loan is made will more than outweigh the favourable movement in the terms of trade when the interest is paid, and country B will obtain less than the nominal yield on her loan (i.e. $\frac{i + t_2 T}{C + t_1 T} < \frac{i}{C}$). But if the making of the loan were spread in a number of small payments over a large number of years and the interest and principal were all repaid in a block at the end of the period, country B would stand to gain more in the final large movement in the terms of trade in her favour than she lost in the small adverse movement in the earlier years. And if the change in the terms of trade is always proportional to the transfer to be made in either direction (i.e. if $\frac{t_2}{t_1} = \frac{i}{C}$) then even in the first example B would ultimately gain when interest was paid as much as she lost when the capital was first transferred.

in order to restore external balance without a deterioration in the terms of trade.[1]

This national interest may in some cases coincide with a world interest. Capital may be flowing from B to A because the nominal yield on capital in A is higher than in B; but the nominal yields to private property owners may not correspond to the real yields to the world as a whole. Suppose, for example, that specially heavy taxes are levied on capital or on the income from capital in B as part of a general fiscal arrangement for the redistribution of income and property in B, and that these arrangements do not exist in A. Then there may be a heavy and continuous outflow of funds from B to A to take advantage of these fiscal arrangements. If the heavy taxes are levied not on property or on income from property situated in B, whoever may own it, but rather on property or on income from property owned by residents of B, wherever the property may be situated, then wealthy residents in B may themselves have to migrate with their property to A in order to avoid the tax in B. This would clearly tend to diminish the flow of capital from B to A.

But whether or not the property owners had to migrate with their property, year after year funds which were first accumulated in B and invested in B's currency might, on a fairly steady scale, be sold in order to be transferred into A's currency. And, it should be noted, any such movement of funds might well be uneconomic from the point of view of total world production in the sense that the real yield on capital (apart from the peculiar tax arrangements) might be higher in B than in A, so that a capital transfer from B to A would mean a transfer from a part of the world in which capital resources were more productive to one in which they were less productive.

If for any of these reasons it is desired to control capital movements, can an exchange control be so devised as to restrict capital transactions while leaving current transactions unrestricted?

In the first place it is impossible strictly to limit capital movements except by an exchange control whose regulations extend to all foreign payments. For example, unless exporters are compelled to surrender to the exchange-control authority all the foreign money which they obtain

[1] From the point of view of relieving an immediate strain on B's balance of payments it would, of course, be equally effective if the authorities in A were to give special encouragement to the movements of capital funds from A to B. Such encouragement might, for example, be given by fiscal measures (the authorities in A might give certain tax exemptions to income earned by residents in A from capital invested in B) or by direct governmental intervention (the authorities in A might themselves borrow funds from private savers in A and invest these funds in various forms of capital in B). But such action would have as adverse an immediate effect upon A's terms of trade as the favourable effect which it would have on B's terms of trade. Except in unusual circumstances it is not, therefore, one which is likely to commend itself to the authorities in A.

from the sale of exports, they could use the proceeds of their exports to invest in foreign securities or other capital assets. In order to restrict capital movements the exchange control must supervise all foreign payments.

Secondly, it may be extremely difficult for an exchange-control authority to distinguish in fact between a capital payment and a current payment. No clear-cut definition can be given, and it must always remain to some extent a matter for the arbitrary decision of the controlling authority whether a particular payment is treated as a capital or current payment. One example must suffice. Suppose it is desired to allow all current payments and to disallow all capital payments; how shall tourists' expenditures be treated? Clearly a genuine tourist's expenditure on a holiday abroad is a current payment; he is deciding merely to consume goods and services abroad instead of consuming them in his own country. But if a man applies to the exchange control authority for $10 m. to finance a week's holiday abroad, it would appear probable that some of the money will not be used to consume goods and services in that week but to invest in some form of capital in the foreign country. But no system of control (short of sending an official abroad with each tourist) can verify how much is intended for genuine current consumption. There must be some arbitrary rule.

If, however, the exchange control authority is prepared to lay down some arbitrary rules as to what constitutes a current payment and if it is given the power to supervise all foreign payments, there is nothing to prevent it from exercising that power so as to forbid all capital movements but to allow in unrestricted amount all payments for current purposes. In that sense there is no technical difficulty in arranging for an exchange control to restrict capital movements without restricting current transactions.

There remains, however, one further question. In previous chapters, and in particular in Chapter XVII, we have found reason for believing that in many cases the most appropriate mechanism for external balance may be to permit exchange rate variations in a free exchange market with a well organized market for forward exchange. Is it technically possible to combine such a free exchange market for current payments with a strict exchange control to restrict capital payments?

At first sight, these two systems would appear incompatible. As we have just seen, an exchange control over capital movements means a strict regulation of all current payments and the monopolization of all foreign exchange dealings by the exchange-control authority. On the other hand, as we argued in Chapter XVII, a free exchange market with well-organized operations in forward exchange involves the free movement of short-term speculative capital funds into and out of the currency in order to set a competitive forward rate of exchange.

Nevertheless, the two desiderata might perhaps be reconciled in a scheme on the following general lines:

(i) The exchange-control authority would grant licences to a fairly large number of competing dealers in foreign exchange to act as agents for the authority. Each licensed dealer would be allowed to hold a certain fund of money for the purpose of foreign exchange dealings and would be permitted to transfer these funds freely into or out of any currency.

(ii) Persons or institutions who were not resident in the exchange-control country could hold 'non-resident' balances in the currency of the exchange-control country, and the exchange-control authority would permit such 'non-resident' balances to be exchanged for foreign currencies at any time for any purpose and not merely to finance a current transaction.

(iii) All residents of the exchange-control country would have to obtain the permission of the exchange-control authority before they could purchase foreign currencies from the licensed dealers in foreign exchange or before they could transfer money from their own 'resident' to foreigners' 'non-resident' accounts.

(iv) All residents of the exchange-control country would have to present evidence to the exchange-control authority that they had sold any foreign money acquired by them (e.g. from the sale of exports in foreign markets) to one of the licensed dealers in foreign exchange.

(v) The exchange-control authority would sanction all requests by residents for the purchase of foreign currencies or for the transfer of balances from 'resident' to 'non-resident' accounts if these were for the purpose of financing a current transaction, but would refuse permits for the purpose of financing capital transactions.

Under a system of this kind, if there were no exchange control in the other country of our two-country world, the free funds allowed to the licensed exchange dealers under (i) and the funds available to non-residents under (ii) would constitute a limited but free competitive market for speculation in the future value of the currency of the exchange-control country; and on the basis of this market there should develop freely fluctuating 'spot' and 'forward' rates for the national currency. But provisions (iii), (iv), and (v) above would ensure that this foreign exchange market could (apart from the funds under (i) and (ii) above) be entered only by those who wished to finance current transactions; and the rate of exchange which would result would, therefore, be that which brought the balance of payments into equilibrium in the absence of any continuing export of capital from the exchange-control country.

It should not, therefore, be technically impossible to arrange for an otherwise free exchange market from which major and persistent capital transactions were excluded by means of exchange control.

CHAPTER XXIII

THE CONTROL OF IMPORTS AND EXPORTS [1]

WE have already pointed out that, in so far as the effects upon trade are concerned, a 10 per cent depreciation of B's currency is equivalent to a 10 per cent duty on B's imports the revenue from which is used to finance a 10 per cent subsidy on B's exports. It is also equivalent to a 10 per cent subsidy on A's imports financed out of the revenue raised from a 10 per cent tax on A's exports. There are in fact four separate fiscal actions which the authorities in the two countries may take in order to put the balance of payments between them into equilibrium:

(i) The authorities in the deficit country may tax or otherwise discourage imports.

(ii) The authorities in the deficit country may subsidize or otherwise encourage exports.

(iii) The authorities in the surplus country may subsidize or otherwise encourage imports.

(iv) The authorities in the surplus country may tax or otherwise discourage exports.

In this chapter we shall examine the efficacy of each of these four types of action in removing a balance-of-payments disequilibrium between A and B. We shall first do so on the assumption that the authorities concerned operate through a general discouragement or encouragement of all imports or exports equally. The simplest examples of this are where the authorities in the deficit country put a 10 per cent *ad valorem* duty on all imports or a 10 per cent *ad valorem* subsidy on all exports, or where the authorities in the surplus country put a 10 per cent *ad valorem* duty on all exports or a 10 per cent *ad valorem* subsidy on all imports. [2] But after considering the effect of such general interventions,

---

[1] The subject matter of this and the following chapter is treated in Sections VIII (viii), (ix), and (x), and X (ii) of the separate mathematical supplement.

[2] We shall in fact carry out this part of our analysis in terms of import and export duties and subsidies; but our analysis is intended to cover restrictions or promotions of trade carried out by other measures as well. For example, we do not intend to confine our discussion of import restriction to the effects of an import duty; we wish to consider also the effects of general import restriction by a system of import quotas or of exchange control. But, as has been pointed out in Chapter XXI, there is one essential difference between the restriction of imports by an import duty and their restriction by a quantitative import quota. Whereas the former will certainly reduce the total amount paid to the foreign suppliers for the imports, the latter will do so to the same extent only if arrangements are such as to ensure that the foreign supplier gains no part of the margin between the selling price and the demand price which will develop as a result of the restriction of supplies on the importing market. From our present point of view a 10 per cent all round *ad valorem* import duty would be

we will then consider the possibilities which arise when the authorities in the deficit country restrict some particular imports more severely than others or pick out particular exports for particular rates of subsidy. Similarly, we shall consider the possibilities which arise when the authorities in the surplus country pick out certain particular imports or exports for special measures of encouragement or discouragement.

Our object in this chapter is to compare the use of direct controls with general price adjustment, as technically effective mechanisms for the restoration of equilibrium to the balance of payments. This is a very limited purpose. The most significant distinction between the methods of general price adjustment and of direct controls lies in the difference which they make (i) to the terms of trade between the two countries and (ii) to the distortion of the flow of trade away from what may be called the 'free-trade position'.

Now both these matters are of first-rate importance. The effect of a particular method of adjustment upon the terms of trade between the two countries will affect the distribution of real income between them. The more favourable the terms of trade to a particular country, the greater the proportion of any given real world income which the residents of that country will enjoy as compared with the residents in the rest of the world. And the effect of a particular method of adjustment upon the 'free-trade position' will affect the level of the total real income which is available for distribution between the two countries. This is not, of course, to imply that the 'free-trade position' necessarily maximizes the real world income. In Volume II we shall have to consider at length the divergences from this position which are to be desired on the grounds of maximizing the real world income. But the use of direct controls as opposed to a general price adjustment as a means of removing a balance-of-payments disequilibrium will necessarily cause some movement to or from the free-trade position and will thus vitally affect the problem of the maximization of the world real income.

These problems will be a main concern of Volume II. In this chapter we intend as far as possible to compare direct controls with the method of variable exchange rates (as the simplest example of a general price adjustment) merely as effective technical instruments for influencing the balance of payments. But it is not possible to divorce this aspect of direct controls completely from their effects upon the terms of trade and upon movements towards or away from the free-trade position. Accordingly, we shall proceed as follows. In this chapter we shall consider in turn

---

equivalent to the limitation of imports through the issue of a limited number of licences to import, these licences (i) being such as to permit a given value (and not volume) of imports to be brought in, (ii) allowing free choice of the particular commodities which should be brought in, and (iii) being issued in such amounts as to be worth in the market 10 per cent of the value of the goods which are thereby permitted to enter the country.

each of the main forms of direct control over trade, primarily as effective technical measures for affecting the balance of payments. But in each case we shall comment on the effect upon the terms of trade and upon movements towards or away from the free-trade position. In the next chapter we shall anticipate briefly some of the analysis of Volume II in order to indicate the grounds upon which the final choice between methods of direct control and of general price adjustment should be based.

We shall assume throughout this chapter that the authorities of the country which is making use of direct controls over trade for the achievement of external balance are simultaneously adopting a financial policy for internal balance. Consider, for example, the case of the deficit country B. The authorities of this country have adopted a financial policy for internal balance and do not, therefore, let the loss of gold which results from the deficit in the balance of payments lead to a deflation of domestic expenditure which would restore external balance through a deflation of imports into B and a reduction in the money costs of B's export products relatively to those of A. Nor do the authorities in B allow the strain on the foreign exchange position to cause a depreciation of the value of B's currency in terms of A's currency. Instead, they restore external balance by a general restriction of B's imports from A or by a general subsidization of her exports to A.

Such action must, of course, be sharply distinguished from the use of import restrictions or export subsidies as an alternative instrument to financial policy for the purpose of achieving internal balance, i.e. in order to give employment at home by diverting demand away from foreign on to home products. Suppose that B is in external balance but is suffering from a deflated national income and heavy unemployment. The authorities in B might attempt to restore internal balance by means of import restrictions or export subsidies. These interventions would cause a favourable movement in B's balance of trade, and the inflationary effect in B of this improvement in the balance of trade (i.e. through the shift of demand of purchasers in B or in A away from A's on to B's products) would help to restore employment and internal balance in B. It would, however, of course exert a deflationary influence in A, since A's balance of trade would move unfavourably as less was sold to B or more bought from B. And even if the authorities in A successfully adopt a financial policy for internal balance and, by a 'policy' inflation of domestic expenditure in A, prevent the unfavourable movement in the balance of trade from causing any net growth of unemployment, A's balance of payments will remain in deficit; for it is the favourable movement in B's balance of trade which has restored internal balance in B.[1]

---

[1] The situation is analogous to that discussed in Chapter XI (pp. 153–4) where the use of the method of price adjustment as a means of 'exporting unemployment' was examined.

Now it is quite another matter if the authorities in B get rid of unemployment in B not by import restriction or export subsidization but by a 'policy' inflation of domestic expenditure in B. But having restored internal balance in this way, the authorities in B will be faced with a deficit on the balance of payments since the internal inflation of demand will have increased the demand for imports in B and may, by raising the demand for, and so the price of, B's exportable products, also have reduced the value of B's exports. If in these circumstances the authorities in B restrict imports or subsidize exports in order to restore external balance, they are not exerting a deflationary pressure on A as a means of solving B's internal difficulties. On the contrary, they are merely preventing the inflation in B from causing an inflationary pressure in A and from upsetting external balance between A and B.

Any direct trade controls imposed by the authorities in B will, of course, be effective in improving B's balance of payments only if they are not offset by retaliatory action by the authorities in A. Of course, if the authorities in A simultaneously imposed equally severe import restrictions or equally severe export subsidies in answer to B's import restrictions or export subsidies, there would be no reason to expect any net change in the balance of trade or the balance of payments between the two countries. Nor, if the action of B's authorities is to be effective, must the authorities in A retaliate by any other 'policy' measure such as a deliberate deflation of domestic expenditure in A or a deliberate depreciation of the exchange value of A's currency, which will offset the effect of B's direct trade controls on the balance of trade and so on the balance of payments between the two countries.

Even if the authorities in A do not adopt any deliberate measures to offset the effect of the direct trade controls imposed by the authorities in B, the extent of the improvement in B's balance of payments which results from the direct trade controls will be much affected by the general policies adopted in A. If the authorities in A are adopting a financial policy for internal balance, there is reason to believe that any given degree of import restriction or export promotion in B will be more effective in improving B's balance of payments than if the authorities in A are adopting what we have called a neutral policy. There are at least two reasons for this.

(i) The authorities in B remove a deficit on B's balance of payments by restricting imports or subsidizing exports. Now this will involve an unfavourable movement in A's balance of trade, which will exert a deflationary pressure in A just as it will exert an inflationary pressure in B. To preserve internal balance the authorities in B must adopt a deflationary financial policy and the authorities in A an inflationary financial policy. This will itself cause some decrease in the demand of

B's purchasers for imports from A and for B's own exportable products; and this will reinforce the direct effect upon B's balance of payments of the import restrictions or export subsidies. The inflationary financial policy in A will similarly reinforce the effect upon the balance of payments between A and B; it will cause some increase in demand in A for the products of B and also for the exportable products of A which might otherwise have been sold to B. If, however, there had been a neutral policy in A the deflationary impact effect upon A's economy of B's trade controls would have caused a general depression to develop in A which would have partially offset, instead of reinforcing, the effect of B's trade controls upon the balance of payments; for the demand of A's purchasers for imports from B and for A's own exportable products would be reduced instead of increased.

(ii) These considerations will be further reinforced if the authorities in A and B are adopting monetary, as opposed to fiscal, measures for the carrying out of their financial policies for internal balance. For in this case the rate of interest will be raised in B to exert a deflationary pressure in B and will be lowered in A in order to exert an inflationary pressure on domestic expenditure in A. These changes in interest rates will encourage a flow of lending from A to B which will reinforce the favourable movement in B's balance of payments. And one half of this influence would be missing if there were a neutral policy and so no reduction in rates of interest in A.

In the analysis which follows we shall assume that the authorities in both A and B adopt financial policies for internal balance. In these conditions the deflation of total domestic expenditure in B which is undertaken as a means of offsetting the inflationary effects of the improvement in B's balance of trade will cause purchasers in B to purchase less imports from A; and the inflation of total domestic expenditure in A which is undertaken to offset the deflationary effect of the adverse movement in A's balance of trade will cause purchasers in A to purchase more imports from B. If the sum of the marginal propensities to import in A and B were as great as unity, these policy inflations and deflations of domestic expenditure in A and B would themselves be sufficient to close the whole of the balance of payments gap without any need for any direct controls on trade (see case i of Table IX). We assume that the sum of the two marginal propensities to import is less than unity. But provided that the marginal propensities to import are not zero, the inflation of domestic expenditure in A and its deflation in B (which will be necessary in order to preserve internal balance when B's balance of trade has been sufficiently improved to remove the deficit on B's balance of payments) will themselves cause a part of the desired improvement in B's balance of trade. It is only the remaining part which has to be brought about by the independent action of the direct controls on trade.

We can now consider in more detail the way in which each of the main forms of direct controls on trade may be expected to operate.

1. *Action by the Authorities in the Deficit Country*

(i) *The imposition of taxes or removal of subsidies on imports in the deficit country.* The authorities in the deficit country B may discourage imports by raising the rate of tax or lowering the rate of subsidy (if any) on its imports. From the point of view of purchasers in B this has a twofold effect.

In the first place, the revenue from the increased import duties in B (or the economy in the budgetary expenditure on import subsidies in B) means that purchasers in B have more free purchasing power to spend. Either private purchasers in B will have a larger tax-free money income to spend on goods and services of all sorts, since the authorities in B can reduce other taxes as the revenue from import duties is increased or the expenditure on import subsidies is reduced. Or else the authorities in B will have a larger net tax revenue from which it can finance increased public expenditure on goods and services. But, secondly, while the total free monetary purchasing power of purchasers in B will have risen by an amount equal to the increase in duties on imports (or reduced subsidies on imports) the market price of imports will, of course, have risen by exactly the same amount. The balance between total purchasing power and total supplies will not thereby have been altered, because the increased monetary purchasing power will have been exactly offset by the increased price of imported supplies.

The net effect will be that the market price of imported products will have risen relatively to that of home-produced products. If there is any possibility of substitution between home products and imported products purchasers in B will shift their demand from A's products on to B's products and this will cause an improvement in B's balance of trade and payments.

The main difference between this mechanism and that of an exchange depreciation of B's currency is that the exchange depreciation will reduce the price of B's exports in A's market whereas the imposition of an import duty or removal of an import subsidy in B will not do so. Now if the elasticity of demand for imports in A is greater than unity, a decline in the price of B's products in A's market would cause an increase in the total amount which purchasers in A would spend on B's products. In this case the method of exchange depreciation of B's currency may be said to be more effective than that of import restriction in B as a means of removing B's deficit, since it will increase the value of B's exports as well as reducing the value of B's imports. But if the elasticity of demand for imports in A is less than unity, the decline in the price of B's products in A's market will reduce the total amount which purchasers in A will spend on B's products. In this case import restriction in B is in a sense a more effective instrument than exchange depreciation, since in the former case the reduction in the value of B's imports is not offset by a reduction in the value of her exports. Indeed, as we have seen above (p. 166), if the sum of the elasticities of demand for imports in the two countries is less than unity, exchange depreciation of B's currency will make B's trade deficit worse; but even in these conditions import restriction by B would improve B's balance of trade.

As far as the terms of trade are concerned, import restriction in B is likely to have a more favourable outcome for B than exchange depreciation of B's currency.[1] If there are no variations in the prices of B's various products relatively to each other and no variations in the prices of A's various products relatively to each other, this is bound to be the case. Financial policies for internal balance in both countries will mean that the prices of B's products will all remain constant in terms of B's currency and the prices of A's products will all remain constant in terms of A's currency. Since with import restriction in B there is no change in the rate of exchange between the two currencies, in this case the real terms of trade will remain unchanged; but with a depreciation of B's exchange rate in terms of A's currency, the prices of B's products will fall relatively to the prices of A's products and the real terms of trade will move against B.

But this conclusion may be somewhat modified if either A's or B's export products (or both) are in particularly inelastic supply to the other country, because in the exporting country there is little or no substitutability either in production or consumption between its export products and its other products. (See p. 238, above.) Suppose, for example, that A's export products are in very inelastic supply to B, because producers in A cannot readily shift to the production of alternative products, and purchasers in A cannot readily shift from the consumption of other A-products on to the consumption of A's export products, when the price offered for A's export products falls relatively to that offered for the other products of A. Then import restriction in B is likely to be even more favourable to B's terms of trade than is exchange depreciation by B. Provided that the elasticity of demand for imports by purchasers in A is greater than one, direct restriction of imports into B will involve a larger restriction of B's imports than will exchange depreciation of B's currency. And if A's exports can be very much depressed in price by a restriction of purchases by B's purchasers, import restriction will greatly turn the terms of trade in B's favour. But suppose, on the other hand, that A's exports were in very elastic supply to B but that

[1] As we shall see in Chapter XXIV this does not mean that import restriction is necessarily preferable even from B's own point of view. We have to take into account the effect on the size of the world real income as well as the effect on the distribution of that income between A and B.

B's exports were in very inelastic supply to A. This will tell in favour of exchange depreciation as a means of turning the terms of trade in B's favour, since exchange depreciation of B's currency, unlike import restriction in B, would stimulate the demand in A for B's exports and thus, with a very inelastic supply of exports from B to A, would cause a marked rise in the price of B's exports as compared with the price of B's other products.

Finally, we may observe that as imports are very rarely subsidized the method of import discouragement by the deficit country is much more likely to take the form of increased import taxes (or other positive import restrictions) rather than of a removal of import subsidies. It is, therefore, likely to take the form of a movement away from the 'free-trade position' in the direction of a more restricted volume of trade.

(ii) *The imposition of export subsidies or the removal of export taxes in the deficit country.* The authorities in the deficit country may attempt to improve the balance of trade by encouraging exports. For this purpose they may subsidize exports[1] or remove an existing tax on exports. It is to be observed that such action will improve E's balance of trade only if the elasticity of the demand for imports in A is greater than one;[2] for only in that case will the decline in the price of B's products in A's market cause purchasers in A to spend a greater total amount on them.

If the elasticity of demand for imports in A is greater than one, then the mechanism of export subsidy in B will work in the following manner. The authorities in B raise additional revenue (e.g. an income tax in B) in order to find the funds to finance the payment of export subsidies. This must be done in order to preserve internal balance in B. The subsidy paid to B's producers when they export to A will be a net addition to the demand for B's products, so that to prevent an internal inflation in B other taxes must be raised to curb domestic expenditure in B.[3] The raising of these taxes will itself cause some reduction in the demand in

---

[1] As we have seen on p. 289, above, a State export organization in B which purchased B's products for export and sold them in such quantities as to make a loss on the trade would have the same effect as an export subsidy.

[2] This is not strictly quite correct. Even if the elasticity of demand for imports in A were only equal to one there would still be some small improvement in B's balance of trade. In order to finance the payment of the export subsidy (or to meet the loss of the export tax) the authorities in B would have to raise an additional revenue from other taxes or to cut down expenditure if they wished to avoid upsetting the existing internal balance between the total demand and supply of B's products. This reduced demand and supply of B's products and services in general would cause some reduction in the demand for imports so that B's balance of trade would improve even without any increase in the value of B's exports.

[3] This is, of course, in addition to the deflation of domestic expenditure which is necessary in B in order to preserve internal balance when the deficit on her balance of trade is reduced, no matter what method is used to effect that reduction.

B not only for B's products but also for imports of A's products, and this will help to reduce B's deficit. But over and above this the price of B's products in A's market will be reduced; and since the elasticity of demand in A is greater than one this will cause an increase in the value of B's exports to A.

The main difference between this mechanism and that of the depreciation of B's currency is that it relies solely upon the elasticity of demand for imports in A. Unlike exchange depreciation it does not cause the price of A's products to rise in B's markets and this influence reducing B's imports is absent. For this reason export subsidy by the authorities in B can be an effective instrument of adjustment only if the elasticity of demand for imports in A is large; and, even so, if the elasticity of demand for imports in B is greater than zero it will be a less efficient instrument than exchange depreciation for reducing B's deficit in terms of A's currency.

The removal of a balance-of-payments deficit by export subsidization in B is likely to cause a larger movement in the terms of trade against B than its removal by the depreciation of B's currency. The latter will reduce the value (in A's currency) of B's imports as well as increasing the value (in A's currency) of B's exports—since we are assuming the elasticity of demand for imports in A to be greater than unity—whereas the former will only increase the value of B's exports. Therefore, if a 10 per cent depreciation of B's currency would have served to remove B's deficit we shall need a greater—say, a 20 per cent—rate of general export subsidy to have the same effect. If the prices of B's products relatively to each other remain unchanged and if the same is true of A's products, it would follow that, while the method of exchange depreciation will mean a 10 per cent movement of the terms of trade against B, the method of export subsidization by B will mean an unfavourable movement of her terms of trade of 20 per cent. For in both cases we are assuming that the operation of financial policies for internal balance maintains the (unsubsidized) prices of A's and B's products constant in terms of A's and B's currency respectively. It follows that a 20 per cent subsidy to the prices of B's products means a 20 per cent movement of the terms of trade against B, while a 10 per cent depreciation of B's currency means a 10 per cent movement of the terms of trade against B. And this relative disadvantage to B of export subsidization would be still greater if the elasticity of supply of A's exports to B was especially low. In this case exchange depreciation which works by restricting B's imports from A as well as by the promotion of B's exports to A would tend to depress the prices of A's export products relatively to her other products and thus keep the terms of trade more favourable to B.

Export taxes are not, in fact, common. Any attempt, therefore, to restore equilibrium to the balance of payments by the encouragement of exports in the deficit country is likely to involve an increase of export subsidies rather than a lowering of existing export taxes. It is, in other words, likely to involve a movement away from the free-trade position in the over-stimulation of world trade.

(iii) *The imposition of taxes or the removal of subsidies on exports in the deficit country.* If the elasticity of demand for imports in A is appreciably less than one, then export restriction by the authorities in B will increase the value of B's exports. The authorities in B should accordingly impose export taxes rather than export subsidies.

The mechanism of this method of adjustment is as follows. The authorities in B receive a net revenue from the proceeds of the new export duties. This absorbs part of the money which the importers in A were spending on B's products. In order to prevent this from causing a net decline in the total demand for B's products, the authorities in B must reduce other forms of taxation or increase the public demand for goods and services out of the proceeds of the export tax. But as this happens there will be some increase in the demand of B's purchasers for imports, the amount depending upon the marginal propensity to import in B. This in itself will tend to cause an adverse movement in B's balance of trade. But the export tax will have made B's products more expensive in A and since the elasticity of demand for imports in A is less than one this will increase the amount spent by purchasers in A on B's products. If this elasticity is sufficiently small, B's balance of trade will improve because the increase in the value of her exports will be greater than the increase in the value of her imports.

This mechanism is, of course, entirely different from that of a depreciation of B's currency. Its effect is, in fact, similar to the effect on B's exports of an appreciation of B's currency which makes B's exports more expensive in terms of A's currency. Here we must distinguish between the case in which the sum of the elasticities of demand for imports in A and B is also less than one and the case in which this sum, unlike the elasticity in A alone, is greater than one.

(*a*) If the sum of the elasticities of demand for imports in A and B were less than one, then an exchange appreciation rather than an exchange depreciation of B's currency would be required in order to improve B's balance of trade. (See p. 166, above.) But in this case an export tax in B would be more efficient than an appreciation of B's currency as a means of improving B's balance of trade, because the latter (unlike the former) would make A's products cheaper in B's markets and would thus cause some increase in the volume (and so in the value in terms of A's currency) of A's exports to B. The increase in the value of B's exports to A would, with exchange appreciation, be partially offset by the increase in the value of B's imports from A (all in terms of A's currency); but with export restriction in B the increase in the value (in terms of A's currency) of B's exports to A would not be accompanied by any increase in B's purchases of A's exports.[1]

(b) If, however, while the elasticity of demand for imports in A is less than one, the sum of the elasticities of demand for imports in A and B is greater than one, then we must compare export restriction by B with exchange depreciation by B. In this case the relative efficiency of the two instruments as means of improving B's balance of trade depends upon the extent to which the elasticity of demand for imports in A is less than one and the extent to which the sum of the two elasticities of demand for imports is greater than one. Suppose, for example, that the elasticity of demand for imports in A is very much lower than one whereas the sum of the two elasticities is only just greater than one. Then the direct restriction of B's exports will have a large and decisive effect in improving B's balance of trade, whereas exchange depreciation of B's currency will have very little favourable effect upon her balance of trade. In the opposite conditions in which the elasticity of demand for imports in A was only very slightly less than one while the sum of the two elasticities of demand for imports was very much greater than one, the direct restriction of B's exports would have very little effect in improving B's balance of trade, whereas the exchange depreciation of B's currency would have a large and decisive effect.

We must also distinguish between these two cases when we consider the effects upon the terms of trade. In case a where the sum of the elasticities of demand for imports in A and B is less than one, both the direct restriction of B's exports and the appreciation of B's currency will move the terms of trade in B's favour, but the former is likely to do so to a lesser extent than the latter. Since the appreciation of B's currency will stimulate the volume of purchases of A's products in B, whereas the taxation of B's exports alone will not do so, a larger appreciation of B's currency (say by 20 per cent) would be required than the rate of taxation of B's exports (say by 10 per cent) for the removal of a given deficit on B's balance of payments. But with financial policies for internal balance to stabilize the price of each country's products in terms of its own currency, the former will involve a 20 per cent and the latter only a 10 per cent movement of the terms of trade in favour of B.

In case b in which the sum of the elasticities of demand for imports in A and B is greater than one we have to compare the restriction of B's exports with the depreciation of B's currency. Now the former will move the terms of trade in B's favour if the (untaxed) price of each country's products is stabilized in terms of the currency of that country, because

---

[1] In those cases (of which this is one) where the elasticities of demand for imports in A is less than one the most efficient combination would be that of import restriction (e.g. import taxes) and export restriction (e.g. export taxes) by B, thereby increasing the value of exports to A and reducing the value of imports from A.

B's products will rise in price in A's market by the amount of the export tax in B. But the depreciation of B's currency will have the reverse effect of moving the terms of trade against B if the price of each country's products remains the same in the currency of that country and more of B's money has to be given to acquire a given amount of A's money. In this case export restriction will have a more favourable effect than exchange depreciation on B's terms of trade.

It is possible that B may start with some export subsidies which she can reduce or remove. But once again the probability is that the method of export discouragement by B will have to rely upon the positive introduction of export taxes (or other restrictions) rather than upon the removal of existing export subsidies. It is probable, therefore, that this method will involve a movement away from the free-trade position in the direction of the artificial restriction of trade.

(iv) *The control of particular imports and exports in the deficit country.* So far we have considered the rather unreal cases in which the authorities in a deficit country restrict evenly all imports or promote or restrict evenly all exports. But in fact a distinctive feature of direct controls as opposed to methods of general price adjustment (such as a variation in exchange rates) is that it enables the authorities to operate differently on imports or on exports of particular products.[1] Indeed, it is precisely this fact which makes the method of direct control in certain respects particularly effective as a means of adjustment of the balance of payments and particularly attractive to deficit countries.

For example, suppose—as is probable—that B exports to A some commodities for which the elasticity of demand in A is very high (much above one) and others for which the elasticity of demand in A is low (somewhat less than one). If the authorities in B subsidize all exports or depreciate the exchange value of B's currency, then the value of A's imports of the former class of goods will increase but the value of the second class of A's imports will decline. On the other hand, if the authorities in B tax all exports or appreciate the exchange value of B's currency, then the value of the former class of A's imports will fall and of the latter class will rise. But if the authorities in B are free to tax the latter class of exports and to use the proceeds to subsidize the former class of exports, the value of both classes of exports will rise. By restricting exports where foreign purchasers cannot easily do without them and by subsidizing exports where they compete closely with the things which foreign producers already produce, the authorities in a deficit country can obtain a much greater and easier increase in the value of total exports than by any method which affects all exports equally.

Moreover, this piecemeal treatment will not only increase B's exports

[1] And, as we shall see in the Part VI, on imports from or exports to particular foreign countries.

most effectively. It will also do so with the most favourable effect upon B's terms of trade. The prices charged for B's exports to A's purchasers will be much raised in those cases (where the elasticity of demand in A is small) in which a considerably higher price can be charged without losing the custom of A's purchasers; and B's exports need be offered at only slightly lower prices in A in those cases where the elasticity of demand in A is great.

In choosing which exports to tax and which to subsidize, the authorities in B can have regard also to the conditions of supply of the commodities in B. An export commodity in B for which not only is the demand in A inelastic but also the supply from B is elastic, will be peculiarly appropriate for export restriction. For the fact that the supply from B to A is elastic means that when, as a result of the export tax, the price of this product in B falls relatively to the price of other products of B, either the producers in B can readily and usefully shift their resources to the production of alternative products or else the final buyers in B can readily and usefully consume greater amounts of this commodity. This will mean that the adjustment can be carried out more smoothly in B and also that the terms of trade will move the more in B's favour, since the (untaxed) price of the commodity in B will be the better maintained, so that the (taxed) price in A's markets will also be kept up.

Similarly, an export subsidy on a product of B for which not only the elasticity of demand in A is great but also the elasticity of supply from B to A is great, will produce a particularly easy improvement in B's balance of trade. As the volume purchased in A increases because of the export subsidy there will be a tendency for the (unsubsidized) price in B to be driven up. If this calls forth a large movement of productive factors from other uses into its production or causes a large reduction in its consumption by final buyers in B, the supplies available for export to A will be much increased; and since the elasticity of demand in A is *ex hypothesi* greater than one, the greater is the increase in the amount exported from B the greater will be the total value of the sales of the product to purchasers in A.[1]

Rather similar considerations arise in the case of B's imports. The authorities in B might pick out for import restriction those particular commodities for which the elasticity of supply from A to B was particularly low. Such commodities would be those from the production of

---

[1] It is true that the terms of trade might be moved somewhat more against B than they would have been if the elasticity of supply in B were very low; for in that case the price of the product in B would have been driven up more quickly by the increased demand for the product in A. But if the terms of trade were the main consideration it would be better to rely upon the taxation of all exports for which the elasticity of demand in A was less than unity and on the taxation of all imports from A of which the elasticity of supply in A was small.

which the producers in A could not readily or usefully withdraw their resources for the production of alternative products and of which the purchasers in A could not readily or usefully consume very much more. If the authorities in B restricted purchases of such commodities from A by a given amount, this would cause a marked and lasting decline in the price of these products in A compared with the price of the rest of A's products. B's balance of trade would be improved not only by the decline in the volume of her imports of these particular products but also by the heavy decline in the price at which she obtained her remaining purchases of them. And by picking out in this way for restriction the imports of those things of which the elasticity of supply in A was particularly small, the authorities in B could most effectively reduce the price of B's imports and so move the terms of trade in B's favour.[1]

Moreover, if imports can be found for which the elasticity of demand in B is particularly high as well as the elasticity of supply in A being particularly low, these will be especially suitable for import restriction in B. The high elasticity of demand in B will mean that the purchasers in B can readily dispense with them or can easily turn to the consumption of some home-produced commodity. In this case only a moderate rise in their price in B will be necessary to bring about a sufficient decline in the demand in B to cause a sharp fall in their price in A. Little hardship will be caused in B; but the value of B's imports will be much reduced and the terms of trade moved much in her favour.

We can imagine, then, a system of direct trade controls in B being used to tax those exports of B for which the demand in A is particularly inelastic, to subsidize those exports of B for which the demand in A is particularly elastic, and to restrict the import into B of those products of A of which the supply from A to B is particularly inelastic and for

---

[1] A given percentage restriction in the volume of B's imports will always reduce the (untaxed) value of B's imports most in those cases in which the elasticity of supply in A is smallest. But it does not follow that a given *ad valorem* import duty on B's imports will always reduce the (untaxed) value of B's imports most in those cases in which the elasticity of supply in A is smallest. If the elasticity of demand in B is greater than one then anything which keeps up the price of B's imports will increase the decline in the expenditure of B's purchasers on imports and so, at a constant *ad valorem* rate of duty, will increase the decline in the untaxed value of B's imports. It is only if the elasticity of demand of the purchasers of imports in B is less than unity that anything which keeps up the price of B's imports will keep up the value of B's imports. It is only in the latter case, therefore, that with a constant *ad valorem* rate of import duty in B a low elasticity of supply in A will be favourable to B's balance of trade. But all that this means is that to achieve a given percentage reduction in the volume of B's imports a high *ad valorem* rate of import duty will be required where the elasticity of demand in B or the elasticity of supply in A is relatively low; and in the latter case though the *ad valorem* rate of duty must be relatively high this will be because the price paid to A's producers falls a lot and not because the price charged to B's final buyers rises much.

which the demand in B is particularly elastic.[1] The above are the obvious ways whereby, in the absence of retaliation, the authorities in B can use a miscellany of trade controls to remove a balance-of-payments deficit; but the reader should at this point remind himself that we are assuming that the authorities in A do not themselves retaliate by any commercial counter-manœuvres. It is, of course, only on this assumption that the authorities in B can by these means obtain a simple solution of the balance-of-payments problem and simultaneously move the terms of trade in B's favour by exploiting A's consumers and producers in the way described above.

2. Action by the Authorities in the Surplus Country

In the real world it is usually the authorities in the deficit country who have employed direct controls on trade to remove the deficit in the balance of payments. But there is nothing in the nature of things to prevent the authorities in a surplus country from using direct controls on trade for the purpose of removing the surplus on the balance of payments. For logical completeness we will briefly enumerate the possibilities on this side. But the discussion may serve a purpose other than that of mere logical completeness; for when we come to consider what action should be taken in the world interest for removing balance-of-payments disequilibria, we shall see that in many cases where direct controls on trade are under consideration action by the authorities in surplus country may be preferable to action by the authorities in the deficit country.

(i) *The imposition of subsidies or the removal of taxes on imports in the surplus country*. Such action will always help to remove a surplus on A's

---

[1] It is often argued that the authorities in a deficit country should not permit the waste of scarce foreign currency on luxuries. It is claimed that the import of necessities (e.g. wheat) should be permitted and that of luxuries (e.g. motor-cars) disallowed. But this is quite erroneous. The standard of living in a deficit country will have to be reduced when the deficit on its balance of payments is removed since its domestic expenditure will have to be reduced to maintain internal balance as its imports decrease and exports increase; and it may well be that when its standard of living is reduced, its residents should give up consuming motor-cars (whether imported or home produced) and should go on consuming wheat. But if, when the balance of payments is once again in balance, motor-cars as well as wheat are still being consumed there is no more reason why wheat should be imported and motor-cars made at home than vice versa. Suppose that (i) the elasticity of supply of motor-cars in A were very great so that the price would not be reduced much if B's purchasers refrained from buying them, (ii) the elasticity of supply of wheat from A to B were very small so that a reduction in B's imports of wheat would cause a large fall in the price charged for wheat by A's producers, and (iii) B's producers could easily shift from producing motor-cars to producing wheat if the price of the latter rose in B because of a restriction on imports of wheat in B; then the authorities in B might achieve a much easier adjustment of the balance of payments and much more favourable terms of trade if they restricted imports of wheat rather than imports of motor-cars.

balance of payments. The authorities in A raise an additional revenue (e.g. by means of an income tax) in order to acquire the funds for the payment of a subsidy on imports or to replace the funds lost through the lowering of an existing duty on imports. Purchasers in A have the same real purchasing power, since the reduction in their buying power due to the increased income tax is exactly offset by the increase in their buying power due to the lower price of imports. But the net effect is to lower the market price of imported products relatively to home products in A and purchasers in A will, therefore, shift their purchases to some extent on to B's products.

An appreciation of A's currency will raise the price of A's products in B's market as well as lowering the price of B's products in A's market. Import subsidization by the authorities in A will do the latter without the former. If, therefore, we consider the size of A's surplus in terms of B's currency, an appreciation of A's currency will be more effective than import subsidization in A in removing A's surplus if the elasticity of demand for imports in B is greater than unity; but if the elasticity of demand for imports in B is less than unity, appreciation of A's exchange will cause an increase in the amount spent in terms of B's currency on A's exports and will, therefore, be less effective than import subsidization in A in removing A's surplus.

If the prices of all A's products are stabilized in terms of A's currency and those of all B's products in terms of B's currency, an appreciation of A's currency will cause the terms of trade to move against B by the amount of the variation in the exchange rate. On the other hand, import subsidization by A would leave the terms of trade unchanged so that, as far as the terms of trade are concerned, the latter would be more favourable from B's point of view. This point would be even more important if the elasticity of supply of exports from B to A were particularly low; for import subsidization by A removes A's surplus solely by increasing the demand in A for B's products and, in this case, it will cause a particularly sharp rise in the price of B's products and so in the terms of trade in B's favour. On the other hand, if the elasticity of supply of A's exports to B is particularly low, the appreciation of A's exchange rate (which operates partly by raising the price of A's products to B's purchasers and so reducing the demand for A's products in B) may result in a sharp fall in the price (in A's currency) of A's exports which would help to turn the terms of trade in B's favour.

Since many countries normally employ import duties and other import restrictions, the method of direct encouragement of A's imports may well mean a movement towards the free-trade position.

(ii) *The imposition of export taxes or removal of export subsidies in the surplus country.* It is only if the elasticity of demand for imports in B is greater than one that a rise in the price of A's products in B's market due to an export tax in A will decrease the amount spent on A's exports by B's purchasers. In this case the mechanism will work in the following way to reduce A's surplus. The purchasers in A find that their purchasing power is increased by the remission of other taxation (e.g. the income tax) which is made possible by the raising of the revenue from export taxes. This increased purchasing power of A's purchasers itself stimulates the demand in A for B's products and thus helps to remove A's surplus. But at the same time the price of A's products is raised in B's markets and, the elasticity of demand for A's products in B being greater than one, the total expenditure by B's final buyers on imports from A is reduced.

A's surplus in terms of B's currency will always be reduced more readily by an appreciation of A's currency than by a general export duty in A. The former method by lowering the price of B's products in A's currency will cause the demand in A for B's products to increase somewhat and will therefore lead to a rise in the value of B's exports to A in terms of B's currency. This part of the mechanism will be absent in the case of an export duty in A, which will have the same effect as an appreciation of A's currency in so far as the value of A's exports in terms of B's currency is concerned.

Since the export tax in A does not have this favourable effect upon B's exports, it will have to be higher than the corresponding appreciation of A's currency necessary to remove a given surplus in A's balance of payments. If the (untaxed) prices of all A's products are stabilized in terms of A's currency and the prices of all B's products are stabilized in terms of B's products, the terms of trade will move against B by the height of the export duty in A or, alternatively, by the extent of the appreciation of A's currency. The terms of trade will, therefore, normally move more unfavourably from B's point of view if the method of direct restriction of exports from A is used instead of that of an appreciation of A's exchange rate.

It is quite possible that a country may have export subsidies which it can remove, so that this method may well mean a movement towards the free-trade position. But more probably it will involve the raising of new export taxes and will, therefore, mean a movement away from the free-trade position in the direction of an artificial restriction on the volume of trade.

(iii) *The imposition of subsidies or the removal of taxes on exports by the surplus country*. If the elasticity of demand for imports in B is much less than unity, then the authorities in A would have to subsidize A's exports in order to cause a reduction in their value. If the elasticity of demand in B is sufficiently below one, then the method of export subsidization in A may remove A's surplus in the following way. The authorities in A must impose additional taxation (e.g. an income tax) in order to raise the funds to pay the subsidies to A's exporters without causing a net inflation of A's national income. This increased rate of income tax will cause some reduction in A in the demand for goods and services of all kinds including the demand for imports from B, and this in itself will tend somewhat to increase A's surplus. But simultaneously the price of A's products will have fallen in B's markets and if the elasticity of demand for imports in B is sufficiently small this will cause a reduction in the total amount spent on imports in B which outweighs the reduction in the demand for imports in A.

If the sum of the elasticities of demand for imports in A and B, as well as the elasticity of demand for imports in B alone, is less than unity, then we must compare the subsidization of A's exports with a depreciation of A's exchange rate as a means for the removal of A's surplus. In these circumstances the subsidization of A's exports will always be more effective than the depreciation of A's exchange rate in removing A's surplus measured in terms of B's currency, because the latter will lead to some rise in the price of B's products in A's market and therefore to some decline in the value of A's imports from B in terms of B's currency. The subsidization of A's exports will have the same effect as a depreciation of A's exchange rate in reducing the value of B's imports in terms of B's currency, but it will not have any effect in reducing the value of A's imports from B in terms of B's currency. For this reason the subsidization of A's exports will not need to be so great as the depreciation of A's currency in order to remove A's surplus; and it follows therefore that the terms of trade (which will move in B's favour in both cases) will move more favourably to B if the method of depreciation of A's currency is chosen than if the method of export subsidization by A is chosen.

It is possible, however, that, although the elasticity of demand for imports in B is less than unity, the sum of the elasticities of demand for imports in A and B is greater than unity. In this case we must compare the subsidization of A's exports with the appreciation of A's currency as means of removing the surplus on A's balance of payments. The subsidization of A's exports will be a more effective method than the appreciation of A's currency if the elasticity of demand for imports in B is much lower than unity but the sum of the elasticities of demand in A and B is only just above unity. On the other hand, the appreciation of A's currency will be the more effective method of removing A's surplus if the elasticity of demand for imports in B is only a little lower than unity whereas the sum of the two elasticities of demand is much above unity.

Since the subsidization of A's exports will move the terms of trade in B's favour whereas the appreciation of A's currency will move the terms of trade against B, there can be no doubt that the former is more favourable to B from this point of view.

As for the comparison with the free-trade position, since export taxes are not in fact common, this method will probably involve the raising of export subsidies, and so will mean a movement away from the free-trade position in the direction of the over-stimulation of trade.

(iv) *The control of particular imports and exports in the surplus country.* It would be possible for the authorities in the surplus country to operate direct controls on particular imports and exports so as to bring about the most effective removal of its surplus. Thus they could pick out for export subsidy those commodities for which the elasticity of demand in B was much below unity and for export tax those commodities for which the elasticity of demand in B was much above unity. And they could pick out for import subsidization those commodities for which the demand by its own final buyers was particularly elastic. In this latter case they could make sure of increasing the value of the exports of the deficit country if they paid high rates of subsidy on the import of commodities for which the supply in the deficit country was very inelastic. By such Quixotic measures they could make quite sure that the surplus on the balance of payments was effectively removed and that simultaneously the terms of trade were moved sharply in favour of the deficit country.

CHAPTER XXIV

DIRECT CONTROLS, PRICE ADJUSTMENT, AND ECONOMIC WELFARE

As we have already observed, it is not possible to decide between direct controls and price adjustments solely on the grounds of their technical efficiency in influencing the balance of payments. Direct controls and mechanisms for price adjustment have at least three aspects, all of which must be considered before the final choice between them is made:

(i) They affect the balance of payments. This is the aspect which is directly relevant to this volume and on which we have concentrated in the preceding chapters.

(ii) They affect the size of the total real income available for distribution among the different countries.

(iii) They affect the distribution of any given real income between the different countries.

Let us first consider aspect i. From the preceding analysis it can be seen that the most important single consideration in deciding between direct controls and price adjustments solely as instruments for influencing the balance of payments is the size of the elasticities of demand for imports in the countries concerned. Price adjustment works by making one set of products cheaper in relation to another. If demand is sensitive to such price changes, then this mechanism will provide an easy adjustment of the balance of payments without too great a change in the terms of trade. If, however, the elasticities of demand are small, normal price adjustments will not readily serve to remove a disequilibrium in the balance of payments and may even make it worse. In such circumstances direct intervention to limit imports, or some similar direct control, will be inevitable if both internal and external balance are to be maintained.

The great issue of fact, therefore, is the actual size of these elasticities. On this question much more statistical and factual research needs to be undertaken; but the presumption is that they will be reasonably large on two conditions.

The first condition is that there should not be a host of barriers to international trade which impede the flow of trade into the new channels which price adjustments would otherwise make profitable. Price adjustment is a mechanism which can be expected to work in a world in which there is not already a host of protective devices in world trade; otherwise direct controls may become inevitable.

The second condition is that some time should be allowed for price adjustments to work out their full effects, since the shift of demand from products which have risen in price on to those which have fallen in price will be much greater if time is given in all the countries concerned for the consumers and producers to adjust their activities to the new price relationships.

This second condition means that some use of direct controls may be necessary if the economy of a country is subjected to extremely violent, sudden, and unexpected external disturbances. The outbreak of a war, or the sudden cessation of hostilities and the return to peace, or a rapid major economic depression in an important country may subject the international markets for imports and exports to catastrophically sudden and great changes. A major economic depression in a major country, for example, may cause a very great and very sudden reduction in the demand for the exports of other countries; and these other countries may thus experience the rapid development of a large and unexpected deficit in their balance of payments. The price adjustment necessary to meet this situation might be very great and might take some time to work itself out. If the deficit countries do not possess sufficient reserves of gold or of other means of payment acceptable to the surplus country to finance these large deficits during the period necessary for a price adjustment to restore external balance, some temporary restriction of imports or other use of direct controls may be difficult to avoid.

The best way to avoid this is, of course, to avoid the catastrophic change in international markets itself. If, to continue our example, the uncontrolled economic depression in the major centre were itself avoided, the need for direct controls as a means of meeting major catastrophic changes in international demand would not arise. Nor should it be taken for granted that the direct control of imports is necessarily a more efficient method than a price adjustment, e.g. a depreciation of the exchange value of the deficit country's currency, as a means of meeting the repercussions from an economic depression in a surplus country. There are other factors which must be taken into account.

Suppose that a major economic depression in country A so reduces the demand for the exports of country B that country B is faced with a sudden and large deficit in the balance of payments. Should the authorities in B depreciate B's currency or should they impose restrictions on imports into B? If the deficit is met by means of exchange depreciation, then exports from B to A will again be stimulated somewhat as well as imports from A into B being discouraged. Now the depression in A is likely to have caused unemployment in B which is particularly concentrated in B's export industries; and this structural unemployment in B is likely to be temporary, since it will disappear again when the economic depression in A is over and the demand for imports in A recovers. In order, therefore, to avoid heavy structural unemployment in B and in order to maintain economic activity in B on a pattern which corresponds as closely as possible to long-run needs, there is much to be said for meeting the external slump by a depreciation of B's currency rather than by a restriction of B's imports, provided that the price adjustment will have any significant effect upon B's exports over the period of time during which the depression in A is likely to last.[1]

We may in any case conclude that if the channels of trade are not clogged up with too great a pre-existing mass of trade barriers and if the most violent changes of economic conditions (such as major wars and major economic depressions) are avoided, price adjustment will probably provide a perfectly adequate technical instrument for the maintenance of external balance.

So much for aspect i of the choice between direct controls and price adjustment. Let us turn next to aspects ii and iii on p. 323. These aspects are properly the subject matter of Volume II. But they are so interwoven with aspect i that it is essential to say something about them here in anticipation of the fuller discussion in Volume II.

We may say that the total world real income is maximized when it is impossible to make the residents in one country better off without making the residents in another country worse off. It should be realized that with this definition the maximization of real world income is not a question solely of maximizing the physical production of commodities, but also a matter of ensuring that the right things are produced in each country and that the right things are exchanged between the countries.

The maximization of real world income has, of course, its purely physical aspect. Suppose, for example, that in country A the resources which are used to produce one motor-car could produce one unit of wheat, whereas in B the resources which are used to producing one unit of wheat could produce two motor-cars. Clearly in this case if resources were moved in A from producing one motor-car to producing one unit of wheat and in B from producing one unit of wheat to producing two motor-cars, the residents in A and B together could have between them the same amount of wheat and one more motor-car. World real income cannot be maximized unless this change is made.

Or to take another example of the maximization of physical output. Suppose that capital equipment is very scarce in B in relation to the available supplies of other economic resources such as labour, land, and

---

[1] The depression in A is likely to have caused some decline in the prices of A's products in terms of A's currency, so that, if internal balance and so the price level are maintained in B and if the exchange rate between A's and B's currency is unchanged, the terms of trade will move in B's favour. Some part of the probable adverse effect of a depreciation of B's currency upon B's real terms of trade would, therefore, merely offset the improvement in B's real terms of trade which would otherwise be the consequence of the depression in A.

other natural resources, with the result that $100 worth of goods invested in capital equipment will add net (i.e. after allowing for the depreciation and replacement of the capital equipment) an annual flow of commodities worth as much as $10 if the investment takes place in B's industries, but worth only $5 if the investment takes place in A's industries. In this case if capital is lent from A to B and, as a result, the investment in capital equipment takes place in B instead of in A, the total physical amount of commodities available for distribution among the residents of A and B will be increased. The residents of one country could be made better off without any reduction of the amount of goods consumed in the other.

Let us now take an example in which the total real income of the world can be increased without any change in the total world production of any commodity but merely by an exchange of commodities between A and B. Suppose that consumers in A are consuming both wheat and motor-cars and that they would be just as well off if they had one less motor-car but one more unit of wheat. Suppose that the consumers in B are also consuming both wheat and motor-cars but that they would be just as well off if they had one more motor-car but two less units of wheat. Then if one motor-car is exported from A to B and one and a half units of wheat from B to A, the consumers in both countries will be better off. The consumers in A will have one less motor-car, but in exchange they will receive one and a half more units of wheat although one more unit of wheat would have been sufficient to make up for the loss of the motor-car. The consumers in B will have one more motor-car but in exchange they will give up one and a half units of wheat, although they would have been prepared to go without two units of wheat in exchange for the one additional motor-car.

Now in Volume II it will be our task to consider to what extent the free forces of competition will bring about all the types of adjustment—namely, those movements of factors from one industry to another within each country, those movements of factors from one country to another, and those exchanges of existing outputs of commodities between the countries—which are necessary to maximize world real income. We shall there conclude that normally the forces in a free competitive market tend to bring about these movements, but that in certain conditions certain interventions in the free market are required in order to achieve them. We will call the position which is reached with all the interventions which are required to lead to a maximum of world real income (but without any interventions which may be undertaken solely to affect the distribution of world real income between the various countries or solely in order to put the balance of payments into equilibrium) the 'modified free-trade position'.

The distribution of world income between countries can be affected by an alteration in the terms of trade in favour of the one country or the other. But it must, of course, be remembered that anything which alters the terms of trade in favour of a country (e.g. the use of import restrictions instead of exchange depreciation by a country to remove a deficit on its balance of payments) is likely also to affect the size of the world real income available for distribution between the two countries. Suppose that the imposition of import restrictions by the deficit country involves a movement away from the 'modified free-trade position'. Then the position with import restrictions in the deficit country is not a position of maximum world real income. It would be technically possible for the residents of both countries to be made better off. But this does not, of course, mean that the substitution of exchange depreciation for import restriction by the deficit country would in fact make the residents of both countries better off. It would merely lead to a position in which it was no longer technically possible to make the residents of one country better off without making the residents of the other worse off; but in this new (exchange depreciation) situation, while the residents in the surplus country might be a great deal better off, the residents in the deficit country might be appreciably worse off than in the old (import restriction) situation. And a situation in which it was technically possible still to make the residents of both countries better off (the import restriction situation) might be preferable to another situation (the exchange depreciation situation) in which it was no longer technically possible to make the residents of one country better off without making the residents of the other worse off, if in the first situation out of a smaller total available income a larger absolute amount went to the poorer country.

But it must also be remembered that intervention in the free market to affect the terms of trade is not the only way in which income can be redistributed internationally. Thus it is always possible for the authorities in one country to raise revenue and to hand it over directly to the authorities in another, so that in effect the residents in the first country are made worse off (by reason of the higher rates of taxation on them) and the residents in the second country are made better off (by reason of the tax remissions which can now be permitted in that country). If this kind of device for the redistribution of income is taken into account, a position (such as that reached through import restriction instead of exchange depreciation by a deficit country) which is removed from the 'modified free-trade position' is always to be avoided. It would always be possible to increase the total real world income by using exchange depreciation instead of import restriction to adjust the balance of payments, and then to achieve the desired redistribution in favour of the deficit country by a direct grant-in-aid from the surplus to the deficit country which will not interfere with the 'modified free-trade position'.[1]

Let us, then, consider the use of direct controls and of price adjustments in the light of the three aspects mentioned on page 323.

Some policies will improve the world position from all three points of view. Let us give three examples of this:

(i) Suppose that the authorities in the surplus country remove an artificial obstacle in the way of the transfer of capital to borrowers in the deficit country, and that residents in the deficit country are poorer than residents in the surplus country. Such action will help to adjust the balance of payments. It may well be a movement towards the modified free-trade position, since it will enable capital resources to move to the country where they have the highest yield. Finally, it will enable the authorities in the deficit country to avoid the necessity for a currency depreciation which would have moved the terms of trade unfavourably to the poor deficit country and in favour of the rich surplus country.

(ii) Similarly, suppose that the authorities in the surplus country remove an import duty or restriction which is not needed in the modified free-trade position, and that residents in the deficit country are poorer than residents in the surplus country. Again this will help to remove the disequilibrium on the balance of payments; it will be a movement towards the modified free-trade position; and it will enable the authorities in the relatively poor deficit country to avoid exchange depreciation and thus to avoid an adverse movement in the real terms of trade.

(iii) Suppose that a balance-of-payments disequilibrium is removed by means of the depreciation of the currency of the deficit country and that residents in the deficit country, as may well be the case, are richer than residents in the surplus country. This will help to put the balance of payments into equilibrium; it will not involve any movement away from the modified free-trade position; and it will involve some movement of the terms of trade against the rich deficit country.

We may now give some illustrations of policies which would be desirable from two of our three aspects but undesirable from the third aspect.

---

[1] This argument is strictly correct only if the taxation necessary in the surplus countries to raise the revenue to make the direct grants to the deficit countries does not itself have any disincentive effects which reduce the size of the real world income. The argument in the text assumes, that is to say, that while import duties will seriously reduce total real world income, income taxes in the rich countries will not do so at all. Only on that extreme assumption are the dogmatic conclusions in the text strictly correct. It will be an important object of Volume II to consider how the argument against direct controls may have to be modified, on grounds of their effects on the distribution of income, if the assumption that redistribution through direct income taxes and subsidies has no serious disincentive effects is modified.

(i) Suppose that the authorities in a deficit country remove the deficit on the balance of payments by exchange depreciation, but that residents in the deficit country are poorer than residents in the surplus country. This will adjust the balance of payments, and it will not involve any movement away from the modified free-trade position. ' But it will move the terms of trade against the poorer country.

(ii) Suppose that the authorities in a deficit country remove the balance of payments deficit by restrictions on the lending of capital abroad or on imports from abroad—restrictions which are not needed in the modified free-trade position—and that the deficit country is poorer than the surplus country. This will adjust the balance of payments and it will avoid the movement of the terms of trade against the poorer country which would result from the alternative policy of exchange depreciation by the deficit country. But it will involve a movement away from the modified free-trade position. In this case it is, of course, possible that the movement away from the modified free-trade position is so extensive and that the movement of the terms of trade against the deficit country which is avoided by the use of restrictions on imports or on capital movements is so slight, that residents in the deficit country (as well as those in the surplus country) would be absolutely better off if the method of exchange depreciation had been used. What would be gained through there being a larger world cake to divide would be greater than what would be lost through having a rather smaller proportionate share of the cake. Conflict of interest would arise only where the deficit country stood to gain absolutely through having a larger proportionate share of a smaller cake.

(iii) Suppose that the authorities in a deficit country were to remove restrictions on imports or on the lending of capital abroad—restrictions which were not needed in the modified free-trade position—and that residents in the surplus country were poorer than residents in the deficit country. This would be a movement towards the modified free-trade position and it would tend to move the real terms of trade in favour of the relatively poor surplus country. But it would, of course, intensify the disequilibrium in the balance of payments.

There is only one way in which all these conflicts can be resolved. The price adjustment mechanism of variable exchange rates or of flexible wage rates must be used to adjust the balance of payments, so that the balance of payments is put into equilibrium without any movement away from the modified free-trade position. Any desirable alteration in the resulting distribution of world income must then be brought about by means of a direct subsidization by the authorities (and so indirectly the residents) in the poorer country by the authorities (and so indirectly the residents) in the richer country.

Such a solution is, of course, possible only when the stage of international economic co-operation is reached at which the distribution of income between countries can begin to be the subject of central international or supranational decision just as the distribution of income between individuals within a nation is the subject of policies adopted by the national authorities. It means not merely that the richer countries must be prepared to consider such an agreed redistribution but that the poorer countries must be prepared to forswear the use of all those purely national instruments (such as import restrictions) which may enable them by their own individual acts to move the terms of trade in their favour. However Utopian—in spite of such recent unprecedentedly generous arrangements as Lend-lease and Marshall Aid—this order of ideas may at the moment seem, the advantages of development on these lines to all concerned should not be underestimated. Suppose the authorities of deficit countries abandoned import restrictions and allowed their exchange rates to depreciate to the extent necessary to restore equilibrium to their balances of payments and that the authorities of the surplus countries filled part of the deficit with direct aid to the deficit countries and thereby made up for the movement of the terms of trade against the latter. In this case the residents in the deficit countries would be unaffected; direct aid if properly estimated would just compensate for the adverse movement in the terms of trade. But the residents in the surplus countries would be better off; the direct fiscal burden would be more than compensated by the movement in the terms of trade in their favour. The world economy would have moved towards the modified free-trade position and everyone could be simultaneously better off.

PART VI.
THE NETWORK OF WORLD PAYMENTS

PART IV

PART VI.

THE NETWORK OF WORLD PAYMENTS

CHAPTER XXV

PAYMENTS BETWEEN MANY COUNTRIES

UP to this point we have concentrated our attention upon the problems which arise in a world of two countries, although the world is in fact made up of a number of countries of different sizes and structures and with fiscal, monetary, wage, foreign-exchange, and commercial policies which are determined in large measure independently. The preceding analysis is not, however, entirely unrealistic. For certain problems of international economic policy it may cover practically all the analysis which is required. For example, we may wish to consider only the restoration of equilibrium between one country and the rest of the world or between one large group of countries (say the 'dollar' countries) and another large group of countries (say the 'sterling' countries) which together cover the greater part of world trade. In such cases we shall not be too wide of the mark if we restrict our analysis to the points covered in Parts I to V of this volume.

But there remains a large class of problems concerning balance-of-payments policies for which our analysis needs to be supplemented in a very important way. There is often a position of world disequilibrium, in which some countries have deficits of various sizes and others surpluses of various sizes in their balances of payments; and we are interested in the question how the authorities in each country should behave so that, when the effects of the policy of each upon the economies of all the others are taken into account, we may attain a final position of world equilibrium in which each country is simultaneously in both internal and external balance.

We have already had occasion to see that, even with only two countries, there are considerable complications in the ways in which the policies adopted in one country may act upon the economy of the other and so react upon its own position. The possible complications are, of course, enormously increased when we allow for the existence of many countries and many independent national policies. The policy adopted in A will act upon the economies of B, C, D, E, etc., in each of which there may be a different 'policy' reaction to the repercussion from A; each of B, C, D, E, etc., may, therefore, send out a new and different impulse into the world economy and so react upon the position of the other countries in various ways. The number of possible outcomes is clearly so innumerably great that it is quite impossible to attempt to cover for a many-country world all the situations, problems, and policies —severely limited though they in fact were—which we have already covered for our two-country world.

Accordingly, we shall proceed as follows. We shall start by outlining in a schematic form some of the principal logical inter-relationships in a network of payments between a number of countries. We shall then proceed on the assumption that the authorities in each country adopt a domestic financial policy for internal balance, and shall consider the implications of this upon the network of world payments. We shall then proceed to consider a few typical sets of consistent rules for the use of wages policy, exchange rate policy, and commercial policy in the various countries so as to obtain a world situation in which each country is also at the same time in external balance.

We start, then, by considering some logical inter-connexions in a system of world payments between a large number of countries. It will be remembered that, in Chapter III, in our analysis of the two-country world, great stress was laid upon the central relationship between the national income, domestic expenditure, and foreign trade of any country namely that domestic expenditure *less* imports *plus* exports = national income. This, we argued, must be true simultaneously of both the countries in our two-country world; and since the one country's exports was the other's imports, there resulted the basic inter-relationship shown in Table VII on p. 36.

In our present many-country world it remains true that for each country domestic expenditure *less* imports *plus* exports = national income; but in this case each country's exports may go to, and imports come from, a large number of other countries. All that one can say is that A's exports to B are B's imports from A, and so on. The resulting relationship is illustrated in Table XVII. This table may be explained as follows.

Our world is now made up of five countries D_1, D_2, S_1, S_2, and B. The balances of trade of D_1 and D_2 are in deficit, of S_1 and S_2 are in surplus, and of B is in balance. The figures in Table XVII illustrate the relationships between the national incomes, domestic expenditures, and the visible and invisible imports and exports of the countries concerned.

Let us illustrate the figures by considering country D_1 in Table XVII. If we consider the figures in column *a* of the Table, the first figure (1,000) shows that persons and institutions in country D_1 are paying \$1,000 m. to other persons and institutions in the same country for goods and services for private or public consumption or investment;

the second figure (65) shows that persons and institutions in D_1 are paying \$65 m. to persons and institutions in D_2, i.e. that imports into D_1 from D_2 or—equally well—exports from D_2 to D_1 are \$65 m.; the third, fourth, and fifth figures show that payments for imports into D_1 from S_1, S_2, and B are \$60 m., \$5 m., and \$25 m. respectively.

TABLE XVII

Network of National and International Payments for Visible and Invisible Trade

$ m.

		Paying Countries					Total, i.e. national income	Total excluding diagonals, i.e. exports	Balance of trade, i.e. exports minus imports
		D_1	D_2	S_1	S_2	B			
		(a)	(b)	(c)	(d)	(e)	(f)	(g)	(h)
Receiving Countries	D_1 (1)	1000	8	56	16	5	1085	85	−70
	D_2 (2)	65	500	5	23	12	605	105	−60
	S_1 (3)	60	47	1000	40	83	1230	230	+95
	S_2 (4)	5	82	53	500	5	645	145	+35
	B (5)	25	28	21	31	700	805	105	0
Total, i.e. domestic expenditure	(6)	1155	665	1135	610	805	4370		
Total excluding diagonals, i.e. imports	(7)	155	165	135	110	105		670	

Now the sum of these first five figures in column *a*—which is shown as \$1,155 m. in row 6 of column *a*—represents the total amount spent by persons and institutions in D_1 on the products of D_1, D_2, S_1, S_2, or B for purposes of private or public consumption or investment. It represents, therefore, the total of what we have called domestic expenditure in D_1. And this sum, excluding the \$1,000 m. which D_1's purchasers spend on D_1's own products, represents the expenditure by D_1's purchasers on imports from other countries, and this amount of \$155 m. is shown in row 7 of column *a*.

By considering the figures in column *a* of the table, we have considered payments by purchasers in D_1 on goods and services whether home produced or imported, and we have thus considered domestic expenditure and imports in D_1. If now we turn to the figures in row 1 of the table we shall be considering the receipts of D_1's producers from the sale of goods and services both to domestic and also to foreign purchasers, and we shall thus be considering the value of the total production of goods and services in D_1 (i.e. D_1's national income) and D_1's exports. Thus the first figure (1,000) in row 1 of the table shows that producers in D_1 are receiving $1,000 m. from the sale of their products to purchasers in D_1; and the figures in columns *b, c, d,* and *e* of row 1 show that producers in D_1 are receiving $8 m., $56 m., $16 m., and $5 m. respectively from exports of their products to purchasers in D_2, S_1, S_2, and B respectively. The total of all the figures in columns *a* to *e* of row 1 thus shows the total value of all production in D_1 or D_1's national income, and this is shown as $1,085 m. in column *f*. And if we exclude from this sum the $1,000 m. of column *a*, which represents what D_1's producers receive from domestic sales, we get the $85 m. of column *g* which represents the total of sales by D_1's producers to foreigners, i.e. of D_1's exports. If, finally, we compare this total of $85 m. with the corresponding total of the imports into D_1 of $155 m. in row 7 of column *a* we see that there is an excess of imports of $70 m. into D_1 which is shown in column *h* of row 1.

To sum up, in Table XVII the figures in any one of the columns *a* to *e* represent the expenditures by the purchasers in the country standing at the head of that column on the products of all the various countries (including, in the diagonal figure, their expenditure on the products of their own country); and the figures in any of the rows 1 to 5 represent the receipts of the producers in the country standing at the beginning of the row from the sale of their products to purchasers in all the various countries (including, in the diagonal figure, receipts from sales to purchasers in their own country). It follows that the total of each column represents each country's domestic expenditure and the total of each row represents each country's national income; and, if the diagonal figures are excluded, the total of each column represents the value of each country's imports and the total of each row represents the value of each country's exports.

Table XVII which we have just described shows the relationships in a many-country world between each country's imports, exports, national income, and domestic expenditure. It is, therefore, relevant to the consideration of the balance of trade. But when we wish to consider the balance of payments we must bring into account two other considerations, as has already been pointed out in Chapter I. First, we must allow for payments and receipts on account of transactions for purposes other than the finance of visible and invisible trade. In Chapter I we enumerated such other payments and receipts under the heading of 'transfers', either 'unrequited transfers' (e.g. reparations payments, indemnities, Marshall Aid, emigrants' remittances, etc.) or 'capital transfers' (e.g. all transfers made now in return for some future repayment in the opposite direction). Secondly, we must distinguish between 'accommodating' and 'autonomous' transactions. As we have seen in Chapter I, if all payments and receipts were brought into the picture each country's total payments would be necessarily equal to its total receipts and there would be no net balance of payments. Accordingly we adopted the method of omitting from the account all 'accommodating' payments and receipts, i.e. all transactions which were undertaken by some monetary or similar authority for the sole purpose of financing a deficit or surplus in the other items of the balance of payments. We were then left with a country's balance of payments on account of autonomous trade and transfers.

These same principles are adopted in drawing up the figures in Table XVIII which illustrates the relationships between the balances of payments of the various countries in a many-country world. Section i of the table represents the network of international payments for autonomous trading transactions. In fact it merely reproduces the figures of Table XVII with the omission of the diagonal figures of that table. In other words we assume, merely for the purposes of illustration, that all the trade transactions of Table XVII were autonomous in character and should enter into our final balance of payments account; and the diagonal figures are omitted because we are no longer concerned with the relationships of these international payments to each country's national income and domestic expenditure.

Section ii of Table XVIII adds figures to illustrate autonomous transfers between the countries concerned. On trading account, i.e. in section i, countries D_1 and D_2 are in deficit and countries S_1 and S_2 in surplus. We suppose that some part of this disequilibrium is covered by autonomous transfers. Thus in section ii of the table we suppose that residents in countries S_1 and S_2 are making autonomous transfer payments (e.g. lending capital on a commercial basis) to residents in the other countries and in particular to residents in the deficit countries D_1 and D_2. Thus the figure of $9 m. in column c of row 7 of the table means that persons or institutions in S_1 are transferring autonomously $9 m. to persons or institutions in D_1. The net result of section ii of the table is that residents in D_1 are receiving $10 m. net by autonomous transfer from the rest of the world, residents in D_2 are receiving $20 m. net and residents in S_1 and S_2 are in each case paying $15 m. net (see column g of section ii).

Section iii of the table merely combines the figures of sections i

TABLE XVIII

Network of International Autonomous Payments

$ m.

			Paying Countries				Total: (i) Autonomous exports (ii) Autonomous transfer receipts (iii) All autonomous receipts	Balance excess receipts (+) or payments (−)
			D_1	D_2	S_1	S_2	B		
			(a)	(b)	(c)	(d)	(e)	(f)	(g)
Section i. Payments for Autonomous Trade (See Table XVII)									
Receiving Countries	D_1	(1)		8	56	16	5	85	−70
	D_2	(2)	65		5	23	12	105	−60
	S_1	(3)	60	47		40	83	230	+95
	S_2	(4)	5	82	53		5	145	+35
	B	(5)	25	28	21	31		105	0
Total autonomous imports		(6)	155	165	135	110	105	670	
Section ii. Payments for Autonomous Transfers									
Receiving Countries	D_1	(7)		1	9	3	1	14	+10
	D_2	(8)	1		11	11	1	24	+20
	S_1	(9)	1	1		5	1	8	−15
	S_2	(10)	1	1	2		1	5	−15
	B	(11)	1	1	1	1		4	0
Total autonomous transfer payments		(12)	4	4	23	20	4	55	
Section iii. All Autonomous Payments									
Receiving Countries	D_1	(13)		9	65	19	6	99	−60
	D_2	(14)	66		16	34	13	129	−40
	S_1	(15)	61	48		45	84	238	+80
	S_2	(16)	6	83	55		6	150	+20
	B	(17)	26	29	22	32		109	0
Total all autonomous payments		(18)	159	169	158	130	109	725	

and ii. Thus the figure of $45 m. in column d row 15 of the table shows that residents in S_2 make total autonomous payments on all accounts of $45 m. to residents in S_1 or, alternatively, that residents in S_1 receive from residents in S_2 $45 m. on account of all autonomous transactions; and this $45 m. is merely the sum of the $40 m. paid by residents in S_2 to residents in S_1 on account of autonomous trade (column d, row 3) and the $5 m. so paid on account of autonomous transfers (column d row 9). Thus when all autonomous transactions are taken into account we find that D_1 has a deficit of $60 m., D_2 a deficit of $40 m., S_1 a surplus of $80 m., S_2 a surplus of $20 m., and B an exact balance (see column g of section iii).

It will be observed that the total world deficits (i.e. $60 m. for D_1 plus $40 m. for D_2) add up to the total world surpluses (i.e. $80 m. for S_1 plus $20 m. for S_2). This is bound to be the case provided that when the residents of any country make an autonomous payment, this is also an autonomous receipt for the receiving country. This is, in fact, the assumption which we have made in Table XVIII and which we shall be tacitly making throughout the remainder of Part VI. It is normally in fact the case; and the assumption greatly simplifies the exposition without essentially distorting the truth.

But as we have argued in Chapter II, this is not necessarily the case. Suppose, for example, that D_1 is a gold-producing country, and that $20 m. of the $65 m. which residents in S_1 are paying to residents in D_1 (column c row 13 of Table XVIII) represents an import of gold into S_1 from D_1. Let us suppose further that this gold is sold by the gold producers in D_1 to S_1's central bank. In this case it would probably represent an ordinary commercial or 'autonomous' export in so far as D_1 was concerned. But it should probably be treated as an 'accommodating' payment in so far as S_1 is concerned, since it would represent merely the financial mechanism whereby the monetary authorities in S_1 receive financial payment for an excess of S_1's receipts for autonomous exports and other autonomous transactions over payments for autonomous imports and other autonomous transactions. In so far as this export of gold from D_1 to S_1 was concerned, D_1 would not appear to be in deficit since gold is being exported from current production and not from monetary reserves, but S_1 would appear to be in surplus since in S_1 gold is being added to monetary reserves.

To meet such a case we should have to enter into column c row 13 of Table XVIII two figures instead of one, viz., a $65 m. which represents D_1's exports and other autonomous receipts from S_1 and a $45 m. which represents S_1 imports and other autonomous payments to D_1. We should have to use the $65 m. when we were adding up row 13 to obtain D_1's autonomous receipts and the $45 m. when we were adding up column c to obtain S_1's autonomous payments, as follows:

$ m.

		Paying Countries					Total autonomous receipts	Balance excess receipts (+) or payments (−)
		D_1	D_2	S_1	S_2	B		
Receiving Countries	D_1		9	45 65	19	6	99	−60
	D_2	66		16	34	13	129	−40
	S_1	61	48		45	84	238	+100
	S_2	6	83	55		6	150	+20
	B	26	29	22	32		109	Nil
Total autonomous payments		159	169	138	130	109	725 705	+20

If this table is compared with section iii of Table XVIII, it is clear that while total world receipts from autonomous transactions (including autonomous exports) have remained at $725 m., total world payments for autonomous transactions (including autonomous imports) are now only $705 m., because the import of gold into S_1 from D_1 no longer counts as an autonomous import for S_1. The result is that world surpluses ($100 m. for S_1 and $20 m. for S_2) now exceed world deficits ($60 m. for D_1 and $40 m. for D_2). The world as a whole has a balance of payments surplus of $20 m.

An examination of section iii of Table XVIII should serve to illustrate a further important point about international payments in a many-country world, namely, the multilateral character of such payments. This point is brought into sharp relief if we consider the relationship of the main deficit country D_1 with the two surplus countries S_1 and S_2. In fact D_1 is in surplus with both S_1 and S_2 individually, although D_1 is in overall deficit and both S_1 and S_2 are in overall surplus. Thus residents in D_1 receive $65 m. from, and pay only $61 m. to, residents in S_1 (column c row 13 and column a row 15), so that D_1 has a surplus of $4 m. with S_1. And residents in D_1 receive $19 m. from, and pay only $6 m. to, residents in S_2 (column d row 13 and column a row 16), so that D_1 has a surplus of $13 m. with S_2. The position described in section iii of the table is one in which D_1 has a surplus with the surplus countries S_1 and S_2 but a still greater deficit with the remaining countries

D_2 and B (and particularly with D_2), so that D_1 is in net deficit. D_2 in turn has this large surplus with D_1, but has large deficits with S_1, S_2, and B and particularly with S_1. Thus D_2 is in deficit with S_1 partly, as it were, on her own right (since D_2 is a net deficit and S_1 a net surplus country), but partly also on behalf of D_1 which, though a net deficit country, is in surplus with the net surplus country S_1 but offsets this by having a large deficit with the net deficit country D_2 which D_2 in turn passes on to the net surplus country S_1.

Now, in order to restore external balance to all our countries we wish somehow or another to alter the figures in section iii of Table XVIII so that the net balances for each country in column g are each reduced to zero.[1] Now there are innumerable ways of doing this, some of which it will be our purpose to consider in the remaining chapters of Part VI. Here, by way of a preliminary observation, we shall merely draw attention to a basic distinction between these various methods, namely, the distinction between bilateral and multilateral solutions. A bilateral solution of a world balance of payments disequilibrium is achieved when every country achieves a balance with each other country separately; and in this case it follows, of course, that each country must also be in equilibrium with the rest of the world, i.e. with all the other countries combined. A multilateral solution is achieved when each country achieves an overall balance with the rest of the world but without achieving a balance with each other country separately; it may have a surplus with one other country provided that it has an equal deficit with another.

Table XIX gives an illustration of a bilateral and of a multilateral solution of the original disequilibrium in world balances of payments which was given in section iii of Table XVIII. Section i of Table XIX merely reproduces the figures of section iii of Table XVIII for ease of reference. This is the disequilibrium in the world network of payments which it is our business to remove.

Section ii of Table XIX shows one possible bilateral solution. In the original position of equilibrium D_1 was in deficit with D_2. Residents in D_1 paid \$66 m. to, but received only \$9 m. from residents in D_2 (column a row 2 and column b row 1). Now D_1's particular balance with D_2 can be brought into equilibrium either by expanding payments from D_2 to D_1 (on exports from D_1 to D_2 or in respect of other autonomous transactions) or by contracting payments from D_1 to D_2. If the balance is achieved in the former manner the figure in column b row 1

---

[1] This is, of course, on the assumption that what is an autonomous payment to one country is an autonomous receipt to another and vice versa. If we were confronted with the figures on p. 340 our purpose would be to reduce all the balancing figures in the right-hand column of that table until we were left only with positive figures adding up to the \$20 m. by which world autonomous receipts necessarily exceed world autonomous payments.

must be raised from $9 m. to $66 m.; if in the latter manner, then the figure in column *a* row 2 must be reduced from $66 m. to $9 m. In the former case there will be a great expansion in the volume of world trade and in the latter case a great contraction. There is, in fact, nothing peculiarly contractionist or expansionist in bilateralism itself. Whether a bilateral solution of a world balance-of-payments disequilibrium will cause a contraction or expansion of world trade, and whether this is a good or a bad thing, are questions the answers to which depend upon the circumstances of the case; and we shall have to consider them in later chapters.

In the illustration in section ii of Table XIX we have supposed that an exact balance is achieved in the payments between each pair of countries partly by a contraction of the payments from the deficit to the surplus member of the pair, and partly by an expansion of the payments from the surplus to the deficit member of the pair. In fact, for the transactions between each pair we have taken the payments and the receipts from section i, have averaged these two figures, and have written down the resulting answer both for payments and for receipts in section ii. Thus we have written down 37\frac{1}{2}$ m. for the payments from D_1 to D_2 (column *a* row 8) and for the payments from D_2 to D_1 (column *b* row 7) in section ii; and this 37\frac{1}{2}$ m. is the average of payments of $66 m. from D_1 to D_2 (column *a* row 2) and of payments of $9 m. from D_2 to D_1 (column *b* row 1) in the original position. And similarly for every other pair of countries in section ii of Table XIX, we have made the payments equal to the receipts at a figure equal to the average of the payments and receipts in the original position. In section ii the total value of world trade and payments remains unchanged at $725 m., because there has been no net expansion or contraction of the total payments and receipts between any pair of countries; and each country is now in balance as a whole (i.e. the deficits and surpluses in column *g* have disappeared), because each country is in balance with each other individual country.

In section iii of Table XIX, however, the position is different. Each country's payments and receipts have been brought into balance in so far as its relations with all the other countries combined are concerned, but not in so far as its relations with each other country separately are concerned. Thus in section iii D_1 is in deficit with D_2 and B but in surplus with S_1 and S_2, and the individual surpluses just offset the individual deficits. The figures in section iii have been obtained in the following way. Country B is in balance in the original position; and accordingly payments from B to each of the other countries are neither expanded nor contracted (i.e. the figures in rows 13 to 17 of column *e* are the same as those in rows 1 to 5 of the same column). But countries D_1 and D_2 are in deficit in the original position;

TABLE XIX

Bilateral and Multilateral Solutions of a Balance of Payments Disequilibrium

$ m.

		Paying Countries					Total autonomous receipts	Balance excess receipts (+) or payments (−)
		D_1	D_2	S_1	S_2	B		
		(a)	(b)	(c)	(d)	(e)	(f)	(g)
Section i. Original Disequilibrium (See Table XVIII Section iii)								
Receiving Countries	D_1 (1)		9	65	19	6	99	−60
	D_2 (2)	66		16	34	13	129	−40
	S_1 (3)	61	48		45	84	238	+80
	S_2 (4)	6	83	55		6	150	+20
	B (5)	26	29	22	32		109	0
Total autonomous payments	(6)	159	169	158	130	109	725	
Section ii. Bilateral Solution								
Receiving Countries	D_1 (7)		$37\frac{1}{2}$	63	$12\frac{1}{2}$	16	129	0
	D_2 (8)	$37\frac{1}{2}$		32	$58\frac{1}{2}$	21	149	0
	S_1 (9)	63	32		50	53	198	0
	S_2 (10)	$12\frac{1}{2}$	$58\frac{1}{2}$	50		19	140	0
	B (11)	16	21	53	19		109	0
Total autonomous payments	(12)	129	149	198	140	109	725	
Section iii. Multilateral Solution								
Receiving Countries	D_1 (13)		7	90	21	6	124	0
	D_2 (14)	51		22	39	13	125	0
	S_1 (15)	48	36		51	84	219	0
	S_2 (16)	5	61	76		6	148	0
	B (17)	20	21	31	37		109	0
Total autonomous payments	(18)	124	125	219	148	109	725	

and accordingly payments from them to all other countries are contracted. Similarly, payments from the surplus countries S_1 and S_2 to all other countries are expanded. Moreover, we assume—merely as a particular illustration of a possible multilateral solution—that the payments from each deficit country are reduced in the same proportion to each other country and that the payments from each surplus country are increased in the same proportion to each other country. Thus in section iii of Table XIX payments from D_1 to D_2, S_1, S_2, and B have each been reduced by approximately 22 per cent; payments from D_2 to D_1, S_1, S_2, and B have each been reduced by approximately 26 per cent; payments from S_1 to D_1, D_2, S_2, and B have each been increased by approximately 39 per cent; and payments from S_2 to D_1, D_2, S_1, and B have each been increased by approximately 14 per cent. These all-round expansions of the payments from the surplus countries, and all-round contractions of the payments from the deficit countries are on a scale which just suffices to put each country into overall balance with the rest of the world as a whole. But no single pair of countries is in bilateral balance.

The multilateral character of the world equilibrium described in section iii of Table XIX is illustrated by the fact that D_1 has an excess of payments for autonomous trade and transfers to D_2; D_2 has an excess of payments to S_2; and S_2 has an excess of payments to D_1. This multilateral chain of payments from D_1 to D_2, D_2 to S_2, and S_2 to D_1 may be in respect of goods. Purchasers in D_1 may purchase raw materials from D_2, whose purchasers purchase foodstuffs from S_2, whose purchasers purchase machinery from D_1; and it might involve considerable loss to balance the trade between each pair of countries. On the other hand, the excess payment from D_1 to D_2 may represent a reparations payment or a normal commercial lending from a developed country with plenty of capital and low interest rates (D_1) to an undeveloped country with a scarcity of capital and the prospect of high yields on development projects (D_2); but the most economical way for this payment to be financed may be for borrowers in D_2 not to spend the loan on the products of D_1, which may not be much wanted in D_2, but to spend it on, say, machinery from S_2, whose purchasers in return can purchase the clothing which they need from D_1. It is this type of multilateralism which is ruled out by the bilateral solution illustrated in section ii of Table XIX.

CHAPTER XXVI

MULTILATERAL INCOME EFFECTS

LET us restate briefly the problem with which we shall deal in this and the following chapters. We assume a world consisting of five countries—D_1, D_2, S_1, S_2, and B. These countries are in internal balance in the sense that the general level of money demand for each country's products in terms of its own national currency is, when taken in relation to the general level of money wage rates and other money costs in that country, sufficiently high to provide a high level of employment but not so high as to cause a progressive inflation of money prices and costs. Moreover, whatever happens as a result of external developments the authorities in each of these countries intend (and have the administrative ability) by means of monetary and fiscal policies so to adjust the domestic money demand for goods and services —i.e. the country's domestic expenditure—as to maintain this internal balance unchanged. But our countries are not in external balance. The position is that which is described in Table XVIII (p. 338). Our problem is to consider the various ways in which external balance might be achieved for all the countries simultaneously, always assuming that in each country the domestic financial policy is so adjusted as to maintain internal balance.

It would, of course, be possible to achieve external balance merely by arranging for some special transfer of funds from the surplus to the deficit countries. The authorities in the surplus countries arrange a flow of Marshall Aid to the deficit countries, and this flow of special funds stops the flow of gold (or of other forms of internationally acceptable means of payment) from the deficit countries. Or the position might possibly be met by an exchange control imposed upon exports of capital by the deficit countries. If there is a gross autonomous flow of capital in process from each deficit country to the surplus countries on a sufficient scale, the authorities in each deficit country might be able to restore the balance of payments merely by stopping the outflow of capital funds. If at the same time any existing inflow of capital funds from the surplus to the deficit countries were allowed to continue, there might result a sufficient increase in the net flow of capital funds from the surplus to the deficit countries to close the whole balance-of-payments gap.

The above methods of dealing with the problem would achieve external balance without any change in any country's visible or invisible imports or in its balance of trade. The whole readjustment would fall on the 'transfer' items and none of the 'trade' items.

But a more probable situation is one in which the greater part of the adjustment has to fall sooner or later upon the trade items. It is probable that in order to achieve external balance the value of the exports of the deficit countries will have, by one means or another, to be expanded and/or the value of their imports contracted, and that the surplus countries will have to undergo the opposite experience.

But if this is so, and if the authorities in each country adopt an effective financial policy for internal balance, then we can immediately reach certain conclusions about the final position of equilibrium which will be achieved in each country. Suppose that in order to achieve external balance there must be a favourable movement in D_1's balance of trade of \$60 m. a favourable movement in D_2's balance of trade of \$40 m., an unfavourable movement in S_1's balance of trade of \$80 m., and an unfavourable movement in S_2's balance of trade of \$20 m.[1] Now for each country domestic expenditure *less* imports *plus* exports = national income; and on our assumptions the authorities in each country in the interests of internal balance are adopting a domestic financial policy which will so adjust domestic expenditure as to maintain national income constant. It follows that the authorities in D_1 will have to bring about a deflation of domestic expenditure in D_1 by \$60 m. in order to offset the inflationary effect which a \$60 m. improvement in D_1's balance of trade would otherwise have upon D_1's national income. Similarly, in the interests of internal balance domestic expenditure will have to be deflated by \$40 m. in D_2, inflated by \$80 m. in S_1, and inflated by \$20 m. in S_2 in order to offset the domestic effects of the adjustments of the balances of trade which must ultimately take place to restore external balance.

But will not these deflations of domestic expenditure in the deficit countries and inflations of domestic expenditure in the surplus countries themselves help to bring about the required adjustments in the balance of trade, the achievement of which makes these deflations and inflations necessary in the interests of internal balance? As the authorities in D_1 and D_2 take steps to deflate domestic expenditure this will cause a reduction in the demand for imported products as well as for home-produced goods and services in these countries; and as the authorities in S_1 and S_2 take steps to raise domestic expenditure, this will cause a rise in the demand for imports as well as for home products in these countries. Is it not possible that the deflation in D_1 and D_2 which is required to offset the domestic inflationary effects of an improvement in their balances of trade, and the inflation in S_1 and S_2 which is

[1] In other words we assume that the whole of the balance of payments disequilibrium shown in column g of section iii of Table XVIII must be met by adjustments in the trade items and none of it by adjustments in the transfer items.

required to offset the domestic deflationary effects of a worsening of their balances of trade, are themselves just sufficient to cause the required improvement in the balances of trade of D_1 and D_2 and the worsening in those of S_1 and S_2? If this were the case, no further action would be required besides the appropriate domestic financial policies in order to restore external balance without disturbing the existing internal balance in each country. An appropriate degree of deflation of domestic expenditure in D_1 and D_2 and of inflation of domestic expenditure in S_1 and S_2 would have the desired twofold effect: (i) it would contract imports into the deficit countries and expand imports into the surplus countries to the extent necessary to restore external balance; and (ii) it would simultaneously reduce the demand within the deficit countries for the deficit countries' home products to the extent necessary to prevent the increased foreign demand for their products from causing a domestic inflation, and similarly it would cause a sufficient expansion of demand within the surplus countries to offset the deflationary effects of their loss of export markets.

We have already seen that in a two-country world this happy result will occur if the sum of the marginal propensities to import in the two countries is equal to unity. The reader is referred to Table IX (see p. 90) and to the argument which is there developed. Let country A of Table IX represent a country in deficit, and country B of Table IX a country in surplus, to the extent of $100 m. Suppose that to regain external balance the balance of trade of A has to be increased, and that of B decreased, by this amount. In anticipation of this adjustment in the balance of trade, the authorities in A, in the interests of internal balance, start to deflate domestic expenditure in A by $100 m. in order to avoid an inflation in A's national income; and the authorities in B start to bring about a similar inflation of domestic expenditure in B. In case i of Table IX we assume that the sum of the marginal propensities to import in A and B add up to unity (i.e. $\frac{40}{100} + \frac{60}{100}$); and in this case it is clear that the very act of deflation of domestic expenditure in A by $100 m. and of inflation of domestic expenditure in B by the same amount both causes the balance of trade to move to exactly the required extent (viz. $100 m.) in A's favour, and also leaves A's and B's national incomes unchanged. Case ii of Table IX illustrates the highly abnormal case where the sum of the marginal propensities to import is greater than unity, and where in consequence the deflation of domestic expenditure in A and its inflation in B causes A's balance of trade to improve by more than $100 m. and causes an *inflation* of A's national income and a *deflation* of B's. Case iii of Table IX shows the normal case where the sum of the propensities to import is less than unity, and where in consequence A's balance of trade improves but improves by less than the required $100 m., and where there is a corresponding net deflation of A's national income and inflation of B's.

Is there anything in our many-country world which corresponds to this critical position at which the sum of the marginal propensities to import is equal to unity? In the two-country world of Table IX a special instance of case i—(where the sum of the marginal propensities to import is unity)—would be where each country's marginal propensity to import is equal to one-half. In case i of Table XX we apply this special case to our five-country world. We are assuming that in order to achieve external balance there must be a favourable movement in D_1's balance of trade of $60 m., a favourable movement in D_2's of $40 m., an unfavourable movement in S_1's of $80 m., and an unfavourable movement in S_2's of $20 m. When these movements have taken place, internal balance will be maintained only if domestic expenditures in D_1 and D_2 have been deflated and in S_1 and S_2 inflated by a similar amount. Accordingly in rows 6, 13, 20, and 27 of Table XX we assume that the domestic expenditures of D_1, D_2, S_1, and S_2 have been changed by −$60 m., −$40 m., +$80 m. and +$20 m. respectively.

In case i of Table XX we are also assuming that the marginal propensity to import in each country is one-half. Thus (column a of case i) we assume that of the reduction of $60 m. in domestic expenditure in D_1 one-half or $30 m. (row 1 of column a) represents a reduced demand for D_1's home products and the other half or $12 m.+$12 m. +$1 m.+$5 m. (rows 2, 3, 4, and 5 of column a) represents a reduced demand for imports from D_2, S_1, S_2, and B. We have assumed for the purposes of illustration that this reduction of $30 m. in the demand in D_1 for imports is spread over imports from D_2, S_1, S_2, and B, roughly in the proportion in which—as illustrated in Table XVII— products are already being imported from those countries.[1] And similarly with the figures in columns b, c, and d of case i of Table XX. We assume that in each case one-half of the change in domestic expenditure falls on the country's own home products, and that the other half which falls on imports is distributed among the various sources of supply roughly in the proportion in which products are already being imported from those sources, as shown in Table XVII. Since country B is already in external balance, no net change in B's domestic expenditure is required in order to preserve her internal balance with the result that the figures in column e of Table XX show no change.

By adding up the figures in each of the first five rows of case i of Table XX we are able to discover the impact effect upon each country's

[1] Thus 12 : 12 : 1 : 5 :: 65 : 60 : 5 : 25 approximately.

TABLE XX

The Impact Effect upon National Incomes and Balances of Payments of Changes in Domestic Expenditures in a Many-country World $ m.

			Increases (+) or decreases (−) in payments by					National income	Exports	Surplus (+) or deficit (−) on balance of payments before the change	after the change
			D₁	D₂	S₁	S₂	B				
			(a)	(b)	(c)	(d)	(e)	(f)	(g)	(h)	(i)

Case i. In each country the marginal propensity to import is one half and changes in imports are in proportion to previous imports

			D₁	D₂	S₁	S₂	B	National income	Exports	before	after
Increase (+) or decrease (−) in	receipts by	D₁	(1)	−30	− 1	+17	+ 1	0	−13	+17	−60	−13
		D₂	(2)	−12	−20	+ 1	+ 2	0	−29	− 9	−40	−29
		S₁	(3)	−12	− 6	+40	+ 4	0	+26	−14	+80	+26
		S₂	(4)	− 1	−10	+16	+10	0	+15	+ 5	+20	+15
		B	(5)	− 5	− 3	+ 6	+ 3	0	+ 1	+ 1	0	+ 1
	Domestic expenditure		(6)	−60	−40	+80	+20	0				
	Imports		(7)	−30	−20	+40	+10	0				

Case ii. In each country the marginal propensity to import is one half. Changes in imports happen to achieve full equilibrium for all countries

			D₁	D₂	S₁	S₂	B	National income	Exports	before	after
Increase (+) or decrease (−) in	receipts by	D₁	(8)	−30	0	+25	+ 5	0	0	+30	−60	0
		D₂	(9)	0	−20	+15	+ 5	0	0	+20	−40	0
		S₁	(10)	−25	−15	+40	0	0	0	−40	+80	0
		S₂	(11)	− 5	− 5	0	+10	0	0	−10	+20	0
		B	(12)	0	0	0	0	0	0	0	0	0
	Domestic expenditure		(13)	−60	−40	+80	+20	0				
	Imports		(14)	−30	−20	+40	+10	0				

Case iii. In each country the marginal propensity equals the average propensity to import from each other country

			D₁	D₂	S₁	S₂	B	National income	Exports	before	after
Increase (+) or decrease (−) in	receipts by	D₁	(15)	−52	0	+ 4	+ 1	0	−47	+ 5	−60	−47
		D₂	(16)	− 4	−30	0	+ 1	0	−33	− 3	−40	−33
		S₁	(17)	− 3	− 3	+70	+ 1	0	+65	− 5	+80	−65
		S₂	(18)	0	− 5	+ 4	+16	0	+15	− 1	+20	+15
		B	(19)	− 1	− 2	+ 2	+ 1	0	0	0	0	0
	Domestic expenditure		(20)	−60	−40	+80	+20	0				
	Imports		(21)	− 8	−10	+10	+ 4	0				

Case iv. In each country the marginal propensity to import is less than one half. Changes in imports happen to achieve equilibrium for one country (D₁)

			D₁	D₂	S₁	S₂	B	National income	Exports	before	after
Increase (+) or decrease (−) in	receipts by	D₁	(22)	−35	0	+30	+ 5	0	0	+35	−60	0
		D₂	(23)	−10	−25	+ 5	0	0	−30	− 5	−40	−30
		S₁	(24)	− 5	− 5	+45	0	0	+35	−10	+80	+35
		S₂	(25)	− 5	− 5	0	+15	0	+ 5	−10	+20	+ 5
		B	(26)	− 5	− 5	0	0	0	−10	−10	0	−10
	Domestic expenditure		(27)	−60	−40	+80	+20	0				
	Imports		(28)	−25	−15	+35	+ 5	0				

national income, exports, and balance of trade resulting from the changes in domestic expenditure given in row 6. If, for example, we add up the figures in columns a, b, c, d, and e of row 1 we obtain the net change in the demand for D_1's products, whether this demand is derived from home sources of demand (column a) or from export markets in D_2, S_1, S_2, or B (columns b, c, d, and e). The result is a net decline in demand for D_1's products of $13 m.; and the impact effect upon D_1's national income will, therefore, be $-$13 m., which is shown in column f of row 1. If we add up the figures in columns b, c, d, and e (i.e. row 1 excluding the diagonal figure in column a) we obtain the change in D_1's exports, and this figure of $+$17 m. is shown in column g of row 1.[1] Finally, D_1's balance of payments deficit which was originally $60 m. will have been improved to a deficit of only $13 m., because D_1's exports have risen by $17 m. (column g row 1) and her imports have declined by $30 m. (column a row 7). This change in D_1's balance of payments from $-$60 m. to $-$13 m., which results from the impact effect of the changes in domestic expenditures shown in row 6 of the table, is recorded in columns h and i of row 1. The figures in columns f, g, h, and i of rows 2, 3, 4, and 5 are derived in a similar manner.

The main result of case i of Table XX should be immediately apparent. In each country the marginal propensity to import is one-half; in the two-country case (case i of Table IX) this would have meant that the adjustments of domestic expenditure would have been sufficient to restore external balance and to maintain internal balance; but in our five-country case this is no longer so; the deficit countries (D_1 and D_2) are still in deficit and have suffered a deflation of their national incomes, while the surplus countries (S_1 and S_2) are still in surplus and have suffered an inflation of

---

[1] D_1's exports thus increase because the increased demand in S_1 and S_2 is greater than the decreased demand in D_2. But in the case of the other deficit country D_2, which sells heavily to D_1, and not so heavily to S_1 and S_2, there is a net *decline* of exports of $9 m. (column g row 2). Similarly while surplus country S_1 experiences a net decline in the demand for exports ($-$14 m. in column g row 3), the other surplus country S_2 experiences a net *increase* in the demand for her exports because S_1 is an important customer (column c row 4 of Table XVII). In case i of Table XX, although D_2's exports fall, nevertheless there is an improvement in D_2's balance of payments because D_2's imports fall still more. Similarly, S_2 experiences a larger rise in imports than in exports, so that S_2's surplus declines. But this need not be so. Suppose, for example, that purchasers in D_1 reduced their demand for D_2's products by $24 m. instead of by $12 m.—(they could do this if they restricted their demand for imports from S_1, S_2, and B by 2, 0, and 3 instead of 12, 1, and 5). Then D_2's exports would fall by $21 m. instead of by $9 m., and the fall in her exports would exceed the fall in her imports by $1 m. One of the deficit countries (D_2) would be in a worse deficit as a result of the adjustments of domestic expenditure, because the deflationary influence on her of the other deficit country (D_1) would be more marked than the combined inflationary effects of the surplus countries (S_1 and S_2).

their national incomes.[1] The result in fact corresponds to the two-country case in which the sum of the marginal propensities to import is less than unity (case iii of Table IX) and in which the deflation of domestic expenditure in the deficit country falls mainly on the deficit country's products (so that its income is severely deflated and its imports do not fall much) and the inflation of the domestic expenditure of the surplus country falls mainly on the surplus country's products (so that its national income rises a lot and its imports do not increase much).

It is easy to see why a situation in which all marginal propensities are equal to one-half in a many-country world should correspond to one in which they are all less than one-half in a two-country world. In Table XX we are in reality dealing with a lack of balance between two groups of countries, the deficit countries D_1 and D_2 on the one hand and the surplus countries S_1 and S_2 on the other hand. Now when domestic expenditure is deflated in D_1 importers in D_1 purchase less of D_2's products as well as less of S_1's and S_2's products. But it is only the reduction of imports into D_1 from S_1 and S_2 which helps to restore external balance. Whereas in the two-country case the whole of the reduced expenditure on imports in the deficit country will help to restore external balance by reducing the exports of the surplus country, in the many-country case it is only a reduction of imports in the deficit countries from surplus countries which helps to restore external balance. The reduction by $12 m. in case i of Table XX of D_1's imports from D_2 merely increases D_2's deficit. It will be seen that in D_1 and D_2 combined in case i of Table XX there is a fall of domestic expenditure of $100 m. and a reduction of total imports

---

[1] It is to be noted that throughout Table XX the figures in column f are the same as those in column i, or in other words that the effect of the changes in domestic expenditure upon a country's national income are exactly the same as the remaining deficit or surplus in that country's balance of payments. The reason is clear. The change in a country's national income = the increase in its domestic expenditure + the increase in its exports — the increase in its imports. Its remaining balance of payments = its initial balance of payments + the increase in its exports — the increase in its imports. But we are examining the results of increases of domestic expenditure which are *ex hypothesi* equal to the initial balance of payments. It follows, therefore, that the resulting change in a country's national income must be equal to its remaining balance of payments. This has a simple, but important, economic significance. As a result of the changes in case i of Table XX country D_1, for example, has suffered a fall of national income of $13 m. and has a remaining balance-of-payments deficit also of $13 m. A shift of demand away from foreign products on to D_1's products of $13 m. is required both to restore D_1's national income to its previous level (i.e. to restore internal balance) and also to remove the remaining balance of payments deficit (i.e. restore external balance). In fact columns f and i of case i of Table XX describe a situation in which a reshuffle of international demand on a given scale (i.e. $13 m. on to D_1's products, $29 m. on to D_2's, $26 m. from S_1's, $15 m. from S_2's, and $1 m. from B's) is required to secure the two objectives of internal and external balance for every country.

from all sources of \$50 m. (i.e. \$30 m.+\$20 m.); but there is a reduction of imports of only \$37 m. (i.e. \$12 m.+\$1 m.+\$5 m.+\$6 m.+\$10 m. +\$3 m.) from countries other than D_1 and D_2. In other words, while the marginal propensities to import in D_1 and D_2 separately are both 50 per cent, the marginal propensity of the deficit part of the world to import from the non-deficit part is only 37 per cent. Similarly, while S_1 and S_2 together have total additional imports from all sources including each other of \$50 m. (\$40 m.+\$10 m.), imports into the joint 'country' S_1-S_2 are only an additional \$30 m. (\$17 m.+\$1 m. +\$6 m.+\$1 m.+\$2 m.+\$3 m.) from the rest of the world when S_1-S_2's joint domestic expenditure rises by \$100 m.

The same point can also be observed by considering, not the relations between the deficit countries and the surplus countries, as is done above, but the relations between country D_1 on the one hand and the rest of the world, i.e. D_2-S_1-S_2-B, on the other. In case i of Table XX in D_1 the marginal propensity to import from D_2-S_1-S_2-B is 50 per cent; imports into D_1 go down by \$30 m. when domestic expenditure in D_1 goes down by \$60 m. But in the joint country D_2-S_1-S_2-B the marginal propensity to import from D_1 is only \$17 m./\$60 m. or 28 per cent; joint domestic expenditure in D_2-S_1-S_2-B goes up by \$60 m. (D_2's being down by \$40 m., S_1's up by \$80 m., S_2's up by \$20 m., and B's unchanged) and imports from D_1 go up by \$17 m. (D_2's imports from D_1 being down by \$1 m., S_1's up by \$17 m., S_2's up by \$1 m., and B's unchanged). Although the marginal propensity to import in each country from the rest of the world is 50 per cent, the sum of the marginal propensity to import into D_1 from D_2-S_1-S_2-B and of the marginal propensity to import into D_2-S_1-S_2-B from D_1 is less than one. In a many-country world each individual country must have a marginal propensity to import which averages more than one-half in order that the income effects which we are examining in this chapter should suffice to restore external balance without disturbing internal balance.

This conclusion is subject to one modification which is illustrated in case ii of Table XX. The marginal propensity to import into each country from the rest of the world is again equal to one-half as in case i of the table. But in this case purchasers in the deficit countries D_1 and D_2 happen to reduce their demand for imports only from the surplus countries S_1 and S_2 and not at all from each other; and similarly, purchasers in the surplus countries S_1 and S_2 happen to increase their demand for imports only from the deficit countries D_1 and D_2 and not at all from each other. In this case the deflation of domestic expenditure by \$100 m. in D_1-D_2 and its inflation by \$100 m. in S_1-S_2 would remove the deficit of \$100 m. of D_1-D_2 and the surplus of \$100 m. of S_1-S_2 without causing any change in the national incomes of D_1-D_2 or of S_1-S_2. In fact the figures are chosen in case ii so that an even more improbable and fortuitous result is achieved. Not only are the two joint countries D_1-D_2 and S_1-S_2 in internal and external balance as a result of the adjustments of domestic expenditure; but each of the individual countries D_1, D_2, S_1, and S_2 are separately in internal and external balance. That is to say, we have chosen figures so that the economies of D_2's purchasers on S_1's products and on S_2's products are so matched with the economies of D_1's purchasers on S_1's products and S_2's products that the total economy of D_1-D_2's purchasers on S_1's products just matches the increased demand of S_1's purchasers for S_1's products, and the total economy of D_1-D_2's purchasers on S_2's products just matches the increased demand of S_2's purchasers for S_2's products. The reader can appreciate the force of this additional condition by reversing, for example, the $-\$15$ m. of column b row 10 with the $-\$5$ m. of column b row 11. In this case S_1-S_2 jointly remains in internal and external equilibrium; but S_1's national income is now $+\$10$ m. and S_2's $-\$10$ m., and S_1's balance of payments is now $\$10$ m. in surplus and S_2's $\$10$ m. in deficit. Whereas D_1-D_2 and S_1-S_2 are again both in full equilibrium, the shift of demand in D_1-D_2 as a result of the deflation in D_1-D_2 has shifted demand too much away from S_2's products and too little away from S_1's products to give both S_1 and S_2 individually full internal and external balance.

Of course, case ii of Table XX is a most improbable fluke. In fact the marginal propensity to import in each country is likely to be less than one-half; and the change in each country's imports is likely to be spread over all other countries whether deficit or surplus. In case iii of the table we assume that, as before, the authorities in countries D_1, D_2, S_1, and S_2 adjust domestic expenditures (row 20) by the amounts necessary to offset the final change required in their balances of payments (column h). But in this case we assume that the changes in the demand in each country both for home-produced goods and services and also for the products imported from each foreign country are roughly in the same proportion as the original demands for home products and for those of each foreign country as shown in Table XVII.[1] In this case, which we may regard as the standard case, we find, as we should expect, that while the deflation of domestic expenditure in the deficit countries and its inflation in the surplus countries does something to reduce the balance-of-payments deficits of the former and surpluses of the latter, it leaves the greater part of these deficits and surpluses to be removed by other means. At the same time it necessarily means that the deflation of domestic expenditure in the deficit countries and its inflation in the surplus countries will cause a

---

[1] Thus $52 : 4 : 3 : 0 : 1$ (column a of case iii of Table XX) :: $1,000 : 65 : 60 : 5 : 25$ (column a of Table XVII) approximately.

marked deflation of national income in the former countries and inflation of national income in the latter. The further measures which are required to shift world demand away from the exports of the surplus countries to those of the deficit countries in the interests of external balance will also serve to maintain internal balance by restricting the total demand for the products of the former and expanding the total demand for the products of the latter.[1]

We shall, therefore, in the remaining chapters of Part VI assume that when the authorities in the deficit countries deflate their domestic expenditures by the amounts of the deficits in their balances of payments, and when the authorities in the surplus countries inflate their domestic expenditures similarly, the deflation of demand in the deficit countries affects mainly the demand for the home products of those countries and the inflation of demand in the surplus countries affects mainly the demand for the home products of those countries. It follows that, though something is achieved through these adjustments of domestic expenditure to expand the imports of the surplus countries and to contract those of the deficit countries and so to restore external balance, the greater part of the external disequilibrium needs other measures for its correction. And these other measures which will shift demand away from the products of the surplus on to those of the deficit countries will, in combination with the domestic 'policy' deflations and inflations of domestic expenditure which have occurred in the deficit and surplus countries respectively, serve to preserve internal as well as external balance.

Table XXI illustrates the position at which we have now arrived. The figures in columns a to e of this table are those of columns a to e of Table XVII with the additions or subtractions shown in columns a to e of case iii of Table XX. In other words we have taken our

---

[1] Case iv of Table XX shows one more special case in the many-country world. In this case the marginal propensity to import is less than one-half in every individual country. In the two-country world, therefore (case iii of Table IX), the deficit country would remain in deficit with a fall in its income and the surplus country would remain in surplus with a rise in its income. But that is not necessarily true of each individual country in the many-country world. In case iv of Table XX the adjustments of domestic expenditure suffice just to put D_1 into external balance and to maintain internal balance in D_1 even though all marginal propensities to import are less than one-half. The clue to the riddle is that although the marginal propensities to import in D_2, S_1, and S_2 are all less than one-half (being $\frac{15}{40}$, $\frac{35}{80}$, and $\frac{5}{20}$ respectively), the marginal propensity to import from D_1 in the joint country D_2-S_1-S_2 is greater than one-half, being $\frac{35}{60}$. This is so because purchasers in D_2 (who have to reduce their imports) reduce them from S_1 and S_2 but not at all from D_1, whereas purchasers in S_1 and S_2 (who have to increase their imports) increase them almost exclusively from D_1. The combined marginal propensity to import in D_2-S_1-S_2 from all sources including D_2, S_1, and S_2 is only $\frac{25}{60}$ (i.e. $\frac{-15+35+5}{-40+80+20}$), but the marginal propensity to import in D_2-S_1-S_2 from D_1 is $\frac{35}{60}$ (i.e. $\frac{0+30+5}{-40+80+20}$).

original position; we have then supposed that in the interests of internal balance the authorities in each deficit country deflate, and in each surplus country inflate, domestic expenditure in their own country by an amount equal to the favourable or unfavourable movement in their balance of trade which is required to restore external balance; and we have then recorded in the new table the levels of demand for the products of each country which result from the impact effects of these changes in domestic expenditure. Columns f and g of Table XXI are obtained in the usual manner by adding up for each row the figures in the previous columns first including, and then excluding, the diagonal figure. Column h shows the difference between the export figure of column g and the import figure of row 7. The transfer payments in column i are taken over directly from column g of section ii of Table XVIII; or in other words, we are assuming that the financial policies employed to bring about the necessary adjustments of domestic expenditure do not make any difference to the volume of autonomous transfer payments between the countries. This assumption we make purely for purposes of simplification; it does not profoundly modify the analysis. We are left in column j of Table XXI with a figure which is the sum of the figures in columns h and i and which represents the deficit or surplus of the country's balance of payments

TABLE XXI

National Incomes and Balances of Trade and Payments after the Adjustment of Domestic Expenditures $ m.

| | | Payments for autonomous trade by | | | | | National income | Exports | Deficit (−) or surplus (+) on balance of autonomous | | |
		D_1 (a)	D_2 (b)	S_1 (c)	S_2 (d)	B (e)	(f)	(g)	trade (h)	trans-fers (i)	pay-ments (j)
Receipts from autonomous trade by	D_1 (1)	948	8	60	17	5	1038	90	−57	+10	−47
	D_2 (2)	61	470	5	24	12	572	102	−53	+20	−33
	S_1 (3)	57	44	1070	41	83	1295	225	+80	−15	+65
	S_2 (4)	5	77	57	516	5	660	144	+30	−15	+15
	B (5)	24	26	23	32	700	805	105	0	0	0
Domestic expenditure	(6)	1095	625	1215	630	805					
Imports	(7)	147	155	145	114	105					

which remains after these adjustments of domestic expenditure have been made.

Let us briefly recapitulate the main points about the position of each country in the original position (Tables XVII and XVIII) and in the new position (Table XXI). This we will do by considering country D_1; the same principles would, of course, apply to all the other countries. In the original position D_1 had a balance of payments deficit of $60 m. (column g section iii of Table XVIII); the authorities in D_1, therefore, deflate domestic expenditure in D_1 by $60 m. because ultimately her balance of trade must improve by $60 m. and domestic expenditure in D_1 must be deflated by this same amount to preserve internal balance (the figure in column a row 6 of Table XXI is $60 m. less than in column a row 6 of Table XVII); this reduction in expenditure is spread *pro rata* over all demands for home products and for imports (the figures in column a of Table XVII are all reduced in approximately the same ratio to obtain those of column a of Table XXI); taking into account also the effects on D_1's exports of similar adjustments of domestic expenditures in D_2, S_1, and S_2 (see the figures in columns b to d of row 1 in Tables XVII and XVIII), we obtain new figures for D_1's national income, exports, balance of trade, and balance of payments (columns f, g, h, i, and j of Table XXI); as a result, D_1's balance of payments has improved from $-$60 m. to $-$47 m. between section iii of Table XVIII and Table XXI; but D_1's national income has also fallen by $47 m. from $1,085 m. to $1,038 m. between Tables XVIII and XXI. In other words, the increase of $47 m. in the demand for D_1's products in preference to those of D_2, S_1, S_2, or B which is still required to restore external balance to D_1 is now also required to restore internal balance to D_1.

In what follows we shall take Table XXI as the arithmetical illustration of the position with which we have to deal. It is one in which we require a shift of international demand ($47 m. on to D_1's products, $33 m. on to D_2's products, $65 m. away from S_1's products, and $15 m. away from S_2's products) for the twofold purpose of achieving simultaneously internal and external balance for each country. We turn now to a consideration of the various ways in which this shift of demand might be brought about.

CHAPTER XXVII

MULTILATERAL PRICE ADJUSTMENTS

WE have reached the following stage in the process of world readjustment of the balance of payments. All our countries started in internal balance, but they were not in external balance; D_1 and D_2 were in deficit and S_1 and S_2 in surplus on their balances of payments; thereupon the authorities in D_1 and D_2 adopted policies of deflation, and those in S_1 and S_2 policies of inflation, for their domestic expenditures in order to preserve internal balance when the balances of trade of the former were increased and of the latter decreased; this caused some deflation of the national incomes of D_1 and D_2 and some inflation of those of S_1 and S_2 and it also caused some increase in the balances of trade of D_1 and D_2 and some decrease in the balances of trade of S_1 and S_2; but these changes in balances of trade were not sufficient completely to restore external balance; a shift of international demand from the products of S_1 and S_2 on to those of D_1 and D_2 is still required both to restore internal balance by deflating again somewhat the national incomes of S_1 and S_2 and inflating those of D_1 and D_2 and also to achieve complete external balance by still further increasing the balances of trade and payments of D_1 and D_2 and decreasing those of S_1 and S_2.

This further shift of international demand away from the products of S_1 and S_2 on to those of D_1 and D_2 might be brought about by the methods of price adjustment which we have discussed at some length in Part IV for the case of the two-country world. As we have seen there, price adjustment may occur through either of two mechanisms.

In the first place, the deflation of the total money national income in D_1 and D_2 which results from the 'policy' deflation of domestic expenditure in those countries represents a net decrease in the total money demand for the products of these countries; this will cause some reduction in output and some growth of unemployment; this reduction in the demand for labour may cause a reduction in the money wage rate and so in money costs and prices in countries D_1 and D_2. Conversely, the inflation of total money demand for the products of S_1 and S_2 may result in a rise in money wage rates, costs, and prices in those countries. As a result D_1's and D_2's products will become cheaper relatively to S_1's and S_2's products. This will cause a shift of international demand away from the more expensive products of S_1 and S_2 on to the cheaper products of D_1 and D_2; and if this shift is on a sufficient scale it will cause a net increase in money expenditure on

D_1's and D_2's products and a net decrease in the money expenditure on S_1's and S_2's products. Thus the balances of trade and the national incomes of D_1 and D_2 will be increased; and simultaneously the balances of trade and the national incomes of S_1 and S_2 will be reduced. This is what we have called the gold-standard mechanism for restoring internal and external balance.

But, in the second place, the price adjustment may be achieved not by an adjustment of domestic money wage rates and costs in D_1, D_2, S_1, and S_2 but by an adjustment of the rates of exchange between their currencies. As we have argued in the last chapter, even after the preliminary downward adjustments of domestic expenditure in the deficit countries D_1 and D_2 and the upward adjustments in S_1 and S_2 there will—in the normal case—remain a deficit on the balances of payments of D_1 and D_2 and a surplus on those of S_1 and S_2. In the foreign exchange market there will remain an excess demand for the currencies of S_1 and S_2 and an excess supply of the currencies of D_1 and D_2. If there is a free exchange market the values of D_1's and D_2's currencies will fall in terms of the currencies of S_1 and S_2. But this will make D_1's and D_2's products cheaper relatively to S_1's and S_2's. As a result international demand will shift away from S_1's and S_2's products on to those of D_1 and D_2; and if any given change in relative prices causes a sufficiently extensive shift of demand, the total money expenditure on D_1's and D_2's products will rise and that on S_1's and S_2's products will fall. This is the variable-exchange-rate mechanism for the restoration of internal and external balance.

In what follows in this chapter we shall confine ourselves to a discussion of the variable-exchange-rate mechanism for the restoration of equilibrium in a many-country world. We shall not repeat those points which have already been made in Part IV on the subject of this mechanism, but shall confine ourselves to the new points which arise in the working of this mechanism when there are more than two countries. In fact these new points arise whether the gold-standard mechanism or the variable-exchange-rate mechanism is adopted. The reader is, however, left to himself after reading the present chapter to apply them to the gold-standard mechanism by means of the general comparison between the gold-standard mechanism and the variable-exchange-rate mechanism which has already been made in Chapter XV.

In order to consider the effect of exchange-rate variations on the balances of trade of the various countries in our many-country world, we must decide which currency we are going to use as the unit of measurement for the balances of trade and payments. When exchange rates are fixed it does not matter in what money we measure balances of trade and payments, since there is a fixed rate of conversion into every other national currency. But when exchange rates between national currencies are varied it does matter in what currency balances of trade and payments are measured; and it is most important to fix on a particular currency as the unit of measurement and to stick to it for all countries at all stages of the problem.

The reason for this may be made clear by means of an example. Suppose D_1 to have a deficit of \$100 m. and S_1 to have a surplus of \$100 m. in the original position; and suppose that the D_1–currency is a D_1–dollar or \$$D_1$ and the S_1–currency is a S_1–dollar or \$$S_1$. Suppose that in the original position the D_1–dollar is at parity with the S_1–dollar so that \$$D_1 1 = $ \$$S_1 1$ and D_1's deficit which equals S_1's surplus is \$$D_1 100$ m. or \$$S_1 100$ m. Suppose then that D_1's dollar depreciates by 10 per cent and S_1's dollar appreciates by 10 per cent in terms of gold so that \$$D_1 1·1 = $ \$$S_1 0·9$. Suppose that as a result of this D_1's deficit and S_1's surplus in terms of S_1's currency moves from \$$S_1 100$ m. to \$$S_1 95$ m.; then in terms of D_1's currency it will have moved from \$$D_1 100$ m. to \$$D_1 116\frac{1}{9}$ m. (i.e. \$$S_1 95$ m. $\times \frac{1·1}{0·9}$ in order to convert the S_1–dollars into D_1–dollars). In other words in this special case while D_1's deficit will have fallen from \$$S_1 100$ m. to \$$S_1 95$ m. in terms of foreign currency it will have risen from \$$D_1 100$ m. to \$$D_1 116\frac{1}{9}$ in terms of the home currency.

In what follows, purely for purposes of convenience, we shall take B's currency or \$B as our unit of measurement. B is a country which starts in external balance. We shall assume that the currencies of the deficit countries D_1 and D_2 depreciate in terms of B's currency and that the currencies of the surplus countries S_1 and S_2 appreciate in terms of B's currency; and we shall measure every country's balance of trade and payments in terms of B's currency.

Our first task is to consider in very general terms the sort of influences which will be at work raising or lowering the value (in terms of B's currency) of the imports and of the exports of each of our five countries when D_1's and D_2's currencies have depreciated and S_1's and S_2's appreciated in terms of B's. These influences are illustrated in Table XXII.

Let us consider the factors affecting the value (in terms of B's currency) of imports into D_1 from D_2 (column a row 2 of Table XXII) when D_1's and D_2's currencies are both depreciated in terms of B's currency. Consider first the effect of the depreciation of the currency of D_2, the exporting country. Here there is a twofold effect: first, the value of imports into D_1 from D_2 tends to fall in so far as purchasers in D_1 can now purchase the same amount from D_2 at a lower price in terms of B's currency (this is the meaning of the first sign—a minus—in column a row 2); but, secondly, the quantity of goods which purchasers in D_1 purchase from D_2 will tend to rise because the deprecia-

TABLE XXII

The General Effect of Exchange-Rate Variations upon the Network of Trade

Case i. The General Case

Exporting Countries		D_1 (a)	D_2 (b)	S_1 (c)	S_2 (d)	B (e)
	D_1 (1)	╲	− + −	− + +	− + +	− + ·
	D_2 (2)	− + −	╲	− + +	− + +	− + ·
	S_1 (3)	+ − −	+ − −	╲	+ − +	+ − ·
	S_2 (4)	+ − −	+ − −	+ − +	╲	+ − ·
	B (5)	· −	· −	· · +	· · +	╲

Case ii. All Elasticities of Demand equal to One

Exporting Countries		D_1 (a)	D_2 (b)	S_1 (c)	S_2 (d)	B (e)
	D_1 (6)	╲	· −	· +	· +	· ·
	D_2 (7)	· −	╲	· +	· +	· ·
	S_1 (8)	· −	· −	╲	· +	· ·
	S_2 (9)	· −	· −	· +	╲	· ·
	B (10)	· −	· −	· +	· +	╲

Case iii. All Elasticities of Demand greater than One

Exporting Countries		D_1 (a)	D_2 (b)	S_1 (c)	S_2 (d)	B (e)
	D_1 (11)	╲	+ −	+ +	+ +	+ ·
	D_2 (12)	+ −	╲	+ +	+ +	+ ·
	S_1 (13)	− −	− −	╲	− +	− ·
	S_2 (14)	− −	− −	− +	╲	− ·
	B (15)	· −	· −	· +	· +	╲

Case iv. All Elasticities of Demand less than One

Exporting Countries		D_1 (a)	D_2 (b)	S_1 (c)	S_2 (d)	B (e)
	D_1 (16)	╲	− −	− +	− +	− ·
	D_2 (17)	− −	╲	− +	− +	− ·
	S_1 (18)	+ −	+ −	╲	+ +	+ ·
	S_2 (19)	+ −	+ −	+ +	╲	+ ·
	B (20)	· −	· −	· +	· +	╲

tion of D_2's currency will tend to lower the price of D_2's products in terms of D_1's currency (this is the meaning of the second sign—a plus— in column a row 2). These two signs may be considered together. If the elasticity of demand in D_1 for D_2's products is greater than unity, then the fall in the price of D_2's products in terms of B's currency will cause purchasers in D_1 to buy so much more in quantity that their total expenditure on D_2's products will rise in terms of B's currency; or, in other words, the first sign in column a row 2 will be outweighed by the second. If the elasticity of demand in D_1 for D_2's products is less than unity, then when the price of D_2's products declines purchasers in D_1 will buy little more in quantity; and the first sign in column a row 2 will outweigh the second. So far we have considered only the influence of the depreciation of D_2's currency in terms of B's currency; but we must now consider the influence of the depreciation of D_1's currency in terms of B's currency. This will tend to raise the price of D_2's products in terms of D_1's currency; and this in turn will tend to cause imports into D_1 from D_2 to fall in quantity and so in value in terms of B's currency (this is the meaning of the third sign—a minus—in column a row 2).[1]

If we consider the demand by any country for the products of any other country, we have then three influences to take into account: first, the fact that the price of the imports in B's currency will have fallen (or risen) as a result of the depreciation (or appreciation) of the *exporting* country's currency; second, the fact that the quantity of the imports will have risen (or fallen) as a result of the depreciation (or appreciation) of the *exporting* country's currency; and thirdly the fact that the quantity of the imports will have fallen (or risen) as a result of the depreciation (or appreciation) of the importing country's currency.[2] In each compartment of case i of Table XXII the three signs show the direction of these three influences: first, the direct influence of the change in the price of the products in question due to the change of the exporting country's currency in terms of B's currency; secondly, the influence of this price change upon the quantity of trade; and thirdly. the influence of the adjustment of the importing country's exchange rate in terms of B's currency upon the quantity of trade.

---

[1] The third sign will outweigh the first and second signs or vice versa according as D_1's or D_2's currency depreciates the more in terms of B_2's currency.

[2] This is, of course, a great simplification. It entirely leaves out of account the fact that the quantity of the imports may change as a result of an adjustment in the exchange rate of a third country, whose products will thus be made more or less expensive and may be specially competitive with or complementary to the products of the exporting country under consideration. We omit these considerations in Table XXII but shall refer to them later. At the moment we consider the demand in D_1 for D_2's products to depend only upon the price of D_2's products relative to that of D_1's and not at all upon the price of S_1's products; and so on.

We will next consider three special cases of these influences (cases ii, iii, and iv of Table XXII). Our special cases are distinguished according as the demand in each importing country for the products of each exporting country has an elasticity equal to, greater than, or less than unity, i.e. according as a depreciation of the currency of the exporting country in terms of B's currency causes so moderate, so large, or so small an increase in the quantity demanded in the importing country that the total value in terms of B's currency of the product imported remains the same, increases, or decreases. If the elasticities of demand are equal to unity, then the first two signs in each compartment of case i of Table XXII cancel out and we have the position shown in case ii. If the elasticities of demand are greater than unity, the first (price) sign in each compartment is weaker than the second (quantity) sign and we have the position shown in case iii; and conversely for case iv.

In case ii it will be seen that the value (in terms of B's currency) of the imports of both deficit countries go down from every source and that the value (in terms of B's currency) of their exports go up to every destination except that they are unchanged to the balanced country B and go down to the other deficit country. In all there are six factors favourable to an increase in their balance of trade (a reduction of imports from all four other countries and an expansion of exports to the two surplus countries) and only one unfavourable factor (a reduction of exports to the other deficit country). Clearly the adjustments are likely to lead to an improvement of each deficit country's balance of payments.

And similarly for the surplus countries. Each surplus country experiences an increase in its imports from each of the other four countries and a reduction of its exports to both of the deficit countries. The only factor tending to increase the surplus of a surplus country is the increase of its exports to the other surplus country. Thus the adjustments are likely to lead to a reduction in the surplus of each of the surplus countries.

Moreover, if one considers the relations between the two deficit countries in combination on the one hand and the two surplus countries in combination on the other hand, i.e. of the payments of the 'country' D_1-D_2 with the 'country' S_1-S_2, there is bound to be a reduction in the joint deficit of the former with the latter. This can be seen from considering the two joint compartments in case ii of Table XXII which are distinguished by heavily printed boundary lines: namely, on the one hand, the joint compartment made up of columns a and b and rows 8 and 9 which shows that purchasers in both D_1 and D_2 reduce their imports from both S_1 and S_2, and, on the other hand, the joint compartment made up of columns c and d and rows 6 and 7 which shows that purchasers in both S_1 and S_2 increase their imports from both D_1

and D_2. The balance of trade between the deficit half of the world, i.e. D_1-D_2, and the surplus half of the world, i.e. S_1-S_2, is bound to improve. The change could increase the deficit of one deficit country e.g. D_1) only if the one unfavourable factor (i.e. the fall in D_1's exports to D_2) was so great as to outweigh all the favourable factors (i.e. the reduced imports into D_1 from D_2, S_1, S_2 and B and the increased exports from D_1 to S_1 and S_2). But in this case the reduction in D_2's imports from D_1 (which is only one of the six factors favourable to D_2's balance of payments) would in itself be greater than D_1's reduced imports from D_2 (which is the only factor unfavourable to D_2). In other words, in the unlikely case of there being a net decrease in D_1's balance of trade there would necessarily be an even greater net increase in D_2's balance of trade. And similarly, if in case ii of Table XXII one of the surplus countries should experience a net increase in its balance of trade the other would necessarily experience an even greater decrease.

In case iii, where the elasticities of demand are all greater than unity, the probability that every deficit country will experience an increase, and every surplus country a decrease, in its balance of trade is even more marked. Thus there are now no less than twelve factors favourable to the balance of trade of each deficit country (or unfavourable to that of each surplus country) and only two factors working in the opposite direction. For example, the value of D_1's imports from B will be reduced on one ground and from S_1 and S_2 on two grounds each; the value of D_1's exports to B will be increased on one ground and to S_1 and S_2 on two grounds each. It is only D_1's trade with the other deficit country D_2 which is in doubt; and in this instance there is one factor increasing and one factor decreasing both D_1's imports from and D_1's exports to D_2. It is only in a very special case indeed that there would be a net deterioration in D_1's balance of payments.[1] Once again it can be seen from the two heavily lined areas in case iii that the balance of trade of the deficit countries jointly with the surplus countries jointly will certainly be improved.

Case iv of Table XXII shows the case where the exchange rate adjustments might have the perverse effects of increasing the deficit of each deficit country and the surplus of each surplus country. In this case each deficit (or surplus) country is subject to seven influences diminishing and to seven influences increasing its deficit (or surplus).

[1] Such a case might arise, for example, if D_2 was D_1's main source of supply, if D_2's products were close substitutes for D_1's products in D_1's market, if D_2's currency depreciated by more than D_1's currency, and if D_2 also provided D_1's main export market. Then the fact that the prices of D_2's products fall relatively to those of D_1's (because D_2's depreciation was greater than D_1's) might cause a considerable net increase in the value of D_1's imports from all sources; and the fact that D_1's products went up in price relatively to D_2's in D_2's market might cause an appreciable net fall in D_1's total exports.

If the elasticities of demand are sufficiently small, the depreciation of the currencies of the deficit countries and the appreciation of the currencies of the surplus countries might have a perverse effect upon the whole network of world payments.

Thus consider the signs in column a row 18 of Table XXII. If the elasticity of demand in D_1 for S_1's products is very small the first sign in this compartment may be a large plus, because the rise in the price in B's currency of S_1's products due to the appreciation of S_1's currency may not be offset by any appreciable diminution in the amount bought in D_1. And for the same reason the second sign in this compartment would be a very small minus, because the further rise in the price of S_1's products in terms of D_1's currency due to the depreciation of D_1's currency would, in these circumstances, cause hardly any decline in the quantity imported into D_1. In circumstances of this kind the net signs in columns a and b rows 18 and 19 might all be important pluses and the net signs in columns c and d rows 16 and 17 might all be important minuses. The exchange-rate adjustments would have caused the value of the deficit countries' imports from the surplus countries to have risen and the value of their exports to those countries to have fallen. The fundamental world lack of balance would have been worsened. And it would be quite possible, indeed probable, that in such circumstances each individual deficit country's deficit and each individual surplus country's surplus would increase as a result of the changes in exchange rates.

But it must not, of course, be concluded from this that with case iv of Table XXII there is necessarily this type of perverse effect. If the elasticities of demand were only a little less than unity, then the first sign would be weaker than the second sign in each of the compartments. We should be back nearly to case ii with its favourable outcome. To obtain a perverse result it is not sufficient that the elasticities of demand should be less than unity; they must be very considerably less than unity.[1]

The preceding discussion may serve as an introduction to some of the more important factors determining the effect of exchange-rate adjustments in a many-country world. But it must now be supplemented in certain very important ways. We have spoken so far of all elasticities of demand being large or small simultaneously. But in the real world some may be large and others small. Moreover, the amount which purchasers in D_1 buy from D_2 may depend not only on the prices of D_1's and D_2's products but also upon the prices of S_1's, S_2's, and B's products. Thus if D_2's products are close substitutes for S_1's products (e.g. both

---

[1] Compare the rule in the two-country world that the sum of the elasticities of demand for imports in the two countries must be less than unity in order to obtain a perverse result.

D_2 and S_1 export cereals) a rise in the price of S_1's products is likely to cause not only a reduction of imports into D_1 from S_1 but also an increase of imports into D_1 from D_2. But if D_2's products are needed jointly with S_1's (e.g. if S_1 produces iron ore which is required with D_2's coal to produce steel) then a rise in the price of S_1's products may cause purchasers in D_1 to reduce their demand for imports from D_2 as well as for imports from S_1

It would be quite impossible to give anything approaching a complete picture of the possibilities which arise in a world of many countries with some countries importing primarily from some, but exporting primarily to other countries, with elasticities of demand varying from instance to instance, and with complicated relationships of competition and of complementarity between the exports of the various countries. All that can be done is to take one or two special instances.

For this purpose we shall give two numerical examples of the effects of exchange-rate adjustments. These examples are both based upon the following assumptions. We start from the position shown in Table XXI (p. 355); that is to say, we assume that the adjustments of domestic expenditure which will ultimately be needed to preserve internal balance have already been made. We measure all changes in the value of imports and exports and so in the balances of trade and payments in terms of B's currency, and we assume that the currencies of deficit countries are depreciated in terms of B's currency and those of surplus countries appreciated in terms of B's currency. We assume, purely for the purposes of convenience, that the transfer payments between the countries are unaffected by exchange-rate variations and remain unchanged in terms of B's currency at the figures shown in column i of Table XXI. The purpose of our examples is to see in what conditions exchange-rate adjustments on these lines will lead to a reduction to zero of all the deficits and surpluses on the balances of payments shown in column j of Table XXI.[1]

---

[1] We have shown above (pp. 353–4) why the reduction of these balances to zero will in the general case restore internal and external balance to every country. But this is not strictly accurate when the method of restoring equilibrium is that of exchange-rate adjustment. Consider the position of country D_1 in its original position of internal and external disequilibrium as shown in Table XVII, where D_1's national income of \$1,085 m. equalled a domestic expenditure of \$1,155 m. less a balance-of-trade deficit of \$70 m. Let us suppose that D_1's currency (\$D_1$) is depreciated by 20 per cent in terms of B's currency (\$B), so that in the new position $\$D_1 1 \times \frac{80}{100} = \$B1$, and that this serves to remove the disequilibrium in the balance of payments. Then we know that in the new position of full internal and external balance, (i) D_1's national income will remain $\$D_1 1,085$ m. in order to maintain internal balance in D_1 so that (ii) it will be equal in value to \$B868 m.; but (iii) D_1's balance of trade will in the new position be equal to $-\$B10$ m., since transfers of \$B10 m. are still made to D_1 so that (iv) D_1's domestic expenditure will be \$B878 m. (i.e. D_1's national income plus D_1's balance of trade deficit) so that (v) D_1's domestic expenditure

Our first numerical example is shown in Table XXIII. In this case we assume that the products of each country are reasonably good substitutes for the products of every other country; and in this case, as can be seen from the table, the method of exchange-rate adjustment will readily restore equilibrium.

In our example, country D_1 starts with a deficit of \$47 m. (column g row 1 of Table XXIII). Let us suppose that D_1's currency is depreciated by an amount sufficient to remove this deficit as shown in adjustment i of the table. The depreciation of D_1's currency raises the price of D_2's, S_1's, S_2's, and B's products in D_1's currency as a result of which purchasers in D_1 buy a smaller amount of each of these countries' products and so spend less on each of them in terms of B's currency (column a rows 1 to 5). As a result of the depreciation of D_1's currency the price of D_1's products falls in terms of B's currency and so in terms of D_1's, S_1's, and S_2's currencies also; and as a result of this purchasers in D_2, S_1, S_2, and B purchase more of D_1's products. Moreover, since D_1's products are fairly readily substitutable for D_2's, S_1's, S_2's, and B's products, purchasers in these latter countries expand their imports of D_1's products quite substantially when the price of D_1's products falls moderately, so that the value in terms of B's currency of their purchases from D_1 goes up (columns b, c, d, and e of row 1). But, since D_1's products are good substitutes for S_1's, S_2's, and B's products as well as for D_2's, purchasers in D_2 not only buy considerably more of D_1's products when the prices of D_1's products fall in D_2's currency but they also purchase somewhat less of S_1's, S_2's, and B's products which they give up for the cheaper products of D_1 (column b rows 3, 4, and 5) ; and purchasers in S_1, S_2

---

converted into D_1 will be $D_1 1,097\frac{1}{2}$ m. and (vi) D_1's balance of trade deficit will be $D_1 12\frac{1}{2}$ m. These changes can be set out thus :

	National Income $m.	=	Domestic Expenditure $m.	+	Trade Balance $m.
Original Position					
D_1 or $B	1,085	=	1,155		−70
New Position $D_1	1,085	=	1,097\frac{1}{2}		−12\frac{1}{2}
New Position $B	868	=	878		−10

In other words, D_1's domestic expenditure in terms of D_1's currency has to be reduced only by $D_1 57\frac{1}{2}$ m. (from $D_1 1,155$ m. to $D_1 1,097\frac{1}{2}$ m.) instead of by $D_1 60$ m. (from $D_1 1,155$ m. to $D_1 1,095$ m.) as has been done between Tables XVII and XXI. The reason for this is apparent. Since D_1 receives certain transfers fixed in \$B, her balance of trade can remain more adverse in terms of D_1 when the D_1 depreciates in terms of \$B than when other methods of adjustment are employed. And, as a result, in order to maintain internal balance domestic expenditure in D_1 needs to be somewhat less deflated in terms of D_1 when the method of exchange depreciation is employed, so that the adjustments of domestic expenditures shown in Table XX are no longer strictly accurate. But if either the extent of the depreciation or the total amount of transfers fixed in terms of \$B are not very great this consideration is of secondary importance—as it is in fact in the above numerical example—and will be neglected in what follows.

TABLE XXIII

The Effect of Exchange-Rate Variations. Case I. High Substitutability between all Products

$B m.

		Increase (+) or decrease (−) in trade payments by					total exports	Deficit (−) or surplus (+) on balance of payments before | after the change	
		D_1	D_2	S_1	S_2	B			
		(a)	(b)	(c)	(d)	(e)	(f)	(g)	(h)
Adjustment i. Depreciation of D_1's Exchange Rate									
Increase (+) or decrease (−) in trade receipts by	D_1 (1)		+ 6	+ 6	+6	+6	+24	−47	0
	D_2 (2)	− 6		− 1	−1	−1	− 9	−33	−45
	S_1 (3)	− 6	− 1		−1	−1	− 9	+65	+53
	S_2 (4)	− 5	− 1	− 1		−1	− 8	+15	+ 4
	B (5)	− 6	− 1	− 1	−1		− 9	0	−12
total imports	(6)	−23	+ 3	+ 3	+3	−3	World disequilibrium falls from 80 to 57.		
Adjustment ii. Depreciation of D_2's Exchange Rate									
Increase (+) or decrease (−) in trade receipts by	D_1 (7)		− 6	− 1	−1	−1	− 9	0	−12
	D_2 (8)	+ 6		+ 6	+6	+5	+23	−45	0
	S_1 (9)	− 1	− 5		−1	−1	− 8	+53	+42
	S_2 (10)	− 1	− 6	− 1		−1	− 9	+ 4	− 8
	B (11)	− 1	− 5	− 1	−1		− 8	−12	−22
total imports	(12)	+ 3	−22	+ 3	+3	+2	World disequilibrium falls from 57 to 42.		
Adjustment iii. Appreciation of S_1's Exchange Rate									
Increase (+) or decrease (−) in trade receipts by	D_1 (13)		+ 1	+ 6	+1	+1	+ 9	−12	0
	D_2 (14)	+ 1		+ 5	+1	+1	+ 8	0	+10
	S_1 (15)	− 6	− 5		−5	−5	−21	+42	0
	S_2 (16)	+ 1	+ 1	+ 5		+1	+ 8	− 8	+ 2
	B (17)	+ 1	+ 1	+ 5	+1		+ 8	−22	−12
total imports	(18)	− 3	− 2	+21	−2	−2	World disequilibrium falls from 42 to 12.		

and B also purchase somewhat less from D_2, S_1, S_2, and B for the same reason (columns c, d, and e rows 2, 3, 4, and 5).

The result of this adjustment is that D_1's deficit of \$B47 m. disappears; but it is passed on to D_2, S_1, S_2, and B more or less equally. In consequence D_2's deficit is increased by \$B12 m. from \$B33 m. to \$B45 m.; and B which was previously in balance now has a deficit of \$B12 m. To this extent (i.e. \$B24 m.) D_1's deficit has been merely added to the deficits of D_2 and B. But the remainder of D_1's deficit (namely \$B23 m.) has been passed on to the surplus countries S_1 and S_2 and has resulted in a reduction of their surpluses, so that to this extent the adjustment has really removed the disequilibrium in world payments.

Adjustment ii of Table XXIII shows what happens when the authorities in D_2, whose deficit has been raised from \$B33 m. to \$B45 m. by D_1's depreciation, in turn depreciate D_2's currency on a scale sufficient to remove this deficit in D_2's balance of payments. As a result of the fall in the price of D_2's products in terms of the currencies of all the other countries and of the rise in the price of the products of all the other countries in terms of D_2's currency, (i) the value of imports into D_2 from each of the other countries falls in terms of B's currency (column b rows 7, 9, 10, and 11), (ii) the value of exports from D_2 to each of the other countries rises in terms of B's currency because their volume increases more than their price falls (columns a, c, d, and e row 8), and (iii) the value of imports into each of the other countries from each of the other countries falls slightly as demand shifts on to the purchase of D_2's competing products (columns a, c, d, and e rows 7, 9, 10, and 11). The net result is that D_2's deficit of \$B45 m. is shifted in more or less equal parts on to D_1, S_1, S_2, and B—namely: \$B12 m. on to D_1, \$B11 m. on to S_1, \$B12 m. on to S_2, and \$B10 m. on to B. The \$B11 m. which is shifted on to S_1 and \$B4 m. of the \$B12 m. which is shifted on to S_2 serve to reduce existing surpluses and thus to reduce by \$B15 m. the total disequilibrium of world payments. But the \$B12 m. which is shifted on to D_1, the \$B10 m. which is shifted on to B, and \$B8 m. of the \$B12 m. which is shifted on to S_2 merely increases the deficits of other countries which are already in deficit or puts a country which was in balance into deficit.

But now in adjustment iii the authorities of country S_1, which is still in surplus to the extent of \$B42 m., appreciate S_1's currency on a scale sufficient to remove this surplus. As a result, (i) imports into S_1 from D_1, D_2, S_2, and B all go up in volume and so in value in terms of B's currency, because their price is lower in terms of S_1's currency (column c rows 13, 14, 16, and 17); (ii) the imports of D_1, D_2, S_2, and B from S_1 all go down in volume more than they rise in price in terms of B's currency so that their value in terms of B's currency falls (columns a, b, d, and e row 15); and (iii) the imports of each of the other countries from each of the other countries rise somewhat in volume and so in value in terms of B's currency as these countries shift their demand on to each other's products away from S_1's more expensive products (columns a, b, d, and e rows 13, 14, 16, and 17). The result is that S_1's surplus of \$B42 m. is shifted in more or less equal parts on to D_1, D_2, S_2, and B. The shift of \$B12 m. on to D_1 removes D_1's deficit of \$B12 m.; the shift of \$B10 m. on to B reduces B's deficit by \$B10 m.; and \$B8 m. of the shift of \$B10 m. on to S_2 removes S_2's deficit of \$B8 m. Thus \$B30 m. of the reduction of \$B42 m. in S_1's surplus is matched by a reduction of the deficits of other countries; and to this extent the world disequilibrium in balances of payments is reduced. The remainder of the shift merely causes a new surplus of \$B10 m. to appear on D_1's balance of payments and of \$B2 m. on S_2's.

The next adjustment would be for the authorities D_2 to appreciate D_2's exchange rate somewhat so as to remove her surplus of \$B10 m. In other words, the depreciation of D_2's currency carried out in adjustment ii of the table now turns out to have been somewhat too large, because of the subsequent favourable effect of the appreciation of S_1's currency in adjustment iii. This appreciation of D_2's currency would tend to reduce B's deficit somewhat, but to raise S_2's surplus and to produce small surpluses for D_1 and S_1. But it is clear that the process of exchange adjustment is, in the conditions of high substitutability between the products of all countries depicted in Table XXIII, calculated fairly rapidly and easily to remove the disequilibrium in the world balance of payments.

The effect is very different in the conditions assumed for our second numerical example in Table XXIV. In this example we assume that the products of the deficit countries D_1 and D_2 are good substitutes for each other and also for the products of the balanced country B, but that they are capable of little or no substitution with the products of the surplus countries S_1 and S_2. Similarly, we assume that the products of the surplus countries S_1 and S_2 are good substitutes for each other and also for the products of the balanced country B, but are capable of little or no substitution for those of the deficit countries D_1 and D_2. An example of this situation would be where D_1 and D_2 produced only primary products which were fairly good substitutes in production or in consumption for each other but which could not be substituted in production or in consumption for the manufactured products which were the only output of S_1 and S_2, though these manufactured goods were good substitutes in production or consumption for each other. B might then represent the rest of the world which could produce both primary products and manufactured goods.

Let us see what happens in these circumstances when, as in adjustment i of Table XXIV, the authorities in D_1 depreciate D_1's exchange

TABLE XXIV

The Effect of Exchange-Rate Variations. Case II. Low Substitutability between the Products of the Deficit Countries and the Products of the Surplus Countries

$B m.

		Increase (+) or decrease (−) in trade payments by					total exports	Deficit (−) or surplus (+) on balance of payments before | after the change	
		D_1	D_2	S_1	S_2	B			
		(a)	(b)	(c)	(d)	(e)	(f)	(g)	(h)
Adjustment i. Depreciation of D_1's Exchange Rate									
	D_1 (1)		+17	− 5	− 5	+17	+24	−47	0
	D_2 (2)	−11		− 1	− 1	− 5	−18	−33	−63
Increase (+) or decrease (−) in trade receipts by	S_1 (3)	− 1	·		·		− 1	+65	+71
	S_2 (4)	− 1	·	·			− 1	+15	+21
	B (5)	−10	− 5	− 1	− 1		−17	0	−29
	total imports (6)	−23	+12	− 7	− 7	+12			
World disequilibrium rises from 80 to 92.									
Adjustment ii. Depreciation of D_2's Exchange Rate									
	D_1 (7)		−15	− 1	+1	− 5	−22	0	−38
	D_2 (8)	+21		− 5	− 5	+21	+32	−63	0
Increase (+) or decrease (−) in trade receipts by	S_1 (9)	·	− 1		·	·	− 1	+71	+77
	S_2 (10)	·	− 1	·		·	− 1	+21	+27
	B (11)	− 5	−14	− 1	− 1		−21	−29	−66
	total imports (12)	+16	−31	− 7	− 7	+16			
World disequilibrium rises from 92 to 104.									
Adjustment iii. Appreciation of S_1's Exchange Rate									
	D_1 (13)		·	+ 1	·	·	+ 1	−38	−44
	D_2 (14)	·		+ 1	·	·	+ 1	0	− 6
Increase (+) or decrease (−) in trade receipts by	S_1 (15)	+ 5	+ 5		−25	−24	−39	+77	0
	S_2 (16)	+ 1	+ 1	+18		+ 5	+25	+27	+72
	B (17)	+ 1	+ 1	+18	+ 5		+25	−66	−22
	total imports (18)	+ 7	+ 7	+38	−20	−19			
World disequilibrium falls from 104 to 72.									
Adjustment iv. Appreciation of S_2's Exchange Rate									
	D_1 (19)		·	·	+ 1	·	+ 1	−44	−50
	D_2 (20)	·		·	+ 1	·	+ 1	− 6	−12
Increase (+) or decrease (−) in trade receipts by	S_1 (21)	+ 1	+ 1		+17	+ 5	+24	0	+42
	S_2 (22)	+ 5	+ 5	−23		−23	−36	+72	0
	B (23)	+ 1	+ 1	+ 5	+17		+24	−22	+20
	total imports (24)	+ 7	+ 7	−18	+36	−18			
World disequilibrium falls from 72 to 62.									

rate. D_1's deficit disappears almost as easily as it did in adjustment i of Table XXIII because D_1's products can now compete on better terms with the close substitutes produced in D_2 and B. To understand the forces at work in this case we will consider each column of Table XXIV (i.e. the changes in the imports of each country) in turn.

As far as D_1's imports are concerned (column a rows 2, 3, 4, and 5), imports from each of the other countries fall in volume and so in value in terms of B's currency because the price of imports rises in terms of D_1's currency. But imports from S_1 and S_2 fall very little because D_1's products cannot readily be substituted for them, whereas imports from D_2 and B fall substantially because they are in close competition with D_1's own products which are now relatively less expensive to purchase.

As far as D_2's imports are concerned (column b rows 1, 3, 4, and 5), imports from D_1 rise very substantially in volume because D_1's products fall in price in terms of B's currency and so in terms of D_2's currency. They rise very substantially in volume because they compete closely with D_2's own products and also with the products which were previously being imported into D_2 from B; and this great rise in their volume outweighs the fall in their price in terms of B's currency so that their total value rises considerably But this is accompanied by an appreciable fall in imports into D_2 from B because D_1's products which have become cheaper are good substitutes for B's products. On the other hand, the fall in the price in D_2's currency of D_1's products leaves unchanged the demand in D_2 for S_1's and S_2's products, which are not in competition with D_1's. Exactly similar factors are at work influencing B's imports (column e rows 1, 2, 3, and 4). Purchasers in B purchase much more from D_1, appreciably less from D_2 and unchanged amounts and values from S_1 and S_2.

We may consider the imports of S_1 and S_2 together (columns c and d rows 1, 2, 3, 4, and 5). Purchasers in both these countries buy a little more in volume from D_1 because the price of D_1's products in terms of B's currency and so in terms of their own currencies has fallen. But since D_1's products do not compete at all strongly with their own, they do not purchase as much more in volume as to compensate for the fall in the price of D_1's products. As a result the value of imports into S_1 and S_2 from D_1 shows a net decline. But as D_1's products compete with D_2's and B's products, purchasers in S_1 and S_2 have shifted somewhat from D_2's and B's products on to D_1's products with the result that the value of their imports from D_2 and B fall somewhat. They continue, however, to purchase unchanged amounts from each other.

The results of this change in the flow of trade should be carefully observed. D_1's deficit has disappeared just as it did in adjustment i of Table XXIII. But no part of D_1's diminished deficit has been matched by a reduced surplus of S_1 or of S_2. On the contrary each of these countries' surpluses has increased by \$B6 m. because the decline in the value of these countries' imports (\$B7 m.) due to the fact that their purchasers can get at a lower price D_1's products for which their demand is inelastic is greater than the decline in the value of exports from S_1 or S_2 (\$B1 m.) due to the fact that purchasers in D_1 are buying a little less from them. As a consequence \$B12 m. more than the whole decline in D_1's deficit of \$B47 m. has been either added to D_2's deficit (which has risen by \$B30 m. from \$B33 m. to \$B63 m.) or has caused a new deficit to appear for B (which country now has a deficit of \$B29 m.). The depreciation of D_1's currency has got rid of D_1's deficit, but at the expense of adding an even greater deficit to the two countries, D_2 and B, which compete closely with D_1 but which happen neither to be in surplus. The total world disequilibrium (i.e. the total either of all surplus countries' surpluses or of all deficit countries' deficits) has risen from \$B80 m. to \$B92 m.

As a result of adjustment i D_2's deficit has grown alarmingly from \$B33 m. to \$B63 m.; and in adjustment ii of Table XXIV the authorities in D_2 depreciate D_2's currency in order to remove this deficit. As a result of this depreciation the price of all foreign products goes up in D_2's currency; and D_2's imports from each foreign country fall in quantity and so in value in terms of B's currency, the fall being large in the case of imports from D_1 and B which compete with D_2's products and small in the case of imports from S_1 and S_2 which do not so compete (column b rows 7, 9, 10, and 11). Imports into D_1 and B from D_2 both increase substantially in volume, since D_2's products compete closely with their own, with the result that the increase in volume outweighs the fall in price and the value of these imports in terms of B's currency rises substantially; but the increased imports into D_1 from D_2 are at the expense of imports of competing products from B, and similarly the increased imports into B from D_2 are at the expense of imports from D_1 (columns a and e rows 7, 8, and 11). Imports into S_1 and S_2 from D_2 go up very little in volume when the price of D_2's products falls, with the result that their value in terms of B's currency actually falls; but there is some increased volume of imports into S_1 and S_2 from D_2 and this is partially at the expense of imports from the competing sources D_1 and B (columns c and d rows 7, 8, and 11).

In consequence of these changes D_2's deficit disappears; but this is wholly at the expense of increased deficits of her competitors D_1 and B whose products purchasers not only in D_2 but also in S_1 and S_2 cease to buy in view of the fact that D_2's competing products are now cheaper. Indeed, S_1 and S_2 now have still larger surpluses because purchasers in these countries economize on imports from D_2 which they purchase in only very slightly increased quantity but at a considerably lower price; and in consequence the depreciation of D_2's currency has to be on a scale sufficient to unload on to D_1 and B not only the whole of D_2's existing deficit of \$B63 m. but also the whole of the increase in the surpluses of S_1 and of S_2 of \$B6 m. each. The total world disequilibrium rises by another \$B12 m. to \$B104 m.

In adjustment iii we examine the effect of an appreciation of S_1's exchange rate. As a result, the price of all foreign products falls in terms of S_1's currency; and purchasers in S_1 increase their demands for D_1's and D_2's products slightly (because these products compete very little with S_1's own products) and for S_2's and B's products very considerably (because these compete very closely with S_1's products) (column c rows 13, 14, 16, and 17). Purchasers in D_1 and D_2 purchase slightly less in volume but more in value of S_1's products because of the rise in the price of S_1's products, but they purchase somewhat more in volume—and so also in value—of S_2's and B's products which compete closely with S_1's more expensive products (columns a and b rows 15, 16, and 17). Purchasers in S_2 and B purchase so much less in volume of S_1's products which compete closely with their own home products that the value of their purchases from S_1 falls in spite of the rise in the price per unit; and they also buy somewhat more from each other's country since their own products tend to replace the more expensive products of S_1 in each others' markets (columns d and e rows 15, 16, and 17). As a result of this S_1 gets rid of her surplus; but it is passed wholly on to S_2 and B, the countries whose products compete with S_1's products. Indeed, the deficits of D_1 and D_2 are each increased by \$B6 m. owing to the rise in the price of imports into these countries from S_1, for whose products the demands in D_1 and D_2 are inelastic. As a result the improvement in the balances of payments of S_2 and B are \$B12 m. more than the reduction of the balance of payments of S_1 from \$B77 m. to zero. But in this case B was already in deficit to the extent of \$B66 m. so that the improvement in B's position of \$B44 m. reduces her deficit from \$B66 m. to \$B22 m., which represents a reduction in world disequilibrium. It is only the shift of a balance-of-payments surplus of an additional \$B45 m. on to S_2 which increases the world disequilibrium. In consequence there is a net fall in the world disequilibrium from \$B104 m. to \$B72 m. as a result of the appreciation of S_1's currency.

Now S_2 is left with a surplus of \$B72 m. Her currency is appreciated in adjustment iv. Once again as a result of the rise in the price of S_2's products with which the products of D_1 and D_2 do not compete, D_1 and D_2 each find their deficits increased by \$B6 m. S_2's currency is appreciated sufficiently to shift the whole of this \$B12 m. as well as S_2's initial surplus of \$B72 m. on to S_1 and B with whose products S_2's more expensive products are in close competition. Of this sum \$B42 m. gives rise to a new surplus for S_1, and the other \$B42 m. turns B's deficit of \$B22 m. into a surplus of \$B 20 m. The net result of the change is to reduce the total world disequilibrium from $B 72m. to $B62 m.

It is interesting to consider what is the net outcome of all the four adjustments of Table XXIV.

At every stage the balance of payments of the two deficit countries D_1 and D_2 with the two surplus countries S_1 and S_2 has become less favourable. This can be seen by confining one's attention to those parts of Table XXIV which are enclosed in heavily printed boundary lines. At each of adjustments i and ii the value of imports into the joint territory D_1-D_2 from the joint territory S_1-S_2 has fallen by $B2 m. because each of these adjustments represents a partial depreciation of D_1-D_2's currency, some rise in the price of imports from S_1-S_2 in terms of D_1-D_2's currencies, therefore some decline in the volume of D_1-D_2's imports from S_1-S_2, and therefore some decline in their value in terms of B's currency. At each of these adjustments i and ii S_1-S_2's imports from D_1-D_2 have fallen in value by $B12 m. because S_1-S_2's imports have risen less in volume than their price has declined in terms of B's currency because of the depreciation of D_1's or D_2's currency. As a result, at each of these adjustments the balance of payments between D_1-D_2 and S_1-S_2 has moved against the deficit area by $B10 m.

And the same thing has happened at each of the adjustments iii and iv. In this case each adjustment has represented a partial appreciation of S_1-S_2's currency. This has caused D_1-D_2's products to fall in price in terms of S_1-S_2's currencies and has thus caused a slight increase in the volume (and so in the value in terms of B's currency) of D_1-D_2's exports to S_1-S_2. But this has been more than outweighed by the increase (of $B12 m. at each adjustment) in the value of D_1-D_2's imports from S_1-S_2 due to the fact that purchasers in D_1-D_2 have had to pay a higher price per unit in terms of B's currency for an almost unchanged volume of imports from S_1-S_2.

Thus, taking all four adjustments together, the balance of payments between D_1-D_2 and S_1-S_2 has moved against D_1-D_2 to the extent of $B40 m. If D_1, D_2, S_1, and S_2 made up the whole of the world this would be a simple case in which the sum of the elasticities of demands in the deficit area for the products of the surplus area and in the surplus area for the products of the deficit area was less than unity. No adjustments by a depreciation of the deficit countries' currencies or an appreciation of the surplus countries' currencies could do anything but worsen the disequilibrium between the two areas. It would, of course, be possible for the authorities in one of the two deficit countries to put their own balance of payments in order by depreciating and undercutting the products of the other deficit country; but in this case the deficit of the second deficit country would be increased by the whole of the deficit of the first deficit country and by something more as well.

But when we allow for another area B with which both D_1-D_2 and S_1-S_2 can compete the picture is changed. The net world disequilibrium at the end of adjustment iv (namely $B62 m.) is less than the original world disequilibrium (namely $B80 m.). This is because the depreciations of D_1's and D_2's currencies in adjustments i and ii have shifted the deficits of D_1 and D_2 to an appreciable extent on to B with whom their products compete. And the appreciations of the exchange rates of S_1 and S_2 in adjustments iii and iv have enabled producers in B, whose products also compete with those of S_1 and S_2, to undercut the producers in S_1 and S_2 and to shift B's deficit on to the surplus countries S_1 and S_2. Thus D_1's and D_2's deficits are indirectly shifted through B on to S_1 and S_2, even though at each adjustment the direct balance of payments between D_1-D_2 and S_1-S_2 becomes less favourable to D_1-D_2.

To what extent this possibility of indirect substitution through B of D_1's and D_2's products for S_1's and S_2's is likely to be important will depend upon the circumstances of each case. If D_1, D_2, S_1, and S_2 make up practically the whole of the world its importance will not probably be great, unless there is very high substitution indeed both of D_1's and D_2's products with B's and also of B's with S_1's and S_2's. But if D_1, D_2, S_1, and S_2 make up only a moderate part of the world and B represents a very large field of possible competition for all these countries' products, the possibility may be a very important one. In the example given in Table XXIV, even after the whole first round of four exchange-rate adjustments the world disequilibrium had been reduced only from $B80 m. to $B62 m. If the depreciations and appreciations required at each of these four stages to get each country in turn into equilibrium were at all large, there would clearly need to be very great exchange adjustments and thus probably a very great movement of the real terms of trade against D_1 and D_2 and in favour of S_1 and S_2 in order to restore external balance by this means alone.

We may briefly sum up the conclusions of this chapter.

If there is a good degree of substitution between the products of all countries, then the successive depreciation of the currencies of all deficit countries and the appreciation of the currencies of all surplus countries will achieve a fairly easy shift of international demand away from the products of the surplus countries and on to the products of the deficit countries. But each deficit country may require a different degree of depreciation and each surplus country a different degree of appreciation. The extent of the depreciation or appreciation required will depend not only upon the size of the original deficit or surplus of each country, but also upon the extent to which each country's products are good substitutes for the products of the other countries, and in particular on the extent to which each deficit country's products are a good substitute for those of the surplus countries, and vice versa.

In a many-country world the process of exchange rate adjustment will, therefore, require the achievement of a whole new set of exchange rates for all countries even if at the start there are only two countries out of equilibrium (one deficit and one surplus). Such a new set can be found only by a process of trial and error in which each country's currency is depreciated so long as it is in deficit and appreciated so long as it is surplus. A method must, therefore, be chosen whereby the authorities in each country, surplus as well as deficit, great as well as small, are prepared continually to make an appropriate contribution to the discovery of the new equilibrium set of exchange rates. The authorities in only one country, the country in terms of whose currency all the other exchange rates are fixed, can be permitted formally to stay out of the game.

For the method of exchange-rate adjustment to work easily there must be a good degree of direct or indirect substitution between the products of the surplus countries on the one hand and of the deficit countries on the other. If there is no such substitution possible, then the method of exchange-rate adjustment will only make the world disequilibrium worse. It is not incompatible with this that the elasticity of demand for imports in every individual country and the foreign elasticity of demand for the exports of every individual country should be so high that the authorities in each individual country acting alone could fairly easily achieve external balance by depreciating the exchange rate if the country is in deficit and by appreciating the exchange rate if it is in surplus. But if these elasticities are high simply because the products of each deficit country compete highly with those of other deficit countries while the products of each surplus country compete highly with those of other surplus countries, exchange-rate adjustments will not remove the world disequilibrium. They will merely shuffle the the deficits round among the deficit countries and the surpluses around among the surplus countries.

The competition between the products of the deficit and the surplus countries may, of course, be direct in production or consumption. That is to say, when the price of the products of the deficit countries falls relatively to that of the products of the surplus countries, *consumers* in the deficit and the surplus countries may readily turn from the purchase of the more expensive products of the surplus countries to the relatively cheaper products of the deficit countries; or *producers* in the deficit countries may readily turn to the production of the relatively expensive things previously imported from the surplus countries (thereby reducing the demand for imports in the deficit countries) or *producers* in the surplus countries may readily turn away from the production of the relatively cheap things previously imported from the deficit countries (thereby increasing the demand for imports in the surplus countries).

But the substitutability between the products of the deficit and the surplus countries may be indirect. It is not necessary that each individual deficit country's products should compete highly with the products of the surplus countries or vice versa. For example, D_1's products may not compete with S_1's or S_2's in production or consumption; but if D_1's compete with D_2's and D_2's compete with S_1's or S_2's, price adjustment will work. D_1's exchange rate is depreciated and D_1's deficit is passed on to D_2. D_2's currency is then depreciated. But the deficit is not thereby merely passed back to D_1; a large part of it is passed on to S_1 or S_2 with whose products D_2's products compete strongly; and thus the world disequilibrium is removed. Nor need the competition of the deficit countries with the surplus countries be as direct as this. The competition may take place through a third group of balanced countries. In this case the currencies of the deficit countries are depreciated and their deficits passed on to the balanced countries; and the currencies of the surplus countries are appreciated and their surpluses passed on to the same group of balanced countries. The balanced countries remain in balance since their increased deficit with the deficit countries is counterbalanced by their increased surplus with the surplus countries; and both the deficit and also the surplus countries gain external balance.

Only the particular circumstances of each case will determine whether in fact there is sufficient substitutability to enable the method of price adjustment to work. But, provided that there is a reasonable absence of rigid controls over trade, there is every presumption that the method can be made to work in view of the facts that substitution may take place in production or consumption and that it may be direct or indirect through third countries.

CHAPTER XXVIII

THE MEANING AND PURPOSE
OF DISCRIMINATION

IN Chapter XXVI we covered the problems which arise when we have to take into account the multilateral effects in a many-country world of inflations and deflations of domestic expenditure in a particular country; or, in other words, we examined the way in which the analysis of Part III must be extended when we allow for a network of payments between many countries. Similarly, in Chapter XXVII we covered the problems which arise when we have to take into account the multilateral effects in a many-country world of price adjustment through the appreciation or depreciation of the exchange rate of a particular country; or, in other words, we examined the way in which the analysis of Part IV must be extended when we allow for a network of payments between many countries.

There remains the extension of the analysis of Part V to the many-country world. The use of direct controls in a many-country world raises the question of discrimination. The authorities in one country decide to impose a particular control over some element of the balance of payments (e.g. a restriction on imports). Should they do so on a non-discriminatory basis (i.e. with 'equal' severity on the imports from all countries)? Or should they, for the purpose of achieving a more direct solution of the balance-of-payments problem, do so on a discriminatory basis (i.e. with 'greater' severity on imports from some sources than on imports from other exporting countries)?

Before we can answer these questions we must consider what is meant by 'non-discrimination' and 'discrimination'. What in the above sentences do the words 'with "equal" severity on imports from all sources' mean? How can one tell whether a direct restriction of A's imports from B and from C has fallen with greater severity on its imports from C than on its imports from B, or vice versa?

There is one case of direct control of A's imports from all sources in which we can say without hesitation that the principle of non-discrimination is observed. That is where the price mechanism is at work in country A and where the amount of imports of all kinds from all countries is restricted solely through the imposition of a uniform *ad valorem* rate of import duty on all imports. In this case all suppliers of all products in all other countries have an equal opportunity to supply A's market. Each supplier has merely to meet the same *ad valorem* charge (say a 10 per cent import duty) on anything which he supplies to purchasers in A.

This would also be the case if the import restriction in A were not by means of an *ad valorem* import duty but by means of the issue of licences to import given quantities of particular commodities from particular sources of supply, provided that the amount of licences issued in each case were determined by a similar principle. This would be achieved if (i) import licences always limited the value and not the quantity of the commodity which might be imported, (ii) the licences were in each case sold by auction to the highest bidders in a perfectly free market by the issuing authority (see pp. 286–7, above), (iii) the auction fee offered in each case were then calculated as an *ad valorem* charge on the value of the particular imports to which it referred, and (iv) the amount of licences issued were always increased (or decreased) according as the *ad valorem* rate of the licence fee as calculated above were above (or below) the average for all imports. In this way the value of imports permitted in each case would be continuously adjusted until in all cases the degree of restriction was the same, in the sense that in each case there remained the same *ad valorem* margin between the price at which the consumers in the importing country were prepared to purchase the restricted amount of imports and the price at which the producers in each supplying country were prepared to make that amount available. Once again each foreign supplier would have an absolutely equal chance of supplying his particular product. He would merely have to be able to meet the same *ad valorem* import charge (in this case the import licence fee) as every other foreign supplier of every other commodity.

But as soon as this simple principle is abandoned some element of discrimination may enter into the system of import control; and it becomes impossible to find any alternative clear-cut criterion to make sure whether or not such discrimination has in fact arisen.

We can, perhaps, best demonstrate this proposition by the following illustrations of deviations from the above principle and by showing how in each case an element of discrimination may have entered into the situation.

(i) Let us first suppose that the system of import duties or of quantitative import restrictions does not apply equally to all commodities. The authorities in A restrict the import of motor-cars but do not restrict the import of wheat. On the face of it there is no discrimination between different exporting countries. The producers in all countries can export motor-cars to A on equal terms, and can export wheat to A on equal terms. But producers in B may produce motor-cars but not wheat, and producers in C may produce wheat but not motor-cars. The authorities in A may have no intention to discriminate between producers in B and C; they may choose to restrict imports of motor-cars and not of wheat on grounds quite unconnected with the sources of foreign supply from which the two commodities proceed. But, nevertheless, in fact the restriction will fall heavily on producers in B and not at all on producers in C.

Moreover, it is impossible to know what were the motives of the authorities in A in imposing the restrictions; they may very well have chosen one commodity and not another for severe restriction simply because it comes from one source of supply rather than another. The possibility of such action is greatly increased by the difficulty of determining what constitutes a given 'commodity'. It is possible to define and redefine a commodity so closely and carefully that one is left with something which comes exclusively from one source of supply. The classical example of this is 'a provision in the German tariff dating from 1902, which is clearly meant to apply to Switzerland and Austria, relating to "brown or dappled cows reared at a level of at least 300 metres above the sea and passing at least one month in every summer at a height of at least 800 metres".'[1] Farmers in countries which possessed no mountains may have felt that they did not obtain completely equal treatment.

(ii) Another case of potential discrimination arises where an import duty is imposed on a specific instead of an *ad valorem* basis. In this case obvious difficulties arise in measuring the degree of restriction as between one commodity and another with the consequences discussed in (i) above. But apart from this, a problem of discrimination arises even in so far as any single commodity is concerned. For example, suppose that a duty is imposed on imports of cotton cloth not at 10 per cent of the value of each parcel of imported cloth but at $1 per square yard of cloth. Then the cloth of fine quality which is worth, say, $10 a square yard will bear a duty equivalent to an *ad valorem* rate of only 10 per cent (i.e. $1 duty on imports worth $10). But the cheap cloth of inferior quality worth, say, only $2 a square yard will bear a duty equivalent to an *ad valorem* rate of 50 per cent (i.e. $1 duty on imports worth $2). Now producers in country B may concentrate on the production of high-quality cloth and those in country C on low-quality cloth; and in this case the specific duty bears more heavily on producers in C than on those in B.

(iii) A very similar point arises where import licences are issued which give permission to import not a certain stated value of a given commodity but a certain stated quantity of that commodity. This also favours the producers of the higher and more expensive grades of the commodity. A licence enabling an importer to import 100 square yards of cloth will enable him to import $1,000 worth of cloth worth $10 a square yard but only $200 worth of cloth worth $2 a square yard. If

[1] Quoted from Gottfried von Haberler, *The Theory of International Trade* 1936, p. 339.

the same rate of profit can initially be obtained on both qualities of cloth, the trader will use the licence for the high-quality cloth rather than for the low-quality cloth, since he can obtain a higher dollar turnover in the former case. The producers of the high quality (who may happen to be residents of B) are favoured at the expense of the producers of the low quality (who may happen to be residents of C).

(iv) It is possible to organize the restriction of imports by means of a global or open quota on the principle of 'first come, first served'. In this case a maximum amount or value is fixed for the imports of any particular commodity or class of commodities; all traders are free to bring the commodity into the country, but as soon as the maximum permissible amount or value has been imported the frontiers are closed to that commodity for the remainder of that quota period and no more may enter. This method has the appearance of non-discrimination, since no particular importers or exporters are favoured. All may take part in the scramble on equal terms. But in fact the suppliers who are geographically nearest the importing country will be favoured. If producers in B are more or less on A's frontier whereas producers in C have to send their products half way round the globe to A, clearly the former can slip their products into A much more expeditiously than the latter. The worst unfairness to producers in C can be overcome if the authorities in A announce the quota of permitted imports well in advance of the quota period during which the stated amount of the commodity may enter A's borders. For in this case producers in C can ship their supplies to A sufficiently in advance to enable them to arrive at A's frontiers at the beginning of the quota period. But even in this case producers in C are at a disadvantage as compared with their rivals in B, because they stand to lose more if they are unsuccessful in getting their goods accepted as part of the quota when they do arrive. Suppose that producers in B and in C have an equal chance of finding that when their products reach A's frontiers the quota will be already full, and they will be turned back. In the former case the products have to return a few miles only to their original source; in the latter case they have to sail half round the world again to return whence they came.

(v) To meet this difficulty it is possible to allocate the licences to import to certain traders in A, but to leave these traders complete freedom to choose from what source they will purchase the commodities which the licences enable them to import. In many cases this may give a fair approximation to the principle of non-discrimination, because the traders may be assumed to purchase from those sources from which they can obtain the supplies most cheaply in relation to the price at which the supplies can be sold in the importing market. But in other cases this may not be so. Some traders may be organized to import certain qualities or brands of the product from certain sources and other traders to import other qualities or brands from other sources. The allocation of the licences among particular importers may thus indirectly amount to an allocation among sources of supply; and in this case the problem of non-discrimination has not been solved.

(vi) The authority which administers the import restriction may itself determine the source of supply in order to achieve non-discrimination by allowing the producers in each supplying country to supply the same percentage of the amount which they supplied in some representative base period. But this does not in fact ensure non-discrimination for at least three reasons. First, there is the problem of deciding what is a representative base period. By choosing one period in which exports from B to A were high producers in B may be favoured; by choosing another period producers in C may obtain a larger quota. And no one can say which period is right. Secondly, even if the base period was truly representative of the past, conditions of supply and demand change as time goes on. The quota fixed on the basis of a past period discriminates more and more against the producers whose costs of producing the particular commodity have fallen most or whose quality or brand of the commodity is becoming more and more fashionable and desired in the importing country. And if periodic adjustments are made to the base period quotas to meet such changes, we are back where we started: on what principles will these adjustments need to be made to ensure that non-discrimination is re-established? Thirdly, even if the base-period supplies were properly representative and there has been no subsequent change in any relevant conditions of supply or demand, it does not follow that the same percentage reduction of imports from each source would be truly non-discriminatory. Producers in B may be able to switch easily to the production of a different commodity or to sell the commodity in another market which is readily available to them; whereas producers in C may not be able to produce anything else or to sell their products elsewhere. In such a case a uniform tax on imports from B and C would result in a large fall in imports from B (as producers in B shifted to alternative lines of production or to alternative markets) and a small fall from C (whose producers could not so shift). And this would be true non-discrimination, since it would allow for the ease of alternative occupations for the two classes of suppliers. But an equal percentage cut would impose much more hardship on C's producers who could not shift than on B's who could.

So far we have considered the problem of defining non-discrimination only in the case of import controls. Precisely similar considerations arise in the case of other direct controls, i.e. controls over exports,[1] capital movements, and any other transfers. In these cases pure non-discrimination can be said to exist when the control is exercised by means of a uniform *ad valorem* duty or subsidy on all the relevant payments or by means of some other instrument (such as an auctioned licence) with a corresponding effect.

The above discussion suggests that only uniform *ad valorem* duties or subsidies on all payments or all receipts can properly be ensured to be non-discriminatory. But this does not, of course, mean that in default of such a system of control nothing can be done to move nearer to a non-discriminatory use of controls. Controls may more or less blatantly discriminate against or in favour of transactions with one foreign country or one group of foreign countries. Common sense and an international organization in which the various points raised above can be argued and applied can certainly help to ensure that controls will be used with less discriminatory effect—if non-discrimination is the accepted goal.

We must turn, then, to the question whether the principle of non-discrimination is to be invariably applied, and, if not, in what circumstances and on what conditions exception to the rule of non-discrimination are to be permitted.

Now there are many purposes which may be served by a discriminatory use of direct controls.

One motive for discrimination may be purely or mainly political. The authorities in one country may prohibit trade in certain commodities with another particular country because it wishes to keep the military potential of that country as low as possible. Or countries which have had close political associations in the past may give preferential treatment to each other largely in order to preserve and promote political cohesion. The full Customs Union or *Zollverein* which is formed largely because the member States feel themselves to have close political ties is the extreme example of such discrimination.

A second motive for discrimination is the use of direct controls as a bargaining weapon in order to induce the authorities in another country

---

[1] It is a little more difficult in the case of export controls than in the case of import controls to tell which country is discriminated-against and which country is discriminated-in-favour-of. An import duty, as we have seen, will (i) make the balance of payments less favourable to the exporting country, (ii) move the real terms of trade against the exporting country, and (iii) hurt the particular producers concerned in the exporting country. An export duty, however, will (i) make the balance of payments less or more favourable to the importing country according as the elasticity of demand for the taxed imports in that country is less or greater than unity, (ii) move the real terms of trade against the importing country, and (iii) be to the advantage of the particular competing producers in the importing country. If, therefore, the authorities in A tax (or subsidize) exports to B but not to C, it is possible to say that they are discriminating, but whether the discrimination is said to be in favour of B or of C will depend upon the point of view from which the favour is judged.

to modify their direct controls. Thus the authorities in country A may reduce import duties on the products of country B if the authorities in country B will agree in return to reduce duties on imports from A. But the authorities in A may refuse to reduce duties on similar imports from C unless the authorities in C will also in return reduce duties on imports from A. Thus the authorities in A may discriminate in favour of producers in B and against producers in C unless and until the authorities in C are also prepared to modify their duties.

A third motive for discrimination may be to attain a favourable movement in the terms of trade. For example, supplies of a certain product may be imported into A from B and C. The producers of this product in B may be easily able to shift to the production of some other product or to sell the product in an alternative market; but the producers in C may be unable to shift either to an alternative line of production or to an alternative market for their product. In this case the authorities in A would be able to turn the terms of trade in A's favour by imposing an import duty on the product when it was imported from C, but not on the product when it was imported from B. If the imports from B were taxed, the producers in B would shift to the production of other commodities or would sell the original product in other markets; the supplies of this product available in A would fall and, as a result, the price offered by consumers of it in A would rise. In the end the consumers in A would be paying most of the duty on imports from B and the producers in B would be getting almost as high a price per unit of their product as they were before the import duty in A was imposed. But if the authorities in A imposed a duty on imports of the product from C, the result would be very different. The producers in C cannot readily shift to alternative production or alternative markets; they would, in competition with each other, supply a practically undiminished amount to A; in consequence, since there is no increased scarcity of the product in A, consumers in A would not be willing to pay a higher price for the product, so that the producers in C would have to accept a price which was reduced by the tax. The community in A would in fact obtain its supplies from C at a lower real cost; or in other words, the real terms of trade would have been moved in A's favour.

Clearly in such circumstances the authorities in A would have an incentive to impose a duty on supplies coming from C but not on supplies coming from B. And similarly, the authorities in A might have an incentive to impose an export duty on exports which were sold to C, if the consumers in C could not obtain their supplies readily from an alternative source and could not satisfy their wants easily by producing a close substitute themselves, since in this case the consumers in C would be ready to pay a higher price (in order to cover the export duty) rather than go without the supplies. If at the same time consumers in B could more readily obtain their supplies from an alternative source or could satisfy their wants by means of an alternative commodity, the authorities in A would have an incentive to impose an export duty which discriminated against the consumers in C.

Both of these last two motives—namely, the use of discriminatory trade controls as an element in commercial bargaining and their use for the purpose of exploiting the most vulnerable sources of supply of a country's imports or the most vulnerable markets for the sale of its exports—are matters which we shall have to consider in Volume II. They are not directly relevant to a consideration of the mechanism of the balance of payments; either or both of them may be operative in conditions in which there is no balance-of-payments problem at all and in which (owing, for example, to a smoothly operating system of price adjustment through variable exchange rates) the question of using direct controls on balance-of-payments grounds does not arise.

But there are circumstances when the problem of discrimination arises directly on balance-of-payments grounds. The monetary authorities in A may for one reason or another find it easier to provide importers in A with the currency which is required to make purchases in B than with the currency which is required to make purchases in C. Here there would be a motive for imposing discriminatory direct controls against imports from C; and this motive would be concerned simply with the technical mechanism of financing payments to B and to C. It is clearly an important part of the subject matter of this volume. The extent to which, and the conditions in which, this balance-of-payments argument is valid will be discussed in Chapter XXX, but before embarking on that discussion we shall in the next chapter briefly enumerate the various methods by which direct controls can be used in a discriminatory manner.

CHAPTER XXIX

THE METHODS OF DISCRIMINATION

IN this chapter we shall consider briefly the way in which the various forms of direct control which were enumerated in Chapters XX and XXI can be employed for the purpose of discrimination.

1. *Exchange Control*

Let us suppose that the authorities in A have instituted a system of exchange control so that any purchaser in A who wishes to import products from outside or to make any payment to a resident in another country must obtain the permission of the exchange-control authority in A to acquire or to use the necessary foreign money. In this case the exchange-control authority in A could discriminate in its administration of the exchange control. It might, for example, allow fairly freely the purchase of B's currency by importers in A for the purpose of importing commodity X into A, but might disallow completely or allow on only a very limited scale the purchase of C's currency for this same purpose.

Such behaviour on the part of A's exchange-control authority would clearly be technical discrimination, but it would not necessarily be effective discrimination. Suppose that B's currency is readily convertible in B into C's currency because there is no system of foreign exchange control in B. In this case the purchasers of X in A can import X from C and pay for it with B's currency, and the sellers of X in C can then convert their receipts of B's money freely into their own money, namely the currency of C. There will be no effective discrimination against imports from C into A. Nor will the position of A's monetary authority be effectively altered by the rule which technically discriminates against C. For when A's exchange control provides B's currency but not C's currency for the finance of the import of X into A, A's monetary authorities will run down their reserves of B's currency instead of running down their reserves of C's currency; but since B's currency is *ex hypothesi* freely convertible into C's, the reserve position in A is not thereby appreciably better than it would have been if the authorities in A had allowed their reserves of C's currency to fall instead of their reserves of B's.

The technical discrimination by exchange control will become somewhat more effective if the rule is not merely that B's currency rather than C's currency may be acquired for the import of X into A, but also that B's currency so acquired must be used for the purpose of purchasing X in B and not in C. The effective discrimination against C may be slight even in this case if commodity X can be freely imported into B from C whether for consumption in B or for re-export to A. In that case importers of X in A can still in effect purchase supplies from C, provided that they are prepared to pay the additional cost of transporting X from C to A via B instead of direct. How much this deters the import of X from C will depend partly upon the extent to which the cost of transport is an important element in the price of X and partly on the extent to which the detour through B from C to A adds to the transport cost.

The discrimination will be still more effective if the rule in A is that foreign currency can be acquired for the purchase of X if X is produced in B but not if X is produced in C.[1] By this means a clear preference is given to the purchase of B's products over C's products.[2] But even in this case the discrimination may not be wholly effective, if X can be freely imported into B from C. For in that case when B's producers sell more X in A and C's producers sell less X in A because of the discriminatory exchange control in A, C's producers may now sell their surplus to the previous consumers (in B, C, D, or E) of B's products which are now being sent to A. In other words, purchasers in A may purchase from B instead of C, producers in C may now sell to the consumers who would have bought the supplies from B which are now going to A. In this case again the only effective change would be the additional transport costs involved in C's producers sending their products to B and B's producers sending their output of the same product to A instead of imports going direct from C to A. But in those cases in which purchasers in A are the largest consumers of X and in which B's home consumption of X is small, these mere re-routings of supplies may be impossible. In this case or in the case where the addition to transport

---

[1] If B's currency is freely convertible into C's there is no point in A's exchange control ruling that only B's currency can be acquired for this purpose. B's currency being convertible into C's is just as useful for making foreign payments as is C's, and needs to be economized by A's exchange control to the same extent as C's. The effective discrimination is brought about by saying that foreign currency, whether B's or C's, can be acquired for purchasing X only if X is produced in B.

[2] This arrangement, like many of the other arrangements for discrimination which will be discussed in this chapter, involves the problem of distinguishing the produce of one country from the produce of another. Suppose, at the one extreme, that commodity X is manufactured in C, transported to B, and there merely packed and branded. Has it become thereby the product of B? Commonsense says No. Suppose, at the other extreme, that the product is wholly manufactured and packed in B out of materials which are all produced in B except one small raw material which is imported from C. Has the product by reason of that one small raw material become the produce of C? Commonsense equally clearly says No. But what percentage of the value of the finished product must be produced in B in order for the commodity to qualify as the produce of B? Some arbitrary criterion must be adopted for the solution of this problem which, as can be seen from a consideration of the rest of this chapter, is fundamental to almost all mechanisms of trade discrimination.

costs is important the discrimination against C's producers may be really effective.

But the discriminatory effect of A's exchange control rules is likely to be greatest where the authorities in B do not permit the free flow of imports into B or of payments for other transactions by residents of B to residents in other countries. Let us consider the simple case where the authorities in B as well as the authorities in A have instituted a general system of exchange control. Purchasers in A can obtain B's but not C's currency for the purchase of X; but B's currency according to the exchange-control regulations in B cannot be freely exchanged into C's currency and must, therefore, be spent upon X produced in B. Nor can the supplies of X in B be replenished any longer by the free import of X from C into B for consumption in B, since importation into B is subject to B's exchange-control regulations. There is now an effective discrimination by A's authorities in favour of B's producers.[1]

Let us therefore consider the problems of discrimination in a world comprised of two deficit countries D_1 and D_2 and one surplus country S, each of the two former having a system of exchange control which prevents the free convertibility of its currency into other currencies but the latter having no exchange control system. The monetary authorities of D_1 and D_2 will both want, at the current rates of exchange, to acquire S's currency more than each others', because S's currency can be used freely to purchase D_1's, D_2's, or S's products (or to make other payments in D_1, D_2, or S) whereas D_1's currency can be used freely only to make payments in D_1 and D_2's currency only to make payments in D_2. Since D_1 and D_2 are deficit countries and S a surplus country, D_1's and D_2's currencies will be easy to acquire while S's currency will be difficult to acquire. Moreover, the use of D_1's or D_2's currency when it is acquired will be limited by D_1's and D_2's exchange control, while that of S's currency will be unlimited. In these circumstances D_1's and D_2's currencies may be called 'soft' currencies and S's a 'hard' currency.

In these conditions the exchange-control authority in either of the soft-currency countries (D_1 or D_2) will treat its foreign exchange relations with the other soft-currency country (D_2 or D_1) differently from its foreign exchange relations with the hard-currency country S. Consider, for example, the exchange-control regulations in D_1. The exchange-control authority in D_1 can no longer lump all foreign currencies together as equal parts of its reserve of foreign exchange. It must distinguish between its reserves of D_2's soft currency and of S's hard currency. For example, persons who are not resident in D_1 from the

---

[1] Except in so far as the increased supplies of X from B to A mean that B's exporters supply less to D, E, F, etc. and that C's producers who are not permitted to supply so much to A merely fill the markets in D, E, F, etc. which are vacated by B's exporters.

point of view of the exchange-control authority in D_1 must be divided by it into D_2 (or soft-currency) non-residents and S (or hard-currency) non-residents. The monetary authorities in D_1 will have to treat non-resident balances of D_1's money as fully convertible into S's currency if they are held by residents of S. In other words, any resident in S who wishes to purchase D_1's currency with S's currency and to hold it on balance in a bank in D_1 will have to be permitted to re-exchange it back into S's currency whenever he wishes; otherwise no one would be prepared to give up holding a hard currency such as S's in order to hold a soft currency such as D_1's. Nor will the monetary authorities in D_1 suffer by such an arrangement. Against the fully convertible non-resident balances held by residents of S the monetary authority in D_1 will hold as a reserve the fully convertible currency of S with which the non-resident balance has been acquired.

But a non-resident balance of D_1's currency acquired by a resident of another soft-currency country such as D_2 must be treated differently. It cannot be treated as fully convertible into any foreign currency including S's currency.[1] Otherwise residents of D_2 could obtain non-resident balances in D_1 by paying in D_2's inconvertible currency to D_1's monetary authorities; and they could then use these non-resident balances to withdraw S's convertible currency from the reserves of D_1's monetary authorities. D_2's residents would indirectly have acquired S's hard currency for their own soft currency at the expense of D_1's monetary authorities who would have lost reserves of S's hard currency and have gained in exchange reserves of D_2's soft currency.

When two countries, such as D_1 and D_2 in our example, both have complete systems of exchange control, their authorities are likely to come to some agreement about the way in which payments should be made between them. Otherwise their independent exchange-control regulations are liable to clash. For example, in the case of a particular import from D_2 into D_1, D_1's exchange-control authority may permit the importer in D_1 to purchase the currency of D_2 which is required for this purpose; but this means that there must be someone in D_2 who is permitted by D_2's exchange-control authority to sell D_2's currency in order to acquire D_1's currency. If there is no flexibility at all, i.e. if each payment from D_1 to D_2 which is permitted by D_1's exchange control has got to be married directly to a payment of the same size from D_2 to D_1 which is permitted by D_2's exchange control, the awkwardness and clumsiness of the control may become intolerable.

The types of payments arrangements which may be concluded between D_1 and D_2 are very varied indeed. Here we will refer merely to

[1] Nor, for the same reason, can D_1's authorities allow a resident of D_2 to transfer a non-resident balance of D_1's currency freely to a resident of S; for in this case the balance would become fully convertible once more.

four main types, leaving the reader to imagine some of the variations which may be made in them.

(i) *The clearing agreement with the waiting principle.* The authorities of D_1 or of D_2, or the two authorities together, may set up a 'clearing office'. All payments which residents in D_1 wish to make to residents in D_2 (and which they are permitted to make by D_1's exchange control) would be paid in D_1's currency into the clearing office. On the other side, all payments made by residents of D_2 to residents of D_1 would be paid in D_2's currency into the clearing office. By this means the clearing office would accumulate a balance of D_1's currency equal to the payments made from D_1 to D_2 and a balance of D_2's currency equal to the payments made from D_2 to D_1. Those residents in D_2 to whom the residents in D_1 wished to make their payments would then be paid by the clearing office out of the balances of D_2's currency which it had acquired as a result of the payments which residents in D_2 were making to residents in D_1. Similarly, those residents in D_1 to whom these residents in D_2 wished to make payment would be paid by the clearing office out of its balance of D_1's currency.

So long as the payments permitted to flow from D_1 to D_2 by D_1's exchange-control authority and the payments permitted to flow from D_2 to D_1 by D_2's exchange-control authority were equal at the current rate of exchange between D_1's and D_2's currencies, the system would work smoothly.

But when the payments in one direction are unequal to the payments flowing in the other direction a complication arises. Suppose that more payments are being made from D_1 to D_2 than from D_2 to D_1. Then the clearing office will run out of D_2's currency as it pays off the many residents in D_2 to whom residents in D_1 are making payments, but it will accumulate an unwanted balance of D_1's currency which is not required in order to pay to the few residents in D_1 to whom residents in D_2 are making payment. One way of dealing with this unbalance is to adopt for the payment of the many creditors in D_2 the principle of 'first come, first served' or what we shall call the 'waiting principle'.[1] In other words, the creditors in D_2 are put in a priority list, the order in the list depending upon the date at which the debtor in D_1 paid in D_1's currency to the clearing office. Each creditor in D_1 will be paid out of the clearing office's large holding of D_1's currency as soon as the debtor in D_2 pays D_2's currency into the clearing office. But when this happens the currency of D_2 which is paid into the clearing office will be used to pay off the creditor in D_2 who is next on the priority list, i.e. who has been waiting longest for payment.

This system will carry with it a self-regulating mechanism. As long

---

[1] Following the terminology used by P. Nyboe Andersen in his excellent book on *Bilateral Exchange Clearing Policy* (Copenhagen, Munksgaard, 1946).

as the payments from D_1 to D_2 exceed the payments from D_2 to D_1 the period during which debtors in D_2 will have to wait for payment will grow longer and longer. The redundant balances of D_1's currency held by the clearing office will become larger and larger. Exporters from D_2 to D_1 (and other creditors in D_2 of debtors in D_1) will have to wait longer and longer for payment until in the end the additional cost and uncertainty of waiting for payment will make them unwilling to export to D_1 or to pile up other credits in D_1. The flow of payments in either direction will approach equality by means of a *contraction* of the exports (and similar transactions) from D_2 to D_1.

(ii) *The clearing agreement with the financing principle.* A clearing agreement between D_1 and D_2 may be run on a different principle in so far as the net accumulation of indebtedness in the one direction or the other is concerned. Suppose, as before, that there is a clearing office and that the payments from D_1 to D_2 exceed those in the opposite direction so that the clearing office is piling up a balance of redundant currency of D_1 and that there is a growing list of creditors in D_2 waiting for payment. An arrangement may be made with the banking system in D_2 that the creditors in D_2 should not have to wait for payment but should have what is owed to them by the clearing office advanced to them by D_2's banks. In this case the creditors in D_2 do not have to wait, but their credits are financed by D_2's banking system which in turn becomes the creditor of the clearing office.[1]

When this 'financing principle' is adopted there will no longer be any automatic regulating mechanism. The exporters of D_2 to D_1 will no longer have to wait increasingly long periods before they receive payment, since their credits will be financed by the banking system in D_2. It is these banking authorities themselves who will find that they are advancing more and more money to their own residents and that in return they are owed more and more by the clearing office, i.e. indirectly by residents in D_1. In short the banking system in D_2 will be lending more and more abroad to D_1 to finance D_2's excess of exports etc. to D_1. Balance in the clearing office account will be reached only if the authorities in D_2 take steps to expand imports from (or other payments to) D_1 or to contract its exports to (or other receipts from) D_1,

---

[1] Andersen (*op. cit.*) calls this the 'financing principle'. In his book there is an interesting discussion of the inflationary effects of the 'financing principle' as opposed to the 'waiting principle' in the surplus country, because the residents in the creditor country will have what is owed to them financed by new lending from their banking system. This distinction is, however, not relevant in the problems which we are discussing in Part VI. We are assuming throughout that either by monetary policy or by fiscal policy the authorities in each country so adjust domestic expenditure as to maintain internal balance. If, therefore, in any surplus country the financing principle is adopted and is exercising a net inflationary influence, we assume that some counter-balancing deflationary act of monetary or fiscal policy is simultaneously adopted.

or if the authorities in D_1 take measures to restrict imports from D_2 or to expand exports to D_2.

This can be achieved by means of the various devices which we shall discuss in greater detail below. The authorities in D_2 can encourage imports from D_1 by setting a new exchange rate for such imports so as to encourage residents in D_2 to purchase D_1's products rather than the products of other countries, or by import subsidies on D_1's products, or by import duties on the products of other countries, or by discriminatory exchange-control regulations or import restrictions which give a preference to the purchase of D_1's products as opposed to the products of other foreign countries, or by a State import organization which simply uses the currency of D_1 which the clearing office owes the banking system in D_2 to make purchases in D_1 of products which it then sells, even at a loss, in D_2. The authorities in D_2 can discourage exports to D_1 by similar devices: fixing a special rate of exchange for such exports so as to make them specially unattractive to producers in D_2; taxing exports to D_1, if the elasticity of demand in D_1 for such products is greater than unity; imposing export restrictions or other obstacles on exports to D_1; using a State export organization in D_2 to purchase the products of D_2 which would otherwise have been sold in D_1 in order to resell them in other markets, even at a loss.

By devices which are the exact opposite of these the authorities in D_1 could take measures to contract imports into D_1 from D_2 or to encourage exports from D_1 to D_2, though there will clearly be less incentive for the authorities in D_1 to take action than for the authorities in D_2, who are making a continual advance of credit to D_1 through the clearing office. In either case, however, the mechanism of the clearing office will have to be supplemented by other devices in order to achieve balance; in either case the mechanism may be contractionist (if the authorities in D_2 restrict exports or the authorities in D_1 restrict imports) or expansionist (if the authorities in D_2 expand imports or the authorities in D_1 expand exports); and in either case these other controls are likely to contain a large element of discrimination as between the other partner of the clearing agreement and third parties.

(iii) *The payments agreement with unlimited credits.* Almost exactly the same result can be achieved by a different type of institutional arrangements. No clearing office is set up; and the exchange transactions which D_1's and D_2's exchange-control authorities permit take place by the actual purchase and sale of foreign currency. In other words, when an importer in D_1 has a payment to make to an exporter in D_2 he does not pay D_1's currency to a special clearing office, but he purchases the necessary amount of D_2's currency direct from D_1's exchange-control authority or one of its licensed agencies. And similarly with payments from D_2 to D_1.

But the authorities in D_1 and D_2, both of whom are operating exchange-control systems, enter into a 'payments agreement' of the following kind. The banking system in the one country (e.g. D_1) agrees to lend to the banking system in the other country (e.g. D_2) as much of its (i.e. D_1's) currency as the other (i.e. D_2's exchange-control authority) requires at the current rate of exchange in order to finance the payments (i.e. from D_2 to D_1) which the other (i.e. D_2's exchange-control authority) permits to take place. With this mechanism a payment from D_2 to D_1 will cause D_2's banking system to become indebted to D_1's banking system to that amount; and a payment from D_1 to D_2 will cause D_1's banking system to become indebted to D_2's to a similar amount. At the end of any period there will be a net indebtedness of the banking system of the one country to that of the other which will measure the net deficit in the balance of payments of the former with the latter.

Under this system there will once again be no automatic mechanism restoring a balance in the payments between the two countries, such as was found to exist under a clearing agreement with the waiting principle. For in this case the private exporter in the surplus country does not have to wait for payment; this is financed by the credit which the banking system of his country extends to the banking system of the importer's country and with which the importer is enabled to pay the exporter. If there are no limits to the net credits which the banking system of the one country undertakes to extend to that of the other, then the result is essentially the same as the clearing agreement with the financing principle. Balance will be restored when the authorities in the surplus country whose banking system is extending an ever-growing credit to the banking system of the deficit country get tired of making this automatic loan abroad and take other measures (of the kind which we have mentioned in the case of the clearing agreement with the financing principle) either to expand its imports from or to restrict its exports to the other country; and the results will be contractionist or expansionist according as the latter or the former method is adopted.

(iv) *The payments agreement with limited credits.* More normally a payments agreement contains stated limits to the credits which the banking system of the one partner undertakes to extend to that of the other. When the net credit in either direction exceeds the agreed limit, then the excess has to be paid by the debtor banking system to the creditor banking system in convertible monetary reserves (e.g. in gold or in the 'hard' currency of a third country whose money is fully convertible). This arrangement alters the incentives of the authorities in the two countries for the restoration of balance. The payments agreement still provides a mechanism for the transfer of funds between the two exchange-control countries, and the sum of the credit which the authorities in D_1 agree to advance if necessary to D_2 and the credit which the authorities in D_2 agree to advance to D_1 represents a margin within which the net balance between the two countries can vary without any transfer of gold or 'hard' currency. But if a net credit appears on one side in excess of the agreed limit, then the incentive is on the authorities in the deficit country to take steps to restrict imports from, or expand exports to, the surplus country[1] in order to reduce the deficit and so to reduce the loss of gold or hard currency from the deficit to the surplus country, whereas with unlimited credits—as we have just seen—the pressure will eventually be on the authorities in the surplus country to take steps to expand imports from, or restrict exports to, the deficit country.[2]

Such, in simple outline, are the types of arrangement which may be made between the authorities in two exchange-control countries as to the mechanism of payments between them. We have, however, so far discussed them, first, as if they must be used to obtain a strict bilateral balance of the payments between the two countries concerned and, secondly, as if such agreements must always be between two and not more exchange-control countries. Neither of these assumptions is correct.

In the first place, the arrangements may be such as to enable one of the partners to have a continual surplus or deficit with the other. Suppose, for example, that D_1 and D_2 are two exchange-control countries while S is a country without exchange control. D_2 may need exchange control because she is a deficit country so far as her overall balance of payments is concerned; but she may, nevertheless, be in surplus with the 'hard' currency country S, this surplus being more than outweighed by D_2's deficit with D_1. This is likely to be the case if in a normal condition of balance purchasers in D_1 buy mainly from S, purchasers in S mainly from D_2, and purchasers in D_2 mainly from D_1. In such circumstances there might be a 'clearing' or 'payments' agreement of the kinds which we have indicated between D_1 and D_2; but the authorities in D_2, having an excess of receipts of 'hard' currency from S, might in the agreement undertake to finance a given amount of D_2's payments to D_1 with gold or S's convertible currency. Only the remainder of the transactions between D_1 and D_2 would need to balance exactly and

---

[1] Once again we cannot say whether the effect will be expansionist or contractionist. It depends upon which of these two methods is adopted.

[2] There is no logical reason why the scheme should be such as to cause such an abrupt change of incentives. If, for example, as a net credit due from D_1 to D_2 piled up, D_1's authorities were under an obligation to pay a certain proportion to D_2's authorities in gold or 'hard' currency, but for the remainder to extend an unlimited credit to D_1, then D_1's authorities would have some incentive to take steps to restore balance (in order to avoid the gold loss on a certain proportion of the deficit) and D_2's authorities would have some incentive to take steps to restore balance (in order to avoid making a compulsory loan to D_1 of the remaining portion of her surplus).

would need to be treated on the principles which we have discussed above. In other words, clearing or payments agreements between pairs of countries can be planned to have any agreed degree of multilateral trade with outside countries if the partner which is planned to have the net surplus with outside countries agrees to finance that much of its payments to the other partner in the currencies of the outside countries.

Nor need clearing or payments agreements necessarily be formed between only two countries. Consider three exchange-control countries D_1, D_2, and D_3. The authorities in D_1, D_2, and D_3 would set up a common clearing office. The importers in each country would pay in their own currency the sums necessary to finance their purchases from the other two; and the exporters in each country would be paid out of the balances of that currency which were accumulated by the clearing office. Suppose that purchasers in D_1 bought exclusively from D_2, those in D_2 from D_3, and those in D_3 from D_1. Even in this extreme case the clearing office could clear all debts if the balance of payments of each one of the three countries was in balance with the other two. Thus producers in D_1 exporting to D_3 would be paid out of the amounts of D_1's currency accumulated by the clearing office from the funds paid into it by the purchasers in D_1, importing from D_2; and so on. Only the net excess of exports of any one of the countries to the other two over its imports from the other two would cause a net credit balance in its favour which would have to be dealt with either by the waiting principle or by the financing principle.

A similar result could be brought about by a tripartite type of payments arrangement. The authorities in the three exchange-control countries would agree to accept for the settlement of payments between them some unit of account which might or might not be the currency of one of them. If an importer in D_1 has a payment to make to an exporter in D_2, he would obtain D_2's currency by purchasing it from his own exchange-control authority, who in turn would acquire it from D_2's authorities in return for a debt from D_1's to D_2's banking system expressed in terms of the accepted unit of account. At the end of a given period, if purchasers in D_1 bought exclusively from D_2, those in D_2 from D_3, and those in D_3 from D_1, D_1's banking system would be indebted to D_2's, D_2's to D_3's, and D_3's to D_1's. A figure could be struck for the net debit or credit of each banking system. Even in this extreme case of triangular payments these net debits and credits would be zero if each country's balance of payments with the other two was in balance; and each country would be left with a net debit or credit according as it had a net deficit or surplus in its balance of payments with the other two. These debits and credits could be either unlimited in amount (in which case the authorities in each surplus country would have an incentive to take steps to increase imports from or to reduce exports to the other two countries) or they could be payable in gold or hard currency above a certain limit or as to a certain proportion (in which case the authorities in each deficit country would to that extent have an incentive to take steps to reduce imports from or to expand exports to the other two countries). Clearly the principle could be applied to a still larger number of countries, in which case the currencies of the countries in the scheme would in effect be convertible as between each other but would remain inconvertible into the 'hard' currencies of the countries outside the scheme.

2. Multiple Exchange Rates

Suppose now that D_1 and D_2 are soft-currency deficit countries, that S is a hard-currency surplus country, that D_1 has a system of exchange control, and that S has a freely convertible currency. We will call the currencies of these countries D_1-dollars, D_2-dollars, and S-dollars. Suppose that the rate of exchange between D_2-dollars and S-dollars is $\$D_21 = \$S1$. The exchange-control authorities in D_1 can now discriminate against imports from S in favour of imports from D_2 by charging to importers in D_1 a higher price for S-dollars (say $\$D_11{\cdot}50$ for $\$S1$) than for D_2-dollars (say $\$D_11$ for $\$D_21$). This is equivalent in its effects to the imposition in D_1 of a 50 per cent *ad valorem* import duty on all products imported from S without a similar duty on products imported from D_2. All transactions in all countries between the three currencies would be at the rate of $\$D_11 = \$D_21 = \$S1$, except that importers in D_1 of the products of S would have to pay $\$D_11{\cdot}50$ for $\$S1$. The authorities in D_1 would receive a revenue from these exchange operations since they would receive $\$D_11{\cdot}50$ for each S-dollar which they had acquired for only $\$D_11$ from exporters of D_1's products to S.

This arrangement, like many other discriminatory devices (see p. 387), would involve the definition of what constituted a product of D_2 as distinguished from a product of S. It would not suffice for the authorities in D_1 to permit importers in D_1 to purchase D_2-dollars at the favourable price of $\$D_11$ for $\$D_21$ for the purchase of all products in D_2's markets, if S's products could in fact be readily transported to D_1 via D_2's markets. In that case no importer in D_1 would pay $\$D_11{\cdot}50$ for $\$S1$ for the purchase of S's products when he need pay only $\$D_11$ to obtain $\$D_21$ with which he could purchase $\$S1$-worth of S's products in D_2's markets. The unfavourable rate of exchange of $\$D_11{\cdot}50$ for $\$S1$ would have to apply to the purchase of S's products in all markets.

An exactly similar type of arrangement would enable the authorities in D_1 to pay what amounted to an export subsidy on exports to S without paying a similar subsidy on exports to D_2. Suppose now that all transactions in all countries are at the rates of $\$D_11 = \$D_21 = \$S1$ except that the exchange-control authorities in D_1 offer $\$D_11\cdot50$ for every $\$S1$ which exporters in D_1 obtain from the sale of products to S. Then the authorities in D_1 lose money on all exports from D_1 to S since they pay $\$D_11\cdot50$ for each $\$S1$ obtained by D_1's exporters but resell this $\$S1$ for only $\$D_11$ to D_1's importers. This is equivalent to an export subsidy on exports to S but not on exports to D_2.

This will raise the problem of the import of the products of D_2 into D_1 for resale in S. A given amount of D_2's products will sell in S for $\$S1$. If the producers in D_2 sell direct in S they will obtain $\$D_21$ in exchange for the $\$S1$ obtained from their sales in S. But if the products were sold to traders in D_1 who then exported them to S, the traders in D_1 would obtain the favourable rate of $\$D_11\cdot50$ for the $\$S1$ obtained in S's markets. They could offer the producers in D_2, say, $\$D_11\cdot25$ (keeping $\$D_10\cdot25$ of exchange profit for themselves) and these producers would obtain $\$D_21\cdot25$ at the rate of exchange of $\$D_21$ for $\$D_11$.

Such an arrangement would clearly be profitable both to the producers in D_2 and to the traders in D_1. If the object of the exchange-rate arrangement in D_1 were to collect as much as possible of S's hard currency rather than of D_2's soft currency, this flow of exports from D_2 to S via D_1 might be very acceptable to the authorities in D_1 as well. But to the authorities in D_2 it would be very unacceptable, since it would mean that D_2's products which had a ready sale in S's hard currency market for $\$S1$ were being sold by the producers in D_2 for the soft currency of D_1, so that the hard currency proceeds in S-dollars were accruing to D_1's instead of to D_2's monetary authorities. The device would in fact cause D_2's monetary authorities to receive inconvertible D_1-dollars instead of convertible S-dollars for these products of D_2. Steps might well be taken by the authorities in D_2 to prevent the export of the products of D_2 to D_1 for resale to S, so that D_1's subsidy on exports to S was in fact confined to D_1's own products.

So far we have examined the case in which the authorities in D_1 fix a rate of $\$D_11\cdot50$ for $\$S1$ either for D_1's imports from (or other payments to) S or else for D_1's exports to (or other receipts from) S. But the authorities in D_1 might, of course, set this rate for both D_1's imports from and also D_1's exports to S. In this case $\$D_21$ would equal $\$S1$ for all transactions between D_2 and S; $\$D_11$ would equal $\$D_21$ for all transactions between D_1 and D_2; but $\$D_11\cdot50$ would equal $\$S1$ for all transactions between D_1 and S. We can think of this in either of two ways: we can say that the authorities in D_1 levy a 50 per cent *ad valorem* duty on imports from S but not on imports from D_2 while they pay a 50 per cent *ad valorem* subsidy on exports to S but not on exports to D_2; or else we can say that the authorities in D_1 have depreciated D_1's exchange rate by 50 per cent in terms of S's currency but have not depreciated it in terms of D_2's currency, although the exchange rate between D_2's and S's currency has remained unchanged.[1]

In the above examples we assumed that D_1 was an exchange-control country; but D_2 as well as S might have had a freely convertible currency. It is clear that for discrimination to be made effective by means of a system of multiple exchange rates one at least of the countries must have an exchange control. Otherwise in the above example importers of the products of S into D_1 would never pay $\$D_1 1 \cdot 50$ for $\$S1$ but would pay $\$D_1 1$ for $\$D_2 1$ and with $\$D_2 1$ would purchase $\$S1$. But this process can be stopped either by an exchange control in D_1 which prevents residents in D_1 from buying D_2-dollars except for the finance of permitted imports of the products of D_2 or by an exchange control in D_2 which prevents D_2-dollars from being convertible into S-dollars except for the finance of permitted imports of the products of S into D_2 for consumption in D_2. If in the above example (with $\$D_2 1 = \$S1$, $\$D_2 1 = \$D_1 1$, but $\$D_1 1 \cdot 50 = \$S1$) D_1 and S had freely convertible currencies, then the free market rates of exchange would be $\$D_1 1 \cdot 50 = \$D_2 1 = \$S1$. The fact that the rate of exchange between D_1-dollars and D_2-dollars was not $\$D_1 1.50 = \$D_2 1$ but $\$D_1 1 = \$D_2 1$ would be due to the fact that D_2's exchange control had set an artificial rate which undervalued D_2's currency in terms of D_1's, i.e. which discriminated in favour of exports from D_2 to D_1 and against imports to D_2 from D_1. As we have just seen, in these circumstances D_2's exchange control would have to take steps to prevent importers in D_2 from financing their imports of the products of D_1 by purchasing S-dollars at $\$D_2 1$ for $\$S1$ and then obtaining D_1-dollars indirectly at $\$D_1 1 \cdot 50$ for $\$S1$.

We have seen in Chapter XX pp. 268–72 that by a system of multiple exchange rates between two countries the exchange-control authority of any country can arrange for any combination of taxes or subsidies on imports or exports by charging different rates of exchange for buying and selling the currency of the other country for various purposes. The principle here is exactly the same. By varying the rates at which it will buy or sell foreign exchange for the finance not of particular imports or exports but of exports to or imports from particular countries, this device can be employed for the institution of any desired system of discrimination.

There is one particular system to which it may be interesting to make reference in passing. Suppose that country A has separate clearing or payments agreements with each of the other countries B, C, D, E, etc. Then the payments and receipts between A and any one of the other individual countries could be brought into balance by means of an

---

[1] The problems arising out of a situation of this kind are known as the problems of disorderly cross-rates. The direct rate of exchange between D_1's and D_2's currency is $\$D_1 1 = \$D_2 1$. The cross-rate through S's currency is $\$D_1 1 \cdot 50 = \$D_2 1$, since $\$D_1 1 \cdot 50$ must be paid for $\$S1$ with which $\$D_2 1$ can be obtained.

THE METHODS OF DISCRIMINATION

alteration in the rate of exchange between A's currency and that of the other country. Suppose that we start with $A1 = $B1 = $C1 = $D1 = $E1 etc., but that A is in deficit with B and C and in surplus with D and E. Then the clearing or payments accounts of A with these countries might be balanced at rates of exchange of, say, $A1·50 = $B1, $A1·30 = $C1, $A0·70 = $D1, and $A0·80 = $E1. The depreciation of A's currency with B's and C's currencies will serve to remove A's deficits with those countries; and the appreciation of A's currency with D's and E's currencies will serve to remove A's surpluses with those countries. Meanwhile, the rates may remain $B1 = $C1 = $D1 = $E1 for all transactions between those other countries.

Indeed, this sort of system could be completely generalized. Every country in the world might have an exchange control; the authorities in each country might operate a clearing or payments agreement with each other country; and balance might be obtained between each pair of countries by adjusting the rate of exchange employed in the appropriate bilateral agreement. In cases of this kind there is an interesting combination of the methods of price adjustment and of direct controls. Direct controls (i.e. exchange controls) must be employed to enable sufficient discrimination of exchange rates to take place in order to force a bilateral balance of payments between each pair of countries; but by allowing a flexible exchange rate between each pair of countries, so that the currency of the surplus member of any pair appreciates in terms of the currency of the deficit member of that pair, a freely operating price adjustment is employed to induce the exact bilateral balance.

3. *Other Measures*

We have been obliged to devote considerable space to the discriminatory aspects of exchange control and multiple exchange rates, because these methods of discrimination raise important new problems of international monetary organization. But we need do little more than catalogue the discriminatory uses of the other direct controls mentioned in Chapters XX and XXI, since no new organizational problems are involved. The reader should, however, beware of gaining the impression that the length of the discussion devoted in this chapter to exchange control and multiple exchange rates on the one hand and to other devices on the other hand in any way measures their relative importance in the real world. This is far from being the case. The discriminatory effects of the devices which we are about to list may be in every way as important as those of the financial devices which we have just discussed.

First in our catalogue come *fiscal measures*. The authorities in A may discriminate against imports from B as opposed to imports from C by imposing a heavier import tax (or paying a smaller import subsidy) on the former than on the latter. Similarly, they may impose export duties or subsidies at different rates according as the exports are being sold to B or to C. Such devices raise all the problems of the definition of the products of different countries and of consumption in different countries. For example, a heavy duty imposed in A on the import of products from B will be evaded if B's products can be sent to A via C. Or subsidies in A on exports to C and taxes on exports to B can be evaded if traders in C are allowed to purchase A's subsidized products not for consumption in C but for re-export to B.

Next we have the discriminatory use of *Quantitative Restrictions* on trade, including the use of *Tariff-Quotas* and similar devices. If the authorities in A set a limit by value or by quantity to the amount of A's imports (or exports) which are allowed into A (or out of A) or which are allowed into A (or out of A) untaxed or at a specially low rate of tax, these quotas can be set by A's authorities so as to permit much trade with B and little trade with C. They can clearly be used to discriminate in favour of one country and against another. Moreover, their use raises the same problem of defining a country's products and a country's consumption as are raised by the discriminatory use of fiscal measures.

Finally, there is the possibility of the discriminatory use of a *State trading organization*. If the State has a monopoly of the country's import or export trade it can use that monopoly to restrict its imports from (or its exports to) one country more severely than in the case of another country. If the State enters into foreign trade even without a monopoly of such trade, it can use its trading organization to expand its imports or its exports beyond the level which would otherwise have been reached, though it must be prepared to face a financial loss if it so over-imports as to flood the home market and so over-exports as to flood the foreign market. It can use this power to subsidize imports or exports in such a way as to expand its trade with one foreign country rather than with another. Here again the problem will arise of preventing the countries against which the State trading organization is discriminating from obtaining the more favourable terms simply by trading via the more favoured foreign country.

CHAPTER XXX

THE USE OF DISCRIMINATORY
AND NON-DISCRIMINATORY CONTROLS

IN Chapter XXVIII we discussed the meaning of discrimination and non-discrimination. In the last chapter we discussed the controls which might be employed for the purpose of discrimination. We come now to the question of substance from the point of view of economic policy. In what conditions, if at all, should the authorities in one country discriminate in their relations with other countries for the purpose of easing the adjustment of the balance of payments?

The simple argument for such discrimination is as follows. The authorities in any country should take discriminatory measures to reduce that country's imports from (or other payments to) and to increase its exports to (or other receipts from) any other country whose currency is abnormally 'hard', i.e. if the authorities in the former country find special difficulty in obtaining the currency of the latter for the finance of foreign payments. Similarly, they should take discriminatory measures to increase imports from and to decrease exports to any country whose currency is abnormally 'soft', i.e. if they can obtain supplies of that currency abnormally easily for the finance of foreign payments.

From this it might appear that if all foreign currencies are freely convertible into each other there would be no question of discrimination on balance-of-payments grounds. If B-dollars are freely convertible into C-dollars and vice versa, it would appear that the authorities in country A could have no reason to discriminate in their control of imports or exports between markets in B and markets in C. If, for example, importers in A purchase more of B's products and less of C's products, the monetary authorities in A may have a deficiency of B-dollars and an excess of C-dollars; but this does not matter since C-dollars can be freely convertible into B-dollars. If all foreign moneys are freely convertible into each other, it would appear quite immaterial to the authorities in any country which foreign currency its exporters earned and which foreign currency its importers used. All that is necessary is to see that the total of foreign currencies earned is as great as the total of foreign currencies used.

But in spite of this there are at least two reasons why a policy of discrimination by the authorities in A between trade with B and trade with C may in fact ease the position of A's balance of payments, even though B's and C's currencies are freely convertible into each other.

In the first place, suppose that the authorities in B adopt a successful financial policy for internal balance, but that C has a neutral economy and suffers from some considerable level of unemployment. Suppose now that the authorities in A adopt a discriminatory control which causes importers in A to switch their purchases from B's markets to C's markets or causes exporters in A to switch their sales in the opposite direction from C's markets to B's markets. This switch will tend to cause a deflationary influence within B's economy (since the demand in A for B's exports has fallen or the supply of A's products competing in B's markets with B's home produce has increased). Conversely, in C there will be an inflationary movement (since the demand in A for C's products has risen or the supply of A's products competing in C's markets has fallen). In B the financial policy for internal balance will offset the deflationary pressure, so that B's national income will not fall and the demand in B for imports—and so for A's exports—will not fall.[1] But in C there is no financial policy for internal balance; and the inflationary influence of the improvement in C's balance of trade will be allowed to generate an inflationary upward movement of C's national income, domestic expenditure, and demand for imports. In consequence there will be a net increase in the demand for A's products in C. As a result of the shift of demand in A from B's products on to C's products, the demand in B for A's products is not allowed to fall but the demand in C for A's products rises as income and expenditure are inflated in C. A's balance of payments is thereby improved.

This same principle might be at work even if both B and C had neutral economies. Suppose that the home leakage in B (see p. 55, above) is larger than in C, that the marginal propensity to import in B is smaller than in C, and that of the marginal propensity to import a smaller proportion represents a propensity to import A's products in B than in C. Then when purchasers in A switch their demand from B's products on to C's products the deflationary influence in B will have a smaller effect in reducing the demand in B for A's exports than the same inflationary influence in C will have in increasing the demand in C for A's exports. As the deflation proceeds in B, (i) it will not go very far because of the high home leakage in B, (ii) it will not affect the demand in B for imports very much because of the low marginal propensity to import in B, and (iii) it will still less affect the demand in B for imports from A because of the small proportion of B's marginal imports which are taken from A. These factors in C will work in the opposite direction: the inflationary influence in C will cause a large

---

[1] Indeed there will be some rise in the demand in B for imports, since the unfavourable movement in B's balance of trade must be offset by an equal increase in B's domestic expenditure, some part of which will be spent on additional imports including imports from A.

increase in C's demand for imports from A because of the small home leakage in C, the high marginal propensity to import in C, and the high proportion of C's marginal imports which are taken from A. The authorities in A can, therefore, improve A's balance-of-payments position, even though all foreign currencies are convertible, by switching the demand for imports away from country B where the resulting deflationary influence will not much reduce the demand for A's products, on to country C where the resulting inflationary influence will increase the demand for A's products considerably.

This phenomenon could not, however, arise in the world on which we are concentrating our attention throughout Part VI, namely, one in which the authorities in all countries are adopting successful financial policies for internal balance. In such circumstances a switch of demand by purchasers in A from B's products on to C's products would not be permitted to cause either a net deflation in B nor a net inflation in C. The demand by purchasers in B for A's products would not fall and the demand by purchasers in C for A's products would not rise, and there would be no net change in A's balance of payments.[1]

But there remains a second important way in which a discriminatory policy by the authorities in one country might improve that country's balance of payments even though there were full convertibility between the currencies of all other countries and even though the authorities in these other countries were all adopting successful financial policies for internal balance. Suppose that both D_1 and D_2 are deficit countries which are attempting to preserve external balance by means of direct controls (e.g. by means of quantitative restrictions of their imports), but that S is a surplus country which has no direct controls (i.e. is not restricting her imports). Then if the authorities in D_1 relax D_1's restrictions on imports from D_2 and the authorities in D_2 simultaneously relax D_2's restrictions on imports from D_1 by a corresponding amount, the authorities in D_1 will find that the increased imports of D_2's products into D_1 do not worsen D_1's balance-of-payments position simply because D_2's imports of D_1's products will expand by the same amount at the same time. In other words, if the authorities in two deficit countries which are employing import restrictions to maintain external balance agree simultaneously to relax their import restrictions on each other's products they can each

---

[1] This is not quite strictly true. There would be some net increase in the demand for A's products by purchasers in B, since domestic expenditure in B (and so B's imports) would be increased to offset the net decline in B's balance of trade; and conversely there would be some net decline in the demand for A's products by purchasers in C. If the marginal propensity to import A's products were higher in B than in C, this would cause some net increase in the demand for A's products by foreign purchasers as a whole and so some improvement in A's balance of payments. But this consideration is of minor importance.

admit larger imports without any increased strain on the balance of payments.

But such relaxations of import restrictions must discriminate against S's products. If the governments of D_1 and D_2 relaxed their import restrictions on S's products when they relaxed their import restrictions on each other's products, each of them would also admit larger imports of S's products. But since the authorities in S have imposed no import restrictions on D_1's or D_2's products, they cannot enter into a simultaneous agreement to relax import restrictions so that imports of D_1's and D_2's products into S may rise as quickly as imports of S's products into D_1 and D_2.

As a general principle we may state that where the authorities in two or more countries are imposing restrictions on imports from each other they can enter into an agreement for a simultaneous relaxation of those restrictions such that each member of the group increases its imports from all the other members of the group to the same extent that it has increased its exports to the other members of the group; and if their currencies are all freely convertible into each other, the authorities in each country in the group will find that they have admitted larger imports without any additional strain on the balance of payments because exports to other members of the group will rise as quickly as imports from other members of the group. But such relaxations of import restrictions must not apply to imports from countries whose authorities (either because they have not previously imposed any import restrictions or because they are not prepared to relax their restrictions) do not join in the general agreement to admit more imports; otherwise the members of the group would experience a strain on their balances of payments because their imports from outside countries would rise without any corresponding rise in their exports to those countries.

As we saw at the beginning of this chapter, the obvious case for discrimination on balance-of-payments grounds is where one foreign currency is inconvertible. Suppose that D_1 is a deficit country whose authorities are attempting to preserve external balance by means of quantitative restrictions over imports from other countries, and suppose that D_2 is a country whose currency is not freely convertible into other currencies. Suppose that purchasers in D_2 find it profitable to purchase on a large scale from D_1, and that they pay for such purchases with inconvertible D_2-dollars; but suppose that purchasers in D_1 (at current rates of exchange and allowing for the imposition of non-discriminatory restrictions by the authorities in D_1 on imports from D_2 as well as from other sources) do not in fact purchase very much from D_2. Then someone in D_1 will be piling up balances of inconvertible D_2-dollars which can be used only for the purchase of additional supplies of D_2's products.

If there is a payments agreement with unlimited credits between the monetary authorities of D_1 and D_2 (see p. 393, above), then the banking system in D_1 will be paying the exporters in D_1 in D_1-dollars and will be piling up a holding of inconvertible D_2-dollars in exchange. There will appear to be a specially strong case why the authorities in D_1 should discriminate in their import restrictions in favour of D_2's products in order that some use may be made of these holdings of D_2-dollars which can be used only for the purchase of D_2's products.

But this necessity is solely due to the type of payments arrangement which is operated by the authorities in D_1 in regard to transactions with D_2. Suppose that the authorities in D_1 simply refused to give D_1-dollars in return for inconvertible D_2-dollars to those exporters who had sold D_1's products in D_2. The exporters would then have to wait until they could themselves find some profitable use for these funds in the purchase of D_2's products. They would soon themselves insist that the importers in D_2 should pay for the products of D_1 either in D_1-dollars or in some freely convertible currency. In this case the authorities in D_2 would find that they were losing hard-currency reserves to finance the excess imports into D_2 of D_1's products.[1]

In this case the authorities in D_2 would be obliged to impose restrictions on imports from D_1 of a sufficiently severe character if they wished (without a change in exchange rates) to remove the drain on their reserves of foreign exchange which was occasioned by the excess imports from D_1 into D_2. But in such a case we should have returned to the argument for discrimination which we have already just examined, namely, that where the authorities in D_1 restrict imports from D_2 and the authorities in D_2 restrict imports from D_1, the authorities in both countries can admit more imports without any additional strain on the balance of payments, if they agree to relax their restrictions on imports from each other's countries without a simultaneous relaxation of their restrictions on imports from third countries. This is the basic argument for discrimination on balance-of-payments grounds in a world in which the authorities in all countries adopt successful financial policies for internal balance.

But, while this principle is fairly clear, the way in which it should be operated in detail is far from simple. The problems which it involves can be made clear if we start from the position of world disequilibrium

---

[1] The same end result would be reached if there were an exchange control in D_1 which laid down the rule that exporters of D_1's products to D_2 must insist upon receiving payment either in D_1-dollars or in other freely convertible currencies which should be surrendered by the exporters of D_1's products to the exchange control in D_1. In this case also the authorities in D_2 would find that they were losing hard-currency reserves in respect of the excess imports from D_1 into D_2.

in balances of payments which is illustrated in Table XXI. From this position external balance is to be reached by the imposition of import restrictions by the deficit countries. Our first problem is to see what happens if these import restrictions are imposed on a non-discriminatory basis; this is illustrated in Table XXV. Our second problem is to see what happens if these import restrictions are imposed on a discriminatory basis, and to examine what different principles of discrimination might be adopted in order to enable the deficit countries to achieve external balance with the minimum destruction of world trade; this is illustrated in Table XXVI.[1]

Let us start, then, with the operation of non-discriminatory import restrictions in Table XXV. Stage i of the table is merely a reproduction from Table XXI for ease of reference of the original position of disequilibrium which remains to be removed by import restrictions. In this position it will be seen that D_1 has a deficit of $47 m. The authorities in D_1 attempt to get rid of this by cutting D_1's imports by $47 m., i.e. from the level of $147 m. shown in row 6, column a of the table to the $100 m. shown in row 12 column a of the table. All D_1's imports in column a, stage ii of the table are $\frac{100}{147}$ of those shown in column a, stage i of the table. Simultaneously the authorities in D_2, the only other deficit country in stage i, cuts imports into D_2 by an amount equal to the existing deficit of $33 m. from $155 m. to $122 m., and the imports into D_2 from each country in column b, stage ii of the table are $\frac{122}{155}$ of the corresponding figures in column b, stage i. Since S_1, S_2, and B have not got deficits on their balances of payments in stage i, the imports of these countries in columns c, d, and e are left unchanged between stages i and ii.

---

[1] In these tables and the discussion which accompanies them we confine our attention to the question of discriminatory and non-discriminatory controls over imports. Similar principles could be applied to controls over other international payments; for example, discriminatory controls over the lending of capital to deficit or surplus countries could be treated in the same manner as discriminatory controls over imports from deficit or surplus countries. Moreover, for the purposes of our present arithmetical illustrations we shall assume that if the authorities in A restrict imports on a non-discriminatory basis this involves the reduction of the value of its imports from B, C, D, E, etc. by the same percentage. As we have already argued in Chapter XVIII, this is not in fact necessarily so. Suppose that purchasers in A import from B products for which the producers in A cannot readily make substitutes and which are indispensable to the purchasers in A; but suppose that purchasers in A import from C products which producers in A can fairly easily produce themselves and with which purchasers in A can in any case fairly easily dispense. Then a uniform 10 per cent *ad valorem* duty on imports into A from B and C would cause a much greater decline in imports from C than in imports from B; and this would be true non-discrimination. The assumption which we shall make in the following arithmetical illustrations, namely, that non-discriminatory import restrictions involve equal percentage cuts on imports from all sources, is made simply for ease of exposition. The principles of the argument would be unaltered if we allowed for a more accurate definition of non-discrimination.

TABLE XXV

Non-Discriminatory Import Restrictions $ m.

		Payments for autonomous trade by					Total exports	Deficit (−) or surplus (+) on balance of autonomous		
		D_1	D_2	S_1	S_2	B		trade	trans-fers	pay-ments
		(a)	(b)	(c)	(d)	(e)	(f)	(g)	(h)	(i)

Stage i. Original Position from Table XXI

Receipts from autonomous trade by	D_1 (1)		8	60	17	5	90	−57	+10	−47
	D_2 (2)	61		5	24	12	102	−53	+20	−33
	S_1 (3)	57	44		41	83	225	+80	−15	+65
	S_2 (4)	5	77	57		5	144	+30	−15	+15
	B (5)	24	26	23	32		105	0	0	0
Total imports	(6)	147	155	145	114	105	666	World disequilibrium = 80		

Stage ii. The Authorities in D_1 and D_2 restrict Imports from all Sources to $\frac{100}{147}$ and $\frac{122}{155}$ respectively of their Original Imports

Receipts from autonomous trade by	D_1 (7)		6	60	17	5	88	−12	+10	−2
	D_2 (8)	42		5	24	12	83	−39	+20	−19
	S_1 (9)	39	35		´41	83	198	+53	−15	+38
	S_2 (10)	3	61	57		5	126	+12	−15	−3
	B (11)	16	20	23	32		91	−14	0	−14
Total imports	(12)	100	122	145	114	105	586	World disequilibrium = 38		

Stage iii. The Authorities in D_1, D_2, S_2, and B restrict Imports from all Sources to $\frac{98}{147}$, $\frac{103}{155}$, $\frac{111}{114}$, and $\frac{91}{105}$ respectively of their Original Imports

Receipts from autonomous trade by	D_1 (13)		5	60	17	4	86	−12	+10	−2
	D_2 (14)	41		5	23	11	80	−23	+20	−3
	S_1 (15)	38	29		40	72	179	+34	−15	+19
	S_2 (16)	3	51	57		4	115	+4	−15	−11
	B (17)	16	18	23	31		88	−3	0	−3
Total imports	(18)	98	103	145	111	91	548	World disequilibrium = 19		

Stage iv. The Authorities in D_1, D_2, S_2, and B restrict Imports from all Sources to $\frac{96}{147}$, $\frac{100}{155}$, $\frac{100}{114}$, and $\frac{88}{105}$ respectively of their Original Imports

Receipts from autonomous trade by	D_1 (19)		5	60	15	4	84	−12	+10	−2
	D_2 (20)	40		5	21	10	76	−24	+20	−4
	S_1 (21)	37	28		36	70	171	+26	−15	+11
	S_2 (22)	3	50	57		4	114	+14	−15	−1
	B (23)	16	17	23	28		84	−4	0	−4
Total imports	(24)	96	100	145	100	88	529	World disequilibrium = 11		

Stage v. Final Position. The Authorities in D_1, D_2, S_2, and B restrict Imports from all Sources to $\frac{93}{147}$, $\frac{93}{155}$, $\frac{95}{114}$, and $\frac{80}{105}$ respectively of their Original Imports.

Receipts from autonomous trade by	D_1 (25)		5	60	14	4	83	−10	+10	0
	D_2 (26)	39		5	20	9	73	−20	+20	0
	S_1 (27)	36	27		34	63	160	+15	−15	0
	S_2 (28)	3	46	57		4	110	+15	−15	0
	B (29)	15	15	23	27		80	0	0	0
Total imports	(30)	93	93	145	95	80	506	World disequilibrium = 0		

The total result of these non-discriminatory import restrictions by the authorities in D_1 and D_2 are shown in the figures for stage ii. The first point to notice is that neither the authorities in D_1 nor the authorities in D_2 have succeeded in fully removing their country's deficit. The non-discriminatory import restrictions in D_1 involved the heavy reduction of D_1's imports from D_2 by \$19 m. (because D_1 is a heavy importer from D_2), so that D_2's exports fell by \$19 m. But the import restrictions imposed by the authorities in D_2 were sufficient only to remove D_2's existing deficit and did not allow for the worsening of D_2's deficit due to the restrictions imposed in D_1 on imports of D_2's products. As a result, in stage ii D_2 still has a deficit of \$19 m. And similarly the non-discriminatory import restrictions imposed in D_2 have reduced D_2's imports from D_1 by \$2 m., so that D_1 is still left in stage ii with a deficit of \$2 m. Moreover, S_2 and B in stage ii have deficits of \$3 m. and \$14 m. respectively, while S_1 is still left with a surplus of \$38 m. The non-discriminatory principle in the import restrictions imposed in D_1 and D_2 has involved cuts in the imports into D_1 and D_2 from B, which was previously in external balance but which now has a deficit of \$14 m.; and it has imposed heavier cuts on the imports of S_2's products into D_1 and D_2 than the original surplus of S_2 so that S_2's original surplus is now changed into a net deficit of \$3 m. On the other hand, the non-discriminatory principle has involved cuts in D_1's and D_2's imports from S_1 which were less than S_1's original surplus of \$65 m. so that S_1 is still left with a surplus of \$38 m. The world disequilibrium has been reduced but not eliminated by the import restrictions imposed by the authorities in D_1 and D_2. Total deficits in the original position amounted to \$80 m. (i.e. \$47 m. for D_1 and \$33 m. for D_2) and were, of course, equal to the total surpluses (i.e. \$65 m. for S_1 and \$15 m. for S_2). In stage ii total deficits have fallen to \$38 m. (i.e. \$2 m. for D_1, \$19 m. for D_2, \$3 m. for S_1, and \$11 m. for B) and are matched by total surpluses of the same amount (i.e. \$38 m. for S_1). That part of the non-discriminatory imports restrictions imposed in D_1 and D_2 which fell on the exports of surplus countries has removed a deficit and a corresponding surplus; but that part which fell on each other's exports or on the exports of countries which were already in external balance has merely shifted a deficit from the restricting country on to another country.

In stage ii we are left then with the following deficits: \$2 m. for D_1, \$19 m. for D_2, \$3 m. for S_1, and \$14 m. for B. The authorities in D_1 and D_2 proceed to tighten up their import restrictions so that their imports are reduced on a non-discriminatory basis by a further \$2 m. and \$19 m. respectively, i.e. in the case of D_1 to \$98 m. instead of the \$100 m. of stage ii and the \$147 m. of stage i, and in the case of D_2 to \$103 m. instead of the \$122 m. of stage ii and the \$155 m. of stage

i. The authorities in S_2 and B now impose restrictions for the first time in order to reduce their imports by $3 m. and $11 m. to $111 m. and $91 m. respectively. These new total import programmes of D_1, D_2, S_2, and B are shown in row 18 columns *a*, *b*, *d*, and *e* of Table XXV. The restrictions are again on a non-discriminatory basis in relation to the imports of the original position so that each of D_1's import figures in column *a* of stage iii is $\frac{98}{147}$ of those in stage i; and similarly for D_2, S_2, and B.

Once again, as the figures in column *i* of stage iii of Table XXV show, these adjustments have further reduced the size of the world disequilibrium but they have not entirely removed it. And the reason for this is simple. In stage ii only one surplus country, namely S_1, was left. All the other countries were deficit countries. In so far as the new non-discriminatory import restrictions imposed in D_1, D_2, S_2, and B involved cuts of imports from the surplus country S_1, the deficits of the deficit countries fell and this was matched by a fall in the surplus of the surplus country. To this extent world disequilibrium was reduced. But in so far as the non-discriminatory import restrictions in D_1 involved a reduction of D_1's imports from the other deficit countries D_2, S_2, and B, this merely reduced D_1's deficit at the expense of increasing the deficits of D_2, S_2, and B. And similarly with the import cuts in D_2, S_2, and B. In so far as they fell upon the exports of another deficit country they merely shuffled the burden of the deficits round among the deficit countries at the expense of cutting each other's export trades, and without putting the restrictions on to the exports of the surplus country.

It will be seen that in stage iii the total deficits have been cut down to $19 m.[1] ($2 m. for D_1, $3 m. for D_2, $11 m. for S_2, and $3 m. for B). Further non-discriminatory cuts of these amounts are imposed in D_1, D_2, S_2, and B and we reach the position shown in stage iv, where once more there has been some further decline in the total deficits (because some of the new imports cuts fell on the exports of the surplus country) but not a total elimination of the deficits (because some of the new import cuts fell on the exports of countries which were already in deficit). This process of cuts will continue until the final position of equilibrium shown in stage v is approached. In this position total world trade (i.e. the total of world exports or of world imports) is only

[1] While the total of world deficits has been reduced from $38 m. to $19 m. between stages ii and iii it is interesting to observe that S_2's deficit alone has increased from $3 m. to $11 m. S_2's new import restrictions are very moderate (she had a deficit of only $3 m. in stage ii to be removed by her stage-iii restrictions) and her imports fall by only $3 m. between the two stages. But D_2 which provides a large market for S_2's products, had the large deficit of $19 m. in stage ii; and the heavy new restrictions imposed in D_2 caused S_2's exports to D_2 alone to fall by $10 m. (from $61 m. to $51 m.).

$506 m. (row 30, column f) as compared with $666 m. in the original position (row 6, column f). In other words, there will have been a decline in total world trade of no less than $160 m. in order to get rid of an original disequilibrium in world payments (i.e. total of world deficits or of world surpluses) of only $80 m.

Now it would appear that if the authorities in the deficit countries cut only their imports from the surplus countries, there need only be one round of cuts. The whole of the first import cut of $80 m. in the deficit countries would cause a direct decline of $80 m. in the exports of the surplus countries. The deficits of the deficit countries and the surpluses of the surplus countries would thereby be simultaneously removed. The total world disequilibrium of $80 m. would have been removed at the cost of a decline in total world imports (i.e. in the imports of the deficit countries) or in total world exports (i.e. in the exports of the surplus countries) of only $80 m.

That this is possible is illustrated in case a of Table XXVI. In this table as in Table XXV stage i merely reproduces from Table XXI for ease of reference the original position of disequilibrium which has to be removed by import restrictions. In case a, stage ii of Table XXVI the authorities in D_2 impose total import cuts equal to D_2's original deficit of $33 m. But they do this by means of discriminatory import restrictions which involve no cuts in D_2's imports from D_1 (a deficit country) or from B (a country already in external balance), but which concentrate D_2's import restrictions upon the two surplus countries S_1 and S_2. The authorities in D_2 impose $15 m. out of the total cuts of $33 m. on imports from S_2. They cannot concentrate more of the cut upon S_2's exports without turning S_2 into a deficit country, because S_2's total surplus is only $15 m. The remaining $18 m. of D_2's cuts are imposed upon imports from the other surplus country S_1, whose surplus is thereby reduced from $65 m. to $47 m. The cuts imposed in D_2 have thus served directly both to reduce D_2's deficit and to reduce surpluses of the exporting countries. D_2's deficit of $33 m. has disappeared by reducing S_2's exports and so S_2's surplus by $15 m. and S_1's exports and so S_1's surplus by $18 m.

We are left then in case a stage ii with a position in which D_1 still has a deficit of $47 m. and S_1 has a surplus of $47 m. If now (case a, stage iii of Table XXVI), the authorities in D_1 impose discriminatory import restrictions of $47 m. on imports from S_1, cutting them from $57 m. to $10 m., D_1's deficit of $47 m. and S_1's surplus of $47m. will both be directly removed. As is apparent from the figures given for stage iii of case a in Table XXVI, all countries are now in external balance and the total of world trade has fallen by only $80 m. (the amount of

TABLE XXVI

Discriminatory Import Restrictions

$ m.

		Payments for autonomous trade by					Total exports	Deficit (−) or surplus (+) on balance of autonomous		
		D_1	D_2	S_1	S_2	B		trade	transfers	payments
		(a)	(b)	(c)	(d)	(e)	(f)	(g)	(h)	(i)
Cases a and b. Stage i Original Position from Table XXI										
Receipts from autonomous trade by	D_1 (1)		8	60	17	5	90	−57	+10	−47
	D_2 (2)	61		5	24	12	102	−53	+20	−33
	S_1 (3)	57	44		41	83	225	+80	−15	+65
	S_2 (4)	5	77	57		5	144	+30	−15	+15
	B (5)	24	26	23	32		105	0	0	0
Total imports	(6)	147	155	145	114	105	666			
Case a. Stage ii. The Authorities in D_2 restrict Imports by 18 from S_1 and by 15 from S_2										
Receipts from autonomous trade by	D_1 (7)		8	60	17	5	90	−57	+10	−47
	D_2 (8)	61		5	24	12	102	−20	+20	0
	S_1 (9)	57	26		41	83	207	+62	−15	+47
	S_2 (10)	5	62	57		5	129	+15	−15	0
	B (11)	24	26	23	32		105	0	0	0
Total imports	(12)	147	122	145	114	105	633			
Case a. Stage iii. The Authorities in D_1 restrict Imports by 47 from S_1										
Receipts from autonomous trade by	D_1 (13)		8	60	17	5	90	−10	+10	0
	D_2 (14)	61		5	24	12	102	−20	+20	0
	S_1 (15)	10	26		41	83	160	+15	−15	0
	S_2 (16)	5	62	57		5	129	+15	−15	0
	B (17)	24	26	23	32		105	0	0	0
Total imports	(18)	100	122	145	114	105	586			
Case b. Stage ii. The Authorities in D_2 restrict Imports by 33 from S_1										
Receipts from autonomous trade by	D_1 (19)		8	60	17	5	90	−57	+10	−47
	D_2 (20)	61		5	24	12	102	−20	+20	0
	S_1 (21)	57	11		41	83	192	+47	−15	+32
	S_2 (22)	5	77	57		5	144	+30	−15	+15
	B (23)	24	26	23	32		105	0	0	0
Total imports	(24)	147	122	145	114	105	633			
Case b. Stage iii. The Authorities in D_1 restrict Imports by 32 from S_1 and by 5 from S_2										
Receipts from autonomous trade by	D_1 (25)		8	60	17	5	90	−20	+10	−10
	D_2 (26)	61		5	24	12	102	−20	+20	0
	S_1 (27)	25	11		41	83	160	+15	−15	0
	S_2 (28)	0	77	57		5	139	+25	−15	+10
	B (29)	24	26	23	32		105	0	0	0
Total imports	(30)	110	122	145	114	105	596			

the original disequilibrium of world payments) from $666 m. to $586 m. Moreover, the main surplus country S_1 has not apparently suffered as a result of the discriminatory policy. S_1's exports at the end of stage iii of case a of Table XXVI are $160 m., i.e. no lower than they are at the end of the process of non-discriminatory import restrictions in stage v of Table XXV. And every other country's exports at the end of stage iii of case a of Table XXVI are higher than at the end of stage v of Table XXV.

But the solution cannot always be as simple as this, as is shown by the figures for case b in Table XXVI. In this case (stage ii of case b) we suppose that the authorities in D_2 choose to get rid of D_2's original deficit of $33 m. by discriminatory import restrictions which impose the whole of the import cut of $33 m. upon imports from S_1. As can be seen from the figures in case b stage ii, this reduces D_2's deficit by $33 m. from $33 m. to zero and reduces S_1's surplus by $33 m. from $65 m. to $32 m. This leaves the following disequilibria: a deficit for D_1 of $47 m. matched by surpluses for S_1 of $32 m. and for S_2 of $15 m.

The authorities in D_1 can now get rid of $32 m. out of D_1's deficit of $47 m. by a discriminatory cut of imports from S_1 of $32 m., i.e. cutting them from $57 m. to $25 m., as is done in stage iii of case b. The authorities in D_1 cannot cut D_1's imports from S_1 any further without putting S_1 into a deficit position, since S_1's total surplus after the adjustment of stage ii of case b was only $32 m. D_1 is now left with a deficit of $15 m. (i.e. the remainder of her deficit of $47 m. after the cut of her imports from S_1 of $32 m.) matched by S_2's surplus of $15 m. But imports into D_1 from S_2 are only $5 m. It is therefore impossible for the authorities in D_1 to get rid of the rest of D_1's deficit of $15 m. by imposing cuts on imports from a surplus country. There is only one surplus country left, namely S_2, and from that country imports into D_1 are only $5 m. Even if the authorities in D_1 cut D_1's imports from S_2 to zero, as is done in stage iii of case b, D_1 is left with a deficit of $10 m.

In stage iii of case b we have reached a position in which D_1's deficit of $10 m. is matched by S_2's deficit of $10 m., but in which D_1's imports from S_2 are zero and cannot therefore be further restricted. In this case the authorities in D_1 can employ import restrictions to remove D_1's deficit only by restricting D_1's imports from D_2, S_1, or B which are in external balance and which will therefore themselves in turn become deficit countries to the extent that D_1's import cuts fall on their exports.

If the authorities in D_1 choose to impose this remaining import cut of $10 m. upon imports from D_2 or S_1, then D_2 or S_1 will be in a deficit of $10 m. instead of D_1. But the authorities in D_2 or S_1 can then cut imports from the surplus country S_2 by \$10 m. and their deficit and S_2's surplus will thereby be reduced. In this case the total of world trade will have fallen to \$576 m. It is \$596 m. at the end of stage iii of case b; it will be reduced by \$10 m. to \$586 m. when the authorities in D_1 restrict imports from D_2 or S_1, and by a further \$10 m. to \$576 m. when D_2's or S_1's imports from S_2 are reduced by \$10 m. The fall in world trade will be \$10 m. more than is necessary in case a where the total fall is only to \$586 m.

But if the authorities in D_1, at the end of stage iii of case b, choose to restrict imports by \$10 m. from B instead of from D_2 or S_1 the fall in world trade will have to be still greater. When D_1's imports from B are reduced by \$10 m., D_1's deficit of \$10 m. will disappear but will be replaced by a deficit of \$10 m. for B whose exports to D_1 have fallen by this amount. The authorities in B must, therefore, impose import restrictions of \$10 m. But B's imports from the only remaining surplus country S_2 are only \$5 m. (row 28 column *e* of Table XXVI.) The authorities in B can, therefore, restrict imports from S_2 by \$5 m; and to this extent B's deficit will be reduced by \$5m. and this will be matched by a reduction of S_2's surplus by \$5 m. But for the removal of the remaining deficit of \$5 m. the authorities in B must restrict imports from D_1, D_2, or S_1, each of which are now in external balance and will be put into deficit by B's import restrictions. If the authorities in B choose to restrict imports from D_2 or S_1 by \$5 m., then the authorities in D_2 or S_1 can restrict imports from S_2 by \$5 m.; and the circle will be closed. In this case world trade will have fallen to \$571 m. It is \$596 m. at the end of stage iii of case b, it is reduced to \$586 m. when D_1's imports from B are reduced by \$10 m.; it is reduced to \$576 m. when B's imports from S_2 are reduced by \$5 m. and from D_2 or S_1 are reduced by \$5 m.; and it is reduced to \$571 m. when D_2's or S_1's imports from S_2 are reduced by \$5 m. But if the authorities in B had chosen to meet B's deficit of \$10 m. in any part by reducing B's imports from D_1 instead of from D_2 or S_1 there would have been a still further fall in world trade, because this would have put D_1 in deficit and D_1 has no imports from the surplus country S_2 to be cut. The authorities in D_1 would in turn have had to cut from D_2, S_1, or B. If they had cut from D_2 or S_1, then the authorities in D_2 or S_1 could have cut from the surplus country S_2, and the circle would have been closed. But if the authorities in D_1 had cut from B, the authorities in B could not cut from the surplus country S_2 because B's imports from S_2 are already zero; they would have had to cut from D, D_2, or S_1. And so on.

The above illustration should serve to show that in order to obtain a minimum reduction in world trade it is not sufficient to work to the simple rule that the authorities in a deficit country must always cut imports from a surplus country, but are otherwise free to choose how they will spread their import cuts. This is insufficient for at least two reasons. First, when a deficit country is importing from two surplus countries it may make a vital difference on which surplus country's exports its authorities decide to concentrate the import cuts. As is shown in the difference between the action of the authorities in D_2 in cases a and b of Table XXVI, the authorities in a deficit country must avoid concentrating their import cuts on the exports of a surplus country if the authorities in some other deficit country need to concentrate their import restrictions on the exports of that surplus country.[1] Secondly, a deficit country may not import at all from any surplus country. In this case, if it is to achieve external balance its authorities must be permitted to restrict imports from another country which is already in deficit or in external balance and thus to pass on its deficit to that other country. But, as is shown by the above discussion of the treatment of the disequilibrium which remains at the end of stage iii of case b of Table XXVI, it makes a great difference which of the existing deficit or balanced countries are chosen as the victims for the necessary cuts on their exports. That one should be chosen which permits the quickest ultimate concentration of the cuts upon the surplus countries.

It is theoretically possible in any pattern of world payments, however complicated, to work out those combinations of discriminatory import or payment restrictions which will restore equilibrium to every balance of payments with the minimum reduction of total world trade and to distinguish these from all other combinations of import or payments restrictions which will restore equilibrium only at the cost of a larger reduction of world trade. Such a solution would require a supranational authority for its achievement. The authorities in individual deficit countries could not be left with freedom of choice as to which imports they should restrict; each would have to confine their restrictions to those which fitted into the general world plan.

Such a solution is, however, itself open to serious objections.

In the first place, the simple criterion of the minimum statistical reduction in world trade is not acceptable. Consider D_1's imports from S_1. In stage v of Table XXV they are $36 m.; that is to say that with

---

[1] The rules are in reality much more complicated even than this. There may be many other deficit countries and many surplus countries. Moreover, the reason why the authorities in a particular deficit country should avoid cutting imports from a particular surplus country may be because another deficit country which imports from no surplus country can nevertheless cut its imports from a balanced country which in turn imports only from this particular surplus country. The various patterns can be indefinitely complex. Nevertheless, there are some patterns of discriminatory import restrictions which will minimize the fall in world trade; and if the figures are all known these can be determined.

a system of non-discriminatory import restrictions they have been reduced by $21 m. from $57 m. to $36 m. In stage iii of case a of Table XXVI they are only $10 m.; thus with a world plan for the minimum reduction of trade, D_1's imports from S_1 have been reduced by as much as $47 m., from $57 m. to $10 m., even though D_1's imports from all sources have fallen less in the case of planned discrimination than in the case of non-discrimination.[1] Now it may be that purchasers in D_1 import their most essential and indispensable supplies from S_1 and that the imports into D_1 from other sources can quite easily be replaced by home products or can quite easily be economized without much hardship. Residents in D_1 may be much better off under the system of non-discrimination with total imports of only $93 m. but imports of $36 m. from S_1 than under a planned discrimination with total imports as great as $100 m. but imports of only $10 m.[2] from S_1.

In other words, no world plan for discrimination could be automatically worked out on the simple basis of bringing about the minimum reduction of world trade. The international officials charged with its formation would have to take into account the relative essentiality of imports from different sources to different countries, a matter which might naturally be the occasion for bitter conflicts of opinion. No national government would allow its citizens to be starved merely as a means of achieving a somewhat smaller reduction in the statistics of world trade.

Moreover, it is important to realize what sort of discrimination the principle of a minimum reduction in the volume of world trade may involve. As we have just seen from our consideration of case a of Table XXVI, in our example it would involve a very heavy cut by the authorities in D_1 of imports from S_1. But in the original position of disequilibrium shown in stage i in Tables XXV and XXVI, D_1 has a surplus in her dealings with S_1. Purchasers in D_1 are importing $57 m. from S_1 (row 3 column a) but producers in D_1 are exporting no less than $60 m. to S_1 (row 1 column c). S_1's currency is not, therefore, 'hard' to the authorities in D_1. Indeed they have a surplus of S_1's currency with which part of D_1's excess imports from other sources are being financed. The principle of the minimum reduction of world trade may thus involve that the authorities in D_1 should concentrate their import cuts on imports from S_1 even though supplies from S_1 are most essential to D_1's purchasers and even though there is a surplus in D_1's balance of

---

[1] A world plan for the minimum reduction of trade could be worked out which allowed purchasers in D_1 to continue to import $15 m. from S_1, if imports into D_1 from S_1 were cut to zero and imports into D_2 from S_1 were cut by $5 m. less and from S_2 by $5 m. more than in stage ii of case a. But imports from S_2 to D_1 of $15 m. remain well below D_1's imports from S_2 under the system of non-discrimination.

[2] Or at the most $15 m. (see preceding footnote).

payments with S_1 whose currency is therefore not 'hard' to D_1's authorities.[1]

There is a second main reason why the principle of discrimination for the minimum reduction of the total imports of the deficit countries cannot be accepted as a rule-of-thumb guide for international economic policy. Throughout the arithmetical examples given of discriminatory and non-discriminatory import restrictions in Tables XXV and XXVI we have assumed that the imports of the surplus countries remain unaffected by the choice of the type of import restrictions to be used by the deficit countries. But this is not at all necessarily the case. With a system of non-discriminatory import restrictions the authorities in the deficit countries D_1 and D_2 will cut down their imports from the territories of each other as well as from country S_1. But the fact that the exporters in D_1 are restricted from D_2's markets may make them seek harder for alternative markets including markets in S_1; and similarly with the exporters of D_2's products who are excluded from D_1's markets. In fact the imports of the surplus countries from the deficit countries may rise because as a result of the non-discriminatory import restrictions which are placed on each other's products the exporters in the deficit countries offer their products on more favourable terms in the

---

[1] This last point shows how completely the use of the principle of discrimination for the minimum reduction of world trade differs from the principle of achieving bilateral balance through import restriction. Under this latter principle the authorities in each country (even though it were in surplus as regards its total balance of payments) which had a deficit in its payments with another particular country would have to restrict imports from that other country until a bilateral balance was achieved. In the original position of disequilibrium shown as stage i in Tables XXV and XXVI we have the following bilateral deficits :—
D_1 imports $61 m. from D_2 and exports $8 m. to D_2 and has a deficit of $53 m. with D_2.
D_1 imports $24 m. from B and exports $5 m. to B and has a deficit of $19 m. with B.
D_2 imports $44 m. from S_1 and exports $5 m. to S_1 and has a deficit of $39 m. with S_1
D_2 imports $77 m. from S_2 and exports $24 m. to S_2 and has a deficit of $53 m. with S_2.
D_2 imports $26 m. from B and exports $12 m. to B and has a deficit of $14 m. with B.
S_1 imports $60 m. from D_1 and exports $57 m. to D_1 and has a deficit of $3 m. with D_1.
S_1 imports $57 m. from S_2 and exports $41 m. to S_2 and has a deficit of $16 m. with S_2.
S_2 imports $17 m. from D_1 and exports $5 m. to D_1 and has a deficit of $12 m. with D_1.
S_2 imports $32 m. from B and exports $5 m. to B and has a deficit of $27 m. with B.
B imports $83 m. from S_1 and exports $23 m. to S_1 and has a deficit of $60 m. with S_1.
If each of these bilateral deficits is removed by a discriminatory import restriction in the deficit country against the products of the surplus member of the pair we should get a total reduction of world trade by the total of these bilateral deficits or by $296 m. to only $370 m.

markets of the surplus countries. This influence would not, of course, be at work in the case of a system of discriminatory import restrictions under which the authorities in the deficit countries did not restrict the demands for each other's products. It follows, therefore, that the comparison between stage v of Table XXV and stage iii of case a of Table XXVI exaggerates the importance of the principle of discrimination for the preservation of world trade. The final equilibrium of Table XXV ought probably to show some increase in the imports of the surplus countries and therefore a smaller fall in the imports of the deficit countries. And this is just what is wanted to restore equilibrium: increase of exports to the surplus countries from the deficit countries combined with a reduction of imports into the deficit countries from the surplus countries. A world in which there is a somewhat greater reduction in total world trade but a greater flow of trade between the deficit and surplus countries may be a world of greater real prosperity, since purchasers in the deficit countries may need the products of the surplus countries more than they need each other's products.

We have in this chapter confined our attention to the problem of restrictions of imports or of other payments by deficit countries and have inquired whether these controls should be on a discriminatory or non-discriminatory basis. Logically to complete the analysis we ought to apply the same methods to the questions whether import subsidies in the surplus countries, export subsidies[1] in the deficit countries, and export restrictions[2] in the surplus countries should be on a discriminatory or non-discriminatory basis, if they are employed as a means of restoring equilibrium to the balance of payments.

The concentration of attention on the restriction of imports or other payments by deficit countries is justified by the fact that this is by far the most important method which is actually employed in the field of direct controls. The reader is left to apply the principles of this chapter to the other types of control if he wishes to do so. A word may, however, usefully be added here on the use of export subsidies for the promotion of exports by the deficit countries, always on the assumption that the elasticity of demand for each deficit country's exports is greater than unity so that the subsidy will in fact increase the value of the country's exports.

Such export subsidies might be on a non-discriminatory or a discriminatory basis. If they were non-discriminatory, export subsidies in the deficit countries D_1 and D_2 would expand their exports to all countries; all the figures in columns a to c of rows 1 and 2 of stage i

---

[1] Or taxes, if the elasticity of demand in the importing country is less than unity.

[2] Or subsidies, if the elasticity of demand in the importing country is less than unity.

of Tables XXV and XXVI would be raised. In so far as the authorities in D_1 and D_2 thereby encouraged exports to each other's country or to B they would merely be shifting their deficits on to each other's country or on to a country, B, which was previously in external balance. But in so far as they encouraged exports to S_1 or S_2 they would be removing their own deficits and removing simultaneously a surplus of a surplus country. There would then have to be a further round of non-discriminatory export subsidization by the authorities in D_1, D_2, and B in order to shift on once more, partly again on to each other, but partly on to the surplus countries that part of D_1's and D_2's original deficits which the first round of non-discriminatory export subsidization had merely shifted around among the deficit or balanced countries. And so the process would go on.

If, however, the export subsidies were discriminatory and related only to exports from the deficit countries to the surplus countries, then the exports of the deficit countries D_1 and D_2 to the surplus countries S_1 and S_2 could be increased at the first round to the extent required to remove directly the deficits of D_1 and D_2 and the surpluses of S_1 and S_2.

But what if the authorities in a deficit country discriminate against imports from a surplus country at the same time that they offer a discriminatory export subsidy on exports to that surplus country? If the degree of the discriminatory import restriction (e.g. a 10 per cent *ad valorem* duty on imports from the surplus country) is equal to the degree of the discriminatory export subsidy (e.g. a 10 per cent *ad valorem* subsidy on exports to that country), the system corresponds, so far as trade between those two countries is concerned, to a depreciation by 10 per cent of the exchange value of the deficit country's currency in terms of the surplus country's currency. This illustration may serve to call attention to an important fact. A system of variable exchange rates such as that discussed in Chapter XXVII above, whereby the currencies of all deficit countries are depreciated and those of all surplus countries are appreciated, will itself bring about just that degree of 'discrimination' which is required both on the import and the export side to restore the balance of payments. When the exchange value of a deficit country's currency is depreciated in terms of a surplus country's currency, this does not merely tend, as in the two-country case examined in Part IV, to reduce the imports of the deficit country from the surplus country because the export products of the surplus country can compete on less favourable terms with the products of the deficit country, and to increase the exports of the deficit to the surplus country because the export products of the deficit country can compete on more favourable terms with the products of the surplus country. It also has an effect similar to that of discriminatory import restrictions and export subsidies. The purchasers in the deficit country buy less imports from the surplus country and more imports from other deficit countries, because the products of the surplus country can compete on less favourable terms with those of the other deficit countries whose currencies have also been depreciated. Similarly, the exporters in the deficit country sell more exports to the surplus country not only because the surplus country is a more profitable market than the home market of the deficit country itself but also because it presents a more profitable market than those of the other deficit countries whose currencies have also been depreciated.

CHAPTER XXXI

DISCRIMINATION AND ECONOMIC WELFARE: CONCLUSION

IN the last sections of the preceding chapter we gave reasons for the view that a rational system of discriminatory controls as a means of restoring equilibrium to world balances of payments would be very difficult to achieve. It would have to take the form of an internationally agreed, or supranationally imposed, plan of control which could not be based upon any automatic rule of thumb because it would involve human judgment on at least two important issues: first, whether one country's imports from a particular country were more or less indispensable to it than another country's imports from another particular country; and, secondly, the extent to which the exporters of the products of one country to the markets of a deficit country would increase their exports to a surplus country if they were prevented from selling in the deficit country.

Nevertheless, in spite of these difficulties and uncertainties, there is a strong case for the use of discriminatory controls if direct controls are selected as the means of achieving external balance. There remains great force in the argument that if the authorities in two deficit countries D_1 and D_2 are going to restore external balance by restricting imports, each should restrict imports more severely from a surplus country S than from each other. For the restriction of imports from the surplus country will directly remove a deficit country's excess of imports and a surplus country's excess of exports, whereas the restriction of imports from a deficit country will directly merely shift the deficit from one deficit country to another.

Moreover, it may also appear at first sight that a properly planned discriminatory use of import restrictions would be likely to be nearer the 'modified free trade position' (as defined on p. 326, above) than the non-discriminatory use of such restrictions for the purpose of restoring external equilibrium. With a non-discriminatory use of import restrictions the authorities in D_1 and D_2 impose, let us say, a 10 per cent *ad valorem* duty on imports from S and also on imports from each other. With a discriminatory use of import restrictions they impose the 10 per cent *ad valorem* import duty on products from S but omit the duty on imports from each other. The difference between the two systems so far is merely that with the non-discriminatory system of duties there must be levied duties of 10 per cent on the trade between D_1 and D_2 which are absent in the case of the discriminatory system of duties. The discriminatory system is, therefore, nearer the free-trade position than the non-discriminatory system; it is in fact the same system except that certain obstacles to trade have been removed.

Indeed the advantage of the discriminatory system as a means of approximating towards the free-trade position may be even greater than this. The imposition of a non-discriminatory import duty of 10 per cent *ad valorem* by the authorities in D_1 on all imports from D_2 and S will have a certain effect in reducing imports into D_1 from the surplus country S, because D_1's own products now have a 10 per cent price advantage (since they are exempt from the import duty) for the purchasers in D_1. But if the duty on imports into D_1 is imposed only on imports from S and not at all on imports from D_2, a lower rate of duty (say a 5 per cent *ad valorem* duty) may be sufficient to bring about the same reduction in imports into D_1 from S, since purchasers in D_1 will now obtain a price advantage in substituting D_2's products as well as D_1's products for S's products. The duty on S's products will now reduce imports from S both because purchasers in D_1 switch to home-produced products and also because they switch to the purchase of imports from D_2. Thus if the authorities in D_1 and D_2 are to achieve a given reduction in the total imports of D_1 and D_2 from S, the use of discriminatory import restrictions will involve not only the complete absence of barriers to the trade between D_1 and D_2 but also a lower rate of duty on imports from S into D_1 and D_2, in so far as the above effect is concerned.

But non-discriminatory import restrictions by imposing restrictions on exports from D_1 into D_2 will almost certainly divert some of D_1's exports into S's market; and similarly, they will divert some of D_2's exports into S's markets instead of D_1's markets. This will be a factor decreasing the height of the non-discriminatory duty that must be imposed by D_1's and D_2's authorities on imports, since with non-discrimination part of the shortage of S's currency in the foreign exchange market will be removed by means of an expansion of the sales of D_1's and D_2's products to purchasers in S. Thus the use of non-discriminatory import restrictions as contrasted with discriminatory restrictions will involve (i) a higher rate of duty on imports from S in so far as there will be less tendency for importers in D_1 (or D_2) to switch from S's products to D_2's (or D_1's) products, and (ii) a lower rate of duty on imports from S in so far as there will be a greater tendency for exporters in D_1 (or D_2) to switch their sales into S's markets instead of into D_2's (or D_1's) markets. It is not possible to say which factor will be the more important. That depends upon the nature of the commodities traded and the ease with which they can be substituted for one another in the consumption or production of the various countries.

Let us suppose, however, that a well-planned system of discriminatory import restrictions would involve not only the complete absence of trade barriers between the deficit countries but also a somewhat lower rate of import duty on imports into the deficit countries from the surplus countries. On both counts it would appear to approach more nearly to the free-trade position than does a system of non-discriminatory import restrictions: all obstacles to trade are lower with the system of discrimination than with the system of non-discrimination. But even in this extreme case it is not certain that economic welfare will be greater with the system of discriminatory import restrictions. It will be one of the objects of Volume II to explain how economic welfare is reduced not only by high protection but also by the independent factor, high discrimination. A system of low import duties which are discriminatory may do more harm to economic welfare than a system of higher import duties which are non-discriminatory.

It is not possible or appropriate to argue this proposition at length; such a discussion belongs to Volume II of this work. Here it must suffice to give a brief indication of its relevance to the choice between discriminatory and non-discriminatory import restrictions. Suppose that with the non-discriminatory system import duties of 10 per cent *ad valorem* on all imports into D_1 and D_2 would suffice to restore external balance, and that with a wisely planned discriminatory system no import duties on trade between D_1 and D_2 would be imposed and import duties of 7 per cent *ad valorem* on imports from S into D_1 and D_2 would be sufficient. In the latter case the total volume of world trade will be greater than in the former; but the volume of trade between S on the one hand and D_1 and D_2 on the other hand will be smaller, because the complete absence of duties on trade between D_1 and D_2 will have diverted some of D_1's (and D_2's) exports away from S's markets into the markets of D_2 (and D_1). Now if the trade between S on the one hand and D_1 and D_2 on the other hand happens to be of particular economic importance the rise in the total of world trade (due to the lower general level of trade barriers with the system of discrimination) may be of less importance to economic welfare than the reduction of the trade with S (due to the discrimination against trade with S).

It may be helpful at this point to compare the effects of (i) an exchange-rate adjustment, (ii) a system of discriminatory import restrictions, and (iii) a system of non-discriminatory import restrictions as a means of removing a balance-of-payments disequilibrium between the two deficit countries, D_1 and D_2, and the surplus country, S.

(i) An exchange-rate depreciation by 10 per cent of the currencies of D_1 and D_2 in terms of the currency of S, so far as trade is concerned, is exactly equivalent to (a) the imposition in D_1 and D_2 of a discriminatory import duty of 10 per cent on imports from S but not on imports from each other, combined with (b) the imposition in D_1 and D_2 of a discriminatory export subsidy on exports to S but not on exports to each other.

(ii) A system of discriminatory import restrictions in D_1 and D_2 may be compared to the imposition of the discriminatory import duty under (i) (a) without the addition of the discriminatory export subsidy under (i) (b).

(iii) A system of non-discriminatory import restrictions in D_1 and D_2 is also like the imposition of the discriminatory import duty under (i) (a) without the addition of the discriminatory export subsidy under (i) (b), but in this case with the addition of an equivalent duty in D_1 (D_2) on imports from D_2 (D_1).

For reasons which will be developed in Volume II we may take the system of exchange-rate adjustment (system i) as providing generally the best principle from the point of view of economic welfare. In this case we should have to answer the following question: suppose we start with system i but then remove the discriminatory export subsidies; shall we get back nearer to, or shall we move still further from, system i if we now proceed to make the import duties non-discriminatory (i.e. if we turn from system ii to system iii)?

Clearly we move further away from system i in so far as we cut off trade between D_1 and D_2 in commodities which would in no case be directly or indirectly exported to S. But we may get nearer to system i if the main effect of the reduction in the demand in D_1 (D_2) for imports from D_2 (D_1) is to release D_2's (D_1's) products for export to S. The former is likely to be the case if the elasticity of demand in S for the products which D_1 and D_2 trade with each other is small. But if the elasticity of demand in S is high, then non-discriminatory import restrictions may approximate more closely than discriminatory import restrictions to the method of exchange-rate adjustment.

It is, therefore, a most difficult matter to determine in any case whether direct controls should be used on a non-discriminatory basis or on the basis of some particular plan of discrimination. But this choice, viz. what one should do if there are to be direct controls, is less funda-mental than the choice whether direct controls should be employed at all in order to achieve external balance, or whether reliance should not rather be placed upon price adjustment in one form or another. If direct controls are not employed, the question of their discriminatory use does not arise.

The author of this work makes no attempt to conceal his own view that, if possible, reliance should be placed upon measures other than direct controls.

First, there must be in each important country reasonably successful financial policies for internal balance, i.e. for the avoidance of large domestic inflations and deflations.

Secondly, there must be an international system (whether of the type of a free exchange market or of the type of an adjustable peg) for the variation of exchange rates on the principle that the currencies of surplus countries should be appreciated and those of deficit countries depreciated.

Thirdly, any measures which may be taken for the protection of national industries—and in Volume II we shall discuss the legitimacy of employing such measures for purposes other than the control of the balance of payments—should take forms (e.g. *ad valorem* import duties rather than rigid quantitative import restrictions) which effectively allow the adjustment of trade flows to subsequent alterations in price relationships.

Such a system, we shall find, would in no way conflict with those other aspects of international economic policy which we shall discuss in Volume II of this work, whereas a system of direct controls devised in the interests of balance-of-payments policy would not allow room for all the policy measures which will recommend themselves in that later discussion.

But is such a system a feasible one?

The answer to this question rests first of all upon a technical question. Are the elasticities of demand for imports (or more strictly the elasticities of substitution between the tradeable products of the various countries) sufficiently great to enable the system of price adjustments to operate smoothly and effectively? This is a question of fact on which the statistical evidence at present is inconclusive. But, as has been stated above (p. 77), to the present author it would appear probable that the degree of substitutability of products in international trade would be amply sufficient on three important provisos: namely, that the commercial-policy obstacles to international trade are not too great or too rigid; that the monetary authorities in each country possess sufficient reserves of gold or of other internationally acceptable means of payment to finance short-term deficits while the long-term effects of price adjustments are working themselves out; and that catastrophic upsets in world markets (due to wars or major economic depressions) are avoided.

Internationally, therefore, this system requires: (i) a reasonable absence of excessive and rigid trade barriers; (ii) some agreed system for the adjustment of exchange rates so that countries do in fact depreciate their exchange rates when they are in deficit and do not depreciate otherwise, and that countries do in fact appreciate their exchange rates when they are in surplus and do not appreciate otherwise; and (iii) a reasonable initial distribution among the countries of the world of an adequate stock of gold or of other internationally acceptable means of payment.

Internally the successful operation of this system requires the fulfilment of at least two basic conditions.

First, the authorities in the major countries at least must effectively operate domestic financial policies for internal balance. A serious uncontrolled slump in an important country might put such a strain on the balance of payments of other countries that they would be driven to the use of import restrictions or other direct controls. Reasonable internal stability achieved primarily by effective domestic financial policies for internal balance are a *sine qua non* for any really satisfactory means of achieving external balance between a number of countries. The detailed methods available for achieving such an internal balance would form one of the most important topics of a Theory of Domestic Economic Policy.

Secondly, if the method of variable exchange rates is to be used effectively as the means of adjustment of disordered balances of payments, from time to time there must be variations in the price of one country's products relatively to that of another's. This means that when the price of a country's imports goes up (e.g. because of a necessary depreciation of its exchange rate) this must not automatically lead to a simultaneous increase in its own money costs. In other words its money-wage rates must not be so tied to the cost of living that domestic costs and prices automatically follow the price of imports. The system will work only if other methods (such as the redistribution of income and property through fiscal policy, the extension of more equal educational and social opportunities to enter the better-paid occupations, and the prevention of monopolistic practices which maintain unduly high incomes) are employed rather than wages policy for the achievement of a tolerably equitable distribution of income and wealth within the community. This also is a matter which would form one of the most important topics of a Theory of Domestic Economic Policy.

The conditions for the successful use of the mechanism of money and prices for the achievement of external balance are, therefore, far-reaching and, in some cases, not at all easy of achievement. But their attainment is worth the effort. Their absence would make inevitable a perpetual structure of direct trade controls whose only justification was the regulation of international payments; and it will be a chief purpose of Volume II to show how great can be the wastes of unnecessary obstacles to world trade.

INDEX

REPRINTED LITHOGRAPHICALLY IN GREAT BRITAIN
AT THE UNIVERSITY PRESS, OXFORD
BY VIVIAN RIDLER
PRINTER TO THE UNIVERSITY